PRINCIPLES OF ACCOUNTING

Revised Edition

Volume I

HARCOURT BRACE JOVANOVICH COLLEGE OUTLINE SERIES

PRINCIPLES OF ACCOUNTING

Revised Edition   Volume I

Terry L. Campbell, DBA, CPA, CMA, CCA

Pennsylvania State University

Peter R. Grierson, PhD, CPA

Slippery Rock University

Doris M. Taylor, MSA, CPA

University of Central Florida

Books for Professionals
Harcourt Brace Jovanovich, Publishers
San Diego   New York   London

Requests for permission to make copies of any part of the work should be mailed to:

Permissions
Harcourt Brace Jovanovich, Publishers
Orlando, Florida 32887

Printed in the United States of America

Library of Congress Cataloging-in-Publication Data

Campbell, Terry, L.
    Principles of accounting / Terry L. Campbell, Peter R. Grierson,
Doris M. Taylor. —Rev. ed.
        p.   cm. —(Harcourt Brace Jovanovich college outline series)
(Books for professionals)
    Includes index.

    ISBN 0-15-601651-6

    1. Accounting   I. Grierson, Peter R.   II. Taylor, Doris M.
III. Title.   IV. Series.   V. Series: Books for professionals.
HF5635.C169   1989
657′.044—dc20   89-11082
                                                                CIP

Revised edition

A B C D E

PREFACE

The purpose of this book is to present the first half of a full year course in introductory accounting theory in the clear, concise format of an outline. The remaining topics generally covered in an accounting principles sequence are presented in the companion text PRINCIPLES OF ACCOUNTING VOLUME II. Although comprehensive enough to be used by itself for independent study, this outline is specifically designed to be used as a supplement to college courses and textbooks on the subject. Notice, for example, the *Textbook Correlation Table* that begins on the inside of the front cover. This table shows how the pages of this outline correspond by topic to the pages of 4 leading textbooks on introductory accounting theory currently in use at major colleges and universities. So, even though the sequence of topics in this outline may differ from your text, you can easily locate the material you want by consulting the table.

Principles of accounting courses typically look closely at the items on the balance sheet and income statement. Questions of valuation, and revenue and expense recognition are examined as well as basic accounting procedures. The student must often differentiate between the results of using several acceptable accounting methods. This book provides numerous straightforward examples and problems to illustrate various accounting standards and concepts.

Regular features as the end of each chapter are specially designed to supplement your textbook and course work in introductory accounting.

• RAISE YOUR GRADES. This feature consists of a checkmarked list of open-ended thought questions to help you assimilate the material you have just studied. By inviting you to compare concepts, interpret ideas, explain concepts, and examine the whys and wherefores of chapter material, these questions help to prepare you for class discussions, quizzes, and tests.

• SUMMARY. This feature consists of a brief restatement of the main ideas in each chapter, including definitions of key terms. Because it is presented in the efficient form of a numbered list, you can use it to refresh your memory quickly before an exam.

• RAPID REVIEW. Like the summary, this feature is designed to provide you with a quick review of the principles presented in the body of each chapter. Consisting primarily of short problems, multiple-choice, and short-answer questions, it allows you to test your retention and reinforce your learning at the same time. Should you have trouble answering any of these questions, you can locate and review the relevant sections of the outline by following the cross references provided.

• SOLVED PROBLEMS. Each chapter of this outline concludes with a set of problems and their step-by-step solutions. Undoubtedly the most valuable feature of the outline, these problems allow you to apply your knowledge of accounting principles to the solution of both numerical and essay type questions. Along with the three examinations, they also give you ample exposure to the kinds of questions that you are likely to encounter on a typical college exam. To make the most of these problems, try writing your own solutions first. Then compare your answers to the detailed solutions provided in the book.

Of course, there are other features of this outline that you will find very helpful. One is the format itself, which serves both as a clear guide to important ideas and as a convenient structure upon which to organize your knowledge. A second is the step-by-step approach to applying various accounting methods. The text lists these steps and illustrates them with straightforward examples. You should be able to solve complex problems by carefully following the steps described in the text.

CONTENTS

PRINCIPLES OF ACCOUNTING

Revised Edition

Volume I

1 INTRODUCTION TO ACCOUNTING

THIS CHAPTER IS ABOUT

- ☑ **The Nature and Purpose of Accounting**
- ☑ **Branches of Accounting**
- ☑ **The Status Elements—The Basic Accounting Equation**
- ☑ **The Owner Elements**
- ☑ **The Performance Elements**
- ☑ **Accounts**

1-1. The Nature and Purpose of Accounting

A. Definitions of accounting once focused on the *nature* of the accounting process.

At one time the American Institute of Certified Public Accountants (AICPA) defined accounting as "the art of recording, classifying and summarizing, in a significant manner and in terms of money, transactions and events which are, in part at least, of a financial character, and interpreting the results thereof."

This early definition recognized that the collection and organization of business data are important parts of accounting. Nevertheless, the AICPA's emphasis on interpretation makes it clear that accounting goes beyond the mere collecting and organizing of information. To be more than a bookkeeper, a person preparing accounting reports must be able to understand the operation of the business and the business environment, as well as organize the selected information in a way that makes that information useful to others.

B. Later definitions of accounting focused on the *purpose* of the accounting process.

By 1970, the AICPA had formulated a new definition that focused on accounting's purpose rather than on its nature. In this new definition, accounting is a service activity whose function is to "provide quantitative information, primarily financial in nature, about economic entities that is intended to be useful in making economic decisions, in making reasoned choices among alternative courses of action."

Thus, an accountant must be able to select the transactions and events that are significant in making economic decisions and portray this information in a way that aids users' decisions.

1-2. Branches of Accounting

Accounting has many branches or specialties.

A. Tax Accounting

Tax accounting is used to prepare tax returns and to examine tax consequences of proposed business transactions. Individuals, partnerships, and corporations prepare their tax returns based upon tax accounting rules.

B. Not-for-profit Accounting

Not-for-profit accounting is used by nonprofit organizations to measure the success of their activities and to ensure strict compliance with all requirements imposed by law, by donors, or by the entity's purposes. The United Way reports its activities to interested parties by using not-for-profit accounting concepts.

C. Governmental Accounting

Governmental accounting is used by all branches of government and by those who receive government funds to oversee the complicated business of providing government services or to report to the government on the use of government funding in compliance with all imposed regulations. Cities and states report the receipt and use of funds granted by the federal government based upon governmental accounting.

D. Managerial Accounting

Managerial accounting is used to aid business managers in managing daily operations and in planning future operations, and to gauge the effects of these management decisions. The decision to open a branch bank requires the use of managerial accounting.

E. Financial Accounting

Financial accounting is used by business managers to record transactions of the business, prepare reports based on those transactions, and thus communicate to owners and creditors the current condition of the company and its success or lack of success. The financial statements provided by General Motors, Inc., to outside parties are prepared on the basis of financial accounting.

This outline will be concerned with financial accounting by business entities. Although financial reporting can be used internally, the focus will be on the accounting reports made by entities to those outside the company.

There are ten elements in financial accounting. These elements represent certain economic information with words and numbers. The ten elements are interrelated, but they can be divided into three elements that report the *status* of an entity, two that report the changes resulting from transactions between the *owners* and the entity, and five that relate to reporting the *performance* of the entity.

1-3. The Status Elements—The Basic Accounting Equation

The three elements of financial accounting that report the status of an entity at a particular time are *assets*, *liabilities*, and *equity*.

A. Assets, liabilities, and equity are linked by the *basic accounting equation*.

The relationship between the status elements is expressed by the basic accounting equation as follows:

BASIC ACCOUNTING EQUATION

$$\text{ASSETS} = \text{LIABILITIES} + \text{EQUITY}$$

or

$$A = L + E$$

B. *Assets* are the economic resources controlled by an accounting entity that are expected to provide future benefits.

Note that this definition differs in three ways from the common definition of an asset as "something owned."

1. It is not necessary for an asset to be tangible. An intangible, such as a trade name, may have *probable future economic benefits* that an obsolete, though still tangible, machine may lack.
2. Ownership is not required. *Control* may be sufficient, as with a leased car.
3. Assets are defined in terms of a *particular entity*. An item may be an asset to one entity and yet not be of benefit to another.

It may help you to think of assets as the *resources* of a particular entity.

C. *Liabilities* **are the obligations of an entity to transfer assets or provide services to other entities in the future as a result of past transactions or events.**

Just as with assets, the accounting definition of liabilities differs from the common definition of a liability as "something owed."

First, as with assets, liabilities are defined in terms of the entity that incurs the obligation.

Second and more important, the accounting concept of liability carries with it none of the common definition's negative connotations, such as hindrance or handicap. Although liabilities in general are defined as obligations, to accountants they are also a means of obtaining assets. Put another way, liabilities are *sources of resources*; the resources, again, referring to assets.

Examples of liabilities are amounts owed to suppliers or other creditors. Some liabilities, such as mortgages, extend over a relatively long period of time.

D. *Equity* **is the owners' residual interest in the assets of an entity that remains after liabilities are deducted.**

As just stated, liabilities are sources of resources provided by creditors. It follows, then, that the equity of an entity is the amount of resources (assets) provided by sources *other* than creditors. Capital, stockholders' equity, and owner's equity are other names for equity. Terms such as preferred stock, common stock, withdrawals, dividends, and retained earnings are also encountered in accounting for equity.

E. The basic accounting equation can be stated in three ways.

Like any algebraic equation, the basic accounting equation can be rearranged in several ways. The form, A = L + E, stresses the entity's resources (assets); however, it can be rearranged to stress the entity's capital or ownership interest (equity) as follows:

$$\text{EQUITY} = \text{ASSETS} - \text{LIABILITIES}$$

A third form of this equation is

$$\text{LIABILITIES} = \text{ASSETS} - \text{EQUITY}$$

Note that by using the appropriate form of the basic accounting equation, the calculation of the dollar amount of the third element is always possible if the dollar amounts of the other two elements are known.

EXAMPLE 1-1: If we know that a firm has $40 in liabilities and $60 in owner's equity, we can calculate the amount of assets as follows:

$$
\begin{aligned}
\text{A} &= \text{L} + \text{E} \\
\text{A} &= \$40 + \$60 \\
\text{A} &= \$100
\end{aligned}
$$

EXAMPLE 1-2: Suppose that the firm in the previous example acquires additional resources (assets) of $50 by incurring additional liabilities (sources of resources). This transaction would be expressed in the basic accounting equation as follows:

$$A = L + E$$
$$(\$100 + \$50) = (\$40 + \$50) + \$60$$
$$\$150 = \$90 + \$60$$

Suppose now that the firm reduces its liabilities by \$20 by using \$20 of its assets to pay a liability. This transaction would appear on both sides of the basic accounting equation as follows:

$$A = L + E$$
$$(\$150 - \$20) = (\$90 - \$20) + \$60$$
$$\$130 = \$70 + \$60$$

Suppose finally that the firm changes one type of asset (\$10 cash) for another type of asset (\$10 worth of typewriter ribbons). This transaction would be expressed in the basic accounting equation as follows:

$$A = L + E$$
$$(\$130 - \$10 + \$10) = \$70 + \$60$$
$$\$130 = \$70 + \$60$$

Note that both sides of the basic accounting equation remain equal throughout the example.

1-4. The Owner Elements

The two elements of financial accounting that report the changes that result from transactions between the owners and the entity are *investments* and *distributions*.

A. *Investments* increase the equity of an entity.

Assets are the most common investments made by owners. Other ways of obtaining an ownership interest include performing services or accepting an ownership interest in exchange for a debt owed; that is, exchange a creditor interest for an ownership interest.

B. *Distributions* to owners are decreases in equity as a result of withdrawing assets, rendering services, or incurring liabilities on behalf of owners.

Owners are willing to give up the use of their assets by investing them in a business if they can expect a return on their investments. The most common return on investment is for a company to distribute cash to owners. Distributions of cash to a sole proprietor (owner) or partners are known as charges to a *drawing* or *withdrawal account*. Decreases in assets as a result of distributions to owners also result in a decrease in the equity of the business.

1-5. The Performance Elements

The five elements of financial accounting that report the changes that result from the performance of an entity are *revenues*, *expenses*, *gains*, *losses*, and *comprehensive income*.

A. *Revenues* are increases in equity resulting from the exchange of goods, services, or other activities involving the entity's central operations.

Examples of revenue are sales revenue, computer service revenue, and rent revenue. Note that revenues are generated by the ongoing operations of the business entity. Thus, the amount taken in by a bookstore chain by selling books is revenue because selling books is the company's central operation. However, selling one of the bookstores at a profit would not be revenue to the firm because selling bookstores is not the company's central operation.

B. *Expenses* **are decreases in equity resulting from the process of earning revenues.**

Expenses are the costs of goods sold or services rendered in earning revenue. Examples of expenses are the cost of goods sold, salary expense, and training expense. Decreases in assets or increases in liabilities as a result of expenses result in a decrease in the entity's equity.

C. *Gains* **are increases in equity resulting from peripheral or incidental transactions affecting the entity.**

It is important to note that gains do not include increases in assets that result from revenues or investments of owners. Only those increases that result from transactions *outside* of the normal operations of the business are recorded as gains. The sale of the bookstore at a profit mentioned in the discussion of revenues would be recorded as a gain.

D. *Losses* **are decreases in equity resulting from peripheral or incidental transactions of the entity.**

Transactions, events, or circumstances occurring outside of the normal operations of a business that result in decreases in assets are recorded as losses. Losses do not include the decreases in assets that result from expenses or distributions to owners. If the bookstore mentioned earlier was sold at a loss that amount would be recorded as a loss, not an expense. A decrease in assets or increase in liabilities as a result of a loss results in a decrease in the equity of a business entity.

E. *Comprehensive* **or** *net income* **is the result of subtracting expenses and losses from revenues and gains.**

Comprehensive (net) income will be discussed in Chapter 2.

1-6. Accounts

A. Many different transactions may be grouped in *accounts.*

Even a small business will engage in hundreds or thousands of transactions involving many different types of assets, liabilities, and equity. Many of these transactions are repetitive and can be grouped in categories with common characteristics. Transactions from the same categories are combined in records known as *accounts.* For example, many transactions involve the receipt or payment of cash. The accountant will establish an account entitled *Cash.* By doing this, the accountant need only look in one place if any questions concerning cash transactions should arise in the future.

B. Account titles are intended to communicate their contents with minimal confusion.

Since accounting is simply a way of communicating information in a useful way, there are no strict rules about how accounts must be titled. The best practice is to choose titles that will convey the most information with minimal confusion. For example, the account for a firm's cash could be titled *Money,* but it is probably best to title it *Cash.* One reason is that the account title *Cash* is traditional, which can help those seeing the accounts for the first time. However, although *Cash* is preferred, *Money* would not be wrong if used consistently. The important thing is that both *Money* and *Cash* describe the category in a way that will prevent confusion with other categories.

C. A *chart of accounts* **is the list of account titles for an entity.**

Each business entity chooses the categories it needs and uses titles that are meaningful to those interested in that entity. A list of the account titles chosen by a particular business entity is known as its *chart of accounts.*

EXAMPLE 1-3: Following is a chart of accounts using traditional account titles.

C. KILROY—SURVEYOR

Chart of Balance Sheet Accounts

Assets:	Cash
	Accounts Receivable
	Office Supplies on Hand
	Buildings
	Equipment
Liabilities:	Accounts Payable
	Notes Payable
	Salaries Payable
	Mortgage Payable
Equity:	C. Kilroy, Capital

RAISE YOUR GRADES

Can you explain...?

☑ the nature and purpose of accounting
☑ the three elements of financial accounting that report the status of an entity
☑ the basic accounting equation and use it to solve for a missing element in the equation
☑ how liabilities are not just obligations but sources of resources as well
☑ the two elements of financial accounting that report the changes resulting from transactions between the owners and an entity
☑ the five elements of financial accounting that report the changes resulting from the performance of an entity
☑ how the owner and performance elements of an entity affect the status elements of that entity
☑ why accounts are needed and how they are titled

SUMMARY

1. Accounting is a means of communicating economic information to a variety of users.
2. Accounting goes beyond the mere collection and organization of information in order to provide assistance in decision making.
3. Financial accounting is used to communicate the current condition of a business entity to owners and creditors.
4. There are ten elements in financial accounting: three report the status of an entity, two report on transactions between the entity and its owners, and five report on the performance of an entity.
5. The three elements that report the status of an entity are assets, liabilities, and equity.
6. The relationship between assets, liabilities, and equity is expressed by the basic accounting equation: ASSETS = LIABILITIES + EQUITY.
7. Given any two elements of the basic accounting equation, the equation may be rearranged algebraically to determine the dollar amount of the missing element of the equation.
8. Assets are economic resources controlled by an accounting entity that are expected to provide future benefits.

9. Liabilities are the obligations of an entity to transfer assets or provide services to other entities in the future. Although liabilities are obligations to others, they are also sources of resources.

10. Equity is the residual interest in the assets of an entity that remains after liabilities are deducted. It is also a source of resources from the owners.

11. The two elements that report the changes resulting from transactions between the owners and the entity are investments and distributions.

12. Investments increase the equity of an entity. Assets are the most common investments made by owners.

13. Distributions to owners are decreases in the equity of a particular entity as a result of withdrawing assets, rendering services, or incurring liabilities on behalf of the owners.

14. The five elements of financial accounting that report the changes resulting from the performance of an entity are revenues, expenses, gains, losses, and comprehensive (net) income.

15. Revenues are increases in equity resulting from the exchange of goods, services, or other activities involving the entity's central operations.

16. Expenses are decreases in equity resulting from the process of earning revenues.

17. Gains are increases in equity resulting from peripheral or incidental transactions affecting the entity.

18. Losses are decreases in equity resulting from peripheral or incidental transactions of the entity.

19. Transactions are recorded in categories with common characteristics. Transactions from the same categories are combined in records known as accounts.

20. An account title is intended to indicate the kinds of transactions recorded in the account.

21. A chart of accounts is a list of the account titles used by a business entity.

RAPID REVIEW   Answers

True or False

1.	Accounting is the process of collecting and organizing quantitative information without interpretation. [Section 1-1]	*False*
2.	Financial accounting is used to communicate the current condition of an entity to its owners and creditors. [Section 1-2]	*True*
3.	Tax accounting is used by government agencies to gauge the effects of their management decisions. [Section 1-2]	*False*
4.	Managerial accounting is used by management to report to governmental agencies. [Section 1-2]	*False*
5.	The three elements of financial accounting that report the status of an entity are assets, liabilities, and equity. [Section 1-3]	*True*
6.	Only tangible economic resources of an entity are assets. [Section 1-3]	*False*
7.	Liabilities are the obligations of an entity to transfer assets or provide services to other entities. [Section 1-3]	*True*
8.	Equity is the measure of fairness regarding the value of an entity. [Section 1-3]	*False*
9.	The basic accounting equation expresses the relationship between the status elements of an entity. [Section 1-3]	*True*
10.	The basic accounting equation is ASSETS = LIABILITIES + EQUITY. [Section 1-3]	*True*
11.	The increase in assets provided by an entity or individual in exchange for an ownership interest is reported as revenue. [Section 1-4]	*False*

12. Distributions of cash to a sole proprietor or partner are known as charges to a drawing account. [Section 1-4] *True*

13. Revenues are generated by the ongoing operations of a business entity. [Section 1-5] *True*

14. Expenses are incurred in the process of earning revenues. [Section 1-5] *True*

15. If a mechanic sold her garage at a profit, the profit would be reported as revenue. [Section 1-5] *False*

16. Accounts are used to record the transactions of a business entity in categories with common characteristics. [Section 1-6] *True*

17. Account titles must be memorized because they are standard in the practice of accounting. [Section 1-6] *False*

18. A chart of accounts is a list of account titles. [Section 1-6] *True*

SOLVED PROBLEMS

PROBLEM 1-1: What are the duties of an accountant?

Answer: An accountant records, classifies, and summarizes the financial transactions and events of an economic entity. Most important, the accountant must present and interpret this information in a way that makes the information useful to others. Thus, the accountant must be able to understand the operation of the business and the business environment in order to select the transactions and events that are significant in making economic decisions and portray this information in a way that aids users' decisions. [Section 1-1]

PROBLEM 1-2: What is the accountant's definition of assets?

Answer: The accountant's definition of assets differs from the common definition in three ways. First, it is not necessary for an asset to be tangible. An intangible, such as a trade name, may have probable future economic benefits that an obsolete, though still tangible, machine may lack. Second, ownership is not required. Control may be sufficient as with a leased car. Third, assets are defined in terms of a particular entity. An item may be an asset to one entity and yet not be of benefit to another. [Section 1-3]

PROBLEM 1-3: What is the equation that links the status elements of an entity and how do transactions affect this equation?

Answer: An equation known as the basic accounting equation expresses the relationship between the three status elements of a business entity. This equation states that

$$\text{ASSETS} = \text{LIABILITIES} + \text{EQUITY}$$

Assets are the resources of a business entity, and liabilities and equity are the sources of those resources. Liabilities are sources of resources from other entities, such as creditors, whereas equity is a source of resources from the owners of the entity. Thus, if the assets (resources) of a business amount to $1,000, then the liabilities and equity (sources of resources) of the business must also amount to $1,000.

Transactions, no matter how complex, can be recorded in terms of the effect they have on these three elements of the basic accounting equation. For example, a transaction that uses cash (an asset) to pay part of a debt (a liability) affects both sides of the basic accounting equation and therefore maintains the balance of the equation. [Sections 1-3 and 1-6]

PROBLEM 1-4: Determine the missing element in each of the following basic accounting equations.

	A	=	L	+	E
1.	$51,295	=	?	+	$39,450
2.	$27,450	=	$10,550	+	?
3.	?	=	$ 7,920	+	$10,985

Answer: 1. $51,295 = LIABILITIES + $39,450
$51,295 − $39,450 = LIABILITIES
$11,845 = LIABILITIES
2. $27,450 = $10,550 + EQUITY
$27,450 − $10,550 = EQUITY
$16,900 = EQUITY
3. ASSETS = $7,920 + $10,985
ASSETS = $18,905

[Section 1-3]

PROBLEM 1-5: New Company begins business today. The owners have invested $5,000 to start the business. What is the basic accounting equation that depicts this transaction?

Answer: The effect of this transaction is to increase assets (Cash) by $5,000 and to increase equity, on the other side of the equation, by the same amount. There are no liabilities of the company yet. Thus, after this transaction, the basic accounting equation for New Company is

ASSETS = EQUITY
$5,000 = $5,000

[Sections 1-3 and 1-5]

PROBLEM 1-6: New Company now borrows an additional $500 from a bank to purchase additional assets. What is the basic accounting equation after this transaction?

Answer: The effect of this transaction is to increase both assets and liabilities by $500. Thus, the basic accounting equation is now

ASSETS	= LIABILITIES	+ EQUITY
$5,000 + **$500** =	**$500**	+ $5,000
$5,500 =	$500	+ $5,000

[Sections 1-3 and 1-5]

PROBLEM 1-7: Next, New Company receives payment for services performed in the amount of $300. What is the resulting effect of this transaction on the basic accounting equation?

Answer: The effect of this transaction is to increase assets by $300 with a resulting increase of $300 in equity (revenue). The effect on the basic accounting equation is thus

ASSETS	= LIABILITIES +	EQUITY
$5,500 + **$300** =	$500	+ $5,000 + **$300**
$5,800 =	$500	+ $5,300

[Sections 1-3 and 1-5]

PROBLEM 1-8: New Company now decreases assets by paying $200 toward its bank loan. What is the effect of this transaction on the basic accounting equation?

Answer: The effect of this transaction is to lower both assets and liabilities by $200, as follows:

ASSETS	=	LIABILITIES	+ EQUITY
$5,800 − **$200** =		$500 − **$200**	+ $5,300
$5,600 =		$300	+ $5,300

[Sections 1-3 and 1-5]

PROBLEM 1-9: The next transaction of New Company is to pay $75 for supplies. What is the effect of this transaction on the basic accounting equation?

Answer: There is no real effect of this transaction on the basic accounting equation because the exchange of one form of asset (cash) for another form (supplies) does not change the total assets, nor does the exchange affect liabilities or equity. The transaction must be recorded, however, so the basic accounting equation is as follows:

ASSETS	= LIABILITIES	+ EQUITY
$5,600 − **$75** + **$75** =	$300	+ $5,300
$5,600 =	$300	+ $5,300

[Sections 1-3 and 1-5]

PROBLEM 1-10: After the first month of operation, New Company pays some business expenses incurred during the month as follows: rent, $500; utilities, $175; and wages, $1,000. How do these payments affect the basic accounting equation?

Answer: The effect of this group of transactions is to decrease assets and decrease equity as follows:

ASSETS	= LIABILITIES +	EQUITY
$5,600 − **$500** − **$175** − **$1,000** =	$300	+ $5,300 − **$500** − **$175** − **$1,000**
$3,925 =	$300	+ $3,625

[Sections 1-3 and 1-5]

PROBLEM 1-11: It is also determined that all of the supplies that were bought for $75 have been used during the first month of operation of the business. What is the effect of this *expense* on the basic accounting equation?

Answer: The effect of this expense is to reduce both assets and equity as follows:

ASSETS	= LIABILITIES +	EQUITY
$3,925 − **$75** =	$300	+ $3,625 − **$75**
$3,850 =	$300	+ $3,550

[Sections 1-3 and 1-5]

PROBLEM 1-12: Sun Company has assets valued at $1,600. It has decided that its basic accounting equation should have liabilities and equity in equal proportions. Thus, one-half of the sources of resources should be liabilities and one-half, equity. What is the resulting equation?

Answer: The resulting basic accounting equation would be

$1,600 *(Assets)* = *Liabilities* + *Equity*
$1,600 *(A)* = [1/2 *(A)* = L] + [1/2 *(A)* = E]
$1,600 *(Assets)* = $800 *(Liabilities)* + $800 *(Equity)*

Sun Company has indicated that its sources of resources should be equally divided between liabilities and equity. Thus, one-half of the assets is equal to the liabilities and one-half of the assets is equal to the equity. [Section 1-3]

PROBLEM 1-13: Sun Company after considerable discussion, has decided to consider changing the proportion of liabilities and equity. The new proportion is that the liabilities should be three times that of the equity. What is the resulting equation?

Answer: The resulting basic accounting equation would be

$$\$1,600 \text{ (Assets)} = 3/4A \text{ (Liabilities)} + 1/4A \text{ (Equity)}$$
$$\$1,600 \text{ (Assets)} = \$1,600(3/4) \text{ (Liabilities)} + \$1,600(1/4) \text{ (Equity)}$$
$$\$1,600 \text{ (Assets)} = \$1,200 \text{ (Liabilities)} + \$400 \text{ (Equity)}$$

Sun Company has indicated that its sources of resources should be in the proportion of three parts of liabilities to one part of equity. Thus, 75% (3/4) of the assets (resources) are provided by liabilities (sources of resources) and 25% (1/4) of the assets (resources) are provided by equity (source of resources). Note that various proportions may be demonstrated. [Section 1-3]

2 *FINANCIAL STATEMENTS*

THIS CHAPTER IS ABOUT

☑ **The Balance Sheet**
☑ **The Income Statement**
☑ **The Statement of Equity**
☑ **The Statement of Cash Flows**
☑ **Guidelines for Preparing Financial Statements**

As was mentioned in Chapter 1, one of the major functions of accounting is to provide reports that aid owners, investors, creditors, and others in making decisions concerning a business entity. There are four principal reports resulting from the process of financial accounting: the balance sheet, the income statement, the statement of equity and the statement of cash flows. All financial statements should be identified in the heading by the name of the entity, the name of the financial statement, and the date or period covered by the statement.

2-1. The Balance Sheet

The basic accounting equation (A = L + E) was introduced in Chapter 1, together with the notion that its algebraic equality or *balance* must be maintained. From this characteristic, the more common name, *balance sheet* equation, was derived. The balance sheet lists the assets, liabilities, and equity of a business entity. It reports the financial position of the entity as of a specific date.

A. Each of the three status elements (assets, liabilities, and equity) is classified by time when presented on the balance sheet.

The accountant uses two time classifications: *current*, also known as *short term*, and *noncurrent*, also known as *long term*. Normally, assets that are used or consumed entirely within one year or obligations due within one year are considered current. Although there are several exceptions to this rule, it follows logical guidelines. For example, firms with an operating cycle of longer than one year use the operating cycle as the measure of those items that are current. The *operating cycle* is the average length of time required to buy merchandise for resale or convert raw materials into a finished product, sell that merchandise or finished product, and receive payment for it. Naturally, any asset or liability that is not current is noncurrent.

B. Assets are classified as current or noncurrent.

1. *Current assets.* Current assets are cash and noncash assets that are readily converted to cash and are available to pay current liabilities, or noncash assets that are consumed in operations within one year or the operating cycle, whichever is longer. There are several traditional accounts that are classified as current assets on the balance sheet.

   - cash
   - marketable securities, such as six-month treasury bills
   - notes or accounts receivable (These are usually due within one year.)
   - inventory, such as supplies on hand
   - prepaid expenses, such as insurance policies and rent paid in advance

2. *Noncurrent assets.* Noncurrent assets include further subcategories of accounts. These include long-term investments, plant assets, intangible assets, natural resources, and other assets.

- *Long-term investments.* Long-term investments are investments that management does not intend to sell within one year as well as any investments that are not readily marketable (easily converted to cash). Long-term investments may include other companies' notes (payables), other companies' stock, or government bonds.

EXAMPLE 2-1: A car dealer with an operating cycle of one year accepts a six-month note receivable in exchange for a used car. This asset (notes receivable) would be reported as a current asset on the balance sheet because it is due within the one-year accounting period.

A distiller with a six-year operating cycle invests in a two-year government bond The bond would be classified as a current asset on the balance sheet because it is payable within the operating cycle of the distiller.

A clothing retailer with a one-year accounting period also invests in a two-year government bond. If the retailer intends to keep the bonds until maturity, the bond would be classified as a long-term investment on the balance sheet because it is due beyond the one-year accounting period.

- *Plant assets.* Tangible noncurrent assets that are used in the operation of the business and are relatively permanent are called *plant assets, operational assets,* or *plant, property, and equipment.* The accounts that are classified as plant assets on the balance sheet include machinery, buildings, the employee parking lot, and the administrative headquarters.
- *Intangible assets.* Assets that are noncurrent and lack physical substance yet confer benefits or rights that are of value to the business are known as *intangible assets.* Common examples of accounts that are classified as intangible assets are patents, copyrights, trademarks, formulas, license franchises, and purchased goodwill.
- *Natural resources.* Natural resources are those assets that are subject to exhaustion by extraction. Natural resources include petroleum deposits, timber stands, and mineral rights.

EXAMPLE 2-2: An oil company purchases two drilling rigs, stores 150,000 gallons of refined oil in tanks ready for delivery to buyers, and discovers oil on its land that has not yet been drilled. When a balance sheet is prepared for the oil company, the purchase of the two drilling rigs will be classified as plant assets because the rigs are equipment that will be used in the operation of the business. The stored oil will be classified as a current asset because it is inventory. The oil that has not yet been removed from the ground will be classified as a natural resource.

- *Other assets.* Some assets do not fit into a classification such as current, long-term investment, plant, or intangible. These assets are simply classified as *other assets* on the balance sheet. An example would be noncurrent assets such as land being held for future use.

C. Liabilities are classified as current or noncurrent.

1. *Current liabilities.* Liabilities that will be paid with current assets within one year or one operating cycle, whichever is longer, are classified as *current liabilities.* There are several accounts that are classified as current liabilities on the balance sheet.

- accounts payable
- notes payable if due within one year or one operating cycle, whichever is longer
- wages payable
- interest payable
- currently due portions of noncurrent liabilities

2. *Noncurrent liabilities.* In general, liabilities that have a due date more than a year beyond

the balance sheet date or beyond one operating cycle, whichever is longer, are classified as *noncurrent liabilities*. Note that a liability that is to be paid from a noncurrent source is considered noncurrent, whatever the due date. There are several accounts that are classified as noncurrent liabilities, such as

- mortgages payable
- bonds payable
- long-term notes payable

EXAMPLE 2-3: Juanita is the sole owner of a small clothing store. She accepts a loan of $10,000 from a friend and agrees to pay the friend back in six months with a car used in her business. She also finances the purchase of a building to use in her business by taking out a 20-year mortgage loan. When the first balance sheet is prepared for the business at the end of the month, the first loan will be classified as a noncurrent liability because it is payable with a noncurrent source (a car). If it was to be paid with cash or inventory, then it would be current because it would be due within one year and be paid with a current asset. The second loan will also be classified as a noncurrent liability because it is due beyond one year. However, any payments on the mortgage to be made within one year would be classified as current liabilities.

D. Equity is the owners' contributions to the business.

Equity represents the noncurrent obligations of the entity to the owners. Because equity equals the amount of assets remaining after subtracting liabilities, equity is sometimes called *net assets*. (The term "net" indicates that at least one amount has been subtracted from another to reach this final amount.) Equity comes from two primary sources: investments by owners and earnings. An unincorporated business (sole proprietorship or partnership) will be illustrated first. Equity is equal to the owners' investments plus net income, less any withdrawals and net losses. The equity section of the balance sheet for incorporated businesses (corporations) is more complex. Corporations are discussed in Chapters 14 and 15.

E. There are two balance sheet formats.

1. *Report format.* The most common balance sheet format is illustrated in Example 2-4, with the liability and equity sections presented below the assets. This is called the *report format*.
2. *Account format.* A second balance sheet format lists the assets on the left and the liabilities and equity on the right, similar to the accounting equation. This is the *account format*.

EXAMPLE 2-4: The balance sheet for Sanford Advertising Company is shown in report format on page 15.

Note that double-ruled lines indicate completion and/or balanced in the accounting language.

2-2. The Income Statement

Recall from Chapter 1 that the performance elements of a business entity are revenues, expenses, gains, losses, and comprehensive income. The *income statement* uses these elements to report the financial results of an entity's operations over a period of time. It is important to note that an income statement does *not* report equity changes that result from the investments of owners or distributions to owners.

Remember that revenues and expenses are the result of transactions involving the central operations of the business, whereas gains and losses are the result of peripheral transactions of the business. Net income is the result of revenue plus gains, less expenses and losses.

```
                        Sanford Advertising Company
                                Balance Sheet
                              December 31, 19x2

                                    Assets

Current assets:
  Cash...........................................................  $  9,500
  Accounts receivable...........................................      6,600
  Supplies on hand..............................................      1,250
  Prepaid Insurance.............................................      3,200
     Total current assets.......................................            $20,550

Noncurrent assets:
  Property, plant, and equipment...............................              13,700

Intangible assets:
  Patent........................................................               1,000
Total assets....................................................            $35,250


                             Liabilities and Equity

Current liabilities:
  Accounts payable..............................................  $  1,720
  Salaries payable..............................................      2,710
  Mortgage, current payment.....................................      1,000
     Total current liabilities..................................            $  5,430

Noncurrent liabilities:
  Mortgage note payable.........................................              19,000
Total liabilities...............................................            $24,430



William Sanford, capital........................................              10,820
Total liabilities and equity....................................            $35,250
```

A. A business entity must decide how to account for its performance elements.

Revenues, expenses, gains, and losses of a business entity can be accounted for in one of two ways: accrual basis or cash basis. *Accrual accounting* reports the revenues, expenses, gains, and losses of an entity in the period in which the transactions giving rise to these elements occur. Under *cash accounting*, these transactions are only reported in the period in which cash is actually received or paid by the entity. It may help to think of accrual accounting as being concerned with the process of generating cash, not just the timing of cash's flow in and out of the firm. This outline will use the accrual basis of accounting.

EXAMPLE 2-5: Servicomp Company generates its revenue by repairing computers. During the current accounting period, the records show cash sales of $2,500 and credit sales of $700, of which $300 has yet to be collected. If the firm uses accrual accounting as the basis for its reports, then it will report $3,200 in revenue on its income statement for the accounting period. If the firm uses the cash basis for its reports, however, it will only report the $2,500 of cash sales plus $400 in credit sales on its income statement for the accounting period, and defer reporting the remaining $300 of credit sales until that amount is actually received in cash.

B. The information that the income statement relays is the net (comprehensive) income of the business for the period.

Recall that "net" indicates that at least one amount has been subtracted from another to reach a final amount. Thus, *net income* is the result of subtracting expenses and losses from revenues and gains. (Of course, a business entity's operations could also result in a *net loss*.) This relationship is expressed by the following equation.

INCOME STATEMENT EQUATION

$$\text{REVENUES} - \text{EXPENSES} + \text{GAINS} - \text{LOSSES} = \text{NET INCOME}$$

or

$$R - E + G - L = NI$$

If there are no nonoperating transactions (gains or losses) over the period of time being reported, then the equation can be expressed as

$$\text{REVENUES} - \text{EXPENSES} = \text{NET INCOME}$$

or

$$R - E = NI$$

EXAMPLE 2-6: During the accounting period January 1, 19x1 through December 31, 19x1, Bob's Car Wash earned revenues of $1,300 and incurred expenses of $900. Using the income statement equation, the net income of the business can be determined as follows:

$$\textbf{R} \quad - \quad \textbf{E} \quad = \quad \textbf{NI}$$

$$\$1,300 - \$900 = \$400$$

Note that since there are no gains or losses (nonoperating items), then the operating income is the same as the net income for the business.

If expenses for Bob's Car Wash had been $1,500, then the income statement equation would show that a net loss was incurred for the accounting period as follows:

$$\textbf{R} \quad - \quad \textbf{E} \quad = \quad \textbf{NI}$$

$$\$1,300 - \$1,500 = (\$200)$$

Note that parentheses indicate negative amounts or deductions.

EXAMPLE 2-7: As of the same date as the company balance sheet presented in Example 2-4, the income statement would be presented as follows:

Sanford Advertising Company
Income Statement
For Year Ended December 31, 19x2

Revenue:		$50,500
Expenses:		
Advertising expenses	$ 530	
Insurance expense	1,900	
Mortgage expense	1,000	
Salaries expense	35,000	
Supplies expense	1,360	
Utilities expense	1,735	
Interest expense	2,300	
Total expenses		$43,825
Net income		$ 6,675

2-3. The Statement of Equity

The *statement of equity* reports the changes in capital that have occurred between the beginning and ending of a given period. This statement serves as a link between the balance sheet and the income statement of a business entity.

EXAMPLE 2-8: Following is the statement of equity for Sanford Advertising Company. Note that the company began the year with $6,145 in the capital account, which would have been reported on the previous year's ending balance sheet. This balance was reduced by withdrawals of $2,000 and increased by the $6,675 net income reported on the year-end income statement in Example 2-7 to give the $10,820 reported on the year-end balance sheet in Example 2-4.

Sanford Advertising Company
Statement of Equity
For Year Ended December 31, 19x2

William Sanford, Capital, January 1, 19x2.	$ 6,145
Add December 31, 19x2 net income	6,675
Subtotal.	$12,820
Deduct withdrawals	2,000
William Sanford, Capital, December 31, 19x2	$10,820

2-4. The Statement of Cash Flows

The fourth basic financial statement of a firm is the *statement of cash flows*. The statement of cash flows focuses on cash receipts and cash payments and also on the financing and investing activities of the firm. This information is not readily obtainable from the balance sheet and income statement. This statement will be discussed in Volume 2 after further information about corporate accounting has been covered.

2-5. Guidelines for Preparing Financial Statements

In order to meet the basic objective of being useful in making financial decisions to those who have a reasonable understanding of business, the information presented in financial statements must be understandable. In addition, the information should have the primary qualities of relevance and reliability, and the secondary qualities of comparability and consistency. To obtain these qualities, the accountant must follow operational guidelines which include basic assumptions, basic principles, and the recognition of certain constraints.

A. Qualities

* The *relevance quality* requires that the information must be capable of making a difference to a decision maker. Relevant information should either help a decision maker predict an outcome or serve as a check on previous predictions in a timely manner.
* The *reliability quality* serves to ensure that the information is a reasonably faithful representation of the entity's financial circumstances and is reasonably free of errors and bias. To be reliable, the information should be verifiable, represent the circumstances as they existed, and treat all interested parties neutrally.
* The *comparability quality* recognizes that the use of different methods makes comparisons among entities difficult. This quality is of concern to those setting accounting standards for the profession.

- The *consistency quality* requires that a business should use consistently the same accounting procedures or methods from one period to the next so that financial data can be compared from one period to the next. This quality does not preclude the implementation of new procedures that improve reporting, but requires that any such change and its effect must be disclosed and explained on financial statements.

B. Operational Guidelines

1. *Basic assumptions.* The basic assumptions are the entity assumption, the continuity assumption, the time-period assumption, and the monetary-unit assumption.

   - The *entity assumption* identifies the business entity's activities as separate from the owner's personal activities and other business entities.
   - The *continuity (going concern) assumption* recognizes that the firm is a going concern and is expected to continue to operate long enough to meet its obligations and fulfill its plans. This assumption justifies the use of historical cost rather than current values.
   - The *time-period (periodicity) assumption* recognizes that timely financial reports must be made to those who need the information in these reports. In other words, although the true financial position of a business cannot be precisely determined until its liquidation, interim financial statements are essential to making ongoing decisions during the operation of the business. Time periods for reporting can be monthly, quarterly, or annually. The year is the basic time unit.
   - The *monetary-unit assumption* holds that business transactions must be recorded and reported in terms of money. In the United States, of course, this monetary unit is the dollar. The problem with this approach is that the dollar—or any other currency—is not a stable or constant unit of measure. Nonetheless, the dollar is treated as stable and no allowance is made for inflation, deflation, or other causes of fluctuation in the value of the dollar.

2. *Basic principles.* The basic principles include the historical-cost principle, the revenue realization principle, the matching principle, and the full disclosure principle.

   - The *historical-cost principle* holds that most assets and liabilities are recorded at their transaction cost. For example, land purchased ten years ago for $20,000 may be worth $75,000 today. Nonetheless, the land would appear on the balance sheet as an asset valued at $20,000. The historical-cost principle provides an objective and verifiable basis for the initial recording of assets and liabilities.
   - The *revenue realization principle* maintains that revenue should not be reported on financial statements until the earning process is complete. In the case of revenue generated by the sale of goods, revenue is realized when title to (ownership of) the goods is passed from the seller to the buyer. In the case of revenue generated by the sale of a service, revenue is realized when the service is rendered.
   - The *matching principle*, when combined with the revenue realization principle, forms the heart of the accrual method. The matching principle requires that, where possible, the entity's operational efforts (expenses) be matched to the entity's operational accomplishment (revenues). By recognizing the revenues when they are realized and matching the related expenses to these revenues, the income statement focuses on the earning process, the purpose of accrual accounting. Note, however, that not all costs can be associated with revenues by rational and systematic means. Some costs will be recognized in the current period as expenses either because they have no anticipated future benefits or because there is no reasonable way to associate these costs with revenues.
   - The *full disclosure principle* requires that the financial statements of a business should be complete and should report sufficient economic information relating to the business entity to make the statements understandable. Information may be on the financial statements themselves or in supplementary attachments.

3. *Constraints.* The primary constraints include cost-benefit relationship and materiality. The secondary constraints are industry practices and conservatism.

   - The *cost-benefit constraint* dictates that the cost of obtaining and distributing information must be considered. That is to say, the accountant must be practical.

Management is not obligated to provide every potentially useful piece of information without regard to cost.

- The materiality constraint is used by accountants to help make decisions about the relative importance of financial data. An item or amount that would not alter a user's decision may be considered immaterial. If an item is considered immaterial, generally accepted accounting principles do not have to be followed in its recording or reporting.

EXAMPLE 2-9: The financial statements of a very large company such as General Motors, Inc., may not show the thousands of dollars because thousands of dollars are immaterial and no bad consequences result from these roundings when decisions are made and implemented based on the financial statements. However, a smaller company, such as Sanford Advertising Company, may be able to ignore cents, but not dollars or hundreds of dollars in presenting financial statements and in making decisions concerning the company.

- The *industry practices constraint* recognizes that there are some circumstances peculiar to a particular industry which require departures from the otherwise accepted practices and methods. Fortunately, these departures are relatively few in number.
- The *conservatism constraint* holds that when equally correct accounting alternatives are available for recording or reporting a transaction, the accountant should select the alternative that will result in the *least* favorable outcome for the business in the current period. The intent of the constraint is to minimize any overstatement of assets and income or understatement of liabilities.

RAISE YOUR GRADES

Can you explain...?

☑ what the balance sheet reports
☑ the subclassifications of assets, liabilities, and equity
☑ the income statement equation
☑ what the income statement reports
☑ the difference between accrual accounting and cash accounting
☑ the advantage of using accrual accounting
☑ what the statement of equity reports
☑ the guidelines for preparing financial statements and why they are important to accountants and users of accounting information

SUMMARY

1. The balance sheet lists the accounts that make up the assets, liabilities, and equity of a business entity in order to report the financial position of the entity as of a specific date.
2. Current assets are cash or noncash assets that are readily converted to cash and expected to be used or consumed through the normal operations of the business within one year or one operating cycle, whichever is longer.
3. Long-term investments are investments that are not readily converted into cash or are intended to be held for more than one year or one operating cycle, whichever is longer.
4. Plant assets are tangible assets that are used in the operation of the business and are relatively permanent.
5. Intangible assets are noncurrent assets that lack physical substance yet confer benefits or rights that are of future value to the business.
6. Other assets are any assets that do not fit any of the other classifications of assets.
7. Current liabilities are liabilities that will be paid with current assets within one year or one operating cycle, whichever is longer.

8. Noncurrent liabilities are liabilities that have a due date more than a year beyond the balance sheet date or beyond the operating cycle, whichever is longer, or will be settled with noncurrent sources.

9. The balance in the equity accounts results from investments, withdrawals, and earnings. It is the owners' contribution to the entity's resources. Equity is sometimes referred to as net assets.

10. There are two balance sheet formats. The most common is the report format which lists the liability and equity sections below the assets. The other is the account format which lists the assets on the left and the liabilities and equity on the right.

11. The income statement uses the performance elements to report the financial results of an entity's activities over a period of time.

12. Based on accrual accounting, businesses report their revenues, expenses, gains, and losses in the period in which the transactions giving rise to these elements occur. Based on cash accounting, these transactions are only reported in the period in which cash is actually received or paid by the entity. Thus, accrual accounting reflects economic events of the period while cash accounting merely reflects cash flows.

13. The income statement equation is REVENUES − EXPENSES + GAINS − LOSSES = NET INCOME. If there are no nonoperating elements to report (gains or losses), then the income statement equation is REVENUES − EXPENSES = NET INCOME.

14. The statement of equity reports the changes in capital that have occurred between the beginning and ending of a given period.

15. The statement of cash flows reports the cash receipts and cash payments along with the financing and investing activities of a firm.

16. There are certain basic assumptions, principles, and constraints about accounting that serve as guidelines to accountants so that they may be objective in preparing, presenting, and analyzing financial statements.

RAPID REVIEW   Answers

True or False

1. Financial statements have the same general heading including the name of the entity, the name of the financial statement, and the date of the financial statement. [Section 2-1]   *True*

2. The balance sheet reports on the financial position of a business entity as of a specific date. [Section 2-1]   *True*

3. Current assets include those assets expected to be used or consumed through operations of the business within one year or one operating cycle, whichever is longer. [Section 2-1]   *True*

4. Property, plant, and equipment are intangible assets with relatively short economic lives. [Section 2-1]   *False*

5. Equity is the owners' contributions to the sources of assets. [Section 2-1]   *True*

6. The report format of the balance sheet lists the assets on the left and the liabilities and equity on the right. [Section 2-1]   *False*

7. The income statement uses the performance elements to report the financial results of an entity's activities as of a specific date. [Section 2-2]   *False*

8. Accrual accounting reports transactions only when cash has been received or paid for them. [Section 2-2]   *False*

9. If there are no nonoperating items to report on the income statement, then operating income is the same as net income. [Section 2-2]   *True*

10. The statement of equity is a link between the balance sheet and the income statement. [Section 2-3]   *True*

11. The statement of cash flows focuses on the cash receipts, cash payments, and the financing and investing activities of a firm. [Section 2-4]

True

12. The entity assumption is used to bring together the owner's activities and the entity's activities. [Section 2-5]

False

13. The conservatism constraint is used to maximize the value of assets and income. [Section 2-5]

False

14. According to the monetary unit assumption, the accountant in the U.S. must treat the dollar as a stable unit of measure. [Section 2-5]

True

15. The consistency quality requires that a business always use the same accounting procedures from one period to the next unless there is justification for change. [Section 2-5]

True

SOLVED PROBLEMS

PROBLEM 2-1: As of June 30, 19x8, Hewitt Company, a small manufacturer of molded plastics with an accounting cycle of one year, has the following balance sheet equation.

$$A = L + E$$

$$\$1,600 = \$1,200 + \$400$$

Upon close examination of the accounts that make up these balances, it is noted that a note payable of $300 is due in 90 days. What is the appropriate classification of this item on the balance sheet and why?

Answer: The appropriate classification of this item on the balance sheet is as a current liability. Current liabilities are any liabilities that are to be paid with current assets within one year or one operating cycle, whichever is longer. In this case, cash is a current asset that will be used to repay the $300 note in 90 days, thus falling within the one-year requirement. [Section 2-1]

PROBLEM 2-2: Another examination of the accounts of Hewitt Company reveals that of the $1,600 in assets, $350 of those assets are represented by a newly issued three-year bond that management plans to hold until maturity. What is the appropriate classification of the bond on the balance sheet and why?

Answer: The appropriate classification of the three-year bond on the balance sheet is as a long-term investment because it is an asset that is to be held for more than the one-year accounting cycle. [Section 2-1]

PROBLEM 2-3: The Hewitt Company also has machinery and equipment that they have acquired over time. The recorded cost of this property is shown in the accounts as $600. What is the appropriate classification of this amount on the balance sheet and why?

Answer: The appropriate classification of the $600 of machinery and equipment (a tangible, long-term asset) is noncurrent. It would thus be classified as a plant asset, operational asset, or plant, property, and equipment on the balance sheet. [Section 2-1]

PROBLEM 2-4: It is noted that Hewitt Company also has a patent on a molding process valued at $250. What is the appropriate classification of this item on the balance sheet and why?

Answer: The appropriate classification of the patent is as an intangible asset because it is a noncurrent asset that lacks physical substance, yet it confers a benefit that is of future value to the business. [Section 2-1]

PROBLEM 2-5: Hewitt Company also has a $400 note payable on its equipment due in two years. What is the appropriate classification of this account on the balance sheet and why?

Answer: Assuming a normal accounting cycle of a year or less, the appropriate classification of the note payable is as a noncurrent liability because it is due beyond one year. [Section 2-1]

PROBLEM 2-6: Suppose that any assets of the Hewitt Company unaccounted for in Problem 2-5 above equal the current asset, Cash. Using this information and that given in the preceding problems, calculate the amount of cash.

Answer: We know from Problem 2-1 that the company's total assets equal $1,600. We also know from other account balances given in Problems 2-2, 2-3, and 2-4 that $1,200 of assets can be classified as $350 of long-term investments, $600 of plant assets, and $250 of intangible assets. Thus, the total assets accounted for equal $1,200 ($350 + $600 + $250), leaving $400 unaccounted for. Hewitt Company therefore has a cash balance of $400. [Section 2-1]

PROBLEM 2-7: Using the account information given in Problems 2-1 through 2-6 above, prepare the balance sheet for Hewitt Company as of June 30, 19x8. Assume that accounts payable has a balance of $500 and the owner is Sam Hewitt. Use report format.

Answer: [Section 2-1]

Hewitt Company
Balance Sheet
June 30, 19x8

Assets		
Current assets:		
Cash		$ 400
Long-term investments:		
Three-year bond		350
Plant assets:		
Machinery and equipment		600
Intangible assets:		
Patent		250
Total assets		$1,600
Liabilities		
Current liabilities:		
Note payable	$ 300	
Accounts payable	500	
Total current liabilities		$ 800
Long-term liabilities:		
Note payable		400
Total liabilities		$1,200
Equity		
Sam Hewitt, Capital		$ 400
Total liabilities and equity		$1,600

PROBLEM 2-8: Classify the following accounts by filling in the blank provided to the left of each account with the letter of the corresponding balance sheet category given on the right.

_____ 1. Capital

_____ 2. Interest payable in 6 months

_____ 3. Ten-year bonds payable

_____ 4. Mortgage payable

_____ 5. Wages payable

_____ 6. Machinery

_____ 7. Inventory

_____ 8. Trademark

_____ 9. Prepaid rent for 1 year

_____ 10. Land

_____ 11. Three-year note payable

_____ 12. Investments to be held for 3 years

Balance Sheet Categories

a. Current assets

b. Long-term investment

c. Plant asset

d. Intangible asset

e. Current liability

f. Noncurrent liability

g. Equity

Answer: 1. *g*;   2. *e*;   3. *f*;   4. *f*;   5. *e*;   6. *c*;   7. *a*;   8. *d*;   9. *a*;   10. *c*;   11. *f*;   12. *b*; [Section 2-1]

PROBLEM 2-9: Motor Bikes Co. has the following account balances. Prepare an income statement for the year ended December 31, 19x3.

Revenue	$16,400	Utilities expense	$1,800
Salary expense	$ 5,500	Advertising expense	$1,000
Rent expense	$ 6,000		

Answer: [Section 2-2]

Motor Bikes Co. Income Statement For Year Ended Dec. 31, 19x3		
Revenue		$16,400
Operating expenses:		
Advertising expense	$1,000	
Rent expense	6,000	
Salaries expense	5,500	
Utilities expense	1,800	
Total operating expenses		14,300
Net income		$ 2,100

3 TRANSACTION ANALYSIS AND THE DOUBLE-ENTRY SYSTEM

THIS CHAPTER IS ABOUT

- ☑ **Transaction Analysis**
- ☑ **The Double-Entry System**

3-1. Transaction Analysis

Transaction analysis is the first critical step in the financial reporting process. All data should be objective and verifiable. Remember, the effects of *every* transaction that are deemed relevant are analyzed and recorded in terms of increases and/or decreases in the elements that make up the accounting equation.

EXAMPLE 3-1: A comprehensive illustration of extended transaction analysis follows. Note that for each transaction analyzed, the first numeric line contains the beginning balances, the second line the changes brought about by the transactions, and the third the resulting balances.

The following transactions occur in May, 19–– the first month of operation of an interior design consulting business known as Interiors Unlimited. These transactions can be analyzed and recorded as follows.

TRANSACTION 1: *The owner, Liz Anderson, invests $10,000 in the business.* Two accounts in the basic accounting equation are affected by this transaction. The asset account, Cash, and the equity account, Liz Anderson, Capital, are both increased by $10,000.

Account	ASSETS =		LIABILITIES +		EQUITY				
	Cash	=		+	Investments	− Withdrawals	+ Revenues	− Expenses	
Beginning bal.	0	=	0	+	0	− 0	+ 0	− 0	
Change	**10,000**		0		**10,000**	0	0	0	
Ending bal.	10,000	=	0	+	10,000	− 0	+ 0	− 0	

TRANSACTION 2: *Interiors Unlimited purchases $600 worth of supplies.* The effect of this transaction is to exchange one type of asset, Cash, for another type of asset, Supplies.

ASSETS		= LIABILITIES +		EQUITY				
Cash	+ Supplies			Investments	− Withdrawals	+ Revenues	− Expenses	
10,000 +	0	= 0	+	10,000	− 0	+ 0	− 0	
− 600	**+ 600**	0		0	0	0	0	
9,400 +	600	= 0	+	10,000	− 0	+ 0	− 0	

TRANSACTION 3: *Interiors Unlimited purchases $3,500 worth of office furniture on account.* In this case, Interiors Unlimited acquires a new asset, $3,500 worth of office furniture, and incurs a liability, accounts payable of $3,500.

	ASSETS			= LIABILITIES +		EQUITY				
Cash +	Supplies +	Office Furn.	=	Accounts Payable	+ Investments	− Withdrawals	+ Revenues	− Expenses
9,400 +	600 +	0 =		0 +	10,000	− 0	+ 0	− 0
0	0	+3,500		+3,500	0	0	0	0
9,400 +	600 +	3,500 =		3,500 +	10,000	− 0	+ 0	− 0

TRANSACTION 4: *Interiors Unlimited pays $400 rent for office space for the current month.* Payment of the rent reduces the asset account, Cash, by $400. The $400 rent is recorded as an expense and a reduction in equity.

	ASSETS			= LIABILITIES +		EQUITY				
Cash +	Supplies +	Office Furn. =		Accounts Payable	+ Investments	− Withdrawals	+ Revenues	− Expenses
9,400 +	600 +	3,500 =		3,500 +	10,000	− 0	+ 0	− 0
−400	0	0		0	0	0	0	+400
9,000 +	600 +	3,500 =		3,500 +	10,000	− 0	+ 0	− 400

TRANSACTION 5: *Interiors Unlimited receives an invoice for $200 of advertising for the current month.* The invoice represents an Accounts Payable liability of $200 that is owed. Since advertising is an expense of the business, it is recorded as another reduction in the equity.

	ASSETS			= LIABILITIES +		EQUITY				
Cash +	Supplies +	Office Furn. =		Accounts Payable	+ Investments	− Withdrawals	+ Revenues	− Expenses
9,000 +	600 +	3,500 =		3,500 +	10,000	− 0	+ 0	− 400
0	0	0		+200	0	0	0	+200
9,000 +	600 +	3,500 =		3,700 +	10,000	− 0	+ 0	− 600

TRANSACTION 6: *Interiors Unlimited receives $3,000 in consulting fees.* This transaction increases the asset account, Cash, and the equity account (revenues) by $3,000.

	ASSETS			= LIABILITIES +		EQUITY				
Cash +	Supplies +	Office Furn. =		Accounts Payable	+ Investments	− Withdrawals	+ Revenues	− Expenses
9,000 +	600 +	3,500 =		3,700 +	10,000	− 0	+ 0	− 600
+3,000	0	0		0	0	0	+3,000	0
12,000 +	600 +	3,500 =		3,700 +	10,000	− 0	+ 3,000	− 600

TRANSACTION 7: *Interiors Unlimited pays an employee a salary of $600 for the month.* This transaction has the effect of reducing both the asset account, Cash, and equity by $600.

	ASSETS			= LIABILITIES +		EQUITY				
Cash +	Supplies +	Office Furn. =		Accounts Payable	+ Investments	− Withdrawals	+ Revenues	− Expenses
12,000 +	600 +	3,500 =		3,700 +	10,000	− 0	+ 3,000	− 600
−600	0	0		0	0	0	0	+600
11,400 +	600 +	3,500 =		3,700 +	10,000	− 0	+ 3,000	− 1,200

TRANSACTION 8: *Interiors Unlimited pays $1,750 of the $3,500 owed for office furniture.* In this transaction, the business is using the asset account, Cash, to reduce the liabilities account, Accounts Payable.

ASSETS			= LIABILITIES +		EQUITY			
Cash	+ Supplies	+ Office Furn. =	Accounts Payable	+ Investments	− Withdrawals	+ Revenues	− Expenses
11,400 +	600	+ 3,500 =	3,700 +	10,000	− 0	+ 3,000	− 1,200
−1,750	0	0	−1,750	0	0	0	0
9,650 +	600	+ 3,500 =	1,950 +	10,000	− 0	+ 3,000	− 1,200

TRANSACTION 9: *Interiors Unlimited discovers through an inventory that 2/3 of the firm's supplies have been used.* The business has consumed a portion of its assets, 2/3 of the supplies or $400 worth. Using these supplies in the operation of the business constitutes an expense and thus results in a decrease in equity as well.

ASSETS			= LIABILITIES +		EQUITY			
Cash +	Supplies	+ Office Furn. =	Accounts Payable	+ Investments	− Withdrawals	+ Revenues	− Expenses
9,650 +	600	+ 3,500 =	1,950 +	10,000	− 0	+ 3,000	− 1,200
0	−400	0	0	0	0	0	+400
9,650 +	200	+ 3,500 =	1,950 +	10,000	− 0	+ 3,000	− 1,600

TRANSACTION 10: *Liz Anderson withdraws $300 for her personal use.* The withdrawal reduces her equity.

ASSETS			= LIABILITIES +		EQUITY			
Cash +	Supplies	+ Office Furn. =	Accounts Payable	+ Investments	− Withdrawals	+ Revenues	− Expenses
9,650 +	200	+ 3,500 =	1,950 +	10,000	− 0	+ 3,000	− 1,600
−300	0	0	0	0	+300	0	0
9,350 +	200	+ 3,500 =	1,950 +	10,000	− 300	+ 3,000	− 1,600

The income statement, statement of equity, and balance sheet for Interiors Unlimited are illustrated on page 28.

Note that the net income for the current period is determined first. Then the statement of equity is prepared using this net income amount of $1,400. The statement of equity summarizes all the transactions affecting the capital account. The ending capital of $11,100 is then shown on the balance sheet.

3-2. The Double-Entry System

In Example 3-1, the effects of each business transaction were depicted as increases and decreases in the accounts that make up the elements of the accounting equation. Each new transaction required all the balances to be brought forward, allowing you to check that the accounting equation was still in balance (Assets = Liabilities + Equity). However, this

Interiors Unlimited
Income Statement
For Month Ended May 31, 19--

Revenues:		$3,000
Expenses:		
Rent expense	$400	
Advertising expense	200	
Salaries expense	600	
Supplies expense	400	
Total expenses		1,600
Net income		$1,400

Interiors Unlimited
Statement of Equity
For Month Ended May 31, 19--

Liz Anderson, Capital, May 1, 19--	$ -0-
Add: Investments	10,000
Net income	1,400
Subtotal	$11,400
Less: Withdrawals	300
Liz Anderson, Capital, May 31, 19--	$11,100

Interiors Unlimited
Balance Sheet
As of May 31, 19--

Assets

Current assets:		
Cash	$9,350	
Supplies	200	
Total current assets		$ 9,550
Property, Plant, and Equipment:		
Office furniture		3,500
Total assets		$13,050

Liabilities

Current liabilities:	
Accounts payable	$ 1,950

Equity

Liz Anderson, capital	11,100
Total liabilities and equity	$13,050

method of transaction analysis is too cumbersome to use in practice. To check the validity of financial statement relationships without having to check account balances and equation balances after every transaction, the *double-entry system* was developed.

A. The double-entry system is two-sided.

Every transaction has a two-fold effect. You may think of these effects as separate parts of the transaction in much the same way as you think of heads and tails as being two sides of a single coin.

1. *Debits.* One side of a transaction is designated the *debit*. The debit (or left) side will be made up of one or more of the following:

   - an increase in an asset, as with buying a building
   - a decrease in a liability, as with repayment of a loan
   - a decrease in equity, as with a distribution to an owner
   - a decrease in a revenue (or gain), as with returned merchandise.
   - an increase in an expense (or loss), as with employee salaries

2. *Credits.* The other side of a transaction is designated the *credit*. The possibilities for the credit (or right) side are a mirror image of the debit side:

   - a decrease in an asset, as with a disbursement of cash
   - an increase in a liability, as with buying on credit
   - an increase in equity, as with an owner's investment
   - an increase in a revenue (or gain), as with a sale of services
   - a decrease in an expense (or loss), as with a tax refund

B. There is a rule for remembering debits and credits for transactions.

With ten possibilities, it is fortunate that the increases and decreases in the accounts of each element follow a pattern that is dependent on their position in the balance sheet.

Memory rule for debits and credits. Items that appear on the *left side* of the balance sheet equation (assets) are increased with *left-side entries* known as *debits*. Items that appear on the *right side* of the balance sheet equation (liabilities and equity) are increased with *right-side entries* known as *credits*.

EXAMPLE 3-2: The following is an illustration of the memory rule for debits and credits. The resemblance to the letter T has led this form of recording the effects of transactions on accounts to be known as *T accounts*.

ASSETS		=	LIABILITIES		+	EQUITY	
Increases	Decreases		Decreases	Increases		Decreases	Increases
+ Debit	− Credit		− Debit	+ Credit		− Debit	+ Credit

Note that the memory rule does not mention decreases. Just remember that decrease rules are opposites of the increase rules. The rule also does not include the performance elements: expenses, losses, revenues, and gains. These elements can be thought of as a subset of the equity element. Remember that the income (or loss) reported on the income statement is the net increase (or decrease) in equity resulting from operations. Thus, since expenses have the effect of decreasing equity, then just as decreases in equity are recorded as debits, increases in expenses are recorded as debits. Furthermore, since revenue has the effect of increasing equity, then just as increases in equity are recorded as credits, increases in revenue are recorded as credits.

EXAMPLE 3-3: The following is an illustration of how the performance elements relate to the equity element.

EQUITY

Decreases – Debit	Increases + Credit

EXPENSES (or loss accounts)	**REVENUE** (or gain accounts)

Increases + Debit	Decreases – Credit	Decreases – Debit	Increases + Credit

C. T accounts are a convenient abbreviated format.

The distinctive T shape used to depict the increases and decreases of each element is commonly used to show the changes for each account.

EXAMPLE 3-4: The following Cash account shows all the cash transactions illustrated in Example 3-1. The transaction number is shown in parentheses beside each entry. All receipts of cash (increases) are shown on the debit (left) side of the account. All payments (decreases) during the same period are shown on the credit (right) side of the account. The financial statements should be prepared for the accounting period, so it is necessary to determine the account balance. Both the debit entries and the credit entries can be totaled and entered below the last entry on each side. This is known as *footing* the account and should be written small and in contrasting pen or pencil so as not to be confused with a transaction entry. The smaller sum is then subtracted from the larger sum to give the *balance of the account*. In this case, the cash account has a balance of $9,350, which is entered to the left of the sum on the debit side, indicating that it is a debit (or positive) balance. Had the payments (credits) totaled more than the receipts (debits) of cash, then the balance would have been entered on the credit side to indicate a credit (or negative) balance. In this case, however, the balance sheet will report the amount of cash as $9,350.

Cash

	(1)	10,000	(2)	600	
Debits	(6)	3,000	(4)	400	*Credits*
increase			(7)	600	*decrease*
assets			(8)	1,750	*assets*
			(10)	300	
	9,350	13,000		3,650	

Verify that this example follows the rules of debits and credits and that the balance is the difference between the sum of the two sides.

In the same example, the T account for Accounts Payable would have looked like this:

Accounts Payable

Debits decrease	(8)	1,750	(3)	3,500	*Credits increase*
liabilities			(5)	200	*liabilities*
			1,950	3,700	

As before, verify that the example follows the rules of debits and credits and that the balance is the difference between the sums of the two sides.

D. The double-entry system is self-balancing.

The double-entry system is self-balancing because each transaction is two sided and both sides must be equal. Thus, if you correctly debit *and* credit an equal amount of dollars for each transaction, then total dollars of debits will aways equal total dollars of credits.

EXAMPLE 3-5: Suppose that a business pays $14,000 cash for a car, Serial Number 1494, on May 3, 19—. The transaction can be analyzed as follows.

Debit asset account, Car, $14,000, and *credit* asset account, Cash, $14,000 for the car.

Note that this transaction is recorded in equal dollar amounts of debits and credits. Asset accounts have been both increased and decreased by $14,000. Liabilities and equity are unchanged.

	ASSETS	=	LIABILITIES	+	EQUITY
Cash	−14,000	=	0	+	0
Car	+14,000		0		0
Net effect	0	=	0	+	0

RAISE YOUR GRADES

Can you explain...?

☑ why transaction analysis is the first critical step in the financial reporting process

☑ a transaction in terms of its effects on the balance sheet equation

☑ the double-entry system and how it reflects the two-sided effect of every transaction

☑ the memory rule for debits and credits

☑ how the performance elements are a subset of the equity element

☑ how to determine an account balance when using the double-entry system

☑ how the double-entry system is self-balancing

SUMMARY

1. Transaction analysis is the first critical step in the financial reporting process.
2. Every transaction can be analyzed and recorded in terms of increases and/or decreases in the accounts that make up the accounting equation.
3. The income statement accounts, revenues and expenses, can be viewed as subsets of the equity accounts. Thus, transactions that affect income statement accounts also affect the equity accounts.
4. Under the double-entry system, every transaction results in at least one debit and one credit entry to accounts.
5. The memory rule for debits and credits states that any items that appear on the left side of the balance sheet equation are increased with left-side entries known as debits, and any items that appear on the right side of the balance sheet equation are increased by right-side entries known as credits.
6. Decreases are recorded as opposites of the memory rule.
7. The performance elements of the income statement—expenses, losses, revenue, and gains—can be thought of as a subset of the equity element: Increases in expense (or loss) accounts result in decreases in equity. Increases in revenue (or gain) accounts result in increases in equity.
8. The balance of an account can be found with the double-entry system by totaling the debit and credit sides of the account and subtracting the smaller sum from the larger sum, keeping in mind whether the larger amount is a debit or a credit.
9. The double-entry system is self-balancing if you correctly debit and credit an equal amount of dollars for each transaction. If so, then debits will always equal credits and the accounting equation will always be balanced.

SOLVED PROBLEMS

PROBLEM 3-1: The following transactions occurred in one month of operation of Juan's Florist Shop. In the space provided, indicate which elements of the accounting equation are increased or decreased as a result of the transaction.

TRANSACTION 1: Juan invested $10,000 in the business.

ASSETS = LIABILITIES + INVESTMENTS − WITHDRAWALS + REVENUE − EXPENSES
_____ = _____ + _____ − _____ + _____ − _____

TRANSACTION 2: Juan's Florist Shop purchased $2,000 worth of flowers, paying $1,000 of the amount and putting the other $1,000 on account.

ASSETS = LIABILITIES + INVESTMENTS − WITHDRAWALS + REVENUE − EXPENSES
_____ = _____ + _____ − _____ + _____ − _____

TRANSACTION 3: Juan's Florist Shop performed services for $3,000 to be billed later.

ASSETS = LIABILITIES + INVESTMENTS − WITHDRAWALS + REVENUE − EXPENSES
_____ = _____ + _____ − _____ + _____ − _____

TRANSACTION 4: Juan's Florist Shop paid rent for the month, $650.

ASSETS = LIABILITIES + INVESTMENTS − WITHDRAWALS + REVENUE − EXPENSES
_____ = _____ + _____ − _____ + _____ − _____

TRANSACTION 5: Juan's Florist Shop paid salaries of $500 for the month.

ASSETS = LIABILITIES + INVESTMENTS − WITHDRAWALS + REVENUE − EXPENSES
_____ = _____ + _____ − _____ + _____ − _____

TRANSACTION 6: Juan made a withdrawal of $1,000 cash from the business for himself.

ASSETS = LIABILITIES + INVESTMENTS − WITHDRAWALS + REVENUE − EXPENSES
_____ = _____ + _____ − _____ + _____ − _____

TRANSACTION 7: Juan received a bill for $300 of advertising during the month.

ASSETS = LIABILITIES + INVESTMENTS − WITHDRAWALS + REVENUE − EXPENSES
_____ = _____ + _____ − _____ + _____ − _____

TRANSACTION 8: Juan's Florist Shop paid the $1,000 balance owed for the flowers bought earlier in the month.

ASSETS = LIABILITIES + INVESTMENTS − WITHDRAWALS + REVENUE − EXPENSES
_____ = _____ + _____ − _____ + _____ − _____

Answer: [Section 3-1]

TRANSACTION 1: Juan's investment has the effect of increasing both the assets and equity of the business by $10,000.

ASSETS = LIABILITIES + INVESTMENTS − WITHDRAWALS + REVENUE − EXPENSES
increase = _____ + increase − _____ + _____ − _____

TRANSACTION 2: The purchase of $2,000 worth of flowers by paying $1,000 and putting $1,000 on account has the effect of increasing assets by the $2,000 worth of flowers, decreasing assets by the $1,000 payment, and increasing liabilities by the $1,000 left on account. Note that the effect of the increase *and* decrease in assets is a net increase overall.

ASSETS = LIABILITIES + INVESTMENTS − WITHDRAWALS + REVENUE − EXPENSES
increase = increase + _____ − _____ + _____ − _____

TRANSACTION 3: The performance of $3,000 in services has the effect of increasing both the assets (accounts receivable) and equity of the business by $3,000. Equity is increased because revenue has been earned.

ASSETS = LIABILITIES + INVESTMENTS − WITHDRAWALS + REVENUE − EXPENSES
increase = _____ + _____ − _____ + increase − _____

TRANSACTION 4: The payment of $650 for rent has the effect of decreasing both the assets and equity of the business by $650. Since rent is an expense of the business, then this transaction decreases equity. Cash is being paid out, thus decreasing assets.

ASSETS = LIABILITIES + INVESTMENTS − WITHDRAWALS + REVENUE − EXPENSES
decrease = _____ + _____ − _____ + _____ − increase

TRANSACTION 5: The payment of salaries has the same effect as the payment of rent. Salary is not a liability but an expense of the business, so both assets and equity are decreased by $500.

ASSETS = LIABILITIES + INVESTMENTS − WITHDRAWALS + REVENUE − EXPENSES
decrease = _____ + _____ − _____ + _____ − increase

TRANSACTION 6: The effect of Juan's making a withdrawal of $1,000 from the business has the effect of decreasing both assets and equity by $1,000. A withdrawal is not an expense of the business but a disbursement.

ASSETS = LIABILITIES + INVESTMENTS − WITHDRAWALS + REVENUE − EXPENSES
decrease = _____ + _____ − increase + _____ − _____

TRANSACTION 7: The $300 for advertising on account during the month has the effect of increasing liabilities and decreasing equity by $300. Accounts Payable and expenses are increased.

ASSETS = LIABILITIES + INVESTMENTS − WITHDRAWALS + REVENUE − EXPENSES
_____ = increase + _____ − _____ + _____ − increase

TRANSACTION 8: The payment of the $1,000 balance owed on the flowers has the effect of decreasing both assets and liabilities by $1,000.

ASSETS = LIABILITIES + INVESTMENTS − WITHDRAWALS + REVENUE − EXPENSES
decrease = decrease + _____ − _____ + _____ − _____

PROBLEM 3-2: In the spaces provided below, refer to the same transactions for Juan's Florist Shop given in Problem 3-1 and indicate the effect of each transaction on the accounting equation elements and performance elements in terms of debits and credits. The number of each transaction is given to the left of the space provided for the transaction.

	ASSETS	LIABILITIES	EQUITY			
			INVESTMENTS	WITHDRAWALS	REVENUE	EXPENSES
1.						
2.						
3.						
4.						
5.						
6.						
7.						
8.						

Answers: Note again that for Transaction 2, although individual asset accounts are both credited and debited, the overall effect on the asset element is a debit of $1,000. [Section 3-2]

	ASSETS		LIABILITIES		EQUITY							
					INVESTMENTS		WITHDRAWALS		REVENUE		EXPENSES	
1.	debit				credit							
2.	debit			credit								
3.	debit									credit		
4.		credit									debit	
5.		credit									debit	
6.		credit					debit					
7.				credit							debit	
8.		credit	debit									

PROBLEM 3-3: Now correctly debit and credit the balance sheet and performance elements with the actual amounts of the transactions of Juan's Florist Shop in the spaces provided below. Determine the balance of the accounts. Does the balance sheet equation balance for the month?

	ASSETS		LIABILITIES		EQUITY							
					INVESTMENTS		WITHDRAWALS		REVENUE		EXPENSES	
1.												
2.												
3.												
4.												
5.												
6.												
7.												
8.												
Totals												
Bal.												

Answer:

	ASSETS		LIABILITIES		EQUITY							
					INVESTMENTS		WITHDRAWALS		REVENUE		EXPENSES	
1.	10,000				10,000							
2.	1,000			1,000								
3.	3,000								3,000			
4.		650.									650	
5.		500									500	
6.		1,000					1,000					
7.				300							300	
8.		1,000	1,000									
Totals	14,000	3,150	1,000	1,300	10,000		1,000		3,000		1,450	
Bal.	10,850			300	10,000		1,000		3,000		1,450	

Totaling the accounts above shows that assets equal liabilities plus equity (investments − withdrawals + revenue − expenses) and that the balance sheet equation is thus balanced for this month of operation of Juan's Florist Shop. [Section 3-2]

PROBLEM 3-4: The following T accounts for Jessica's Boutique show ten transactions that have been recorded for the month of June. The number of each transaction is shown in parentheses to the left of each transaction entry.

Cash			
(1)	10,000	(2)	500
(6)	3,000	(3)	1,000
(10)	800	(5)	500
		(7)	1,000
		(8)	1,000

Fixtures	
(3)	3,000

Jessica Cooper, Drawing	
(7)	1,000

Accounts Receivable			
(4)	7,000	(6)	3,000
		(10)	800

Accounts Payable			
(8)	1,000	(3)	2,000

Sales Revenue			
		(4)	7,000

Supplies			
(2)	500	(9)	150

Jessica Cooper, Capital			
		(1)	10,000

Rent Expense	
(5)	500

Supplies Expense	
(9)	150

Next to the number of each transaction given below, indicate the type of account affected (asset, liability, investment, withdrawal, revenue, or expense). Then indicate whether the effect of the transaction is to increase or decrease the account.

	ACCOUNT DEBITED		ACCOUNT CREDITED	
	Type	Effect	Type	Effect
(1)	_____	_____	_____	_____
(2)	_____	_____	_____	_____
(3)	_____	_____	_____	_____
	_____	_____	_____	_____
(4)	_____	_____	_____	_____
(5)	_____	_____	_____	_____
(6)	_____	_____	_____	_____
(7)	_____	_____	_____	_____
(8)	_____	_____	_____	_____
(9)	_____	_____	_____	_____
(10)	_____	_____	_____	_____

Answer: [Section 3-2]

	ACCOUNT DEBITED		ACCOUNT CREDITED	
	Type	Effect	Type	Effect
(1)	asset	increase	investment	increase
(2)	asset	increase	asset	decrease
(3)	asset	increase	asset	decrease
			liability	increase
(4)	asset	increase	revenue	increase
(5)	expense	increase	asset	decrease
(6)	asset	increase	asset	decrease
(7)	withdrawal	increase	asset	decrease
(8)	liability	decrease	asset	decrease
(9)	expense	increase	asset	decrease
(10)	asset	increase	asset	decrease

PROBLEM 3-5: In the space provided below, determine the balance of the accounts for **Jessica's Boutique** given in Problem 3-4 for the month of June. Does the accounting equation **balance** for the month? What was the net income of the store for the month?

Cash			Fixtures		Jessica Cooper, Drawing	
10,000	500		3,000		1,000	
3,000	1,000					
800	500					
	1,000					
	1,000					

Accounts Receivable			Accounts Payable		Sales Revenue	
7,000	3,000		1,000	2,000		7,000
	800					

Supplies			Jessica Cooper, Capital		Rent Expense	
500	150			10,000	500	

Supplies Expense	
150	

Answer: [Section 3-2] To determine the balance of an account, total both the debit entries and **the credit** entries for each account and enter the sums below the last entry on each side as shown **below.** Then subtract the smaller sum from the larger sum to get the balance of the account. **Enter this** amount beside the sum of the correct side of the account to indicate a debit or credit **balance.**

Cash			Fixtures		Jessica Cooper, Drawing	
10,000	500		3,000		1,000	
3,000	1,000					
800	500					
	1,000					
	1,000					
9,800	*13,800*	*4,000*				

Accounts Receivable			Accounts Payable		Sales Revenue	
7,000	3,000		1,000	2,000		7,000
	800			*1,000*		
3,200	*3,800*					

Supplies			Jessica Cooper, Capital		Rent Expense	
500	150			10,000	500	
350						

Supplies Expense	
150	

Plugging the correct accounts and their balances into the balance sheet equation, you get

	ASSETS			=	LIABILITIES	+		EQUITY			
Cash	+ Accounts Receivable	+ Fixtures	+ Supplies	=	Accounts Payable	+	J. Cooper, Capital	− J. Cooper, Drawing	+ Revenue	− Expenses	
9,800 +	3,200	+ 3,000	+ 350	=	1,000	+	10,000	− 1,000	+ 7,000	− 650	
			16,350	=	1,000	+			15,350		

Thus, the balance sheet equation for Jessica's Boutique balances for the month of June.

To determine the net income for the store, plug the income statement account sums into the income statement equation and you get

$$\text{NET INCOME} = \text{REVENUE} - \text{EXPENSES}$$
$$6{,}350 = 7{,}000 - 650$$

PROBLEM 3-6: Following is the list of accounts for Smith Co.

1. Accounts Payable
2. Accounts Receivable
3. Advertising Expense
4. Cash
5. Equipment
6. Revenue
7. Rent Expense
8. Barney Smith, Capital
9. Barney Smith, Drawing
10. Salaries Expense
11. Supplies
12. Utilities Expense

The following transactions occurred in one month of operations of Smith Company. Indicate which accounts are to be debited and credited as a result of each transaction by inserting the number of the account in the space provided to the right of each transaction.

	Debit	Credit
a. Owner invested $10,000 in business.	____	____
b. Rent payment made for the month.	____	____
c. Provided a service and received cash.	____	____
d. Received cash for accounts owed.	____	____
e. Bought equipment on account.	____	____
f. Bought supplies on account.	____	____
g. Paid salaries for month.	____	____
h. Paid part of balance due on equipment purchase.	____	____
i. Billed customer for service provided.	____	____
j. Paid water, phone, and electric bills.	____	____
k. Paid for ad placed in newspaper.	____	____
l. Owner withdrew $1,000.	____	____

Answer: [Sections 3-1 and 3-2]

	Debit	Credit
a.	4	8
b.	7	4
c.	4	6
d.	4	2
e.	5	1
f.	11	1
g.	10	4
h.	1	4
i.	2	6
j.	12	4
k.	3	4
l.	9	4

PROBLEM 3-7: The following accounts show the transactions of Karl Slosberg's accounting firm for the month. The number of each transaction is given to the left of each entry.

Cash

(1)	5,000	(3)	700
(4)	5,000	(6)	500
		(7)	1,000
(11)	3,500	(9)	250

Accounts Payable

| (9) | 250 | (2) | 500 |

K. Slosberg, Drawing

| (7) | 1,000 | | |

Accounts Receivable

| (5) | 6,000 | (11) | 3,500 |
| (10) | 400 | | |

Notes Payable

| (6) | 500 | (4) | 5,000 |

Revenue

| | | (5) | 6,000 |
| | | (10) | 400 |

Supplies

| (2) | 500 | (8) | 100 |

K. Slosberg, Capital

| | | (1) | 5,000 |

Rent Expense

| (3) | 700 | | |

Supplies Expense

| (8) | 100 | | |

Next to the number of each transaction given below, analyze the transaction by describing it, then filling in the type of balance sheet element (asset, liability, or equity) affected by the transaction and whether the effect is to increase or decrease the account. The first transaction is analyzed for you as an example.

	Effect on Account Debited	Effect on Account Credited
1. Karl invested $5,000 cash in the business.	increase asset	increase equity
2.		
3.		
4.		
5.		
6.		
7.		
8.		
9.		
10.		
11.		

Answer: [Sections 3-1 and 3-2]

	Effect on Account Debited	Effect on Account Credited
1. Karl invested $5,000 cash in the business.	increase asset	increase equity
2. Bought $500 worth of supplies on account.	increase asset	increase liability
3. Paid office rent of $700 for the month.	decrease equity	decrease asset
4. Took out a loan for $5,000, signing a note for the amount.	increase asset	increase liability
5. Provided accounting services for clients for $6,000 on account.	increase asset	increase equity
6. Made payment on note of $500.	decrease liability	decrease asset
7. Owner withdrew $1,000 for personal use.	decrease equity	decrease asset
8. Supplies worth $100 had been used during the month.	decrease equity	decrease asset
9. Paid $250 on accounts payable.	decrease liability	decrease asset
10. Provided services for $400 to a client on account.	increase asset	increase equity
11. Received $3,500 cash from clients on account.	increase asset	decrease asset

PROBLEM 3-8: The following transactions occurred in one month of business of the private practice of Dr. Anna Boyer, a family practitioner. Correctly record the effects of each transaction in the T accounts provided.
1. Boyer invested $5,000 in the business.
2. Bought $1,000 worth of equipment, paying $500 cash and putting the remaining balance on account.
3. Billed patients for $9,000 of services provided during the month.
4. Paid medical insurance for the next month of $3,000.
5. Paid office salaries for the month of $1,200.
6. Received $6,000 from patients on account.
7. Paid office rent for the month of $1,100.
8. Paid $300 on accounts owed.
9. Paid $175 for repairs needed on X-ray equipment.
10. Paid $200 for office supplies.

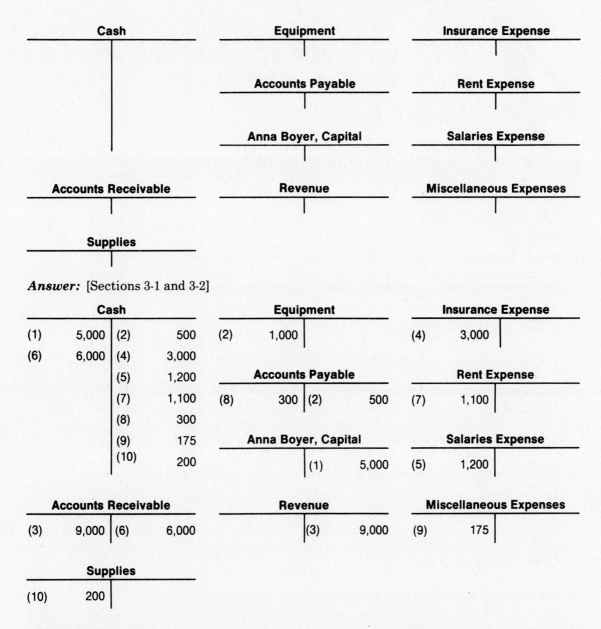

Answer: [Sections 3-1 and 3-2]

PROBLEM 3-9: Determine the balance of accounts given in Problem 3-8 for Dr. Boyer's medical practice. Group the accounts into an extended transaction analysis balance sheet equation and determine if the equation balances for the month.

Answer: Total the debit and credit side of each account and subtract the smaller amount from the larger amount to determine each account balance. Be aware of whether each account has a debit or credit balance. [Sections 3-1 and 3-2]

ASSETS				=	LIABILITIES	+			EQUITY				
Cash +	Accts. Rec. +	Supp. +	Equip. =		Accounts Payable +		Anna Boyer, Capital +	Revenue −	Ins. Exp. −	Sal. Exp. −	Rent Exp. −	Misc. Exp.	
4,525 +	3,000 +	200 +	1,000 =		200 +		5,000	+ 9,000 −	3,000 −	1,200 −	1,100 −	175	
			8,725 =		200 +				8,525				

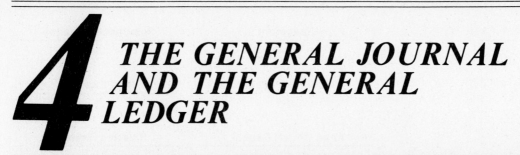

4 THE GENERAL JOURNAL AND THE GENERAL LEDGER

☑ **The General Journal**
☑ **The General Ledger**
☑ **Posting**
☑ **Trial Balance**

4-1. The General Journal

So far, you have concentrated on transaction analysis, which is the first critical step of the financial reporting process. The simple T account, with its debit and credit entries, was introduced as an easy method for illustrating the monetary effects of transactions on a business entity's accounts. However, a simple T account does not provide all the information about a transaction that a company needs. The necessary transaction information is first recorded in a journal and then posted to the ledger accounts (T accounts).

A. *Journalizing* is the second critical step in the financial reporting process.

A *journal*, also known as the *book of original entry*, is used by a business to chronologically record the effects of all transactions on company accounts along with brief explanations of each transaction. The design of a journal or the number of journals used by a business can vary. The *two-column general journal* is described in this chapter. Some special journals are discussed in Chapter 7.

B. The general journal provides a standardized place for each entry.

There is a standard procedure for journalizing, or recording, a transaction in a general journal. Suppose that on August 2, 19—, a construction company purchased a truck for $22,500, Serial No. 1776, using $5,000 as a cash down payment and signing a 15% note from First City Trust Bank for $17,500. The journal entry for this transaction would read as follows:

	DATE		DESCRIPTION	POST. REF.	DEBIT	CREDIT	
	JOURNAL					PAGE 16	
1	19-- Aug.	2	Equipment		2 2 5 0 0 00		1
2			Cash			5 0 0 0 00	2
3			Notes Payable			1 7 5 0 0 00	3
4			Truck, Serial No. 1776;				4
5			15% note, First City Trust Bank				5

1. *Date.* The year and month are recorded once at the top, left side of the date column for each page unless, of course, the month changes within the page. The day is recorded on

the right side of the date column on the first line of *each* transaction entry, even if several transactions occur on the same day.

2. *Account titles.* The name of the account to be debited is recorded on the first description line next to the date entry. The name of the account to be credited is recorded on the line below and indented. Debit entries are made first, then the credit entries. There can be more than one account that requires debiting or crediting, like the credit entries shown on page 42. This type of journal entry is known as a *compound journal entry.*

3. *Posting reference.* This column is not filled in until the transaction entry is posted, or entered, in the ledger. Posting references are discussed in Section 4-3 of this chapter.

4. *Amounts.* The amounts to be debited and credited are recorded in the appropriate debit and credit columns on the same line as their respective account titles. Again, more than one debit or credit amount may need to be recorded.

5. *Supplemental explanation.* A brief explanation of the transaction is usually recorded below the account entries in the description column and indented slightly. The explanation may be omitted if the transaction is obvious. Lengthy explanations of complex transactions can be omitted by referring to the supporting business document instead. The next line after an entry can be left blank to separate the entries.

Note the extensive amount of information recorded by the journal entry on page 42 and how easy it is to verify it. The date is easily verified by the supporting documents (the loan papers and the receipt for the cash down payment). The supplementary explanation makes it easy to determine the particular truck purchased and the source of the loan. The equality of debits and credits (in dollars, *not* number) is easily verified as $22,500. It is also simple to confirm that the effect of the transaction maintains the balance of the balance sheet equation as shown below.

	ASSETS =	LIABILITIES +	EQUITY
Cash	−5,000	0	0
Equipment	22,500	0	0
Notes Payable	0	17,500	0
Net Effect	17,500 =	17,500 +	0

EXAMPLE 4-1: In Example 3-1 on page 25, the transactions of Interiors Unlimited were analyzed for the company's first month of operation. Those same transactions are dated, expanded, and journalized as follows.

TRANSACTION 1: *May 1, the owner, Liz Anderson, invests $10,000 in the business.*

	JOURNAL				PAGE 1
	DATE	DESCRIPTION	POST. REF.	DEBIT	CREDIT
1	19-- May 1	Cash		1 0 0 0 0 00	
2		Liz Anderson, Capital			1 0 0 0 0 00
3		Owner invests in business			

TRANSACTION 2: *May 3, Interiors Unlimited purchases $600 worth of supplies from Daniel's Designs, Inc., Invoice No. 09543.*

7	3	Supplies		6 0 0 00	
8		Cash			6 0 0 00
9		Purchased from Daniel's Designs,			
10		Inc., Invoice No. 09543			

TRANSACTION 3: *May 3, Interiors Unlimited purchases $3,500 worth of office furniture on account from Best Furniture, Invoice No. 78114.*

12		3	Office Furniture			3 5 0 0	00					12
13			Accounts Payable					3 5 0 0	00			13
14			Purchased from Best Furniture,									14
15			Invoice No. 78114									15

TRANSACTION 4: *May 3, Interiors Unlimited pays $400 rent for office space.*

17		3	Rent Expense			4 0 0	00					17
18			Cash					4 0 0	00			18
19			Current month rent only									19

TRANSACTION 5: *May 7, Interiors Unlimited receives an invoice for $200 worth of advertising for the current month, from Hometown News, Invoice No. 41662.*

21		7	Advertising Expense			2 0 0	00					21
22			Accounts Payable					2 0 0	00			22
23			Bill for first month's adver-									23
24			tising from Hometown News,									24
25			Invoice No. 41662									25

TRANSACTION 6: *May 10, Interiors Unlimited receives $3,000 in consulting fees from North County Pediatric Group, Inc., Account No. 08.*

27		10	Cash			3 0 0 0	00					27
28			Consulting Fees					3 0 0 0	00			28
29			Received from North County Pedi-									29
30			atric Group, Account No. 08									30
31												31
32												32

TRANSACTION 7: *May 28, Interiors Unlimited pays an employee, Pat Jones, a salary of $600 for the month.*

			JOURNAL				PAGE 2	
	DATE		DESCRIPTION	POST. REF.	DEBIT		CREDIT	
1	19-- May	28	Salaries Expense		6 0 0 00			1
2			Cash				6 0 0 00	2
3			Current month wages paid Pat Jones					3
4								4

TRANSACTION 8: *May 29, Interiors Unlimited pays $1,750 of the $3,500 owed for office furniture to Best Furniture; Invoice No. 78114.*

6	29	Accounts Payable			1	7	5	0	00						6
7		Cash								1	7	5	0	00	7
8		Partial payment to Best Furni-													8
9		ture, Invoice No. 78114													9

TRANSACTION 9: *May 29, Interiors Unlimited discovers through an inventory that 2/3 of the firm's supplies have been used.*

11	29	Supplies Expense				4	0	0	00						11
12		Supplies									4	0	0	00	12
13		Supplies used in current month													13
14		based on physical inventory													14

TRANSACTION 10: *May 30, Liz makes a personal withdrawal of $300.*

16	30	Liz Anderson, Drawing				3	0	0	00						16
17		Cash									3	0	0	00	17
18		Withdrawal of cash for personal													18
19		use													19

4-2. The General Ledger

The general ledger is comprised of the accounts of a business entity. T accounts have been used to illustrate the ledger accounts up to now.

A. Accounts in the ledger are generally classified by common characteristics.

The accounts in the ledger are numbered, generally in the order that they are presented in the balance sheet and income statement, and using a system that reflects their common characteristics.

EXAMPLE 4-2: The eleven accounts of Interiors Unlimited (see Example 4-1) can be grouped as follows:

ASSET ACCOUNTS
11 Cash
12 Supplies
13 Office Furniture

LIABILITY ACCOUNTS
21 Accounts Payable

EQUITY ACCOUNTS
31 Liz Anderson, Capital
32 Liz Anderson, Drawing

REVENUE ACCOUNTS
41 Consulting Fees

EXPENSE ACCOUNTS
51 Rent Expense
52 Advertising Expense
53 Salaries Expense
54 Supplies Expense

This listing is usually referred to as the chart of accounts and is helpful in locating an account in the ledger. In this case, a two-digit number has been assigned to each account. The first digit represents the type of the account—1 for assets, 2 for liabilities, 3 for equity, 4 for revenue, and 5 for expenses. The second digit gives the position of accounts within each grouping. New accounts can be added at any time using this system of numbering. Each account would constitute a page in the general ledger. Ledgers are generally maintained in a binder so that new accounts can easily be added.

B. The four-column account is the most widely used in the general ledger.

The ledger account form is similar to the simple T account that was used to introduce you to the practice of debiting and crediting accounts. In addition to a column for debit entries and one for credit entries, debit and credit *balance* columns are used. This is known as the *four-column account.* Its main advantage is that it allows for a running balance of each account to be maintained at all times. (See page 47.)

C. The balance of the account should be entered in the first line of a ledger account.

Obviously, if an account is being opened for the first time, there is no balance of the account to enter in the first line. However, many firms begin a new page for each account at the beginning of a new accounting period as follows:

- The first day of the new accounting period is entered in the date columns of the ledger.
- The balance of the account as of the beginning of the accounting period is entered in the balance columns to indicate whether it is a debit or credit balance.
- The word "Balance" is written in the description column.
- A check mark is entered in the posting reference column to show that the entry is not the result of a transaction.

If, on the other hand, a new page must be started for an account *during* the accounting period, the balance is brought forward from the previous page, dated as of the last entry on the previous page, and the words "Balance brought forward" are entered in the description column.

4-3. Posting

The process of transferring information from the journal to the ledger is known as *posting.* Posting is the third critical step in the process of preparing financial reports.

A. The timing of the posting process can vary.

Many businesses have mechanical or electronic equipment that does the posting from the journal to the ledger and automatically enters new balances along with each entry. When posting manually, posting of a journal entry may be done immediately, at the end of each day, or even at the end of a week or month, depending on the size of the company and the number of transactions.

B. The four-column account provides a standardized procedure for posting each entry.

There is a standard procedure for posting a general journal entry to the general ledger. Shown below is the journal entry for the purchase of a 3/4-ton truck by a construction company that was shown on page 42. The posting of the debit to the Equipment account is illustrated immediately below the journal entry. Note that the balance of the account at the beginning of the accounting period has been recorded on the first line of the ledger page. In this case, there is a debit balance of $50,434.

1. *Date.* The date (year, month, day) is recorded in the date columns in the same manner as it is recorded in the journal entry.
2. *Amounts.* The amount is entered in the correct debit or credit column of the account.
3. *Ledger posting reference.* The number of the journal page from which the entry is posted is recorded in the posting reference column of the account.
4. *Journal posting reference.* The number of the ledger account to which the posting is made is recorded in the posting reference column of the journal.

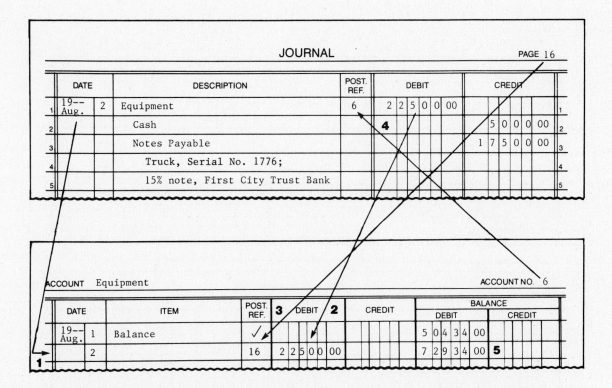

		JOURNAL														PAGE 16	
	DATE		DESCRIPTION	POST. REF.		DEBIT						CREDIT					
1	19-- Aug.	2	Equipment	6		2	2	5	0	0	00						1
2			Cash	**4**									5	0	0	0	00	2
3			Notes Payable									1	7	5	0	0	00	3
4			Truck, Serial No. 1776;															4
5			15% note, First City Trust Bank															5

ACCOUNT Equipment													ACCOUNT NO. 6						
	DATE		ITEM	POST. REF. **3**	DEBIT **2**				CREDIT			BALANCE							
												DEBIT					CREDIT		
1	19-- Aug.	1	Balance	✓								5	0	4	3	4	00		
		2		16	2	2	5	0	0	00		7	2	9	3	4	00 **5**		

5. *Balance of account.* The new balance of the account is entered in the proper debit or credit balance column.

C. Posting references provide a trail for each transaction.

Note that the cross-indexing of the journal page to the ledger and the account number to the journal provides a trail. A transaction can always be traced from the journal to the ledger or the ledger to the journal. This cross-indexing can help in error analysis, aid in auditing the books, facilitate internal control, or merely indicate which was the last journal entry posted.

EXAMPLE 4-3: All of the transactions for the month of May for Interiors Unlimited were journalized in Example 4-1 on pp. 43–45. At the end of the month, the entries must be posted in the ledger. The ledger will appear as shown below. Since this is a new business, there are no opening balances in the accounts. Refer back to Example 4-1 to trace each entry from the journal to the ledger and to better understand the posting process. Remember that in practice, each account is on a separate page. The accounts are numbered as shown in Example 4-2 on page 45.

ACCOUNT Cash													ACCOUNT NO. 11					
DATE		ITEM	POST. REF.	DEBIT					CREDIT				BALANCE					
													DEBIT					CREDIT
19-- May	1		1	1	0	0	0	0	00					1	0	0	0	0	00
	3		1							6	0	0	00	9	4	0	0	00
	3		1							4	0	0	00	9	0	0	0	00
	10		1		3	0	0	0	00					1	2	0	0	0	00
	28		2							6	0	0	00	1	1	4	0	0	00
	29		2							1	7	5	0	00	9	6	5	0	00
	30		2							3	0	0	00	9	3	5	0	00

ACCOUNT Supplies   ACCOUNT NO. 12

DATE		ITEM	POST. REF.	DEBIT	CREDIT	BALANCE	
						DEBIT	CREDIT
19-- May	3		1	600 00		600 00	
	29		2		400 00	200 00	

ACCOUNT Office Furniture   ACCOUNT NO. 13

DATE		ITEM	POST. REF.	DEBIT	CREDIT	BALANCE	
						DEBIT	CREDIT
19-- May	3		1	3500 00		3500 00	

ACCOUNT Accounts Payable   ACCOUNT NO. 21

DATE		ITEM	POST. REF.	DEBIT	CREDIT	BALANCE	
						DEBIT	CREDIT
19-- May	3		1		3500 00		3500 00
	7		1		200 00		3700 00
	29		2	1750 00			1950 00

ACCOUNT Liz Anderson, Capital   ACCOUNT NO. 31

DATE		ITEM	POST. REF.	DEBIT	CREDIT	BALANCE	
						DEBIT	CREDIT
19-- May	1		1		10000 00		10000 00

ACCOUNT Liz Anderson, Drawing   ACCOUNT NO. 32

DATE		ITEM	POST. REF.	DEBIT	CREDIT	BALANCE	
						DEBIT	CREDIT
19-- May	30		2	300 00		300 00	

ACCOUNT Consulting Fees   ACCOUNT NO. 41

DATE		ITEM	POST. REF.	DEBIT	CREDIT	BALANCE	
						DEBIT	CREDIT
19-- May	10		1		3000 00		3000 00

ACCOUNT Rent Expense   ACCOUNT NO. 51

DATE		ITEM	POST. REF.	DEBIT	CREDIT	BALANCE	
						DEBIT	CREDIT
19-- May	3		1	400 00		400 00	

ACCOUNT   Advertising Expense   ACCOUNT NO. 52

DATE		ITEM	POST. REF.	DEBIT	CREDIT	BALANCE	
						DEBIT	CREDIT
19-- May	7		1	2 0 0 00		2 0 0 00	

ACCOUNT   Salaries Expense   ACCOUNT NO. 53

DATE		ITEM	POST. REF.	DEBIT	CREDIT	BALANCE	
						DEBIT	CREDIT
19-- May	28		2	6 0 0 00		6 0 0 00	

ACCOUNT   Supplies Expense   ACCOUNT NO. 54

DATE		ITEM	POST. REF.	DEBIT	CREDIT	BALANCE	
						DEBIT	CREDIT
19-- May	29		2	4 0 0 00		4 0 0 00	

4-4. Trial Balance

To test the accuracy of the ledger entries, the equality of the debits and credits should be checked periodically. This test is done by preparing a *trial balance*.

A. There are four steps to preparing a trial balance.

1. Determine the balance of each account in the ledger.
2. List the accounts and their balances with the debit balances in one column and the credit balances in another.
3. Total the debit balances and then total the credit balances.
4. Compare the sums of the debit and credit balances to see if they are equal.

EXAMPLE 4-4: The following trial balance was prepared at the end of May from the accounts of Interiors Unlimited (see Example 4-3).

Interiors Unlimited

Trial Balance

May 31, 19--

Cash	9 3 5 0 00	
Supplies	2 0 0 00	
Office Furniture	3 5 0 0 00	
Accounts Payable		1 9 5 0 00
Liz Anderson, Capital		1 0 0 0 0 00
Liz Anderson, Drawing	3 0 0 00	
Consulting Fees		3 0 0 0 00
Rent Expense	4 0 0 00	
Advertising Expense	2 0 0 00	
Salaries Expense	6 0 0 00	
Supplies Expense	4 0 0 00	
	1 4 9 5 0 00	1 4 9 5 0 00

B. A trial balance that balances does not absolutely prove the accuracy of the ledger.

A trial balance that balances proves only that there is an equal dollar amount of debits and credits. It is still possible that an error exists in the ledger accounts, such as

- a correct amount may have been debited or credited to the wrong account
- an incorrect amount may have been debited and credited to two accounts
- a transaction may not have been posted at all
- the same transaction may have been recorded more than once

These errors would not affect the equality of the debits and credits. Even so, a trial balance is useful because most errors *do* result in an inequality of debits and credits. Remember, however, that a trial balance that balances is not assumed proof of the accuracy of the ledger.

C. There are methods for discovering errors if a trial balance does not balance.

If the trial balance does not balance, the general procedure for detecting the error or errors is to work backward from the trial balance to the original journal entry using the steps below. Usually, any errors will be discovered before all steps are completed.

1. Re-add the trial balance columns to confirm the discrepancy between the totals.
2. Make sure that no accounts have been omitted by comparing the account listings and balances in the trial balance with the account listings and balances in the general ledger.
3. Recalculate the balance of each account in the ledger.
4. Check the postings in the ledger against the entries in the journal by placing a check mark by each item in both the ledger and the journal. If no error in posting is detected, check that each entry in the journal has a check mark in case an entry was not posted at all.
5. Check the equality of the debits and credits in the journal.

RAISE YOUR GRADES

Can you explain...?

☑ how a journal entry provides more information about a transaction than a T account
☑ how to journalize a transaction
☑ the purpose of the general ledger
☑ why accounts are classified by common characteristics
☑ what is the advantage of a four-column general ledger account
☑ when posting should be done
☑ how to post a general journal entry
☑ the importance of posting references
☑ how to prepare a trial balance and when it should be prepared
☑ what proof is provided by a trial balance
☑ how to discover errors if a trial balance does not balance

SUMMARY

1. Journalizing is the second critical step in the financial reporting process.
2. A journal, also known as the book of original entry, is used to chronologically record the effects of transactions on company accounts along with a brief explanation of each transaction.
3. The general journal provides a standardized place for entering information about a transaction.
4. The purpose of the general ledger is to accumulate and summarize the transactions that affect a particular account.
5. Accounts in the ledger are generally numbered using a system that reflects their common characteristics. A listing of the account titles and their numbers is usually called a chart of accounts.
6. The four-column account is the most widely used in the general ledger. It includes debit and credit entry and balance columns.
7. Posting is the third critical step in the financial reporting process.
8. Posting of journal entries may be done at any time, depending on the size of the company and the number of transactions.
9. The four-column account provides a standardized place for recording all journal entries affecting the account.
10. The cross-indexing of the journal page to the ledger and the account number to the journal provides a means of tracing a transaction from the journal to the ledger or the ledger to the journal. This tracing can help in error analysis, aid in auditing the books, facilitate internal control, or merely indicate which was the last journal entry posted.
11. A trial balance is prepared periodically to determine the equality of the dollar amount of debits and credits in the general ledger.
12. It is still possible that an error exists in the ledger accounts even though the debits and credits are equal. Thus, a trial balance is not assumed proof of the accuracy of the ledger.
13. If a trial balance does not balance, the general procedure for detecting the error or errors is to work backward from the trial balance to the original journal entry, checking all entries and balances as you go.

RAPID REVIEW   Answers

True or False

1. The design of a journal or the number of journals used by a business can vary. [Section 4-1] — *True*

2. A compound journal entry is one in which more than one account requires debiting or crediting. [Section 4-1] — *True*

3. Supplemental information about a transaction can always be omitted from the journal entry. [Section 4-1] — *False*

4. The general ledger is comprised of the accounts of a business entity. [Section 4-2] — *True*

5. The main advantage of the four-column ledger account is that multiple debits or credits can be posted to an account at one time. [Section 4-2] — *False*

6. Posting may be done from the journal to the ledger or from the ledger to the journal. [Section 4-3] — *False*

7. Posting should be done at least once a month. [Section 4-3] — *True*

8. Each succeeding page of an account in the ledger should begin with the beginning balance of the account or the balance brought forward from the preceding page. [Section 4-3] — *True*

9. The number of the ledger account to which a posting is made is recorded in the posting reference column of the journal entry. [Section 4-3] — *True*

10. The new account balance must be entered immediately after each posting of a journal entry. [Section 4-3]   *False*

11. If an amount has been debited to the wrong account in the general ledger, then the equality of the debits and credits in the trial balance will be affected. [Section 4-4]   *False*

SOLVED PROBLEMS

PROBLEM 4-1: What are the steps in the financial reporting process?

Answer: The steps involved in the financial reporting process can be illustrated as follows:

TRANSACTION → ANALYSIS → JOURNALIZING → POSTING → FINANCIAL REPORT

First, a transaction occurs that affects the accounts of a business. These effects, evidenced by business documents, are then analyzed to determine exactly what accounts are affected and in what way. This information, plus a brief explanation of the transaction, is journalized in chronological order. Often, the explanation of the transaction refers to the supporting documents of the transaction. The amount of the debits and credits in the journal are then posted to the accounts in the general ledger. The account accumulates and summarizes the effects of similar transactions on that account. Financial reports are then prepared from the information recorded in the general ledger.

PROBLEM 4-2: The Thompson Company has the following accounts in its ledger: Cash; Accounts Receivable; Supplies; Office Equipment; Accounts Payable; Emily Thompson, Capital; Emily Thompson, Drawing; Fees Revenue; Utilities Expense; Rent Expense; Miscellaneous Expense.

The following transactions of the Thompson Company took place in January of the current year. Enter these transactions in the two-column journal provided below.

Jan. 3   Paid $300 cash for supplies.
      5   Withdrew $1,500 cash for personal use.
      8   Received and paid $174 electric bill for the month.
      9   Paid $750 rent for the month.
     11   Received $3,487 in fees from customers.
     13   Bought desk, Serial #29856, on account, $2,300.
     13   Received $2,950 from customers on account.
     24   Paid creditor $600, Invoice #698.
     27   Paid $220 advertising expense, Invoice #32.
     30   Paid previously recorded telephone bill, $340.

	JOURNAL			PAGE *12*

DATE	DESCRIPTION	POST. REF.	DEBIT	CREDIT

Answer: [Section 4-1]

JOURNAL

PAGE 12

DATE		DESCRIPTION	POST. REF.	DEBIT	CREDIT
19-- Jan.	3	Supplies		300 00	
		Cash			300 00
		Paid cash for supplies			
	5	Emily Thompson, Drawing		1500 00	
		Cash			1500 00
		Withdrawal for personal use			
	8	Utilities Expense		174 00	
		Cash			174 00
		Paid electric bill for month			
	9	Rent Expense		750 00	
		Cash			750 00
		Paid rent for month			
	11	Cash		3487 00	
		Fees Revenue			3487 00
		Fees from customers			
	13	Office Equipment		2300 00	
		Accounts Payable			2300 00
		Bought desk; Serial #29856			
	13	Cash		2950 00	
		Accounts Receivable			2950 00
		Received from customers on account			
	24	Accounts Payable		600 00	
		Cash			600 00
		Paid creditor; Invoice #698			
	27	Miscellaneous Expense		220 00	
		Cash			220 00
		Paid advertising; Invoice #32			
	30	Utilities Expense		340 00	
		Accounts Payable			340 00
		Paid telephone bill			

PROBLEM 4-3: Sterling Co., a new business, has determined that the following accounts are necessary to start its beginning chart of accounts: John Sterling, Capital; Accounts Payable; Salaries Expense; Accounts Receivable; Land; Supplies; John Sterling, Drawing; Notes Payable; Supplies Expense; Equipment; Utilities Expense; Cash; Prepaid Insurance; and Fees Earned. In the space provided below, use the system discussed in Example 4-2 on page 45 to list and number the accounts in the order that they should appear in the ledger.

No.	Account	No.	Account
___	_____	___	_____
___	_____	___	_____
___	_____	___	_____
___	_____	___	_____
___	_____	___	_____
___	_____	___	_____
___	_____	___	_____

Answer: The system used in Example 4-2 to number accounts in the ledger is a two-digit system. The first digit represents the element—1 for assets, 2 for liabilities, 3 for equity, 4 for revenue, and 5 for expenses. The second digit consecutively numbers the accounts, beginning with 1, in the order that they would appear on the balance sheet or the income statement. Thus, the correct order and numbering of the accounts in the ledger of Sterling Co. is as follows*:

No.	Account	No.	Account
11	Cash	22	Notes Payable
12	Accounts Receivable	31	John Sterling, Capital
13	Supplies	32	John Sterling, Drawing
14	Prepaid Insurance	41	Fees Earned
15	Land	51	Salaries Expense
16	Equipment	52	Supplies Expense
21	Accounts Payable	53	Utilities Expense

* The sequence *within an element* can vary for some accounts; so may your answer. [Section 4-2]

PROBLEM 4-4: The following trial balance of Ziskin Company does not balance.

Ziskin Company

Trial Balance

October 31, 19--

Account	Debit	Credit
Cash	6 1 7 0 0 00	
Accounts Receivable	9 7 0 0 00	
Supplies	4 2 0 0 00	
Accounts Payable		7 6 5 0 00
Mike Ziskin, Capital		4 5 0 0 0 00
Mike Ziskin, Drawing		3 0 0 0 00
Fees Income		1 2 8 6 0 00
Utilities Expense	3 2 0 00	
Advertising Expense		5 0 0 00
	7 5 9 2 0 00	6 9 0 1 0 00

A review of the ledger and journal entries reveals the following:

1. The debits and credits in the Cash account equal $61,700 and $11,910 respectively.
2. A payment of $1,200 to a creditor was not posted to the Accounts Payable account.
3. The advertising expense for the month, $500, was credited to the Advertising Expense account.
4. The receipt of $1,400 from a customer on account was not posted to the Accounts Receivable account.
5. The balance of the Supplies account is $2,400.
6. The balance of the Mike Ziskin, *withdrawals* account is shown as a credit in the trial balance.

Based on these discoveries, prepare a corrected trial balance for Ziskin Company, using the form provided below.

```
                              Ziskin Company
                               Trial Balance
                              October 31, 19--

    Cash
    Accounts Receivable
    Supplies
    Accounts Payable
    Mike Ziskin, Capital
    Mike Ziskin, Drawing
    Fees Income
    Utilities Expense
    Advertising Expense
```

Answer: Each error requires a change in the account balances given in the trial balance, as follows:

1. The debit amount was given for the Cash account without subtracting the credits. Therefore, the cash balance should be $61,700 − $11,910, or $49,790.
2. A payment of $1,200 to a creditor would result in a debit to the Accounts Payable account that was not posted. This debit must be subtracted from the credit balance shown in the trial balance to give a new Accounts Payable balance of $6,450.
3. The advertising expense of $500 should have been debited to the Advertising Expense account, not credited.
4. The receipt of $1,400 from a customer on account would result in a credit to the Accounts Receivable account that was not posted. This credit must be subtracted from the debit balance shown in the trial balance to give a new Accounts Receivable balance of $8,300.
5. The balance of the Supplies account was incorrectly reported as $4,200 instead of $2,400. This is a common error known as a transposition when two digits are unintentionally reversed.
6. The normal balance of a Drawing account should be shown as a debit balance, not a credit balance.

Following is the corrected trial balance for Ziskin Company. [Section 4-4]

Ziskin Company

Trial Balance

October 31, 19--

Cash	4 9 7 9 0 00	
Accounts Receivable	8 3 0 0 00	
Supplies	2 4 0 0 00	
Accounts Payable		6 4 5 0 00
Mike Ziskin, Capital		4 5 0 0 0 00
Mike Ziskin, Drawing	3 0 0 0 00	
Fees Income		1 2 8 6 0 00
Utilities Expense	3 2 0 00	
Advertising Expense	5 0 0 00	
	6 4 3 1 0 00	6 4 3 1 0 00

PROBLEM 4-5: The following transactions of Haller Concrete Works occurred and were journalized in February of the current year. In the space provided below each entry, write a brief explanation of the transaction that has been entered as it might appear in the journal.

JOURNAL — PAGE 13

	DATE		DESCRIPTION	POST. REF.	DEBIT	CREDIT	
1	19-- Feb.	2	Accounts Receivable		2 9 0 0 00		1
2			Services Revenue			2 9 0 0 00	2
3							3
4							4
5		5	Equipment		1 4 0 0 0 00		5
6			Cash			4 0 0 0 00	6
7			Accounts Payable			1 0 0 0 0 00	7
8							8
9							9
10							10
11		10	Don Haller, Drawing		1 5 0 0 00		11
12			Cash			1 5 0 0 00	12
13							13
14							14
15		17	Utilities Expense		5 0 0 00		15
16			Cash			5 0 0 00	16
17							17
18							18
19		23	Accounts Payable		1 0 0 0 00		19
20			Cash			1 0 0 0 00	20
21							21

Answer: [Section 4-1]

	DATE		DESCRIPTION	POST. REF.	DEBIT	CREDIT	
1	19-- Feb.	2	Accounts Receivable		2 9 0 0 00		1
2			Services Revenue			2 9 0 0 00	2
3			*Services on account*				3
4							4
5		5	Equipment		1 4 0 0 0 00		5
6			Cash			4 0 0 0 00	6
7			Accounts Payable			1 0 0 0 0 00	7
8			*Equipment purchased with*				8
9			*$4,000 cash, $10,000 on account*				9
10							10
11		10	Don Haller, Drawing		1 5 0 0 00		11
12			Cash			1 5 0 0 00	12
13			*Owner withdrawal*				13
14							14
15		17	Utilities Expense		5 0 0 00		15
16			Cash			5 0 0 00	16
17			*Paid utility bill*				17
18							18
19		23	Accounts Payable		1 0 0 0 00		19
20			Cash			1 0 0 0 00	20
21			*Payment to creditor*				21

JOURNAL   PAGE 13

PROBLEM 4-6: The following errors occurred in posting from the journal to the ledger of Cox Company. In the space provided, indicate whether the trial balance would be out of balance as a result of the error.

1. A debit of $300 to Supplies was posted as a debit to Cash.   _____
2. A debit of $550 to Accounts Receivable was posted twice.   _____
3. A debit of $1,000 to Mortgage Payable was not posted.   _____
4. A sale of $400 was debited and credited as a sale of $600.   _____
5. A credit of $200 to Accounts Payable was posted as a debit.   _____

Answer: 1. No; 2. Yes; 3. Yes; 4. No; 5. Yes   [Section 4-4]

5 COMPLETING THE ACCOUNTING PROCESS

5-1. Accrual Accounting and Timing of Revenue and Expense

A. Accrual accounting emphasizes performance.

Accrual accounting attempts to measure the performance of an enterprise during a particular period. It does this by trying to associate accomplishment (revenue) recognized in a period with the effort (expense) related to that accomplishment. Generally, accrual accounting provides a better indication of performance than information about the period's cash receipts and cash payments.

B. Revenue realization and expense matching bring together the separate income elements.

1. *Revenue realization.* There are various points in the earning process when revenue could be recognized. Revenue is generally realized (recognized) when an exchange has taken place; that is, revenue is realized when

   • the *business provides* the goods or services *and*
   • the *buyer provides* either payment or a promise to pay for the goods or services.

2. *Expense matching.* Matching expenses to the correct period or revenue brings into play the remainder of the income elements.

   (a) Some revenues and expenses result simultaneously from the same transaction. Because the revenue and the expense are *directly related*, the matching of such expenses in the same period is relatively easy; for example, a sales representative's commission with sales revenue.

   (b) Some costs incurred are not directly related to particular revenues but are allocated to a particular period by means of *systematic and rational allocation*; for example, depreciation expense for store equipment in a retail store.

59

(c) Other costs are incurred to obtain benefits which expire in the same period, but cannot be directly associated with revenues, such as insurance. Still other costs may have future benefits, but they cannot be related directly to future revenues or systematically and rationally allocated to a particular period; for example, advertising expense. These costs are *immediately recognized* as expense.

5-2. Adjusting Entries

Adjusting entries are made at the end of the accounting period to bring the accounts up to date so that the balances will more accurately reflect the financial position at the end of the period and the net income for the period. The financial statements are prepared after the adjusting entries are made.

A. There are two types of adjusting entries that should be made at the end of the accounting period.

1. *Deferral adjusting entries.* A deferral *delays* recognition of an expense or a revenue to a time period later than the one in which the cash was paid or the liability incurred.
2. *Accrual adjusting entries.* An accrual adjusting entry recognizes revenues and expenses prior to a transfer of cash. No transaction has as yet been recorded.

In either case, the adjustment affects the balance sheet in either an asset or liability account *and* the income statement in either a revenue or expense account.

B. The two types of adjusting entries may be further subdivided into four classes.

1. *Asset/expense adjustments.* These adjustments transfer the cost of an asset to expense as the asset is used. For example, the cost of a three-year insurance policy will be allocated to expense over three years.
2. *Asset/revenue adjustments.* These adjustments record revenues earned but not yet collected or billed to customers (receivables); for example, interest revenue on a note receivable earned but not yet received.
3. *Liability/expense adjustments.* These adjustments record the liability for costs for which the service potential has already expired; for example, wages earned but not paid by the last day of the accounting period.
4. *Liability/revenue adjustments.* These adjustments record the liability for revenue collected in advance of its being earned; for example, rent received in advance of the rental period.

5-3. Asset/Expense Adjustments

Asset/expense adjustments are required to allocate expenses over more than one accounting period. The amount in the asset account may have been recorded in this period or in some prior period. This amount represents the cost of benefits acquired for the future. Asset/expense adjustments involve determining the appropriate portion of the cost that has expired and allocating it to an expense at the end of the period. Remember that the determination of the amount of cost to allocate to expense may be direct, systematic and rational, or immediate.

A. The cost of consumable assets is directly matched to a period.

Every business keeps an inventory of consumable assets used in the day-to-day operation of the business, such as stationery, floppy discs, paper, and cleaning materials. While it would be possible to record each item as an expense when it was removed from inventory, this is not practical. Instead, the supplies on hand at the end of the period are reported as current assets and the supplies used during the period are reported as expense. This is an example of direct matching of an expense to a period.

EXAMPLE 5-1: At the beginning of December, Creative Consulting, an art consulting firm, had $200 of supplies on hand. During the month, supplies were purchased for $300. At the end of the accounting period, December 31 of the current year, a count of the supplies still on hand revealed that supplies costing $100 were available for use in the next accounting period. The supplies used during the current period will be transferred to expense, as illustrated below:

Supplies Available During Period	=	Used Portion (Expired Cost or Expense)	+	Unused Portion (Unexpired Cost or Asset)
$500		$400		$100

The purchase of the supplies during the accounting period was recorded as an increase to the asset account, Supplies. At the end of the accounting period, the journal entry made to adjust the accounts, recognizing a portion of the supplies as expense would be

		JOURNAL				PAGE --
DATE		DESCRIPTION	POST. REF.	DEBIT	CREDIT	
19-- Dec.	31	Supplies Expense	52	4 0 0 00		1
		Supplies	14		4 0 0 00	2
		Adjustment of account based on				3
		December 31 physical inventory				4

Note that the expense account is increased (debited) $400 for the cost of the supplies used. The asset account is decreased (credited) $400. Thus, the asset account, Supplies, will show a balance of $100, the cost of supplies on hand. The ledger entries made for the accounting period that reflect this information are shown in T account format.

Supplies				Supplies Expense	
Beg. bal. 200	adj. 400		adj. 400		
purch. 300					
bal. 100					

B. Prepayments may require adjustments to allocate cost to expense.

Another type of cost that must be allocated to expense over more than one accounting period is the expiration of prepayments. An asset is created when an expense is paid for before it is actually incurred. The asset is reduced and an expense is recognized as the asset is used up. Examples are Prepaid Taxes, Prepaid Rent, and Prepaid Insurance. This adjustment has features of both direct, and systematic and rational matching of expense to a period.

EXAMPLE 5-2: On December 1, Creative Consulting bought a one-year insurance policy for $1,200. At that time, the asset account, Prepaid Insurance, was increased (debited). At the end of the accounting period, December 31, one month of the right to insurance protection had been used. The analysis for making the adjusting entry to reflect this information allocates the insurance between expense and asset:

Insurance Available	=	Used Portion (Expired Cost or Expense)	+	Unused Portion (Unexpired Cost or Asset)
$1,200		$1,200 × 1/12 = $100		$1,100

The adjusting journal entry would be

		DATE		DESCRIPTION	POST. REF.	DEBIT	CREDIT	
JOURNAL							PAGE --	
1	19-- Dec.	31	Insurance Expense		53	1 0 0 00		1
2			Prepaid Insurance		15		1 0 0 00	2
3			Adjustment to account for one					3
4			month's expiration of policy					4

Note that the expense account is increased (debited) $100, the cost of insurance used or expired in one month. The asset account is decreased (credited) $100. Thus, the asset account, Prepaid Insurance, will show a balance of $1,100 at the end of the accounting period—the amount of insurance protection that the company has the right to for the next eleven months.

The ledger entries made for the accounting period that reflect this information are shown below in T account format.

Prepaid Insurance				Insurance Expense	
12/1	1,200	*adj.*	100	*adj.*	100
bal.	1,100				

C. As some assets are used, the cost is systematically and rationally expensed.

Depreciation is the periodic allocation of the cost of a long-lived asset to expense over its useful life. Plant and equipment are expected to benefit a business for a relatively predictable period of time. This period of time is called the *useful life* or *economic life* of the asset. During this useful life, the usefulness of the asset decreases due to wear and tear or obsolescence. Because the cost of using these items cannot be directly related to revenues, the cost is allocated to expense using a systematic and rational method. Depreciation is based on the asset cost, the estimated useful life, and the estimated salvage (or residual) value. The salvage value is the amount the company estimates the asset will be worth at the end of its useful life.

1. *Determining depreciation.* The simplest method for determining depreciation is the straight-line method. Straight-line depreciation assumes that an equal portion of depreciable cost is allocated to each period that the asset is expected to benefit the business. Straight-line depreciation is computed using the following formula:

$$\frac{\text{Depreciation}}{\text{Expense}} = \frac{\text{Cost} - \text{Estimated Salvage Value}}{\text{Estimated Years of Useful Life}}$$

Other methods for determining depreciation costs will be discussed in Chapter 12.

2. *Contra accounts.* The adjusting entry to recognize depreciation expense for the period is *not* credited directly to the asset account. Instead, the accountant credits a contra asset account called Accumulated Depreciation or Allowance for Depreciation. A *contra account* is used to reduce an associated account. This contra asset account and its related asset account are irrevocably linked—they will always appear together in the financial statements. The use of a contra account provides more information than reducing the asset account directly. It is more informative to state that a truck cost $10,000 and has accumulated depreciation of $6,000 than to simply report the truck's balance of $4,000.

EXAMPLE 5-3: Tiffany Neal; owner of Creative Consulting, purchased office equipment at the beginning of the year for $12,000. The equipment has an estimated useful life of ten years and an estimated salvage value of $2,000. At the end of the accounting period, December 31, 1/10 of the depreciable cost is transferred to expense, using the straight-line method of determining depreciation. The adjusting journal entry to recognize the use of the office equipment for one year would be

	DATE		DESCRIPTION	POST. REF.	DEBIT	CREDIT	
	JOURNAL					PAGE --	
1	19-- Dec.	31	Depreciation Expense	56	1 0 0 0 00		1
2			Accumulated Depreciation	17		1 0 0 0 00	2
3			One-year straight-line deprecia-				3
4			tion; $12,000 equipment; esti-				4
5			mated 10-yr. life; $2,000 salvage				5

Note that the expense account is increased (debited) $1,000, the estimated cost of using the office equipment for one year. The contra asset account is increased (credited) $1,000. The ledger entries made that reflect this information are shown below in T account format.

Equipment	Accumulated Depreciation	Depreciation Expense
1/3 12,000	*adj.* 1,000	*adj.* 1,000

3. *Book value.* The balance in the contra asset account is subtracted from the balance in its related asset account when presented on the balance sheet. This yields what is called the *book value* of the asset.

EXAMPLE 5-4: The information given in Example 5-3 would be presented on the company's balance sheet as shown below. Note that the book value of the equipment is $11,000.

```
Plant assets:
  Equipment ............................................. $12,000
  Less accumulated depreciation.........................   1,000   $11,000
```

5-4. Asset/Revenue Adjustments

Asset/revenue adjustments are required to recognize revenue that would otherwise not be recorded in the proper accounting period. A business may have earned the right to revenue that has not yet been collected or billed to customers. The revenue should be recognized to more accurately reflect the true results of the period's operations. The adjusting entry for an accrued revenue increases both an asset account and a revenue account. The asset account is normally a receivable account, indicating that the cash will not be received until some later period. Examples of accounts that may require these end-of-the-period adjustments are Interest Receivable, Rent Receivable, and Accounts Receivable.

EXAMPLE 5-5: Creative Consulting performed services for $4,000 for Tuscaw Galleries on November 1 in exchange for a $4,000 note stating that the fee would be paid at the end of three months plus 12% interest. The note plus the interest will be due on January 31. Therefore, as of December 31, no interest on this loan has been received. The simple interest calculation on the loan is .12 × $4,000 = $480 interest or $40 per month over the three-month period. At the end of the accounting period, interest has been earned for two months—November and December. This amount would be reported as revenue earned during this accounting period, even though it will not be received until the next accounting period. Thus, the adjusting journal entry at the end of the accounting period would be

	DATE		DESCRIPTION	POST. REF.	DEBIT	CREDIT	
	JOURNAL					PAGE --	
1	19-- Dec.	31	Interest Receivable	18	8 0 00		1
2			Interest Revenue	45		8 0 00	2
3			Two months' interest; 3-month,				3
4			$4,000, 12% note				4
5							5

Note that the asset account is increased (debited) $80 and the revenue account is increased (credited) $80, the amount of interest earned in November and December but not yet received. When the note is paid on January 31, the entry to record the payment would be

	DATE		DESCRIPTION	POST. REF.	DEBIT	CREDIT	
	JOURNAL					PAGE --	
1	19-- Jan.	31	Cash	11	4 1 2 0 00		1
2			Note Receivable	17		4 0 0 0 00	2
3			Interest Receivable	18		8 0 00	3
4			Interest Revenue	45		4 0 00	4
5			Principal & interest on $4,000,				5
6			3-month note				6
7							7

The asset account, Cash, is increased (debited) $4,120, the amount of cash received. The asset account, Note Receivable, is decreased (credited) $4,000. The asset account for the interest accrued for November and December, Interest Receivable, is decreased (credited) $80. The revenue account, Interest Revenue, is increased (credited) $40, the amount of interest earned from January 1 to January 31.

5-5. Liability/Expense Adjustments

Liability/expense adjustments are required to recognize expenses that would otherwise not be recorded in the proper accounting period. A business may incur liabilities during the accounting period that will not be paid until a later period. The adjusting entry for the accrued expenses increases both a liability and an expense account. The liability account is usually a payable account, indicating that the expense will be paid later. Examples of accounts that may require these adjustments at the end of the accounting period are Interest Payable and Wages Payable.

EXAMPLE 5-6: Creative Consulting borrowed $10,000 from First State Bank on July 1. The $10,000 note will be due in nine months plus 10% interest ($10,000 × .10 × 9/12 = $750 interest).

The adjusting journal entry for this accrued expense would be

	DATE		DESCRIPTION	POST. REF.	DEBIT	CREDIT	
1	19-- Dec.	31	Interest Expense	57	5 0 0 00		1
2			Interest Payable	23		5 0 0 00	2
3			Six months' interest on $10,000,				3
4			10%, 9-month note				4

JOURNAL — PAGE --

Here, the expense account in increased (debited) $500, the amount of interest accrued for six months. The liability account is increased (credited) $500, the amount of interest owed on December 31.

At the end of March, the journal entry to record the payment of the note would be

JOURNAL — PAGE --

	DATE		DESCRIPTION	POST. REF.	DEBIT	CREDIT	
1	19-- Mar.	31	Note Payable	21	1 0 0 0 0 00		1
2			Interest Payable	23	5 0 0 00		2
3			Interest Expense	57	2 5 0 00		3
4			Cash	11		1 0 7 2 0 00	4
5			Principal and interest				5
6			on $10,000, 10%, 9-month note				6
7							7

Note that the liability account for the money borrowed on July 1 is decreased (debited) $10,000 because it is being paid. The liability account for the interest accrued for six months is decreased (debited) because it is being paid. The expense account is increased (debited) $250 for the months of January, February, and March. The asset account, Cash, is decreased (credited) $10,750, representing the amount borrowed plus interest at 10% for nine months.

EXAMPLE 5-7: The weekly payroll of $1,000 for a five-day work week at Creative Consulting is paid every Friday. The accounting year-end of December 31 falls on a Wednesday. The wages earned by the employees for Monday, Tuesday, and Wednesday would be an expense of the accounting period ending December 31, even though the employees will not be paid until Friday, January 2. Three days of wages would be $600 ($1,000 ÷ 5 days = $200 per day × 3 days = $600). The adjusting journal entry for this accrued expense would be

JOURNAL — PAGE --

	DATE		DESCRIPTION	POST. REF.	DEBIT	CREDIT	
1	19-- Dec.	31	Wage Expense	51	6 0 0 00		1
2			Wages Payable	24		6 0 0 00	2
3			Three days' wages since Dec. 28				3

Here, the expense account is increased (debited) $600, the amount of wage expense for three days. The liability account is increased (credited) $600, the amount owed to the employees for three days.

On January 2, when the employees are paid, the journal entry would be

	DATE		DESCRIPTION	POST. REF.	DEBIT	CREDIT	
	JOURNAL					PAGE --	
1	19-- Jan.	2	Wage Expense	51	4 0 0 00		1
2			Wages Payable	24	6 0 0 00		2
3			Cash	11		1 0 0 0 00	3
4			Wages as of Dec. 31				4

Note that the expense account is increased (debited) $400, the amount of wage expense for two days (January 1 and 2). The liability account is decreased $600, the amount recorded as a liability on December 31. The asset account, Cash, is decreased (credited) by $1,000, the amount the employees received on Friday, January 2.

5-6. Liability/Revenue Adjustments

Liability/revenue adjustments are necessary to allocate revenues over more than one accounting period. When revenue is collected in advance of its being earned, the company has the liability to provide goods or services or to reimburse the customer. The recognition of revenue is deferred. The Cash account is debited and the unearned revenue (liability) account is credited when the payment is received in advance of its being earned. As goods or services are provided, the revenue is no longer unearned and may now be realized. The adjusting entry for the realization of the earned revenue increases a revenue account and decreases a liability. Examples are Unearned Rent Revenue, Unearned Commissions, and Unearned Subscription Revenue.

EXAMPLE 5-8: On November 1, Creative Consulting received $1,800 from the Winter Springs Art Center. Tiffany Neal agreed to provide consulting services to the center for six months. The fee of $1,800 represents payment in advance ($300 per month). This transaction was recorded on November 1 by debiting (increasing) Cash and crediting (increasing) a liability account— Unearned Fees.

On December 31, consulting services have been provided for two months—November and December. The revenue earned during the current period will be transferred to the revenue account as illustrated below:

Fees Received in Advance	=	**Unearned Portion (Liability)**	+	**Earned Portion (Revenue)**
$1,800		$1,200		$1,800 × 1/3 = $600

The adjusting journal entry to record this information would be

	DATE		DESCRIPTION	POST. REF.	DEBIT	CREDIT	
	JOURNAL					PAGE --	
1	19-- Dec.	31	Unearned Fees	26	6 0 0 00		1
2			Consulting Fees	43		6 0 0 00	2
3			Earned 2 months' fees received				3
4			in advance				4

The liability account is decreased (debited) $600. The revenue account is increased (credited) $600, the amount of revenue earned. The liability account will show a balance of $1,200, the amount that will be recognized as revenue in the next accounting period.

5-7. The Work Sheet

A small company may journalize and post adjusting entries and then prepare financial statements directly from the ledger balances. Errors in adjusting accounts and preparing financial statements are less likely to occur, however, if the accountant prepares a work sheet.

A. A *work sheet* is a tool to assist the accountant in preparing financial statements.

The work sheet is not a part of the formal accounting system (or "books") of the company. It is an accountant's work area or "scratch pad." A work sheet helps the accountant

- determine the need for, and record the effect of, adjusting entries *before* journalizing and posting the adjustments
- separate the adjusted account balances into their proper financial statement categories
- check the mathematical accuracy of the calculations
- prepare the financial statements and enter the adjusting entries in the journal and the ledger

B. The work sheet focuses attention on the adjusting process.

Work sheets vary according to the needs of the accountant. The work sheet on page 68 is one form of a ten-column work sheet. Study the work sheet prepared for Creative Consulting as of December 31, the end of the accounting period. The name of the company, the name of the form, and the accounting period involved are placed at the top of the work sheet. Next to the Account Title column are five pairs of columns. Each pair of columns serves a separate function.

1. *Trial Balance columns.* The ending balances from the general ledger are used to prepare a trial balance in the first pair of columns. This is an *unadjusted trial balance*. Check that the trial balance does balance; that is, the dollar amount of debits equals the dollar amount of credits.

2. *Adjustments columns.* Enter the adjustments needed in the next pair of columns. A letter code is generally placed by each debit and credit of an adjusting entry to help anyone who may review the work sheet and to refer to any explanations of adjustments written on the bottom of the work sheet. If the titles of any accounts requiring adjustment are not given in the trial balance, insert these accounts below the trial balance totals. Again, total the debits and credits to determine if the adjustments columns balance.

Note: The adjusting entries illustrated in this chapter appear on the work sheet on page 68 in the adjustments columns in the following order:

ADJUSTMENT	EXAMPLE
a	5-1
b	5-2
c	5-8
d	5-7
e	5-3 and 5-4
f	5-5
g	5-6

3. *Adjusted Trial Balance columns.* Compute and enter the adjusted balance for each account in the third pair of columns. To determine the adjusted balance, the amount in the trial balance (if any) is combined with its adjustments (if any). Once again, before going on to the next step, check to insure that the dollar total of the debits equals the dollar total of the credits.

Creative Consulting
Ten-Column Work Sheet
December 31, 19xx

ACCOUNT TITLE	TRIAL BALANCE		ADJUSTMENTS		ADJ. TRIAL BAL.		INCOME STATEMENT		BALANCE SHEET	
	DEBIT	CREDIT	DEBIT	CREDIT	DEBIT	CREDIT	DEBIT	CREDIT	DEBIT	CREDIT
Cash	13,200				13,200				13,200	
Accounts Receivable	7,150				7,150				7,150	
Notes Receivable	4,000				4,000				4,000	
Supplies	500			400 (a)	100				100	
Prepaid Insurance	1,200			100 (b)	1,100				1,100	
Office Equipment	12,000				12,000				12,000	
Accounts Payable		6,180				6,180				6,180
Notes Payable		10,000				10,000				10,000
Unearned Fees		1,800	600 (c)			1,200				1,200
Tiffany Neal, Capital		10,000				10,000				10,000
Tiffany Neal, Drawing	8,000				8,000				8,000	
Consulting Fees		62,000		600 (c)		62,600		62,600		
Rent Expense	3,100				3,100		3,100			
Utilities Expense	2,580				2,580		2,580			
Wage Expense	38,250		600 (d)		38,850		38,850			
	89,980	89,980								
Supplies Expense			400 (a)		400		400			
Insurance Expense			100 (b)		100		100			
Depreciation Expense			1,000 (e)		1,000		1,000			
Accumulated Depreciation				1,000 (e)		1,000				1,000
Interest Receivable			80 (f)		80				80	
Interest Revenue				80 (f)		80		80		
Interest Expense			500 (g)		500		500			
Interest Payable				500 (g)		500				500
Wages Payable				600 (d)		600				600
			3,280	3,280	92,160	92,160	46,530	62,680		
Net Income							16,150			16,150
							62,680	62,680	45,630	45,630

4. *Income Statement and Balance Sheet columns.* Transfer the account balances to the columns for the individual financial statements. Debits are transferred as debits and credits are transferred as credits. Revenue and expense accounts are transferred to the Income Statement columns. Asset, liability, capital, and drawing accounts are transferred to the Balance Sheet columns. Then compute the subtotal for each of the four columns.

The net income (or loss) for the period is the difference between the subtotals of the Income Statement columns. If the company is profitable, the credits (increases to income) will be greater than the debits (decreases to income). To transfer income from the Income Statement to the Balance Sheet, place a debit in the Income Statement columns equal to the net income and a credit for the same amount in the Balance Sheet columns. If there were a net loss, the amount would be entered as a credit in the Income Statement columns and a debit in the Balance Sheet columns.

Compute the resulting totals of the four columns again after transferring net income (or loss) from the Income Statement to the Balance Sheet. Check again that the total debits equal the total credits in both the Income Statement columns and the Balance Sheet columns.

C. The work sheet provides the information that is reported on financial statements.

1. *Income statement.* The work sheet provides the quantitative information reported in the income statement.

2. *Statement of equity.* The work sheet provides most of the information reported in the statement of equity.

In preparing a statement of equity, it is necessary to refer to the ledger to determine the beginning balance and any other investments made by the owner(s) during the accounting period. Then the net income and withdrawals given in the balance sheet columns of the work sheet are used to determine the ending capital.

3. *Balance sheet.* The work sheet provides the quantitative information reported on the balance sheet except for the amount of ending capital, which can be taken from the statement of equity.

Financial statements are discussed and illustrated in Chapter 2.

D. Adjusting entries are usually journalized and posted after the work sheet is completed and the financial statements have been prepared.

The adjusting entries that were made on the work sheet in the Adjustments columns are now journalized and posted in the same manner as the journal entries shown in the early part of this chapter. Adjusting entries are usually dated "as of" the last day of the accounting period. In the journal, each entry should contain an explanation. In addition, a heading such as "Adjustments" or "Adjusting Entries" may be written above the first entry.

5-8. Closing Entries

After the financial statements for an accounting period are prepared and the books have been updated (adjusting entries have been journalized and posted), then the books must be prepared for the next accounting period.

A. Closing entries eliminate balances in temporary accounts.

Revenue, expense, gain, loss, and drawing accounts are *nominal* or *temporary* accounts. The balance sheet accounts (assets, liabilities, and equity) are real or permanent accounts. Temporary accounts are used to record and summarize changes in equity during the accounting period. These accounts must be made to equal zero for the beginning of each new accounting period in order to reflect just one period's revenues, expenses, gains, losses, and withdrawals. This is done by transferring the temporary account balances (except for withdrawals) to a summary account.

B. A *summary account* is used to clear the amounts in the income statement accounts.

This summary account is usually called Income Summary. Other titles for the summary account are Revenue and Expense Summary, or Profit and Loss Summary. Check to see that the balance in the summary account is the same as the income found on the work sheet to insure that all accounts have been closed. Both the summary and drawing account balances are then transferred to the owner's capital account. This is because both income and withdrawals affect equity. Thus, the net effect of the income and withdrawals during the accounting period is now recorded in the capital account. The summary account is used only at the end of the accounting period and is both opened and closed during the closing process.

C. Closing involves a four-step process.

The four steps in closing the temporary accounts are

1. Every revenue and gain account is debited for an amount equal to its balance and the summary account is credited for the same amounts.
2. Every expense and loss account is credited for an amount equal to its balance and the summary account is debited for the same amounts.
3. The balance in the summary account is calculated. The balance should be the same as the net income (or loss) shown on the work sheet and income statement. If the summary account has a credit balance (net income), debit the summary account for an amount equal to its balance and credit the capital account. If the summary account has a debit balance (net loss), credit the summary account for an amount equal to its balance and debit the capital account.
4. The drawing account is credited for an amount equal to its balance and the capital account is debited.

   Note: All revenue accounts, all expense accounts, the income summary account, and the drawing account should have a zero balance and be ready to start a new period.

D. Closing entries must be journalized and posted.

The income statement columns plus the drawing account on the work sheet can be used to determine what accounts require closing entries. Closing entries are journalized and posted in the same manner as adjusting entries. They also are dated "as of" the last day of the accounting period. In the journal, they are either explained individually or listed under the heading "Closing Entries." When posting, the entry may be identified as a closing entry in the item section of the account.

EXAMPLE 5-9: Refer to the work sheet on page 68 that was prepared for Creative Consulting at the end of the accounting period, December 31. Based on the income statement columns shown on the work sheet, the closing entries shown on page 71 must be entered in the company's general journal in order to prepare the books for the next accounting period.

First, the revenue accounts, Consulting Fees and Interest Revenue, are debited for the balances shown in the Income Statement Credit column and the Income Summary account is credited for the same amounts. Next, all of the expense accounts are credited for their balances shown in the Income Statement Debit column, and the Income Summary account is debited for the same amounts. The balance of the Income Summary account is then determined ($62,680 − $46,530) to give a credit balance of $16,150. Note that this amount is equal to the net income shown in the income statement columns of the work sheet. Since the Income Summary account has a credit balance, it is debited for an amount equal to that balance and the same amount is credited to the capital account, Tiffany Neal, Capital. Finally, since the business is a sole proprietorship, it is necessary to credit the drawing account for the amount equal to its balance, and debit the capital account for the same amount.

All of the revenue and expense accounts now have a zero balance.

	DATE		DESCRIPTION	POST. REF.	DEBIT	CREDIT	
1			Closing Entries				1
2	19-- Dec.	31	Consulting Fees	43	6 2 6 0 0 00		2
3			Interest Revenue	41	8 0 00		3
4			Income Summary	33		6 2 6 8 0 00	4
5							5
6		31	Income Summary	33	4 6 5 3 0 00		6
7			Wages Expense	51		3 8 8 5 0 00	7
8			Supplies Expense	52		4 0 0 00	8
9			Insurance Expense	53		1 0 0 00	9
10			Rent Expense	54		3 1 0 0 00	10
11			Utilities Expense	55		2 5 8 0 00	11
12			Depreciation Expense	56		1 0 0 0 00	12
13			Interest Expense	57		5 0 0 00	13
14							14
15		31	Income Summary	33	1 6 1 5 0 00		15
16			Tiffany Neal, Capital	31		1 6 1 5 0 00	16
17							17
18		31	Tiffany Neal, Capital	31	8 0 0 0 00		18
19			Tiffany Neal, Drawing	32		8 0 0 0 00	19

JOURNAL PAGE --

EXAMPLE 5-10: Refer again to the work sheet on page 68 that was prepared for Creative Consulting at the end of the accounting period, December 31. Based on the adjusted trial balance shown on the work sheet, all of the ledger account balances of the business are shown below in T account format. To fully prepare the books for the next accounting period, the closing entries journalized in Example 5-9 are also posted (shown in bold type).

Cash
bal. 13,290 |

Accounts Receivable
bal. 7,150 |

Notes Receivable
bal. 4,000 |

Interest Receivable
bal. 80 |

Supplies
bal. 100 |

Prepaid Insurance
bal. 1,100 |

Office Equipment
bal. 12,000 |

Accumulated Depreciation
| bal. 1,000

Accounts Payable
| bal. 6,180

Notes Payable
| bal. 10,000

Wages Payable
| bal. 600

Unearned Fees
| bal. 1,200

Interest Payable
| bal. 500

Tiffany Neal, Capital
8,000 | bal. 10,000
| **16,150**
| bal. 18,150

Tiffany Neal, Drawing
bal. 8,000 | **8,000**

Consulting Fees		Interest Revenue		Depreciation Expense	
62,600	*bal.* 62,600		*bal.* 80	*bal.* 1,000	**1,000**

Interest Expense		Insurance Expense		Rent Expense	
bal. 500	**500**	*bal.* 100	**100**	*bal.* 3,100	**3,100**

Supplies Expense		Utilities Expense		Wage Expense	
bal. 400	**400**	*bal.* 2,580	**2,580**	*bal.* 38,850	**38,850**

Income Summary	
46,530	62,680
16,150	

Note that after closing entries have been journalized and posted, the temporary accounts (revenue, expense, and drawing) have zero balances, and the permanent accounts (assets, liabilities, and equity) have balances to be carried over to the new accounting period.

5-9. Post-Closing Trial Balance

A post-closing trial balance is prepared after the temporary accounts have been closed. The purpose of the post-closing trial balance is to make sure that the ledger is in balance at the beginning of the new accounting period. The accounts and their balances should agree exactly with the balance sheet that was prepared at the end of the period. Only the permanent accounts appear on the post-closing trial balance.

EXAMPLE 5-11: The post-closing trial balance for Creative Consulting is shown below.

Creative Consulting

Post-Closing Trial Balance

December 31, 19--

	Debit	Credit
Cash	13,200 00	
Accounts Receivable	7,150 00	
Notes Receivable	4,000 00	
Interest Receivable	80 00	
Supplies	100 00	
Prepaid Insurance	1,100 00	
Office Equipment	12,000 00	
Accumulated Depreciation		1,000 00
Accounts Payable		6,180 00
Notes Payable		10,000 00
Unearned Fees		1,200 00
Interest Payable		500 00
Wages Payable		600 00
Tiffany Neal, Capital		18,150 00
	37,630 00	37,630 00

RAISE YOUR GRADES

Can you explain...?

☑ why adjusting entries are necessary
☑ how to make adjusting entries
☑ what the account Accumulated Depreciation is, and why it is used in recording depreciation
☑ the reason for preparing a work sheet at the end of the accounting period
☑ how to prepare the financial statements from the work sheet
☑ what types of accounts are temporary (or nominal) and what types of accounts are permanent (or real)
☑ why closing entries are necessary
☑ the four steps in closing the accounts
☑ why a post-closing trial balance is prepared

SUMMARY

1. Adjusting entries are made to bring accounts up to date at the end of the accounting period.
2. There are two types of adjusting entries that must be made at the end of the accounting period: deferral entries that delay the recognition of revenues and expenses; and accrual entries that accelerate the recognition of revenues and expenses.
3. There are four subsets of adjusting entries that should be made at the end of the accounting period: asset/expense adjustments; asset/revenue adjustments; liability/expense adjustments; and liability/revenue adjustments.
4. Asset/expense adjustments are required to allocate expenses over more than one accounting period.
5. Asset/revenue adjustments are required to recognize revenue that would otherwise not be recorded in the proper accounting period.
6. Liability/expense adjustments are required to recognize expenses that would otherwise not be recorded in the proper accounting period.
7. Liability/revenue adjustments are required to allocate revenues over more than one accounting period.
8. Depreciation is the periodic allocation of the cost of a long-lived asset to expense over its useful life. Rather than directly crediting the asset account for depreciation, a contra asset account is credited.
9. A contra account is used to reduce a related account. The contra account is subtracted from its related account when presented on the balance sheet.
10. A work sheet is prepared at the end of the accounting period to help determine the need for and record adjusting entries, to separate the adjusted account balances into their proper financial statement categories, to check the mathematical accuracy of the calculations, and to prepare the financial statements.
11. The trial balance columns on the work sheet are prepared from the ending balances of the general ledger accounts.
12. The adjustments columns on the work sheet are used to enter adjusting entries that need to be made to the trial balance.
13. The Adjusted Trial Balance columns on the work sheet are prepared by combining each amount in the trial balance with its adjustment, if any.
14. Revenue, expense, gain, and loss accounts are transferred to the Income Statement columns. Asset, liability, equity, and drawing accounts are transferred to the Balance Sheet columns.
15. The net income (or loss) for the period is the difference between the subtotals of the Income

Statement columns. If the company is profitable, debit the Income Statement columns for the net income amount and credit the same amount to the Balance Sheet columns. Do the reverse if the company has a net loss.

16. The work sheet provides all of the quantitative information necessary to prepare the income statement.

17. The work sheet provides the quantitative information necessary to prepare a statement of equity. In preparing a statement of equity, it is necessary to refer to the ledger to determine the beginning balance and if any other investments have been made by the owner(s) during the accounting period.

18. The work sheet provides the quantitative information necessary to prepare a balance sheet except for the amount of capital, which can be taken from the statement of equity.

19. Adjusting entries are usually journalized and posted after the financial statements are prepared.

20. Preparing the books for the next accounting period is known as closing. Closing entries eliminate balances in temporary accounts by transferring their effects to the capital account. Revenue, expense, gain, loss, and drawing accounts are temporary accounts. Asset, liability, and equity accounts are permanent accounts.

21. A summary account is used to clear the amounts in the revenue, expense, gain, and loss accounts. It is used only at the end of the accounting period and is both opened and closed during the closing process.

22. Closing involves a four-step process as follows:

   • Revenue and gain accounts are debited for their balances and the summary account is credited for the same amounts.

   • Expense and loss accounts are credited for their balances and the summary account is debited for the same amounts.

   • The balance in the summary account (net income) is calculated and the amount is debited to the summary account and credited to the capital account. The opposite is done if the summary account shows a net loss.

   • The drawing account is credited for its balance and the capital account is debited.

23. After closing entries are journalized and posted, a post-closing trial balance is prepared to make sure that the ledger is in balance for the beginning of the new accounting period.

RAPID REVIEW   Answers

True or False

1. Adjusting entries are only necessary if errors have been made in the journal during the accounting period. [Section 5-2]   *False*

2. Some assets become expenses because they are used up in the accounting period. [Section 5-2]   *True*

3. A contra account is an account that will be shown as a subtraction from its related account in the financial statements. [Section 5-3]   *True*

4. The adjusting entry for an accrued expense increases both a liability and an expense account. [Section 5-5]   *True*

5. The balance of a temporary or nominal account should be carried forward to the next accounting period. [Section 5-8]   *False*

6. An Income Summary account is always closed by debiting it. [Section 5-8]   *False*

Multiple Choice

7. Expired costs incurred to obtain benefits are called (*a*) net income, (*b*) prepaid expenses, (*c*) expenses, (*d*) revenue. [Section 5-1]   *c*

8. An accrued revenue is (*a*) revenue received but not recorded, (*b*) revenue earned but not received, (*c*) unearned revenue, (*d*) the same as an accrued liability. [Section 5-2]

b

9. If a business collects rent revenue in advance of its being earned, this revenue is recorded in (*a*) a rent revenue account, (*b*) an accrued revenue account, (*c*) a rent receivable account, (*d*) an unearned (deferred) revenue account. [Section 5-6]

d

10. Which of the following accounts would *not* be closed in the closing process? (*a*) Sales Revenue (*b*) Wages Expense, (*c*) Equity (*d*) Income Summary [Section 5-8]

c

11. Which of the following accounts would appear on the post-closing trial balance? (*a*) revenue and expense accounts only (*b*) revenue, expense, and drawing accounts only (*c*) asset, liability, and capital accounts only [Section 5-9]

c

SOLVED PROBLEMS

PROBLEM 5-1: On June 1, a new business purchases supplies for $900. On June 30, at the end of the accounting period, an inventory shows supplies worth $300 remaining. Make the appropriate adjusting entry in the following journal.

	JOURNAL				PAGE
DATE	DESCRIPTION	POST. REF.	DEBIT	CREDIT	
1					1
2					2
3					3

Answer: Subtract the amount of supplies on hand at the end of the accounting period from the amount purchased on June 1 to get the amount of supplies used during the accounting period ($900 − $300 = $600). Thus, supplies worth $600 have been used during the accounting period. Therefore, the Supplies Expense account is increased (debited) $600, and the Supplies account is decreased (credited) $600. [Section 5-3]

	JOURNAL					PAGE - -
	DATE	DESCRIPTION	POST. REF.	DEBIT	CREDIT	
1	19-- June 30	Supplies Expense		600 00		1
2		Supplies			600 00	2
3		Supplies used in current period				3

PROBLEM 5-2: On July 1, the Supplies account in the general ledger of a company has a debit balance of $150. On July 9, supplies worth $300 are purchased for cash. On July 19, supplies worth $200 are purchased on credit. On July 31, the end of the accounting period, an inventory shows supplies worth $350 remaining. Make the appropriate entries for the purchases of July 9 and July 19 in the journal on page 76; then make the appropriate adjusting entry for July 31 (omit explanations).

	DATE		DESCRIPTION	POST. REF.	DEBIT	CREDIT	
1							1
2							2
3							3
4							4
5							5
6							6
7							7
8							8

JOURNAL   PAGE

Answer: The July 9 purchase of supplies for cash increases the Supplies account $300 and decreases the Cash account $300. The July 19 purchase of supplies increases the Supplies account by $200 and increases a liability account (Accounts Payable) $200 since these supplies were purchased on credit. The $350 worth of supplies remaining on July 31 must be subtracted from the amount of supplies available to determine the amount of expired cost of supplies used. The $150 balance as of July 1 plus the two purchases of $300 and $200 during July are added to give $650 for supplies available during July. Thus, $650 (supplies available) − $350 (supplies remaining) = $300 (supplies used during the month of July). The adjusting entry for July 31 would therefore increase (debit) Supplies Expense by $300 and decrease (credit) Supplies by $300. [Section 5-3]

JOURNAL   PAGE – –

	DATE		DESCRIPTION	POST. REF.	DEBIT	CREDIT	
1	19-- July	9	Supplies		300 00		1
2			Cash			300 00	2
3							3
4		19	Supplies		200 00		4
5			Accounts Payable			200 00	5
6							6
7		31	Supplies Expense		300 00		7
8			Supplies			300 00	8

PROBLEM 5-3: Post the transactions described in Problem 5-2 in the following blank T accounts. Do not forget to include the opening balance in the Supplies account. An opening balance is provided for the Cash account. Indicate the balance of each account after all entries have been posted.

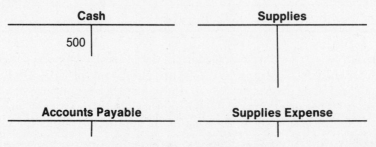

Cash		Supplies
500		

Accounts Payable		Supplies Expense

Answer: [Section 5-3]

	Cash				Supplies	
	500	300			150	300
bal.	200				300	
					200	
				bal.	350	

	Accounts Payable			Supplies Expense	
	bal.	200	bal.	300	

PROBLEM 5-4: On February 1, the McGregor Company paid $1,800 for a three-year fire insurance policy. If the company uses monthly accounting periods, what adjusting entry would be made on February 28? Journalize your answer below.

	JOURNAL				PAGE

	DATE		DESCRIPTION	POST. REF.	DEBIT	CREDIT	
1							1
2							2
3							3

Answer: The $1,800 purchase of the three-year policy would be recorded as an asset, Prepaid Insurance. Since the insurance was purchased for a 36-month period, 1/36 of the premium (1,800 ÷ 36), or $50, will be debited to an Insurance Expense account each month, and the Prepaid Insurance account will be decreased (credited) $50 each month. Thus, the adjusting entry for February 28 (and for the last day of every month during the 36-month period) would be as shown below. [Section 5-3]

	JOURNAL				PAGE - -

	DATE		DESCRIPTION	POST. REF.	DEBIT	CREDIT	
1	19-- Feb.	28	Insurance Expense		50 00		1
2			Prepaid Insurance			50 00	2
3			One month's expiration of policy				3

PROBLEM 5-5: The rent on Katherine's store is $600 per month, due on the first of each month. On May 1, Katherine pays three months' rent in advance. The journal entry for this transaction is shown below.

	JOURNAL				PAGE --

	DATE		DESCRIPTION	POST. REF.	DEBIT	CREDIT	
1	19-- May	1	Prepaid Rent		1 8 0 0 00		1
2			Cash			1 8 0 0 00	2
3			May, June, & July rent paid in				3
4			advance				4

On June 30, Katherine's accounting period ends. What adjusting entry does she need to make at this time? Record your answer below. (Assume the monthly adjusting entries have not been made.)

	DATE	DESCRIPTION	POST. REF.	DEBIT	CREDIT	
1						1
2						2
3						3
4						4

JOURNAL — PAGE

Answer: June 30 is two months after May 1, so two-thirds of the three-month prepaid rent period has expired. Thus, two-thirds of the $1,800 in prepaid rent has expired, or $1,200 (1,800 × 2/3). Therefore, Katherine would increase (debit) $1,200 to her Rent Expense account and decrease (credit) her Prepaid Rent account by $1,200. [Section 5-3]

JOURNAL — PAGE - -

	DATE	DESCRIPTION	POST. REF.	DEBIT	CREDIT	
1	19-- June 30	Rent Expense		1 2 0 0 00		1
2		Prepaid Rent			1 2 0 0 00	2
3		Two months rent expired;				3
4		prepaid on May 1				4

PROBLEM 5-6: A firm purchases equipment for $25,000 at the beginning of the year. The equipment has a useful life of ten years and will depreciate at a rate of $2,500 for each year of use. Prepare the adjusting journal entry needed after one year in the journal provided below (the company's year end is December 31). Is the Equipment account affected by the adjusting entry?

JOURNAL — PAGE

	DATE	DESCRIPTION	POST. REF.	DEBIT	CREDIT	
1						1
2						2
3						3
4						4

Answer: Depreciation Expense is increased (debited) $2,500, the cost of using the equipment for one year. Depreciation is *not* credited directly to the asset account, Equipment. Instead, a contra account, Accumulated Depreciation, is increased (credited) $2,500. [Section 5-3]

	JOURNAL						PAGE - -
DATE	DESCRIPTION	POST. REF.	DEBIT		CREDIT		
1	19-- Dec. 31	Depreciation Expense - Equip.		25 00 00			1
2		Accumulated Depreciation Equip.			25 00 00		2
3		One-yr. depreciation; $25,000					3
4		equipment; estimated 10-yr. life					4

PROBLEM 5-7: After using the equipment purchased in Problem 5-6 for seven years, what is the amount of depreciation that would be accumulated in the contra asset account? How would this information be presented on the balance sheet?

Answer: Depreciation of $2,500 would have been recorded each year for seven years, so the Accumulated Depreciation account would be credited seven times for $2,500. The amount accumulated would thus be $2,500 × 7 = $17,500. This information would be presented on the balance sheet as follows:

Plant assets:
Equipment $25,000
Less accumulated depreciation.. 17,500 $7,500

The $7,500 represents the remaining amount to be depreciated over the next three years (assuming there is no salvage value). The net amount is commonly called the asset's book value. [Section 5-3]

PROBLEM 5-8: On December 1, an accountant receives payment of $3,600 for accounting services to be provided during December and January. The accountant records this transaction by increasing (debiting) the Cash account and increasing (crediting) the liability account, Unearned Professional Fees, as follows:

	JOURNAL						PAGE --
DATE	DESCRIPTION	POST. REF.	DEBIT		CREDIT		
1	19-- Dec. 1	Cash		3 6 0 0 00			1
2		Unearned Professional Fees			3 6 0 0 00		2
3		Payment for Dec. & Jan. services					3

By December 31, the accountant has provided one-half of the agreed-upon accounting services. What adjusting entry does the accountant need to make to record this information? Use the following journal to record your answer.

	JOURNAL						PAGE
DATE	DESCRIPTION	POST. REF.	DEBIT		CREDIT		
1							1
2							2
3							3
4							4

Answer: On December 31, the accountant has performed one-half of the liability and thus earned one-half of the prepaid fee ($3,600 ÷ 2 = $1,800). The adjusting journal entry to record this information would therefore be as shown below. [Section 5-6]

	DATE		DESCRIPTION	POST. REF.	DEBIT	CREDIT	
	JOURNAL					PAGE – –	
1	19-- Dec.	31	Unearned Professional Fees		1800 00		1
2			Professional Fees Earned			1800 00	2
3			Fees earned in Dec.; payment				3
4			received Dec. 1				4

PROBLEM 5-9: Based on the information given in Problem 5-8, if the accountant provides the balance of the agreed-upon accounting services by January 31, what adjusting journal entry will the accountant make on that date? Record your answer in the following journal.

	DATE	DESCRIPTION	POST. REF.	DEBIT	CREDIT	
		JOURNAL			PAGE	
1						1
2						2
3						3
4						4

Answer: The account will show the second half of the liability as performed and the second half of the prepaid fee as earned. [Section 5-6]

	DATE		DESCRIPTION	POST. REF.	DEBIT	CREDIT	
	JOURNAL					PAGE – –	
1	19-- Jan.	31	Unearned Professional Fees		1800 00		1
2			Professional Fees Earned			1800 00	2
3			Fees earned in Jan.; payment				3
4			received Dec. 1				4

PROBLEM 5-10: The Wilson Company uses monthly accounting periods. Assume that one of its two-week pay periods covers the ten working days from Monday, October 29, through Friday, November 9, which is payday. What adjusting entry would be needed on Wednesday, October 31, if the total payroll on November 9 will be $10,000? Record your answer in the following blank journal.

	DATE	DESCRIPTION	POST. REF.	DEBIT	CREDIT	
		JOURNAL			PAGE	
1						1
2						2
3						3
4						4

Answer: First, calculate the wages expense that accrues each day by dividing $10,000 (the total payroll) by 10 (the number of days in the pay period) to get $1,000 (the wages expense accrued per day). Thus, for the three October days in the pay period, a total of $3,000 in wages expense will accrue. The adjusting entry for October 31, including the increase in the Wages Payable liability since the wages have not actually been paid yet, is therefore as shown below. [Section 5-5]

	DATE		DESCRIPTION	POST. REF.	DEBIT	CREDIT	
			JOURNAL			PAGE - -	
1	19-- Oct.	31	Wages Expense		3 0 0 0 00		1
2			Wages Payable			3 0 0 0 00	2
3			Accrued wages for Oct. 29, 30,				3
4			and 31 at $1,000 per day				4

PROBLEM 5-11: Based on the information given in Problem 5-10, what will be the journal entry on payday, November 9? Remember that $3,000 of the $10,000 payroll has already been charged to Wages Expense. Record your answer in the journal provided below.

	DATE	DESCRIPTION	POST. REF.	DEBIT	CREDIT	
		JOURNAL			PAGE	
1						1
2						2
3						3
4						4
5						5

Answer: By November 9, the Wilson Company will have accrued an additional $7,000 in wages expense for the seven November working days. The $3,000 in Wages Payable liability will be paid off (debited) as the company pays out the full $10,000 payroll (recorded as a credit to Cash). Following is the journal entry that will therefore be made on November 9. [Section 5-5]

	DATE		DESCRIPTION	POST. REF.	DEBIT	CREDIT	
			JOURNAL			PAGE - -	
1	19-- Nov.	9	Wages Payable		3 0 0 0 00		1
2			Wages Expense		7 0 0 0 00		2
3			Cash			1 0 0 0 0 00	3
4			Wages payable for 2 weeks,				4
5			Oct. 29 - Nov. 9				5

PROBLEM 5-12: The Taylor Company uses an accounting period ending December 31. On July 1, the company borrows $6,000 in cash for one year at 10% interest by signing a note to First State Bank. The journal entry for this transaction is shown on page 82.

		JOURNAL				PAGE --	
	DATE	DESCRIPTION	POST. REF.	DEBIT		CREDIT	
1	19-- July 1	Cash		6 0 0 0 00			1
2		Notes Payable				6 0 0 0 00	2
3		One-year, 10% loan, First State					3

On December 31, the end of the accounting period, what would be the adjusting journal entry to record accrued interest expense? Record your answer in the following journal.

		JOURNAL				PAGE	
	DATE	DESCRIPTION	POST. REF.	DEBIT		CREDIT	
1							1
2							2
3							3
4							4
5							5

Answer: The interest expense for the entire one-year term of the loan is calculated as follows: $6,000 (principal) × 10% (rate) = $600 (interest). The period from July 1 to December 31 is six months, so in that period, one-half of the total interest expense, or $300, has accrued. The adjusting entry to record this information would thus increase (debit) Interest Expense and increase (credit) the liability account, Interest Payable, by $300. [Section 5-4]

		JOURNAL				PAGE --	
	DATE	DESCRIPTION	POST. REF.	DEBIT		CREDIT	
1	19-- Dec. 31	Interest Expense		3 0 0 00			1
2		Interest Payable				3 0 0 00	2
3		Six-months' accrued interest					3
4		expense on $6,000, 10%, 1-year					4
5		note; First State					5

PROBLEM 5-13: The First State Bank, which made the loan described in Problem 5-12, will make the following journal entry on July 1 to record the loan.

		JOURNAL				PAGE --	
	DATE	DESCRIPTION	POST. REF.	DEBIT		CREDIT	
1	19-- July 1	Notes Receivable		6 0 0 0 00			1
2		Cash				6 0 0 0 00	2
3		One-year, 10% loan to Taylor Co.					3

This entry records an increase in the asset account, Notes Receivable, and a decrease in the Cash account. At the end of the lender's yearly accounting period, December 31, what will be the adjusting entry to record the accrued interest revenue on the loan? Record your answer in the following blank journal.

	DATE	DESCRIPTION	POST. REF.	DEBIT	CREDIT	
1						1
2						2
3						3
4						4
5						5

JOURNAL — PAGE

Answer: The bank's adjusting entry will show an increase of $300 (the amount of interest owed to First State as of December 31 that was calculated in Problem 5-12) in the asset account, Interest Receivable. The revenue account, Interest Income, will show an increase of $300 also, reflecting the amount of interest earned in the accounting period. [Section 5-4]

JOURNAL — PAGE - -

	DATE	DESCRIPTION	POST. REF.	DEBIT	CREDIT	
1	19-- Dec. 31	Interest Receivable		300 00		1
2		Interest Income			300 00	2
3		Six-months' accrued interest;				3
4		1-year, $6,000, 10% loan to				4
5		Taylor Co.				5

PROBLEM 5-14: When the Taylor Company pays back the loan described in Problem 5-12 on June 30 of the following year, what will be the entry the company makes in its journal to record the transaction? Record your answer in the journal below.

JOURNAL — PAGE

	DATE	DESCRIPTION	POST. REF.	DEBIT	CREDIT	
1						1
2						2
3						3
4						4
5						5
6						6

Answer: When the Taylor Company pays back the loan on June 30, it will decrease (debit) its liability account, Notes Payable, for $6,000. It will also pay the full $600 interest (calculated in Problem 5-12). To record the $600 cash interest payment, the liability account, Interest Payable, will be decreased (debited) by $300 because Taylor Company will no longer owe the $300 in interest that was accrued and recorded in this account on December 31. Interest Expense will be increased (debited) by $300 to reflect the interest accrued since January 1. Remember that the $300 in interest that accrued prior to December 31 was already debited to Interest Expense. The total cash outlay is thus $6,600, so the Cash account is decreased (credited) $6,600. The June 30 entry will therefore appear as shown below. [Section 5-4]

	DATE		DESCRIPTION	POST. REF.	DEBIT	CREDIT	
1	19-- June	30	Notes Payable		6000 00		1
2			Interest Payable		300 00		2
3			Interest Expense		300 00		3
4			Cash			6600 00	4
5			Principal and interest on $6,000,				5
6			10%, 1-yr. loan, First State				6

JOURNAL — PAGE --

PROBLEM 5-15: When the Taylor Company pays back the loan as described in Problem 5-12, what will be the entry that the bank makes in its journal to record the transaction? Record your answer in the following journal.

	DATE		DESCRIPTION	POST. REF.	DEBIT	CREDIT	
1							1
2							2
3							3
4							4
5							5
6							6
7							7

JOURNAL — PAGE

Answer: When the loan is paid back, the bank will receive $6,600 in cash, representing the full amount of both principal and interest. Repayment of the principal results in a decrease (credit) of $6,000 to the asset account, Notes Receivable. The asset account, Interest Receivable, is decreased (credited) by $300 because the lender is no longer owed the $300 in interest that accrued prior to December 31 and that was recorded in Problem 5-13. Interest Income is increased (credited) by $300 to reflect the interest accrued since January 1. Remember that the $300 in interest accrued prior to December 31 was already credited to Interest Income in Problem 5-13. The June 30 entry would thus appear as shown below. [Section 5-4]

	DATE		DESCRIPTION	POST. REF.	DEBIT	CREDIT	
1	19-- June	30	Cash		6600 00		1
2			Notes Receivable			6000 00	2
3			Interest Receivable			300 00	3
4			Interest Income			300 00	4
5			Collection of July 1 Taylor Co.,				5
6			1-yr., 10% loan, including				6
7			6 months' accrued interest				7

JOURNAL — PAGE --

PROBLEM 5-16: The work sheet on page 86 shows the trial balance for Watson Company prepared from the ledger account balances at the end of the accounting period, December 31, 19--. Complete the work sheet as follows:

1. Enter the adjustments needed in the adjustments columns to reflect the following transactions. Be sure to identify each entry by its letter on the work sheet.

   (a) An inventory on December 31 shows supplies worth $100 were used during the accounting period.
   (b) It is determined that $5,000 worth of the prepaid advertising has been used during the accounting period.
   (c) Depreciation expense was $60.
   (d) $600 in prepaid rent for the months of November and December expired.

2. Compute and enter the adjusted account balances in the Adjusted Trial Balance columns.
3. Transfer the account balances to their correct financial statement columns.
4. Determine the net income of the company and transfer it to its correct financial statement column.

Answer: The completed work sheet is shown on page 87. Note the following for each step required in this problem. [Section 5-7]

1. Note that when making the adjusting entries, it is necessary to add the three expense accounts (Supplies Expense, Depreciation Expense, and Advertising Expense) to the worksheet.
2. The adjusted trial balance should combine the original amounts shown in the trial balance with any adjustments made to those amounts. Note that the accounts whose balances change as a result of the adjusting entries are Supplies, Prepaid Advertising, Prepaid Rent, Accumulated Depreciation, Rent Expense, and the three added expense accounts.
3. For Step 3, be sure that you have transferred revenue and expense accounts to the Income Statement columns, and asset, liability, capital, and drawing accounts to the Balance Sheet columns.
4. To determine the net income of the company, you should first subtotal the Income Statement columns. The net income is the difference between these subtotals. Net income is also shown in the Balance Sheet columns. This is necessary for the Balance Sheet columns to balance.

PROBLEM 5-17: Use the Income Statement columns and drawing account for Watson Company in Problem 5-16 to determine the closing entries needed to prepare the company's books for the next accounting period. Record your entries in the journal provided on page 88.

Answer: Each step in the closing is numbered next to the journal entries for that step and explained below and illustrated on page 88. [Section 5-8]

1. The revenue account is debited for an amount equal to its balance and the summary account is credited for the same amount.
2. The expense accounts are credited for the amounts equal to their balances and the summary account is debited for an amount equal to their totals.
3. The summary account balance is calculated and then debited for the amount of its balance and the capital account is credited for the same amount. This amount is equal to the net income.
4. The drawing account is credited for its balance and the capital account is debited for the same amount.

Watson Company

Work Sheet

For Period Ending December 31, 19--

ACCOUNT TITLE	TRIAL BALANCE		ADJUSTMENTS		ADJUSTED TRIAL BALANCE		INCOME STATEMENT		BALANCE SHEET	
	DEBIT	CREDIT	DEBIT	CREDIT	DEBIT	CREDIT	DEBIT	CREDIT	DEBIT	CREDIT
Cash	7 0 0 00									
Accounts Receivable	8 3 0 00									
Supplies	2 0 0 00									
Prepaid Advertising	5 1 1 0 00									
Prepaid Rent	6 0 0 00									
Equipment	6 0 0 00									
Accumulated Depreciation		6 0 0 00								
Accounts Payable		3 0 0 00								
J. D. Watson, Capital		1 1 5 0 00								
J. D. Watson, Drawing	3 0 0 0 00									
Services Revenue		1 2 0 0 0 00								
Rent Expense	3 0 0 0 00									
Miscellaneous Expense	1 0 0 00									
	1 3 5 1 0 00	1 3 5 1 0 00								

86

Watson Company

Work Sheet

For Period Ending December 31, 19--

ACCOUNT TITLE	TRIAL BALANCE DEBIT	TRIAL BALANCE CREDIT	ADJUSTMENTS DEBIT	ADJUSTMENTS CREDIT	ADJUSTED TRIAL BALANCE DEBIT	ADJUSTED TRIAL BALANCE CREDIT	INCOME STATEMENT DEBIT	INCOME STATEMENT CREDIT	BALANCE SHEET DEBIT	BALANCE SHEET CREDIT
Cash	700 00				700 00				700 00	
Accounts Receivable	500 00				500 00				500 00	
Supplies	200 00			(a) 100 00	100 00				100 00	
Prepaid Advertising	5110 00			(b) 5000 00	110 00				110 00	
Prepaid Rent	600 00			(d) 600 00						
Equipment	3000 00				3000 00				3000 00	
Accumulated Depreciation		60 00		(c) 60 00		120 00				120 00
Accounts Payable		300 00				300 00				300 00
J. D. Watson, Capital		1150 00				1150 00				1150 00
J. D. Watson, Drawing	300 00				300 00				300 00	
Services Revenue		12000 00				12000 00		12000 00		
Rent Expense	3000 00		(d) 600 00		3600 00		3600 00			
Miscellaneous Expense	100 00				100 00		100 00			
	13510 00	13510 00								
Supplies Expense			(a) 100 00		100 00		100 00			
Advertising Expense			(b) 5000 00		5000 00		5000 00			
Depreciation Expense			(c) 60 00		60 00		60 00			
			5760 00	5760 00	13570 00	13570 00	8860 00	12000 00	4710 00	1570 00
Net Income							3140 00			3140 00
							12000 00	12000 00	4710 00	4710 00

JOURNAL PAGE

	DATE	DESCRIPTION	POST. REF.	DEBIT	CREDIT	
1						1
2						2
3						3
4						4
5						5
6						6
7						7
8						8
9						9
10						10
11						11
12						12
13						13
14						14
15						15
16						16

JOURNAL PAGE - -

	DATE	DESCRIPTION	POST. REF.	DEBIT	CREDIT	
1		Closing Entries				1
2	19-- Dec. 31	Services Revenue		1200000		2
3		Income Summary			1200000	3
4						4
5	31	Income Summary		886000		5
6		Rent Expense			360000	6
7		Miscellaneous Expense			10000	7
8		Supplies Expense			10000	8
9		Advertising Expense			50000	9
10		Depreciation Expense			6000	10
11						11
12	31	Income Summary		314000		12
13		J. D. Watson, Capital			314000	13
14						14
15	31	J. D. Watson, Capital		30000		15
16		J. D. Watson, Drawing			30000	16

PROBLEM 5-18: The following T accounts show the ledger balances of all accounts in the adjusted trial balance of Watson Company given in Problem 5-16. Post the closing entries to these accounts and compute all new balances.

Cash	Accounts Receivable	Supplies
bal. 70	bal. 830	bal. 100

Prepaid Advertising		Equipment		Accumulated Depreciation	
bal. 110		*bal.* 600			*bal.* 120

Accounts Payable		J. D. Watson, Capital		J. D. Watson, Drawing	
	bal. 300		*bal.* 1,150	*bal.* 3,000	

Services Revenue		Rent Expense		Miscellaneous Expense	
	bal. 12,000	*bal.* 3,600		*bal.* 100	

Advertising Expense		Depreciation Expense		Supplies Expense	
bal. 5,000		*bal.* 60		*bal.* 100	

Income Summary	

Answer: The closing entries and new balances are shown below in bold type. Note that after posting all of the closing entries, the balance of the temporary accounts (revenue, expense, and drawing) equal zero. [Section 5-8]

Cash		Accounts Receivable		Supplies	
bal. 70		*bal.* 830		*bal.* 100	

Prepaid Advertising		Equipment		Accumulated Depreciation	
bal. 110		*bal.* ·600			*bal.* 120

Accounts Payable		J. D. Watson, Capital		J. D. Watson, Drawing	
	bal. 300	**3,000**	*bal.* 1,150	*bal.* 3,000	**3,000**
			3,140		
			bal. **1,290**		

Services Revenue		Rent Expense		Miscellaneous Expense	
12,000	*bal.* 12,000	*bal.* 3,600	**3,600**	*bal.* 100	**100**

Advertising Expense		Depreciation Expense		Supplies Expense	
bal. 5,000	**5,000**	*bal.* 60	**60**	*bal.* 100	**100**

Income Summary	
8,860	**12,000**
3,140	
—0—	

PROBLEM 5-19: Prepare a post-closing trial balance for Watson Company in the space provided on page 90.

Answer: Note that only the permanent accounts (assets, liabilities, and equity) appear on the post-closing trial balance. The balance in these accounts will be carried forward to the next accounting period. [Section 5-9]

Watson Company
Post-Closing Trial Balance
December 31, 19--

Cash	7000	
Supplies	10000	
Accounts Receivable	8300	
Prepaid Advertising	11000	
Equipment	60000	
Accumulated Depreciation		12000
Accounts Payable		30000
J. D Watson, Capital		129000
	171000	171000

PROBLEM 5-20: The following accounts of Wood's Lawn Care Company are taken from an adjusted trial balance as of the end of the accounting period, June 30. They are presented in alphabetical order. Record the closing entries necessary to prepare these accounts for the next accounting period. Use the journal provided on page 91 and explain each entry.

Accounts Payable		$ 10,000
Accounts Receivable	$ 12,000	
Accumulated Depreciation—Equipment		15,000
Advertising Expense	850	
Cash	5,000	
Depreciation Expense	7,500	
Equipment	75,000	
Office Salaries Expense	3,500	
Rent Expense	5,000	
Service Revenue		25,000
Telephone Expense	1,500	
Wood, Capital		62,350
Wood, Drawing	2,000	
	$112,350	$112,350

JOURNAL

	DATE		DESCRIPTION	POST. REF.	DEBIT	CREDIT	
1							1
2							2
3							3
4							4
5							5
6							6
7							7
8							8
9							9
10							10
11							11
12							12
13							13
14							14
15							15
16							16
17							17
18							18
19							19
20							20

Answer: All temporary accounts now have a zero balance. [Section 5-8]

JOURNAL

PAGE - -

	DATE		DESCRIPTION	POST. REF.	DEBIT	CREDIT	
1			Closing Entries				1
2	19-- June	30	Service Revenue		2 5 0 0 0 0		2
3			Income Summary			2 5 0 0 0 0	3
4			To close the revenue account				4
5							5
6		30	Income Summary		1 8 3 5 0 0		6
7			Advertising Expense			8 5 0 0 0	7
8			Depreciation Expense			7 5 0 0 0	8
9			Office Salaries Expense			3 5 0 0 0	9
10			Rent Expense			5 0 0 0 0	10
11			Telephone Expense			1 5 0 0 0	11
12			To close the expense accounts				12
13							13
14		30	Income Summary		6 6 5 0 0 0		14
15			Wood, Capital			6 6 5 0 0 0	15
16			To close the summary account				16
17							17
18		30	Wood, Capital		2 0 0 0 0		18
19			Wood, Drawing			2 0 0 0 0	19
20			To close the drawing account				20

PROBLEM 5-21: The balances of the accounts given in Problem 5-20 are presented below in T account format. Post the journal entries to these T accounts. Be sure to record all new balances.

Cash		Accounts Receivable		Equipment	
bal. 5,000		*bal.* 12,000		*bal.* 75,000	

Accumulated Depreciation		Accounts Payable		Wood, Capital	
	bal. 15,000		*bal.* 10,000		*bal.* 62,350

Wood, Drawing		Service Revenue		Advertising Expense	
bal. 2,000			*bal.* 25,000	*bal.* 850	

Depreciation Expense		Office Salaries Expense		Rent Expense	
bal. 7,500		*bal.* 3,500		*bal.* 5,000	

Telephone Expense		Income Summary	
bal. 1,500			

Answer: The closing entries and new balances are shown in bold type. [Section 5-3]

Cash		Accounts Receivable		Equipment	
bal. 5,000		*bal.* 12,000		*bal.* 75,000	

Accumulated Depreciation		Accounts Payable		Wood, Capital	
	bal. 15,000		*bal.* 10,000	**2,000**	*bal.* 62,350
					6,650
					bal. **67,000**

Wood, Drawing		Service Revenue		Advertising Expense	
bal. 2,000	**2,000**	**25,000**	*bal.* 25,000	*bal.* 850	**850**

Depreciation Expense		Office Salaries Expense		Rent Expense	
bal. 7,500	**7,500**	*bal.* 3,500	**3,500**	*bal.* 5,000	**5,000**

Telephone Expense		Income Summary	
bal. 1,500	**1,500**	**18,350**	**25,000**
		6,650	
		—0—	

PROBLEM 5-22: Use the information given in Problem 5-21 to prepare a post-closing trial balance for Wood's Lawn Care Company. A form is provided on page 93.

Answer: [Section 5-4]

Woods Lawn Care Company Post-Closing Trial Balance June 30, 19--		
Cash	500000	
Accounts Receivable	1200000	
Equipment	7500000	
Accumulated Depreciation		1500000
Accounts Payable		1000000
Wood, Capital		6700000
	9200000	9200000

EXAMINATION I (CHAPTERS 1 THROUGH 5)

True or False

1. Assets, liabilities, and equity are the three elements that report on the status of an entity at a particular time. (Section 1-3)

2. The basic accounting equation is: Assets + Liabilities = Equity. (Section 1-3)

3. Revenues are increases in equity from the exchange of goods, services, or other activities. (Section 1-5)

4. Liabilities and equity are resources of a business. (Section 1-3)

5. Notes and accounts receivable due within one year are classified as current assets on the balance sheet. (Section 2-1)

6. Using the accrual method of accounting, expenses are recognized only when cash has been paid. (Section 2-5)

7. Debit entries increase asset accounts and decrease liability and equity accounts. (Section 3-2)

8. Increases to revenue accounts are recorded as credits. (Section 3-2)

9. The trial balance proves that the general ledger has been correctly posted. (Section 4-4)

10. A contra asset account is a liability. (Section 5-3)

Fill in the blanks

Fill in the missing word or words.

1. The _____ principle maintains that revenue should not be reported on financial statements until the earning process is complete. (Section 2-5)

2. The _____ principle holds that most assets and liabilities are recorded at their transaction cost and not adjusted for future changes in market value until sold. (Section 2-5)

3. The _____ is sometimes referred to as the book of original entry. (Section 4-1)

4. After the closing entries have been posted, revenue and expense accounts will have a _____ balance. (Section 5-8)

5. The two types of adjusting entries are _____ and _____. (Section 5-2)

6. The periodic allocation of the cost of a long-lived asset to expense over its useful life is called _____. (Section 5-3)

7.

	Assets	Liabilities	Equity
(a)	$ 40,000	$15,000	?
(b)	?	$32,000	$12,500
(c)	$100,000		$30,000

Problems

PROBLEM 1: The following transactions were completed by Sun Company, a lawn service, during the first month of operation.

(1) Shawn Briggs, owner, invested $10,000 in the business.   _____
(2) Purchased mowing equipment on credit for $2,500.   _____
(3) Purchased additional equipment with cash, $300.   _____
(4) Provided lawn service to customers and collected cash, $600.   _____
(5) Paid $1,000 of amount owed to creditor in (2) above.   _____

Indicate the effect of each of these transactions on the basic accounting equation by inserting the appropriate letter from the following list in the space provided to the right of each transaction.

(*a*) increase in asset, increase in liability

(*b*) increase in asset, increase in equity

(*c*) increase in one asset, decrease in another asset

(*d*) decrease in asset, decrease in liability

(*e*) decrease in asset, decrease in equity

PROBLEM 2: Classify the following accounts by filling in the blank provided to the left of each account with the letter of the corresponding balance sheet category given on the right.

Balance Sheet Categories

_____ 1. Patent	(a) Current assets
_____ 2. Cash	(b) Long-term investment
_____ 3. Sam Jones, Capital	(c) Plant and equipment
_____ 4. Notes Payable, due in 5 yrs.	(d) Intangible asset
_____ 5. Accounts Receivable	(e) Current liability
_____ 6. Building	(f) Noncurrent liability
_____ 7. Wages Payable	(g) Equity
_____ 8. Equipment used in business	

PROBLEM 3: Below is a list of accounts of Taylor Company. For each of the transactions below indicate the accounts that would be debited and credited by placing the number of the appropriate account in the debit and credit column.

1. Cash	6. Accounts Payable
2. Accounts Receivable	7. James Taylor, Capital
3. Office Supplies	8. James Taylor, Drawing
4. Office Equipment	9. Revenues
5. Accumulated Depreciation–Office Equipment	10. Expenses

Transactions	Accounts Debited	Accounts Credited
Example: Owner invested $10,000 cash in the business	1	7
1. Purchased office supplies on account.	___	___
2. Paid this month's rent.	___	___
3. Billed customers for services rendered during the current month.	___	___
4. Owner withdrew cash from the business.	___	___
5. Additional office equipment is purchased; $100 cash is paid now and the balance is to be paid in 30 days.	___	___
6. Received cash from customers for services rendered and billed in prior month.	___	___
7. Paid employees wages.	___	___
8. Received cash from customer at time service was rendered.	___	___
9. Paid balance due on office equipment in (5) above.	___	___
10. Recorded depreciation on office equipment for current month.	___	___

PROBLEM 4: The Dee Jay Company began operations on March 2, 19x1. The management company had the following transactions. Record these transactions in the general journal provided on page 96.

March 2 Jay Royer invested $50,000 in the business

March 2 Rent of $300 was paid in cash for office space for March

March 3 Office equipment was purchased an account for $4,350.

March 5 Office Supplies in the amount of $750 were puchased for cash

March 8 Purchased automobile for use in business. Paid cash of $1,000 and signed a 6-month note for the balance of $7,500.

March 15 Sent invoice for $450 to Bliss & Company for management services performed March 9.

March 20 Paid for office equipment purchased March 3.

March 30 Received $300 payment for management services–balance to be paid in 15 days

	DATE	DESCRIPTION	POST. REF.	DEBIT	CREDIT	
1						1
2						2
3						3
4						4
5						5
6						6
7						7
8						8
9						9
10						10
11						11
12						12
13						13
14						14
15						15
16						16
17						17
18						18
19						19
20						20
21						21
22						22
23						23
24						24
25						25
26						26
27						27
28						28
29						29
30						30
31						31
32						32
33						33
34						34
35						35
36						36
37						37
38						38

JOURNAL   PAGE *1*

PROBLEM 5: Prepare the appropriate adjusting entries on December 31, 19x1 for each of the following transactions in the form provided. No adjusting entries have been made during the year. Explanations may be omitted.

A three-year fire insurance policy was purchased on October 1, 19x1, at a cost of $3,600. The premium, which was paid in cash, was debited to Prepaid Unexpired Insurance.

	DATE	DESCRIPTION	POST. REF.	DEBIT	CREDIT	
1						1
2						2
3						3

JOURNAL — PAGE 1

The office supplies on hand on December 31, 19x1 total $330. The beginning balance in the office supplies account was $600. Purchases made during the year and debited to the office supplies account amounted to $150.

4						4
5						5
6						6
7						7

Weekly salaries are paid each Friday in the amount of $7,000. December 31, 19x1, the last day of the accounting period, falls on a Wednesday. Make the necessary adjusting entry on December 31, 19x1. (Assume a 5-day work week beginning on Monday.)

8						8
9						9
10						10
11						11

On December 1, 19x1, the company borrowed the sum of $10,000 from the bank. Interest is payable at 12% per year and is due when the note matures November 30, 19x2.

12						12
13						13
14						14
15						15

PROBLEM 6: The following accounts of Heath Company are taken from the adjusted trial balance as of December 31, the end of the accounting period. They are presented in alphabetical order. Record the necessary closing entries to prepare the accounts for the next accounting period. Use the general journal on page 98.

Accounts Payable		$ 7,800
Accounts Receivable	$ 6,200	
Accumulated Depreciation: Equipment		8,000
Advertising Expense	500	
Cash	2,500	
Depreciation Expense	2,000	
Equipment	40,000	
John Heath, Capital		23,920
John Heath, Drawing	1,500	
Office Salaries Expense	10,300	
Rent Expense	6,000	
Revenue		31,600
Telephone Expense	620	
Utility Expense	1,700	
	$71,320	$71,320

	DATE		DESCRIPTION	POST. REF.	DEBIT	CREDIT	
1							1
2							2
3							3
4							4
5							5
6							6
7							7
8							8
9							9
10							10
11							11
12							12
13							13
14							14
15							15
16							16
17							17
18							18
19							19
20							20
21							21
22							22
23							23
24							24

JOURNAL   PAGE *1*

ANSWERS

True or False

1. True   2. False   3. True   4. False   5. True   6. False   7. True   8. True   9. False
10. False

Fill in the Blanks

1. revenue recognition
2. historical cost
3. journal
4. zero
5. accrual; deferral
6. depreciation
7. (*a*) $25,000
   (*b*) $44,500
   (*c*) $70,000

Problems

1. (1) b—Cash (asset) is increased and equity is increased.
   (2) a—Equipment (asset) is increased and liabilities are increased.
   (3) c—Equipment (asset) is increased and Cash (asset) is decreased.
   (4) b—Cash (asset) is increased. The service provided to customers is revenue. Revenue increases equity.
   (5) d—Cash (asset) is decreased and liabilities are decreased.

2. (1) D   (5) A
   (2) A   (6) C
   (3) G   (7) E
   (4) F   (8) C

3.

Transaction	Account Debited	Account Credited
(1)	3	6
(2)	10	1
(3)	2	9
(4)	8	1
(5)	4	1 and 6
(6)	1	2
(7)	10	1
(8)	1	9
(9)	6	1
(10)	10	5

4.

	DATE		DESCRIPTION	POST. REF.	DEBIT	CREDIT	
1	March	2	Cash		5 0 0 0 00		1
2			J. Royer, Capital			5 0 0 0 00	2
3			Owner invests in company				3
4		2	Rent Expense		3 0 0 00		4
5			Cash			3 0 0 00	5
6			Paid office rent for				6
7			March				7
8		3	Office Equipment		4 3 5 0 00		8
9			Accounts Payable			4 3 5 0 00	9
10			Purchased office				10
11			equipment on account				11
12		5	Office Supplies		7 5 0 00		12
13			Cash			7 5 0 00	13
14			Purchased office supplies				14
15			for cash				15
16		8	Automobile		8 5 0 0 00		16
17			Cash			1 0 0 0 00	17
18			Notes Payable			7 5 0 0 00	18
19			Purchased automobile				19
20			for use in business. Paid				20
21			$1,000 cash and signed				21
22			6-month note				22
23		15	Accounts Receivable		4 5 0 00		23
24			Management Fees			4 5 0 00	24
25			Sent invoice for services				25
26			performed on March 9				26
27		20	Accounts Payable		4 3 5 0 00		27
28			Cash			4 3 5 0 00	28
29			Paid for office equipment				29
30			purchased March 3				30
31		30	Cash		3 0 0 00		31
32			Accounts Receivable			3 0 0 00	32
33			Received payment for				33
34			services billed March 15				34
35							35
36							36
37							37
38							38

JOURNAL   PAGE 1

5.

JOURNAL   PAGE 1

	DATE		DESCRIPTION	POST. REF.	DEBIT	CREDIT	
1	19x1 Dec.	31	Insurance Expense		3 0 0 00		1
2			Prepaid Insurance			3 0 0 00	2
3							3

$3,600 ÷ 36 months × 3 months = $300

			POST. REF.	DEBIT	CREDIT	
4						4
5	31	Supplies Expense		4 2 0 00		5
6		Office Supplies			4 2 0 00	6
7						7

$600 beginning balance
150 purchases during the year
$750 supplies available for use
330 supplies on hand—12/31
$420 supplies used during the year

8						8
9	31	Wages Expense		4 2 0 0 00		9
10		Wages Payable			4 2 0 0 00	10
11						11

$7,000 ÷ 5 days = $1,400 per day
$1,400 × 3 days = $4,200

12						12
13	31	Interest Expense		1 0 0 00		13
14		Interest Payable			1 0 0 00	14
15						15

$10,000 × .12 × 1/12 = $100

6.

	DATE		DESCRIPTION	POST. REF.	DEBIT	CREDIT	
			JOURNAL			**PAGE 1**	
1			Closing Entries				1
2	Dec.	31	Revenue		3 1 6 0 0 00		2
3			Income Summary			3 1 6 0 0 00	3
4		31	Income Summary		2 1 1 2 0 00		4
5			Advertising Expense			5 0 0 00	5
6			Depreciation Expense			2 0 0 0 00	6
7			Office Salaries Expense			1 0 3 0 0 00	7
8			Rent Expense			6 0 0 0 00	8
9			Telephone Expense			6 2 0 00	9
10			Utility Expense			1 7 0 0 00	10
11		31	Income Summary		1 0 4 8 0 00		11
12			John Heath, Capital			1 0 4 8 0 00	12
13		31	John Heath, Capital		1 5 0 0 00		13
14			John Heath, Drawing			1 5 0 0 00	14
15							15
16							16

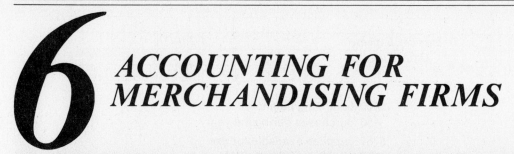

6 ACCOUNTING FOR MERCHANDISING FIRMS

THIS CHAPTER IS ABOUT

☑ **Merchandising Firms**
☑ **Accounting for the Sale of Merchandise**
☑ **Accounting for the Cost of Goods Sold**
☑ **The Work Sheet**
☑ **Financial Statements**

6-1. Merchandising Firms

A. A merchandising firm buys goods for resale.

A merchandising firm may be a *wholesaler*, which buys goods for resale to retailers, or a *retailer*, which buys goods for resale to final customers. The goods purchased and held for resale, whether wholesale or retail, are known as *merchandise inventory*, or *inventory*, and are held apart from all other inventories.

B. Accounting for a merchandising firm involves determining sales revenue and the cost of goods sold.

The gross profit of a merchandising firm is computed by subtracting the cost of goods sold from sales revenue. Before the subtraction can be made, however, the revenue from sales and the cost of goods sold must be determined. Accounting for the sale of merchandise and for the cost of goods sold is what differentiates the accounting for a merchandising firm from that of a service organization.

EXAMPLE 6-1: The income statement of a merchandising firm typically has the following format.

Merchandising Firm
Condensed Income Statement
For Year Ended December 31, 19--

Sales (net)	$60,000
Less cost of goods sold	25,000
Gross profit from sales	$35,000
Less operating expenses	15,000
Net income	$20,000

In this example, a merchandising firm sold goods for $60,000 that cost $25,000, thus earning a gross profit from sales of $35,000. A net income of $20,000 is then computed by subtracting operating expenses of $15,000 from the gross profit.

6-2. Accounting for the Sale of Merchandise

A. Revenue from the sale of merchandise is usually recorded in the ledger as Sales or Sales Revenue.

A sale consists of an exchange of merchandise for some other asset, usually cash or a receivable.

1. *Sales for cash.* Sales of merchandise for cash are totaled and recorded in the journal by debiting Cash and crediting Sales.

EXAMPLE 6-2: Media Market sold a video cassette recorder to a customer for $1,000 cash; Invoice No. 10. The journal entry for this sale would be recorded as follows:

Dec.	9	Cash	1,000	
		Sales		1,000
		Invoice No. 10		

Note that the recording of the invoice number would provide reference to the details of the transaction, such as the model number of the recorder.

Sales to customers who use bank credit cards (such as Visa or MasterCard) are usually recorded as cash sales also. Most banks charge a fee for handling credit card sales. This fee should be debited to an expense account.

2. *Sales on account.* Sales of merchandise on account are recorded in the journal by debiting Accounts Receivable and crediting Sales. When the account is paid, Cash is debited and Accounts Receivable is credited.

EXAMPLE 6-3: Media Market sold a portable computer to a customer on credit for $1,500; Invoice No. 11. The journal entry for this sale would be recorded as follows:

Dec.	9	Accounts Receivable	1,500	
		Sales		1,500
		Invoice No. 11		

When Media Market receives payment for the computer, the following journal entry will be made.

Dec.	19	Cash	1,500	
		Accounts Receivable		1,500
		Invoice No. 11		

Sales to customers who use nonbank credit cards (such as American Express) must usually be reported to the credit card company before cash is received, therefore a receivable is created with the card company and the sale is recorded in the same manner as a sale on account. However, the credit card company generally deducts a service fee before it pays the cash, which should be debited to an expense account.

EXAMPLE 6-4: Media Market sold a $400 turntable to a customer who charged the amount on her American Express card; Invoice No. 12. The sale was recorded in the journal as a receivable. When payment was received from the credit card company, a service fee of $8 was deducted from the cash amount. The journal entry for the receipt of payment would be recorded as follows:

Dec.	10	Cash	392	
		Credit Card Collection Expense	8	
		Accounts Receivable		400
		Receipt of cash from American Express for payment of Invoice No. 12		

B. Sales returns and allowances result in a reduction to gross sales.

Occasionally, goods are returned for a refund or an allowance (reduction in the original price of the goods) is granted to a customer for defective or damaged goods. It is important that such returns and allowances be recorded because they result in a reduction in sales and a reduction in Cash or Accounts Receivable. Thus, a contra sales account, Sales Returns and Allowances, is set up in which to debit returns and allowances. Management should monitor the numbers of and reasons for returns and allowances so that action can be taken if they become excessive.

EXAMPLE 6-5: Media Market has a guaranteed policy of having the lowest prices in town. The customer who purchased the $400 turntable in Example 6-4 returned several days after purchasing it and presented an ad from a competing store offering the same turntable for $350. Consequently, the manager of Media Market granted the customer a $50 refund for the difference in price. The journal entry for this transaction would be recorded as follows:

Dec. 12	Sales Returns and Allowances	50	
	Cash		50
	Allowance given to customer to		
	match ad appearing in paper,		
	Invoice No. 12		

C. Sales discounts result in a reduction to gross sales.

The terms of a credit sale should be clearly specified on the sales invoice given by the seller to the purchaser. The terms granted usually depend on the custom of the trade. For example, trade terms for sales to another business may specify full payment in 30 days by saying "net 30" or simply "n/30."

Some sellers may offer *cash discounts* for prompt payment. A common cash discount is a two percent discount if paid within ten days, or full (net) payment in thirty days, commonly written "2/10, n/30." The full amount of a sale made on these terms is recorded as a debit to Accounts Receivable and a credit to Sales because it is not yet known if the customer will pay within the discount period. If payment is received within the discount period, Cash is debited for the amount received and a contra sales account, Sales Discounts, is debited for the amount of the discount. Accounts Receivable is then credited for the full amount. If payment is not received within the discount period, then the payment is recorded in the same manner as any sale on account.

EXAMPLE 6-6: Media Market sold a set of speakers to a customer for $500. The terms of the sale were 2/10, n/30 on Invoice No. 1012. The journal entry for this sale would be recorded as follows:

May 1	Accounts Receivable	500	
	Sales		500
	Invoice No. 1012; 2/10, n/30		

If payment is received on May 11, the last day within the discount period, then the following journal entry would be made.

May 11	Cash	490	
	Sales Discounts	10	
	Accounts Receivable		500
	Invoice No. 1012, paid within		
	discount period		

If payment is received on May 31, the date due, then the following journal entry would be made.

May 31	Cash	500	
	Accounts Receivable		500
	Invoice No. 1012, paid after		
	discount period		

A 2% discount for paying between days 1–10 can be looked at as a 2% penalty for paying between days 11–30. There are 18.25 20-day periods in a year ($365 \div 20 = 18.25$). If 2% is charged for a 20-day period, the annual interest rate is almost 37% ($18.25 \times .02 = 36.5$). If a customer regularly pays late, thus borrowing at such a high rate of interest, then it may be an indication to management that the customer has exhausted other sources of credit and is a high risk.

Net sales is computed as shown below:

$$\text{Sales} - \text{Sales Discounts} - \text{Sales Returns and Allowances} = \text{Net Sales}$$

D. Trade discounts do not result in a reduction to gross sales.

A *trade discount* is a discount from the list price of merchandise given to a certain class of customers (such as those who buy in quantity) before consideration of credit terms. A trade discount is thus given without regard to the time of payment. The use of trade discounts allows a business to vary prices in a catalog by varying the trade discount offered, thus permitting the issue of only one catalog to both wholesale and retail customers.

For accounting purposes, list prices and their trade discounts do not need to be listed separately in the accounts. This is because trade discounts reflect the original agreed upon price of an item rather than an optional price for early payment, as is the case with sales discounts.

6-3. Accounting for the Cost of Goods Sold

A merchandising firm must account for the cost of the goods that it sells in a given accounting period. There is more to accounting for the cost of goods sold than simply recording the invoice price of the goods purchased for resale during a given period. Adjustments must be made for the cost of transportation in, purchase returns and allowances, and purchase discounts. It is also necessary to determine the amount of goods on hand at the beginning and ending of the accounting period. All of this information is reported on the income statement of a merchandising firm.

A. The cost of transportation in is included in the cost of goods sold.

An agreement to purchase goods usually specifies who is to pay for the cost of transporting the goods to the merchandising firm. The terms are stated *FOB destination* if the seller is to pay for transportation. The terms are stated *FOB shipping point* if the purchaser is to pay for transportation. There are two ways that a merchandising firm may record transportation costs for the goods it purchases for resale.

1. *Debit Purchases account.* A merchandising firm may simply debit its Purchases account for any transportation costs (in addition to the cost of the goods) and credit Accounts Payable or Cash.
2. *Debit Transportation In account.* Some merchandising firms maintain a separate Transportation In account to record the transportation costs on goods they purchase. This account is debited for the amount and Accounts Payable or Cash is credited Transportation In is included in determining the costs of goods sold.

EXAMPLE 6-7: Media Market agreed to purchase 100 television sets, terms FOB shipping point. It later received a bill in the amount of $175 from Cannonball Trucking for shipment of the sets, Invoice No. 55. Assuming that Media Market keeps a separate record of transportation costs, the following journal entry would be made upon receipt of the bill.

May 15	Transportation In	175	
	Accounts Payable		175
	Invoice No. 55		

B. Discounts, returns, and allowances are recorded by a merchandising firm.

The discounts, returns, and allowances given by the seller are also recorded on the books of the purchaser. Cash discounts given by the seller are credited to Purchase Discounts by the purchaser.

EXAMPLE 6-8: In Example 6-6, Media Market sold a set of speakers to a customer for $500, terms 2/10, n/30, on Invoice No. 1012. Assuming that the speakers were purchased by the customer as merchandise inventory (if they were not, then they would not be recorded as Purchases), the following journal entry would be made by the customer to record the purchase.

May 1	Purchases	500	
	Accounts Payable		500
	Invoice No. 1012; 2/10, n/30		

The following journal entry would be made by the purchaser to record a payment mailed to arrive on May 11, the last day of the discount period.

May 9	Accounts Payable	500	
	Cash		490
	Purchase Discounts		10
	Invoice No. 1012, paid within discount period		

The following journal entry would be made by the purchaser to record a payment mailed to arrive on May 31, after the discount period.

May 29	Accounts Payable	500	
	Cash		500
	Invoice No. 1012, paid after discount period		

Sales returns and allowances given by the seller are credited to Purchase Returns and Allowances by the purchaser.

EXAMPLE 6-9: In Example 6-4, Media Market sold a turntable to a customer for $400 and later gave the customer a $50 return on the purchase, Invoice No. 12 (Example 6-5). Assuming that the turntable was purchased as merchandise inventory, the following journal entry would be made by the customer to record the purchase allowance.

Dec. 12	Cash	50	
	Purchase Returns and Allowances		50
	Invoice No. 12, refund to match advertised price of competing store		

Net purchases is computed as shown below:

Purchases − Purchase Discounts − Purchase Returns and Allowances = Net Purchases

C. The beginning and ending merchandise inventory is determined by a merchandising firm.

The amount of inventory on hand at the end of an accounting period is determined by a physical count and is available for sale during the next period. The merchandise on hand at the end of one period is also the beginning balance for the next period. Beginning and ending inventories are used in determining the cost of goods sold in the income statement. Ending inventory also appears on the balance sheet as an asset. It is therefore necessary to determine the cost and quantity of goods on hand at the end of a period. There are various methods for determining the cost of goods that remain in inventory based on different cost flow assumptions. These are discussed in Chapter 10. There are two basic methods of accounting for merchandise inventory on hand.

1. *Perpetual inventory method.* The perpetual inventory method consists of keeping records of the cost of each item in Inventory and deducting the cost from Inventory and debiting it to the Cost of Goods Sold account as each item is sold. Purchases are debited to the Inventory account, rather than the Purchases account, when this system is used.

Merchandising firms that sell large items of high value, such as cars or furniture, would use the perpetual inventory method. When this method is used, a firm is able to closely estimate the inventory and cost of goods sold throughout the accounting period. A physical inventory at the end of the period can be compared to the perpetual inventory records and, if necessary, adjustments can be made. (Computers have made it possible for more companies to maintain a perpetual inventory.)

EXAMPLE 6-10: Media Market purchased cassette recorders for $1,000 on account. Under the perpetual method of inventory, the following journal entry would be made.

Apr. 19	Inventory	1,000	
	Accounts Payable		1,000
	To record purchase of inventory on account		

Assume that each cassette recorder costs $50 and will be sold for $75. As each recorder is sold, the following two journal entries will be made.

June 9	Accounts Receivable	75	
	Sales		75
	To record sale of merchandise		
9	Cost of Goods Sold	50	
	Inventory		50
	To record the cost of goods sold and reduce inventory		

2. *Periodic inventory method.* Merchandising firms that sell many items of low value, such as grocery stores or bookstores, may find it impractical to use the perpetual inventory method. They would simply take a physical count of inventory at the end of the accounting period. Under the periodic inventory method, no entries are made in the Inventory or Cost of Goods Sold accounts during the period. Instead, the purchase of merchandise is recorded as a debit to Purchases and a credit to Accounts Payable. A sale is simply debited to Accounts Receivable (or Cash) and credited to Sales.

EXAMPLE 6-11: In Example 6-10, Media Market purchased cassette recorders for $1,000. Using the periodic inventory method, the following journal entry would be made to record the purchase.

Apr. 19	Purchases	1,000	
	Accounts Payable		1,000
	To record purchase of inventory on account		

As each recorder is sold, the following journal entry will be made.

June 9	Accounts Receivable	75	
	Sales		75
	To record sale of merchandise		

No adjustments to Inventory or Cost of Goods Sold are made until the end of the year. A physical count of inventory is made at that time.

D. The income statement of a merchandising firm reports the final calculation of the cost of goods sold during a given period.

The basic form of the cost of goods sold computation is presented in the cost of goods sold section of the income statement of Media Market, as shown on page 108. The complete income statement is shown on page 111.

Cost of goods sold:			
Beginning inventory, January 1, 19—			$32,100
Purchases		$72,650	
Less: Purchase discounts	$1,360		
Purchase returns and allowances	2,200	3,560	
Net purchases		$69,090	
Add: Transportation In		1,890	70,980
Cost of goods available for sale			$103,080
Less: Ending inventory, December 31, 19—			36,500
Cost of goods sold			$66,580

6-4. The Work Sheet

The work sheet was presented in Chapter 5 as a tool to assist the accountant in preparing financial statements. To illustrate accounts that are unique to a merchandising firm, the complete work sheet for Media Market is presented on page 109. These accounts are indicated in bold type.

A.   The trial balance, adjustments, and adjusted trial balance columns are completed as for any company.

As discussed in Chapter 5, the account balances at the end of the accounting period are entered in the trial balance columns. Any adjustments to these accounts are then entered in the adjustments columns. In this case, adjustments are entered for expired insurance, equipment depreciation, and salary expense accrued but not paid. The adjusted trial balance columns are then completed.

B.   The income statement columns contain the adjusted amounts for expenses and revenues.

Recall that revenue and expense accounts are transferred to the income statement columns. The cost of goods sold accounts are all either expenses or adjusting expense accounts. The sales accounts are all either revenue or adjusting revenue accounts. Thus, it should be obvious that they are all listed in the income statement columns. In this case, the Sales, Sales Discounts, Sales Returns and Allowances, Purchases, Purchase Discounts, Purchase Returns and Allowances, and Transportation In accounts are entered in their appropriate income statement columns.

We know that the beginning inventory appears in the cost of goods sold computation on the income statement and must be removed from the Inventory account at the end of the period. Thus, the beginning inventory balance is transferred as a debit to the income statement columns. Ending inventory appears as a reduction from the cost of goods available on the income statement. Thus, the ending inventory balance is transferred as a credit to the income statement columns.

C.   The balance sheet columns include ending inventory as an asset.

Recall that assets, liabilities, equity, and drawing accounts are transferred to the balance sheet columns. Ending inventory is not only recorded as a reduction in the cost of goods sold section of the income statement, but as a remaining asset at the end of the period on the balance sheet. Thus, the ending inventory balance is entered as a debit in the balance sheet columns of the work sheet in addition to appearing in the credit column of the income statement section of the work sheet.

MEDIA MARKET
WORK SHEET
FOR YEAR ENDED DECEMBER 31, 19—

ACCOUNT TITLE	TRIAL BALANCE DEBIT	TRIAL BALANCE CREDIT	ADJUSTMENTS DEBIT	ADJUSTMENTS CREDIT	ADJUSTED TRIAL BALANCE DEBIT	ADJUSTED TRIAL BALANCE CREDIT	INCOME STATEMENT DEBIT	INCOME STATEMENT CREDIT	BALANCE SHEET DEBIT	BALANCE SHEET CREDIT
Cash	10600 00				10600 00				10600 00	
Accounts Receivable	11450 00				11450 00				11450 00	
Inventory, January 1	32100 00				32100 00		32100 00			
Prepaid Insurance	3600 00			(b) 1200 00	2400 00				2400 00	
Equipment	68000 00				68000 00				68000 00	
Accumulated Depr., Equipment		20400 00		(a) 6800 00		27200 00				27200 00
Accounts Payable		28170 00				28170 00				28170 00
Vern Massey, Capital		52120 00				52120 00				52120 00
Vern Massey, Drawing	3000 00				3000 00				3000 00	
Sales		145400 00				145400 00		145400 00		
Sales Discounts	7100 00				7100 00		7100 00			
Sales Returns & Allowances	5300 00				5300 00		5300 00			
Purchases	72650 00				72650 00		72650 00			
Purchase Discounts		1360 00				1360 00		1360 00		
Purchase Returns & Allow.		2200 00				2200 00		2200 00		
Transportation In	1890 00				1890 00		1890 00			
Rent Expense	5200 00				5200 00		5200 00			
Salary Expense	25550 00		(c) 1525 00		27025 00		27025 00			
Utilities Expense	3260 00				3260 00		3260 00			
	249650 00	249650 00								
Insurance Expense			(b) 1200 00		1200 00		1200 00			
Depreciation Expense			(a) 6800 00		6800 00		6800 00			
Salaries Payable				(c) 1525 00		1525 00				1525 00
			9525 00	9525 00	257975 00	257975 00				
Inventory, December 31								36500 00	36500 00	
							162525 00	185460 00	131950 00	109015 00
Net Income							22935 00			22935 00
							185460 00	185460 00	131950 00	131950 00

Adjustments::
(a) Depreciation on equipment during the year.
$68,000 ÷ 10-year life = $6,800 depreciation per year.
(b) Insurance premium expired during the year.
(c) Salaries accrued at end of year.

D. The work sheet can now be completed.

All that is left to complete the work sheet is to sort the accounts into their proper financial statement columns, calculate the net income, transfer net income to the proper balance sheet column, and total the columns as a final check.

E. After the financial statements are prepared, adjusting and closing entries are journalized and posted to the ledger.

The same procedures are followed to make adjusting and closing entries for a merchandising firm as were presented in Chapter 5. Note, however, that one of the effects of the closing entries for a merchandising firm is to remove the beginning inventory balance from the Inventory account and enter the ending inventory balance.

EXAMPLE 6-12: The closing entries for the debit column of the income statement columns of the work sheet are shown below for Media Market.

Dec. 1	Income Summary	162,525	
	Inventory		32,100
	Sales Discounts		7,100
	Sales Returns and Allowances		5,300
	Purchases		72,650
	Transportation In		1,890
	Rent Expense		5,200
	Salary Expense		27,025
	Utilities Expense		3,260
	Insurance Expense		1,200
	Depreciation Expense		6,800
	To close out beginning inventory and temporary accounts with debit balances		

The Sales Discounts, Sales Returns and Allowances, Purchases accounts, and so forth, now have a zero balance. The beginning inventory has been eliminated from the inventory account.

EXAMPLE 6-13: The closing entries for the credit column of the income statement columns of the work sheet are shown below for Media Market.

Dec. 31	Sales	145,400	
	Purchase Discounts	1,360	
	Purchase Returns and Allowances	2,200	
	Inventory	36,500	
	Income Summary		185,460
	To record ending inventory and close out temporary accounts with credit balances		

All income statement accounts with credit balances now have zero balances. The ending inventory appears in the Inventory account, which now shows a debit balance of $36,500, as shown below.

Inventory			
bal. 1/1	32,100	*12/31*	32,100
12/31	36,500		

The Income Summary account and the Drawing account are now closed in the same manner as for any firm.

6-5. Financial Statements

As discussed in Chapter 5, all of the information needed to prepare the income statement, balance sheet, and statement of equity is available in the income statement and balance sheet columns of the work sheet.

EXAMPLE 6-14: The income statement, balance sheet, and statement of equity for Media Market are presented below. Trace the accounts from the work sheet to the financial statements to verify your understanding of the work sheet as a tool for preparing these financial statements.

Media Market
Income Statement
For Year Ended December 31, 19—

Revenue from sales:			
Gross Sales		$145,400	
Less: Sales discounts	$ 7,100		
Sales returns and allowances	5,300	12,400	
Net sales			$133,000
Cost of goods sold:			
Inventory, January 1, 19—		$ 32,100	
Purchases	$72,650		
Less: Purchase discounts	$1,360		
Purchase returns and allowances	2,200	3,560	
Net purchases	$69,090		
Add: Transportation in	1,890	70,980	
Cost of goods available for sale		$103,080	
Less: Inventory, December 31, 19—		36,500	
Cost of goods sold			66,580
Gross profit			$ 66,420
Operating expenses:			
Rent expense		$ 5,200	
Salary expense		27,025	
Utilities expense		3,260	
Insurance expense		1,200	
Depreciation expense		6,800	
Total operating expenses			43,485
Net income			$ 22,935

Media Market
Statement of Equity
For Year Ended December 31, 19–

Vern Massey, capital, January 1, 19––	$52,120
Add December 31, 19–– net income	22,935
Subtotal...	$75,055
Deduct withdrawals	3,000
Vern Massey, capital, December 31, 19––	$72,055

Media Market
Balance Sheet
December 31, 19––

Assets

Current assets:		
Cash...	$10,600	
Accounts receivable	11,450	
Inventory...	36,500	
Prepaid insurance.......................................	2,400	
Total current assets		$ 60,950
Plant assets:		
Equipment	$68,000	
Less: Accumulated depreciation....................	27,200	40,800
Total assets...		$101,750

Liabilities and Equity

Current liabilities:		
Accounts payable	$28,170	
Salaries payable	1,525	
Total current liabilities...............................		$ 29,695
Vern Massey, capital		72,055
Total liabilities and equity		$101,750

RAISE YOUR GRADES

Can you explain...?

☑ what a merchandising firm is

☑ how to record sales, sales returns and allowances, and sales discounts

☑ how to record purchases, purchase returns and allowances, and purchase discounts

☑ how to compute net sales
☑ how to compute the cost of goods sold
☑ the perpetual and periodic methods of inventory
☑ how to prepare a work sheet for a merchandising firm and use it to prepare financial statements
☑ the effect of closing entries on the Inventory account

SUMMARY

1. A merchandising firm buys merchandise for resale to customers.
2. The sale of merchandise is the source of sales revenue. Gross profit is computed by subtracting the cost of goods sold from net sales.
3. Sales for cash are debited to Cash and credited to Sales.
4. Sales on account are debited to Accounts Receivable and credited to Sales. When the account is paid, Cash is debited and Accounts Receivable is credited. Any collection fees charged by credit card companies are debited to an expense account.
5. Sales returns and allowances and sales discounts result in a reduction in gross sales. They are debited to accounts of the same titles and credited to Cash or Accounts Receivable.
6. Trade discounts reflect the original agreed upon price of an item.
7. Net Sales = Gross Sales − Sales Returns and Allowances − Sales Discounts.
8. The cost of goods sold is the cost of merchandise sold to customers during a given period.
9. The cost of transportation in is debited to Transportation In. Purchase returns and allowances and purchase discounts are credited to accounts of the same titles. Some firms may choose to record the cost of transportation in along with the invoice price of goods in the Purchases account.
10. Net Purchases = Purchases − Purchase Returns and Allowances − Purchase Discounts.
11. Ending inventory of merchandise on hand is determined by a physical count and is also the beginning inventory balance for the next period.
12. There are two methods of accounting for merchandise inventory on hand. Under the perpetual inventory method, records are kept of the cost of each item in Inventory and the cost is deducted from Inventory and debited to Cost of Goods Sold as each item is sold. Under the periodic inventory method, a physical inventory is taken to determine the ending inventory balance. No entries are made during the period.
13. Cost of Goods Sold = Beginning Inventory + Net Purchases + Transportation In − Ending Inventory.
14. The work sheet for a merchandising firm is prepared in the same manner as for any firm. The cost of goods sold accounts are entered in the appropriate income statement columns. Beginning and ending inventory are also entered in the appropriate income statement columns. The balance sheet debit column includes the ending inventory balance as an asset.
15. The information needed to prepare the income statement, balance sheet, and statement of equity is available in the income statement and balance sheet columns of the work sheet.
16. After the financial statements are prepared, adjusting and closing entries are journalized and posted to the ledger. The effect of the closing entries for a merchandising firm is to remove the beginning inventory balance from the Inventory account and enter the ending inventory balance. All revenue and expense accounts will have a zero balance after the closing entries.

RAPID REVIEW

1. What is the principal activity of a merchandising firm? [Section 6-1]
2. What is the difference between gross profit and net income? [Section 6-1]
3. What is the difference between sales revenue and net income? [Section 6-1]

4. What is the meaning of (a) 2/10, n/30; (b) n/30? [Section 6-2]

5. When defective merchandise is returned by a customer, what accounts are debited and credited? [Section 6-2]

6. What is a trade discount? [Section 6-2]

7. A cash discount affects both seller and buyer. (a) What account does the seller use to record the discount? (b) the buyer? [Section 6-3]

8. What is the difference between gross sales and net sales? [Section 6-2]

9. Where do transportation in costs appear on the income statement? [Section 6-3]

10. What type of expenditures are recorded in the Purchases account? [Section 6-3]

11. What are the perpetual inventory and periodic inventory methods? [Section 6-3]

Answers:

1. Buying goods for resale to customers.

2. Sales Revenues less Cost of Goods Sold equals Gross Profit. To arrive at net income, gross profit is reduced by the amount of operating expenses.

3. Sales revenue is the total amount of sales. Cost of goods sold and operating expenses have not been subtracted. Net income is determined by subtracting cost of goods sold and operating expenses from net sales.

4. (a) A 2% discount is granted if the invoice is paid within 10 days, or the net invoice amount is due 30 days after the invoice date.

   (b) No discount is offered. The net amount of the invoice is due 30 days after the invoice date.

5. Sales Returns and Allowances is debited. Accounts Receivable or Cash is credited.

6. A trade discount is a reduction in the list price of goods. It is given to certain customers, such as those who buy in quantity, and is not entered in the accounting records as a discount. Only the amount billed is entered in the accounting records.

7. The seller debits cash discounts to the Sales Discount account. The buyer credits cash discounts to the Purchase Discounts account.

8. Gross sales equals total sales. Net Sales equals Gross Sales less Sales Returns and Allowances and Sales Discounts.

9. Transportation in costs appear on the income statement in the cost of goods sold section.

10. Only purchases of merchandise for resale to customers are entered in the Purchases account.

11. The perpetual inventory method provides a continuous record of inventory on hand by recording the cost of each item in Inventory, and by crediting Inventory and debiting Cost of Goods Sold as each item is sold. The periodic inventory method consists of simply taking a physical count of the inventory on hand at the end of the period. No entries are made in the Inventory or Cost of Goods Sold accounts during the period.

SOLVED PROBLEMS

PROBLEM 6-1: Record the following transactions for June in the journal provided. The periodic inventory method is being used. From this point on, do not skip a line between journal entries in problems.

June 1 Purchased merchandise for $600 on credit, terms 2/10, n/30.
      4 Sold merchandise for $100 on credit, terms 2/10, n/30.
      6 Returned $50 of the merchandise purchased June 1 for credit.
      9 Paid for merchandise purchased June 1, less return and discount.
     10 Received payment from the customer of June 4, less discount.
     15 Sold merchandise for $200 on credit, terms 2/10, n/30.
     19 Customer of June 15 returned $20 of merchandise for credit.
     24 Purchased merchandise for $350 on credit, terms n/30.

	DATE	DESCRIPTION	POST. REF.	DEBIT	CREDIT	
1	19— June					1
2						2
3						3
4						4
5						5
6						6
7						7
8						8
9						9
10						10
11						11
12						12
13						13
14						14
15						15
16						16
17						17
18						18
19						19
20						20
21						21
22						22
23						23
24						24
25						25
26						26
27						27
28						28
29						29
30						30
31						31
32						32
33						33
34						34
35						35
36						36
37						37
38						38

JOURNAL PAGE *31*

Answer: [Sections 6-2 and 6-3]

	DATE		DESCRIPTION	POST. REF.	DEBIT				CREDIT				
1	19— June	1	Purchases		6	0	0	00					1
2			Accounts Payable						6	0	0	00	2
3			Purchased merchandise;										3
4			2/10, n/30										4
5		4	Accounts Receivable		1	0	0	00					5
6			Sales						1	0	0	00	6
7			Sold merchandise on credit;										7
8			2/10, n/30										8
9		6	Accounts Payable			5	0	00					9
10			Purchase Returns and							5	0	00	10
11			Allowances										11
12			Returned merchandise										12
13			purchased 6/1										13
14		9	Accounts Payable		5	5	0	00					14
15			Cash						5	3	9	00	15
16			Purchase Discounts							1	1	00	16
17			Payment of 6/1 purchase,										17
18			less 6/6 return and discount										18
19		10	Cash			9	8	00					19
20			Sales Discounts				2	00					20
21			Accounts Receivable						1	0	0	00	21
22			Received payment for 6/4										22
23			sales, less discount										23
24		15	Accounts Receivable		2	0	0	00					24
25			Sales						2	0	0	00	25
26			Sold merchandise on credit;										26
27			2/10, n/30										27
28		19	Sales Returns and Allowances			2	0	00					28
29			Accounts Receivable							2	0	00	29
30			Customer returned										30
31			merchandise										31
32		24	Purchases		3	5	0	00					32
33			Accounts Payable						3	5	0	00	33
34			Purchased merchandise;										34
35			n/30										35

JOURNAL   **PAGE** *31*

For the entry on June 9, determine the amount paid as follows:

$600 (purchase June 1)
− 50 (merchandise returned June 6)
  550 (gross amount payable)
× .02 (discount rate)
$ 11 (purchase discount)

Subtract the purchase discount amount of $11 from the gross amount payable of $550 to get the amount paid of $539.

For the entry on June 10, determine the amount received as follows:

$100 (gross sales June 4)
× .02 (discount rate)
$ 2 (sales discount)

Subtract the sales discount amount of $2 from the gross sales amount of $100 to get the amount received of $98.

PROBLEM 6-2: Calculate the cost of goods available for sale using the following data.

Purchases	$80,000
Transportation In	3,000
Purchase Returns and Allowances	3,200
Beginning Inventory	31,000
Purchase Discounts	2,100

Answer: The cost of goods available for sale is computed by taking beginning inventory plus purchases, less purchase returns and allowances, less purchase discounts, to get net purchases. Then add transportation in to net purchases to get the cost of goods available for sale. [Section 6-3]

Beginning inventory			$ 31,000
Purchases		$80,000	
Less: Purchase discounts	$2,100		
Purchase returns and allowances	3,200	5,300	
Net purchases		$74,700	
Add: Transportation in		3,000	77,700
Cost of goods available for sale			$108,700

PROBLEM 6-3: Calculate the cost of goods sold using the following information.

Purchases (Net)	$106,200
Beginning Inventory	37,500
Ending Inventory	42,150

Answer: The cost of goods sold is computed by taking beginning inventory plus net purchases, less ending inventory. [Section 6-3]

Beginning inventory	$ 37,500
Net purchases	106,200
Cost of goods available for sale	$143,700
Less: Ending inventory	42,150
Cost of goods sold	$101,550

Note that the cost of goods sold may also be calculated by adjusting purchases by the change in inventory. In this problem, inventory increased from $37,500 to $42,150, an increase of $4,650. An inventory increase results in less expense (cost of goods sold) than the net purchases amount. Purchases of $106,200, less the difference of $4,650 equals cost of goods sold of $101,550. This provides a method for verifying the cost of goods sold calculation.

The following information is to be used to solve Problems 6-4 through 6-7. Tiffany Company is a merchandising firm. Below is the trial balance prepared for the period ending December 31, 19––

Tiffany Company
Trial Balance
December 31, 19––

Cash	$ 6,360	
Accounts Receivable	6,870	
Inventory, January 1	19,260	
Prepaid Insurance	2,160	
Equipment	40,800	
Accumulated Depreciation: Equipment		$ 12,240
Accounts Payable		16,902
Tiffany O'Neal, Capital		31,272
Tiffany O'Neal, Drawing	1,800	
Sales		87,240
Sales Discounts	4,260	
Sales Returns and Allowances	3,180	
Purchases	43,590	
Purchase Discounts		816
Purchase Returns and Allowances		1,320
Transportation In	1,134	
Rent Expense	3,120	
Salary Expense	15,300	
Utilities Expense	1,956	
Totals	$149,790	$149,790

A physical inventory taken at the close of business on December 31, 19––, showed inventory on hand of $21,900. Depreciation expense for the year was $4,080. Expired insurance was $720. Salaries earned by employees but not paid were $915. Using the information provided above, complete the following problems on the work sheet provided.

PROBLEM 6-4: Enter the trial balance for Tiffany Company.

PROBLEM 6-5: Enter the adjustments for Tiffany Company.

PROBLEM 6-6: Complete the adjusted trial balance columns for Tiffany Company.

PROBLEM 6-7: Transfer the account balances for Tiffany Company to the appropriate income statement and balance sheet columns and complete the work sheet.

ACCOUNT TITLE	TRIAL BALANCE		ADJUSTMENTS		ADJUSTED TRIAL BALANCE		INCOME STATEMENT		BALANCE SHEET	
	DEBIT	CREDIT	DEBIT	CREDIT	DEBIT	CREDIT	DEBIT	CREDIT	DEBIT	CREDIT

119

Answer to Problems 6-3–6-6: [Section 6-4]

TIFFANY COMPANY
WORK SHEET
DECEMBER 31, 19—

ACCOUNT TITLE	TRIAL BALANCE DEBIT	TRIAL BALANCE CREDIT	ADJUSTMENTS DEBIT	ADJUSTMENTS CREDIT	ADJUSTED TRIAL BALANCE DEBIT	ADJUSTED TRIAL BALANCE CREDIT	INCOME STATEMENT DEBIT	INCOME STATEMENT CREDIT	BALANCE SHEET DEBIT	BALANCE SHEET CREDIT
Cash	636000				636000				636000	
Accounts Receivable	687000				687000				687000	
Inventory, January 1	1926000				1926000		1926000			
Prepaid Insurance	216000			(b) 72000	144000				144000	
Equipment	4080000				4080000				4080000	
Accumulated Depr., Equip.		1224000		(a) 408000		1632000				1632000
Accounts Payable		1690200				1690200				1690200
Tiffany O'Neal, Capital		3127200				3127200				3127200
Tiffany O'Neal, Drawing	1800000				1800000				1800000	
Sales		8724000				8724000		8724000		
Sales Discounts	426000				426000		426000			
Sales Returns & Allowances	318000				318000		318000			
Purchases	4359000				4359000		4359000			
Purchase Discounts		81600				81600		81600		
Purchase Returns & Allow.		132000				132000		132000		
Transportation In	113400				113400		113400			
Rent Expense	312000				312000		312000			
Salary Expense	1530000		(c) 91500		1621500		1621500			
Utilities Expense	195600				195600		195600			
	14979000	14979000								
Insurance Expense			(b) 72000		72000		72000			
Depreciation Expense			(a) 408000		408000		408000			
Salaries Payable				(c) 91500		91500				91500
			571500	571500	15478500	15478500				
Inventory, December 31								2190000	2190000	
							9751500	11127600		
Net Income							1376100			1376100
							11127600	11127600	7917000	7917000

Adjustments:
(a) Depreciation on equipment during the year.
(b) Insurance premium expired during the year.
(c) Salaries accrued but not paid at end of year.

PROBLEM 6-8: Prepare the income statement for Tiffany Company using the information available in the income statement columns of the completed work sheet.

Answer: [Section 6-5]

Tiffany Company
Income Statement
For Year Ended December 31, 19—

Revenue from sales:			
Gross sales..		$87,240	
Less: Sales discounts	$ 4,260		
Sales returns and allowances	3,180	7,440	
Net sales			$79,800
Cost of goods sold:			
Inventory, January 1, 19—..........................		$19,260	
Purchases	$43,590		
Less: Purchase discounts..........................	$ 816		
Purchase returns and allowances	1,320	2,136	
Net purchases	$41,454		
Add: Transportation in..............................	1,134	42,588	
Cost of goods available for sale.....................		$61,848	
Less: Inventory, December 31, 19—		21,900	
Cost of goods sold			39,948
Gross profit			$39,852
Operating expenses:			
Rent expense		$ 3,120	
Salary expense		16,215	
Utilities expense		1,956	
Insurance expense..................................		720	
Depreciation expense...............................		4,080	
Total operating expenses........................			26,091
Net income...			$13,761

PROBLEM 6-9: Prepare the balance sheet for Tiffany Company using the information available in the balance sheet columns of the completed work sheet.

Answer: [Section 6-5]

Tiffany Company
Balance Sheet
December 31, 19—

Assets

Current assets:
Cash .... $ 6,360
Accounts receivable... 6,870
Inventory... 21,900
Prepaid insurance.. 1,440
   Total current assets.. $36,570

Plant assets:
Equipment $40,800
   Less: Accumulated depreciation................................ 16,320   24,480
Total assets $61,050

Liabilities

Current liabilities:
Accounts payable $16,902
Salaries payable 915
   Total current liabilities $17,817

Equity

Tiffany O'Neal, Capital 43,233
Total liabilities and equity....................................... $61,050

PROBLEM 6-10: Prepare the statement of equity for Tiffany Company using the information available on the completed work sheet.

Answer: [Section 6-5]

Tiffany Company
Statement of Equity
For Year Ended December 31, 19—

Tiffany O'Neal, Capital, January 1, 19—	$31,272
Add December 31, 19— net income	13,761
Subtotal	$45,033
Deduct withdrawals	1,800
Tiffany O'Neal, Capital, December 31, 19—	$43,233

PROBLEM 6-11: Journalize the closing entries for Tiffany Company using the information available on the completed work sheet. Date the entries for December 31.

	DATE	DESCRIPTION	POST. REF.	DEBIT	CREDIT	
1	19— June					1
2						2
3						3
4						4
5						5
6						6
7						7
8						8
9						9
10						10
11						11
12						12
13						13
14						14
15						15
16						16
17						17
18						18
19						19
20						20
21						21
22						22
23						23
24						24
25						25
26						26
27						27
28						28
29						29
30						30

JOURNAL   **PAGE** *31*

Answer: [Section 6-4]

	DATE		DESCRIPTION	POST. REF.	DEBIT						CREDIT						
			JOURNAL										**PAGE** *31*				
1			*Closing Entries*														1
2	19— Dec.	*31*	Income Summary		97	5	1	5	00								2
3			*Inventory, January 1*							19	2	6	0	00			3
4			*Sales Discounts*							4	2	6	0	00			4
5			*Sales Returns and*														5
6			*Allowances*							3	1	8	0	00			6
7			*Purchases*							43	5	9	0	00			7
8			*Transportation in*							1	1	3	4	00			8
9			*Rent Expense*							3	1	2	0	00			9
10			*Salary Expense*							16	2	1	5	00			10
11			*Utilities Expense*							1	9	5	6	00			11
12			*Insurance Expense*								7	2	0	00			12
13			*Depreciation Expense*							4	0	8	0	00			13
14			*To close out beginning*														14
15			*inventory and all*														15
16			*temporary accounts with*														16
17			*debit balances*														17
18		*31*	Sales		87	2	4	0	00								18
19			*Purchase Discounts*			8	1	6	00								19
20			*Purchase Returns and*														20
21			*Allowances*		1	3	2	0	00								21
22			*Inventory, December 31*		21	9	0	0	00								22
23			*Income Summary*							111	2	7	6	00			23
24			*To record ending inventory*														24
25			*and close out all temporary*														25
26			*accounts with credit*														26
27			*balances*														27
28		*31*	Income Summary		13	7	6	1	00								28
29			*Tiffany O'Neal, Capital*							13	7	6	1	00			29
30			*To transfer net income to*														30
31			*the capital account*														31
32		*31*	Tiffany O'Neal, Capital		1	8	0	0	00								32
33			*Tiffany O'Neal, Drawing*							1	8	0	0	00			33
34			*To close the drawing*														34
35			*account*														35

7 SPECIAL JOURNALS, DATA PROCESSING, AND INTERNAL CONTROL

THIS CHAPTER IS ABOUT

☑ **Control Accounts and Subsidiary Ledgers**
☑ **The Need for Special Journals**
☑ **Data Processing**
☑ **Internal Control**

7-1. Control Accounts and Subsidiary Ledgers

A. A *control account* is a summary account in the general ledger that represents numerous accounts with a common title.

Up to now, we have recorded each business transaction in its own individual account in the ledger. In a large business that deals with numerous transactions, this individual posting makes the ledger quickly unmanageable. To avoid this problem, a firm will often group accounts concerning like transactions, such as accounts receivable and accounts payable, and summarize them in one account called a *control account*. The control account is placed in the general ledger instead of the numerous individual accounts.

B. The individual accounts that are summarized in a control account are maintained in a *subsidiary ledger*.

A subsidiary ledger is established when it is necessary for a business to keep a separate record of similar accounts. A business may set up a subsidiary ledger for almost any account in the general ledger. For example, a business may have numerous transactions involving notes payable and would set up a subsidiary ledger called the notes payable ledger. The control account in the general ledger would be Notes Payable. At this point, we will discuss subsidiary ledgers that are established for transactions involving accounts receivable and accounts payable.

1. *Accounts Receivable.* The individual accounts for credit customers are maintained in alphabetical order in a subsidiary ledger called the *account receivable subsidiary ledger.* The control account in the general ledger that summarizes the debit and credit entries to customers' accounts is Accounts Receivable. The sum of the subsidiary ledger account balance must agree with the balance of the Accounts Receivable control account at the end of each period.

EXAMPLE 7-1: Suppose a company has 40 customers who each owe $1,000 for a total of $40,000. The subsidiary ledger would have an account for each of the forty customers where the accountant would record details of additional charges, returns and allowances, and customer payments. The control account in the general ledger would also reflect the changes mentioned, but would only show the total for all forty accounts contained in the subsidiary ledger.

2. *Accounts Payable.* The individual accounts for creditors are maintained in numerical or alphabetical order in a subsidiary ledger called the *accounts payable subsidiary ledger.* The control account in the general ledger that summarizes the debit and credit entries to creditors' accounts is Accounts Payable. The sum of the subsidiary ledger account balances must agree with the balance of the Accounts Payable control account in the general ledger at the end of each period.

EXAMPLE 7-2: The relationship between the Accounts Receivable control account in the general ledger and accounts receivable subsidiary ledger is shown in the following diagram. Below the diagram is a *schedule of accounts receivable.* It is necessary to prove that a subsidiary ledger is in agreement with its controlling account at the end of each accounting period by preparing a schedule similar to the one illustrated.

ACCOUNTS RECEIVABLE SUBSIDIARY LEDGER

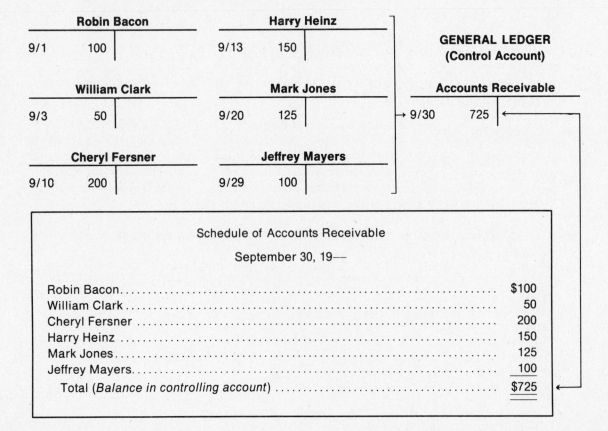

EXAMPLE 7-3: The following diagram illustrates the relationship between the Accounts Payable control account in the general ledger and the accounts payable subsidiary ledger. The schedule of accounts payable prepared to check that the subsidiary ledger agrees with the control account is also illustrated.

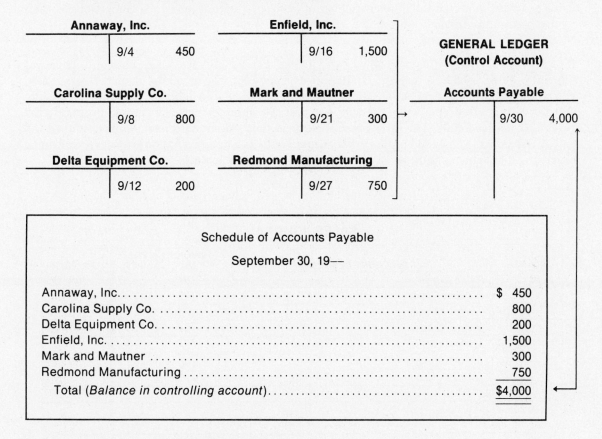

ACCOUNTS PAYABLE SUBSIDIARY LEDGER

Schedule of Accounts Payable

September 30, 19—

Annaway, Inc.	$ 450
Carolina Supply Co.	800
Delta Equipment Co.	200
Enfield, Inc.	1,500
Mark and Mautner	300
Redmond Manufacturing	750
Total (*Balance in controlling account*)	$4,000

7-2. The Need for Special Journals

A. Special journals reduce and simplify work and allow for a division of labor.

Up to now, you have learned to journalize all transactions as they occur in one book—the general journal. Most businesses use special journals to simplify the journalizing and posting of transactions. Any number of special journals can be utilized by a business.

Special journals make summary posting possible. *Summary posting* is the posting of a column total from a special journal to the ledger. A business with numerous special journals may even assign different employees to be in charge of a particular special journal and its summary posting.

The majority of the transactions of a merchandising firm can generally be broken down into four categories—sales on credit, purchases on credit, cash receipts, and cash payments. Thus, a special journal may be used for each category. The following are special journals commonly used by merchandising firms:

- sales journal
- purchases journal
- cash receipts journal
- cash payments journal (or cash disbursements journal)

B. The sales journal is used to record all sales of merchandise on credit.

Recall that each sale of merchandise on credit is recorded as a debit to Accounts Receivable and a credit to Sales. There is only one column in the sales journal (shown below) to enter the amount of each sale of merchandise on credit at the end of the period. The column *total* is posted as a debit to Accounts Receivable and a credit to Sales. In addition, an extra column is provided to record the invoice number of each sale, so that lengthy explanations of each entry are unnecessary.

EXAMPLE 7-4: Let us illustrate how a sales journal can simplify work. Suppose only a general journal is being used by a business. If 100 sales of merchandise on credit occurred in one day, you would make 100 journal entries of at least two lines each—a debit to Accounts Receivable and a credit to Sales. You would then have to post 200 amounts from the general journal to the general ledger accounts. The sales journal requires only one line for each transaction. At the end of the month, you would post *only the column total* as a debit to Accounts Receivable and a credit to Sales. Time is thus saved in both journalizing and posting.

		SALES JOURNAL			PAGE 23	
DATE		ACCOUNT DEBITED	INVOICE NO.	POST. REF.	AMOUNT	
Sept.	1	Robin Bacon	101	✓	100	00
	3	William Clark	102	✓	50	00
	10	Cheryl Fersner	103	✓	200	00
	13	Harry Heinz	104	✓	150	00
	20	Mark Jones	105	✓	125	00
	29	Jeffrey Mayers	106	✓	100	00
	30	Totals			725	00

The amount of each transaction must still be posted to the individual customer accounts in the accounts receivable subsidiary ledger daily. Remember, the total from the Accounts Receivable control account in the general ledger appears in the balance sheet. The subsidiary ledger is only a backup which shows transactions with each customer in detail, such as the purchases, purchase returns and allowances, and payments. The subsidiary ledger should be posted daily.

EXAMPLE 7-5: The following diagram illustrates how sales of merchandise on credit are journalized in the sales journal, posted to the individual customer accounts in the subsidiary ledger, and then posted to the accounts in the general ledger. Note that a check mark (✓) is placed in the sales journal next to each amount posted to a customer's account to indicate that the posting has been made to the subsidiary ledger. The numbers shown in parentheses below the column total in the sales journal (4 and 41) indicate that the column total has been posted to the Accounts Receivable control account (4) as a debit, and to the Sales account (41) as a credit in the general ledger.

The ledgers are shown in T account form. Although not illustrated in the diagram, when transactions are posted from a special journal to a subsidiary ledger and then to the general ledger, the special journal and page number of the transaction being posted should be entered in the posting reference columns of both the subsidiary ledger and the general ledger. The sales journal is usually indicated by the letter "S." Thus, the posting reference column entry in the subsidiary ledger and general ledger for each of the following transactions would be

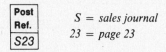

S = *sales journal*
23 = *page 23*

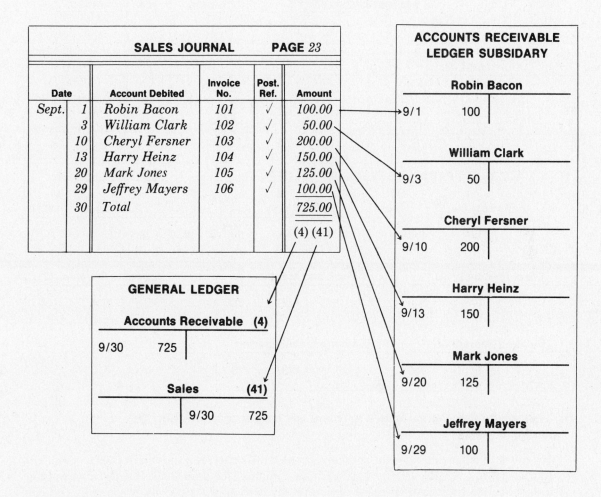

C. The purchases journal is used to record all purchases of merchandise on credit.

In its most simplified form (see page 132), a purchases journal includes a column for transaction dates, a column for the name of the vendor from whom the purchase was made (account credited), a column for invoice dates, a column to put the check mark to indicate the amount has been posted to the subsidiary ledger, and an amount column.

At the end of the day, amounts are posted to the individual vendors' accounts in the accounts payable subsidiary ledger. At the end of each month, the amount column is totaled and posted as a debit to the Purchases account and a credit to the Accounts Payable control account in the general ledger.

Any time transactions occur frequently, columns may be added to the purchases journal or to any of the other special journals to save posting time.

EXAMPLE 7-6: The following diagram shows how purchases of merchandise on credit are journalized in a simple purchases journal and illustrates the posting procedures. The letter used in the posting reference column of the subsidiary ledger to indicate that a transaction is posted from the purchases journal is "P."

PURCHASES JOURNAL				PAGE *31*		
DATE		ACCOUNT CREDITED	INVOICE DATE	POST. REF.	AMOUNT	
Sept.	*4*	*Annaway, Inc.*	*9/1*	✓	*450*	*00*
	8	*Carolina Supply Co.*	*9/6*	✓	*800*	*00*
	12	*Delta Equipment Co.*	*9/8*	✓	*200*	*00*
	16	*Enfield, Inc.*	*9/15*	✓	*1,500*	*00*
	21	*Mack and Mautner*	*9/18*	✓	*300*	*00*
	27	*Redmond Manufacturing*	*9/23*	✓	*750*	*00*
	30	*Total*			*4,000*	*00*
					(51)	(21)

ACCOUNTS PAYABLE SUBSIDIARY LEDGER

Annaway, Inc.		Enfield, Inc.	
9/4	450	9/16	1,500

Carolina Supply Co.		Mack and Mautner	
9/8	800	9/21	300

Delta Equipment Co.		Redmond Manufacturing	
9/12	200	9/27	750

GENERAL LEDGER

Purchases	(51)
9/30 4,000	

Accounts Payable	(21)
	9/30 4,000

D. The cash receipts journal is used to record any transactions involving the receipt of money.

Even if only a partial payment is received, the transaction is recorded in the cash receipts journal (CRJ). A CRJ usually has multiple columns (see page 133). It must always have a debit column for cash. If sales discounts are frequently given by a company, a debit column for sales discounts can be included.

The number of credit columns needed in the CRJ is determined by the frequency of transactions for which money is received. If the business is involved in merchandising, columns are usually included for sales (to record cash sales), and for accounts receivable (to record receipt of cash payment for sales on credit). The account to which the amount to be credited is entered in the account column. As with any special journal, summary posting can be done at the end of each month.

Other Accounts debit and credit columns can be included and used for transactions that occur infrequently, such as additional investments of cash in a business or receipt of cash from notes receivable. The name of the other account to be debited or credited is entered in the account column. Because the Other Accounts columns include a number of different accounts, a summary posting cannot be made. It is necessary to post the individual accounts from the Other Accounts columns directly to the general ledger, inserting the account number in the posting reference column of the journal.

The totals in the CRJ are checked at the end of the period. The total of the debit columns should equal the total of the credit columns.

EXAMPLE 7-7: The following transactions would be recorded in the CRJ because they all involve receipts of cash. The diagram following the transactions illustrates the entries for each of these transactions in the CRJ and the posting procedures. Note how separate columns are provided for the credits resulting from receipts of payment on account, receipts of cash for sales, and receipts of cash from other sources. Also, note that each transaction results in equal debits and credits.

Nov. 1   *The owner, R. Mims, invested $50,000 cash in the business.* This transaction is recorded as a credit in the Other Accounts column, and as a debit to Cash. The account title to be credited, R. Mims, Capital, is entered in the account column. Since there is no subsidiary ledger containing this account, it would be posted directly to the general ledger and the account number is entered in the posting reference column. When posting directly to the general ledger, the letters "CR" are usually used along with the page number in the posting reference column of the general ledger to indicate that the amount has been posted from the cash receipts journal.

    7   *Received $180 from A. Jefferson in payment of his October 27 purchase.* The title of the account to be credited is entered in the account column and the amount is entered as a credit to Accounts Receivable. Cash is debited for the amount. A check mark is shown in the posting reference column to indicate that the amount has been posted to Jefferson's account in the accounts receivable subsidiary ledger.

  11   *Received $294 from J. Rasch in payment of her November 2 purchase of $300, less the 2% discount.* This transaction is recorded by crediting Accounts Receivable for $300, debiting Cash for $294, and debiting Sales Discounts for $6. A check mark is placed in the posting reference column to indicate that the amount has been posted to the subsidiary ledger.

  15   *Sold merchandise for cash, $2,000.* When cash registers are used, the total cash sales are recorded as one transaction and the cash register tape is used as the backup. Thus, the total sales are recorded as a debit to Cash and a credit to Sales.

  20   *A note payable was issued in the amount of $6,000 for a loan from the bank.* The $6,000 is debited to Cash and credited to Notes Payable. Because notes payable are not issued frequently, the CRJ does not have a Notes Payable credit column. Instead, the transaction is recorded in the Other Accounts credit column and posted individually to the Notes Payable account in the general ledger.

  26   *Received $200 from R. Able. Able paid for $300 worth of merchandise purchased October 1 by sending a check for $200 and signing a note for the balance of $100.* This transaction is recorded by debiting Cash for $200 and Notes Receivable for $100 (Notes Receivable must be entered in the Other Accounts debit column). Accounts Receivable is credited for $300 to complete the recording of this transaction.

CASH RECEIPTS JOURNAL									PAGE *16*		
DATE	ACCOUNT	POST REF.	OTHER ACCOUNTS DEBIT		OTHER ACCOUNTS CREDIT		ACCOUNTS REC. CREDIT		SALES CREDIT		SALES DISCOUNT DEBIT		CASH DEBIT	
Nov. 1	R. Mims, Capital	30			50,000	00							50,000	00
7	A. Jefferson	✓					180	00					180	00
11	J. Rasch	✓					300	00			6	00	294	00
15	Cash sales	✓							2,000	00			2,000	00
20	Notes Payable	21			6,000	00							6,000	00
26	{ R. Able	✓					300	00					200	00
	{ Notes Receivable	3	100	00										
30	Total		100	00	56,000	00	780	00	2,000	00	6	00	58,674	00
			(✓)		(✓)		(12)		(40)		(42)		(1)	

Daily:

    Post to Accounts Receivable accounts in the subsidiary ledger and put a check mark in the Post Ref. column. Other accounts should be posted individually during the month, preferably as they occur.

Monthly:

- Add columns.
- Check to be sure total debits equal total credits. The debit/credit check for the CRJ on page 133 is shown below.

Debits	Credits
$ 100	$56,000
6	2,000
58,674	780
$58,780	$58,780

- Post column totals.

(1) A check mark was placed below the $100 total in the Other Accounts debit column to indicate that the amount in this column was posted individually.

(2) A check mark was placed below the $56,000 total in the Other Accounts credit column to indicate that amounts in this column were posted individually.

(3) The $780 in the Accounts Receivable column was credited to Account #12, Accounts Receivable (the control account in the general ledger).

(4) The $2,000 in the Sales column was credited to Account #40, Sales.

(5) The $6 in the Sales Discounts column was debited to Account #42, Sales Discounts, in the general ledger.

(6) The $58,674 in the Cash column was debited to Account #1, Cash, in the general ledger.

E. The cash payments journal is used to record all payments of cash.

The number of columns to be provided in the cash payments journal (CPJ) is determined by the kind of transactions to be recorded and the frequency of their occurrence (see page 135). A credit column for Cash is always necessary. Most purchases are made on account, so an Accounts Payable debit column is usually included. The account to be debited in the accounts payable subsidiary ledger is entered in the Account column. A business that does not use the net method of recording purchases should include a Purchase Discounts credit column. Debit and credit columns for Other Accounts are included for transactions that occur infrequently. The other account to be debited or credited is entered in the Account column. Amounts in the Other Accounts columns are posted individually. There is also a column included to record the number of the check used to make the payment.

EXAMPLE 7-8: The following transactions should be recorded in the CPJ because they all involve the payment of cash. The diagram following the transactions illustrates the entries for each of these transactions in the CPJ and the posting procedures.

Dec. 1 *Paid Ingram, Inc., $441 on a $450 purchase on account, less 2% discount of $9, Check #120.* Accounts Payable is debited for the full amount of $450. Purchase Discounts is credited for $9 and Cash is credited for $441. A check mark is placed in the posting reference column to indicate that the amount has been posted to the accounts payable subsidiary ledger. This is done at the time the subsidiary ledger is posted.

  3 *Paid freight bill of $40 to Huckabee Transport Company for November 2 delivery, Check #121.* This amount is debited in the Other Accounts column and the account to be debited, Transportation In, is entered in the Account column. Cash is credited for the amount. The account number is entered in the posting reference column at the time the amount is posted to the general ledger. When posting directly to the general ledger, the letters "CP" are usually used along with the page number in the posting reference column of the general ledger to indicate that the amount has been posted from the CPJ.

  4 *Paid Reese Manufacturing $735 on a $750 purchase on account, less 2% discount of $15, Check #122.* Accounts Payable is debited for the full amount of $750. Purchase Discounts is credited for $15 and Cash is credited for $735. A check mark is placed in

the posting reference column at the time the accounts payable subsidiary ledger is posted.

9 *Purchased merchandise for $700 cash from Carolina Supply Co., Check #123.* The purchase of merchandise for cash is recorded as a debit to Purchases of $700 in the Other Accounts column. Cash is credited for $700. The account number is entered in the posting reference column to indicate that the amount has been posted directly to the general ledger.

16 *Purchased store equipment from Delta Equipment Co. for $7,000, giving $2,000 cash and a note payable for $5,000, Check #124.* The Store Equipment account title is entered and the $7,000 is recorded in the Other Accounts debit column. The Notes Payable account title is entered in the Account column and $5,000 is recorded in the Other Accounts credit column. Cash is credited for $2,000. The account numbers are entered in the posting reference column to indicate that these amounts have been posted directly to the general ledger.

17 *Purchased store supplies for $90 cash from King Supply Company, Check #125.* The Supplies account title is entered and shown as a $90 entry in the Other Accounts debit column. Cash is credited for $90. The account number is entered in the posting reference column to indicate that the amount has been posted directly to the general ledger.

		CASH PAYMENTS JOURNAL							PAGE 24		
DATE	CHECK NO.	ACCOUNT	POST REF.	OTHER ACCOUNTS				ACCOUNTS PAYABLE DEBIT		PURCH. DISCOUNT CREDIT		CASH CREDIT	
				DEBIT		CREDIT							
Dec. 1	120	Ingram, Inc.	✓					450	00	9	00	441	00
3	121	Transportation In	59	40	00							40	00
4	122	Reese Manuf.	✓					750	00	15	00	735	00
9	123	Purchases	60	700	00							700	00
16	124	{ Store Equipment	14	7,000	00							2,000	00
		{ Notes Payable	21			5,000	00						
17	125	Supplies	13	90	00							90	00
30		Total		7,830	00	5,000	00	1,200	00	24	00	4,006	00
				(✓)		(✓)		(20)		(61)		(1)	

Daily:

Post to Accounts Payable accounts in the subsidiary ledger and put a check mark in the column. Other accounts should be posted individually during the month as time permits.

Monthly:

• Add columns.
• Check to be sure total debits equal total credits. The debit/credit check for the above CPJ is shown below.

Debits	Credits
$7,830.00	$5,000.00
1,200.00	24.00
$9,030.00	4,006.00
	$9,030.00

• Post column totals.

(1) A check mark was placed below the totals in the Other Accounts debit and credit columns to indicate that the amounts in these columns were posted individually.
(2) The $1,200 in the Accounts Payable column was posted to Account #20, Accounts Payable.

(3) The $24 in the Purchase Discounts column was posted to Account #61, Purchase Discounts.

(4) The $4,006 in the Cash column was posted to Account #1, Cash.

F. The general journal is used to record transactions that cannot be recorded in any of the four special journals.

Transactions most frequently recorded in the general journal are sales returns and allowances, purchase returns and allowances, adjusting entries, and closing entries. You can decide which transactions should be recorded in the general journal by using the following method of elimination.

First, try to place the transaction in a special journal by asking these questions.

• Is the transaction a sale of merchandise on credit? If yes, record the transaction in the sales journal.
• Is the transaction a purchase of merchandise on credit? If yes, record it in the purchases journal.
• Does the transaction involve the receipt of cash? If yes, record the transaction in the cash receipts journal.
• Does the transaction involve the payment of cash? If yes, record it in the cash payments journal.

If the answer is "no" to all of the above questions, the transaction should be recorded in the general journal.

G. If a certain type of transaction appears frequently in the general journal, a new special journal may be set up.

For example, if sales returns and allowances or purchase returns and allowances occur frequently, a sales returns and allowances journal and/or a purchase returns and allowances journal may be added. Remember that each transaction can only be recorded in one journal. Select the journal and record the complete transaction in that journal.

If a transaction must be recorded in the general journal that also affects a subsidiary ledger account, it is necessary to indicate the subsidiary ledger account to which it must be posted, and to indicate that the posting has been done to both the subsidiary and general ledgers.

EXAMPLE 7-9: Comtech, Inc. returned $100 of damaged goods to Merle Company. Comtech debited Accounts Payable and credited Purchase Returns and Allowances for $100. Comtech, Inc., does not record purchase returns in a special journal; thus, the transaction must be recorded in the general journal. The company does, however, maintain an individual account in an accounts payable subsidiary ledger for Merle Company. The general journal entry and the posting procedure for this transaction are illustrated below.

DATE		DESCRIPTION	POST. REF.	DEBIT		CREDIT	
Aug.	1	Accounts Payable/Merle Company	✓ 21	100	00		
		Purchase Returns and Allowances	53			100	00
		Return of damaged merchandise					

GENERAL JOURNAL — PAGE 32

Note that next to the Accounts Payable account entry in the description column, the individual account title maintained in the subsidiary ledger is also entered. When posting to the subsidiary ledger and general ledger is done, a check mark is entered in the posting reference column to indicate that the amount has been posted to the subsidiary ledger. The account number of Accounts Payable in the general ledger is also entered in the posting reference column to indicate that the amount has also been posted to the general ledger.

7-3. Data Processing

A. The processing of accounting data is made easier through the use of machines.

Handwritten records like the ones described thus far are used by many small businesses. However, many small businesses have enough transactions to warrant the use of electronic devices for processing accounting data. Machines enable mankind to process enormous amounts of data quickly and efficiently. For example, when used in accounting for a credit sale, an electronic machine can enter the sale in the sales journal, post the sale to the customer's account, update the account balance, enter the sale on the customer's month-end statement, and update the statement with only one entry of the initial transaction.

B. A progression of machines preceded the modern-day computer.

The early accounting machines used punched cards for input. With punched cards, machines could manipulate large amounts of data for record keeping. However, the first automatic computer, Mark I, was possibly the major discovery toward development of the modern-day computer. The Mark I used electromagnetic relays and mechanical counters instead of the mechanical gears used in earlier machines. The computers that have evolved from the Mark I have capabilities that boggle the mind.

C. Electronic Data Processing (EDP) refers to data processing by electronic computers.

The heart of a computer system is the Central Processing Unit (CPU). Data is transferred into the CPU by a person using an input device. An output device produces information in words or numbers on a screen or printer, or it communicates to other computer devices. The CPU consists of three units—an arithmetic/logic unit (ALU), a primary storage unit, and a control unit.

1. *Arithmetic/logic unit.* The ALU adds, subtracts, multiplies, divides, and compares numbers. An example of a logical operation would be to compare one number to another to determine which is less. The ALU is the unit within which data is manipulated but not stored.
2. *Primary storage unit.* The primary storage unit (or memory unit) stores not only data but also the instructions on how to use it. The computer knows exactly where data is stored and finds the information when it is needed.
3. *Control unit.* The control unit maintains order and guides the computer along each step of the operation. The control unit interprets and executes the instructions programmed into it. Not only does the control unit communicate with an input device to begin transfer of and input of data into storage, it also communicates with an output device to start the transfer of results from storage.

EXAMPLE 7-10: The diagram shown below illustrates an EDP system.

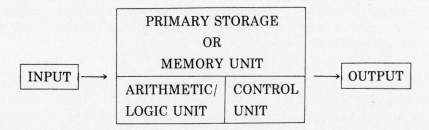

4. *Programs.* The instructions which tell a computer what to do are called programs. Programs may be fed directly into the computer by using input devices to place the program into primary storage. Also, primary storage can be supplemented with secondary or auxiliary storage in the form of magnetic tapes or magnetic disk units. A wide variety of supplemental "packaged programs," known as software, is available to businesses.

EXAMPLE 7-11: Basic computer accounting application software includes a general ledger, accounts receivable, accounts payable, payroll, and fixed assets. This wide variety of packaged software has eliminated much of the need for "in-house" programming to handle accounting procedures.

7-4. Internal Control

Businesses must protect data and assets from improper use. All plans and procedures used to promote efficiency of operation and protect resources from improper use are part of *internal control.*

A. Most companies protect stored data by controlling access to it.

Code words are assigned and changed often to prevent access to data within a computer by unauthorized persons. In many firms only persons whose job requires it, have access to a specific portion of a data base. The use of badges, keys, and specially coded cards also restricts access to the data processing department. One of the most important controls is to screen carefully when selecting employees who have access to data systems. It is important to be certain that employees are aware of company rules and to discharge employees who violate them.

B. The assets most in need of internal controls are cash, accounts receivable, and inventory.

1. *Cash.* Procedures must be in place to control the receipt and payment of cash. Employees who handle cash must be selected carefully. Authority and responsibility must be clearly defined. Two or more people responsible for cash makes a division of duties possible whereby no one person would ever be in charge of a complete transaction. When two or more people are involved, discrepancies and errors are more likely to be discovered.

   To help prevent theft or misuse of cash, written instructions should control authorization of payment of cash, state exactly when deposits have to be made following receipt of cash, and include instructions to record all cash receipts intact. An excellent control on disbursements is to set up a *voucher system* and require that each payment be made by check. A simplified explanation of the voucher system (see Chapter 8) requires that the person who writes company checks have a voucher in hand before the check may be issued. The voucher is simply an authorization for payment. For minor payments, a petty cash fund (see Chapter 8) can be used.

2. *Accounts receivable.* Accounts receivable must be handled in much the same way as cash. One person's work should be verified by another. Along every step, there should be a division of duties; for example, the person receiving cash from customers should not be the person to record the transaction.

EXAMPLE 7-12: Control over cash and receivables must start at the point of the sale. Sequentially numbered sales tickets (all must be accounted for), printed cash register tapes, and written instructions along every step through shipping, billing, collecting, and recording are effective methods for internal control.

3. *Inventory.* Inventory is usually one of the most costly assets. Merchandise carried in inventory must be purchased, paid for, stored, and issued. At every step, the possibility of theft, loss, or misappropriation exists. Examples of effective internal controls for inventory are a division of duties and assigned inventory responsibilities.

C. Many businesses have internal auditors who periodically audit any units that handle cash or are responsible for inventory.

Auditing involves reviewing accounting records to determine their fairness and reliability. Businesses that do not have internal auditors may hire independent auditors to examine the accounting records in detail and give suggestions to strengthen internal control.

RAISE YOUR GRADES

Can you explain...?

☑ the purpose of a control account
☑ the relationship of the subsidiary ledger to the control account
☑ the need for special journals
☑ the transactions recorded in a sales journal
☑ the transactions recorded in a purchases journal
☑ the transactions recorded in a cash receipts journal
☑ the transactions recorded in a cash payments journal
☑ examples of transactions that must be recorded in the general journal
☑ summary posting
☑ the components of a computer system and the purpose of each component
☑ various internal control procedures to protect data and assets

SUMMARY

1. A control account is a summary account in the general ledger that gives one total for numerous accounts with a common title, such as Accounts Receivable or Accounts Payable.
2. The individual accounts that are summarized in a control account are maintained in a subsidiary ledger. A business may set up a subsidiary ledger for almost any account in the general ledger.
3. The individual accounts for credit customers are maintained in alphabetical order in a subsidiary ledger called the accounts receivable subsidiary ledger. The control account in the general ledger for these accounts is Accounts Receivable.
4. The individual accounts for creditors are maintained in alphabetical order in a subsidiary ledger called the accounts payable subsidiary ledger. The control account in the general ledger for these accounts is Accounts Payable.
5. A special journal can be used to simplify work and allow for a division of labor.
6. An advantage of special journals is summary posting. Since like transactions are all recorded in one column in a special journal, much time is saved by being able to post the total of the column rather than each individual amount.
7. Although summary posting is made to control accounts in the general ledger, individual amounts need to be posted to accounts in the subsidiary ledger. A check mark in the posting reference column of the special journal indicates that the amount has been posted to the subsidiary ledger.
8. The sales journal is used to record all sales of merchandise on account. Column totals in the sales journal are posted as a debit to Accounts Receivable and a credit to Sales.
9. The purchases journal is used to record all purchases of merchandise on credit. Column totals in the purchases journal are posted as a debit to Purchases and a credit to Accounts Payable.
10. The cash receipts journal is used to record any transactions involving the receipt of cash. The number of debit and credit columns needed in the cash receipts journal is determined by the frequency of transactions for which money is received. It must always have a debit column for Cash. Summary posting of account columns should be done at the end of each month. Other Accounts columns should be posted individually throughout the month.
11. The cash payments journal is used to record all payments of cash. The number of debit and credit columns needed in the cash payments journal is determined by the frequency of transactions for which money is paid. It must always have a credit column for Cash. Summary posting of account columns should be done at the end of each month. Other Accounts columns should be posted individually throughout the month.

12. The processing of accounting data is made easier through the use of machines. The electronic computer uses programs to give the computer instructions on how to manipulate data and feed it back to the user in usable form.

13. A computer system has three components—input, the central processing unit (CPU), and output. The CPU consists of three units—the arithmetic/logic unit, the primary storage or memory unit, and the control unit.

14. Businesses must protect data and assets from improper use by establishing procedures to promote efficiency and protect resources, known as internal control. Examples of internal control procedures are

- Have two or more people responsible for each transaction.
- Set up adequate access control procedures.
- Carefully screen persons being considered for employment that involves access to assets.
- Discharge employees who violate company rules.
- Establish a voucher system.

RAPID REVIEW

Multiple Choice

1. Your company has two control accounts backed up by subsidiary ledgers. What titles would the control accounts most likely have?
   (*a*) Assets and Liabilities
   (*b*) Debits and Credits
   (*c*) Accounts Receivable and Accounts Payable
   (*d*) Capital and Dividends
   (*e*) Liabilities and Capital

2. At the end of an accounting period, a schedule of accounts receivable is prepared. The schedule is prepared
   (*a*) to show management the condition of accounts receivable
   (*b*) to verify the total in the Accounts Receivable control account
   (*c*) to make it easier to prepare the end-of-the-period bills
   (*d*) to make it easier to transfer each account total to statements
   (*e*) to show the results of doing business in the accounting period

3. All cash received in a business using the following journals is recorded in a
   (*a*) general journal
   (*b*) cash payments journal
   (*c*) sales journal
   (*d*) purchases journal
   (*e*) cash receipts journal

4. All checks written for a business using the following journals are recorded in a
   (*a*) general journal
   (*b*) cash payments journal
   (*c*) sales journal
   (*d*) purchases journal
   (*e*) cash receipts journal

5. All sales on credit for a business using the following journals are recorded in a
   (*a*) general journal
   (*b*) cash payments journal
   (*c*) sales journal
   (*d*) purchases journal
   (*e*) cash receipts journal

6. All purchases on credit for a business using the following journals are recorded in a
   (*a*) general journal
   (*b*) cash payments journal
   (*c*) sales journal
   (*d*) purchases journal
   (*e*) cash receipts journal

7. A purchase return for a business using the following journals is recorded in a
   (*a*) general journal
   (*b*) cash payments journal
   (*c*) sales journal
   (*d*) purchases journal
   (*e*) cash receipts journal

8. The advantage(s) of having special journals in addition to a general journal is/are
   (*a*) summary posting
   (*b*) saving time in journalizing
   (*c*) a division of labor
   (*d*) all of the above

9. The definition of summary posting is
    (a) posting each debit and credit monthly
    (b) posting column totals from special journals
    (c) posting debit and credit totals from the general journal
    (d) posting from the journal to the ledger
    (e) posting from the ledger to the trial balance

10. Electronic data processing is a term associated with
    (a) the electronic computer
    (b) any type of filing system
    (c) rotary calculators
    (d) the abacus
    (e) manually manipulated punched cards

11. Businesses protect assets from improper use by
    (a) a division of duties
    (b) sequentially numbered documents
    (c) a voucher system
    (d) care in hiring personnel
    (e) all of the above

Answers: 1. (c); 2. (b); 3. (e); 4. (b); 5. (c); 6. (d); 7. (a); 8. (d); 9. (b); 10. (a); 11. (e)

SOLVED PROBLEMS

PROBLEM 7-1: The following are the T accounts in the subsidiary ledger and control account for Accounts Receivable in the general ledger as of December 31, 19—, the end of the accounting period. Prepare a schedule of accounts receivable in the space provided.

ACCOUNTS RECEIVABLE SUBSIDIARY LEDGER

Candy Able — 100
Linda Carr — 205
Sam Baker — 350
Donald Davis — 56

GENERAL LEDGER

Accounts Receivable — 711

Answer: A schedule of accounts receivable is a listing of the individual accounts and their balances in the subsidiary ledger. The total should equal the total in the Accounts Receivable control account in the general ledger. [Section 7-1]

Schedule of Accounts Receivable

December 31, 19—

Candy Able...	$100
Sam Baker	350
Linda Carr...	205
Donald Davis	56
Total	$711

PROBLEM 7-2: Tiffany Company uses the following journals: (a) general; (b) cash receipts; (c) cash payments; (d) sales; and (e) purchases. Select the journal in which each of the following transactions would be recorded and put the letter of that journal in the space provided to the right of each transaction.

1. Purchase of merchandise on credit.   _____
2. Adjusting entry for depreciation.   _____
3. Purchase of office equipment for cash.   _____
4. Sale of merchandise for cash.   _____
5. Payment of utility bill.   _____
6. Payment of salaries   _____
7. Purchase of office equipment on credit.   _____
8. Sale of merchandise on credit.   _____
9. Purchase of merchandise for cash.   _____

Answers: 1. (e); 2. (a); 3. (c); 4. (b); 5. (c); 6. (c); 7. (a); 8. (d); 9. (c) [Section 7-2]

PROBLEM 7-3: The following sales on credit were made by Tiffany Company in May. Record the sales in the sales journal provided below.

May 2 Sold merchandise to James Bean for $85, Invoice #101.
　　　5 Sold merchandise to Alice Copper for $308, Invoice #102.
　　　8 Sold merchandise to Kelly Smith for $500, Invoice #110.
　　15 Sold merchandise to Robert Holmes for $415, Invoice #115.
　　27 Sold merchandise to James Dee for $710, Invoice #136.

SALES JOURNAL				PAGE *35*	
DATE		ACCOUNT DEBITED	INVOICE NO.	POST. REF.	AMOUNT

Answer: [Section 7-2]

SALES JOURNAL					PAGE 35	
DATE		ACCOUNT DEBITED	INVOICE NO.	POST. REF.	AMOUNT	
May	2	James Bean	101		85	00
	5	Alice Copper	102		308	00
	8	Kelly Smith	110		500	00
	15	Robert Holmes	115		415	00
	27	James Dee	136		710	00

PROBLEM 7-4: Total the following sales journal Amount column as of May 31. Post the transactions to the subsidiary ledger and general ledger provided below.

SALES JOURNAL					PAGE 35	
DATE		ACCOUNT DEBITED	INVOICE NO.	POST. REF.	AMOUNT	
May	2	James Bean	101		85	00
	5	Alice Copper	102		308	00
	8	Kelly Smith	110		500	00
	15	Robert Holmes	115		415	00
	27	James Dee	136		710	00

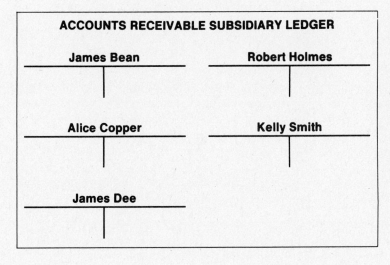

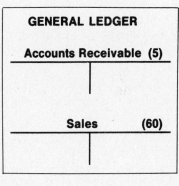

Answer:

		SALES JOURNAL				PAGE *35*	
DATE		**ACCOUNT DEBITED**	**INVOICE NO.**	**POST. REF.**		**AMOUNT**	
May	*2*	*James Bean*	*101*	√		*85*	*00*
	5	*Alice Copper*	*102*	√		*308*	*00*
	8	*Kelly Smith*	*110*	√		*500*	*00*
	15	*Robert Holmes*	*115*	√		*415*	*00*
	27	*James Dee*	*136*	√		*710*	*00*
	31	*Total*				*2,018*	*00*
						(5)	(60)

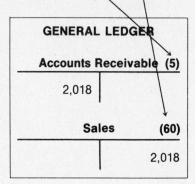

ACCOUNTS RECEIVABLE SUBSIDIARY LEDGER

James Bean		Robert Holmes	
85		415	

Alice Copper		Kelly Smith	
308		500	

James Dee	
710	

GENERAL LEDGER

Accounts Receivable	(5)
2,018	

	Sales	(60)
		2,018

As each subsidiary ledger account is posted, a check mark is placed in the posting reference column. At the end of May, the general ledger accounts are posted for the total amount of sales on credit. Accounts Receivable in the general ledger is debited for $2,018 and Sales is credited for $2,018. The general ledger page numbers for these two accounts are placed below the column total in the sales journal to indicate that the posting has been done. The (5) on the left indicates Accounts Receivable has been debited. The (60) on the right indicates the Sales account has been credited. [Sections 7-1 and 7-2]

PROBLEM 7-5: The following purchases of merchandise were made by Tiffany Company in May. Record the purchases in the purchases journal and compute the total.

May   1   Purchased merchandise worth $150 from Miller, Inc., invoice dated 4/28.
      10   Purchased merchandise worth $205 from Spotts Company, invoice dated 5/6.
      13   Purchased merchandise worth $790 from All Pool, invoice dated 5/11.
      18   Purchased merchandise worth $400 from Ace Homes, invoice dated 5/15.

		PURCHASES JOURNAL			PAGE *4*	
DATE		**ACCOUNT CREDITED**	**INVOICE DATE**	**POST. REF.**	**AMOUNT**	

Answer: [Section 7-2]

PURCHASES JOURNAL					PAGE 4	
DATE		ACCOUNT CREDITED	INVOICE DATE	POST. REF.	AMOUNT	
May	*1*	*Miller, Inc.*	*4/28*		*150*	*00*
	10	*Spotts Company*	*5/6*		*205*	*00*
	13	*All Pool*	*5/11*		*790*	*00*
	18	*Ace Homes*	*5/15*		*400*	*00*

PROBLEM 7-6: Total the following purchases journal amount column as of May 31. Post the transactions to the subsidiary ledger and general ledger provided below.

PURCHASES JOURNAL					PAGE 4	
DATE		ACCOUNT CREDITED	INVOICE DATE	POST. REF.	AMOUNT	
May	*1*	*Miller, Inc.*	*4/28*		*150*	*00*
	10	*Spotts Company*	*5/6*		*205*	*00*
	13	*All Pool*	*5/11*		*790*	*00*
	18	*Ace Homes*	*5/15*		*400*	*00*
	31	*Total*				

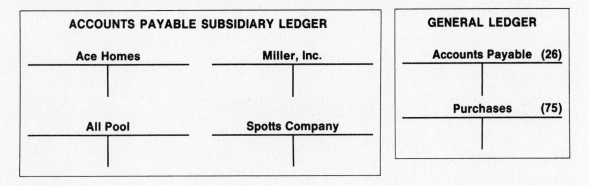

ACCOUNTS PAYABLE SUBSIDIARY LEDGER

Ace Homes   Miller, Inc.

All Pool   Spotts Company

GENERAL LEDGER

Accounts Payable (26)

Purchases (75)

Answer:

PURCHASES JOURNAL					PAGE 4	
DATE		ACCOUNT CREDITED	INVOICE DATE	POST. REF.	AMOUNT	
May	*1*	*Miller, Inc.*	*4/28*	✓	*150*	*00*
	10	*Spotts Company*	*5/6*	✓	*205*	*00*
	13	*All Pool*	*5/11*	✓	*790*	*00*
	18	*Ace Homes*	*5/15*	✓	*400*	*00*
	31	*Total*			*1,545*	*00*
					(75)	(26)

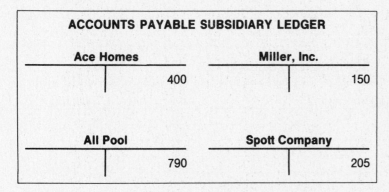 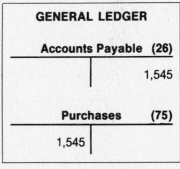

Each subsidiary ledger is posted during the month and a check mark is placed in the posting reference column of the journal. At the end of the month, the total is posted as a credit to the Accounts Payable control account in the general ledger and the account number (26) is placed below the total in the purchase journal. The Purchases account is debited and the account number (75) is placed below the total in the purchases journal. [Sections 7-1 and 7-2]

PROBLEM 7-7: Adams Company had the following cash transactions during August. Record the transactions in the cash receipts journal and total the columns.

Aug. 1 Received payment from Adam Jones for account receivable. The amount of the check was $58.80. A 2% discount of $1.20 was taken.

   8 Cash sales for the week amounted to $1,015.

  10 Juan Taylor, the owner, invested an additional $5,000 in the company.

  20 Received payment from Cap Allen for account receivable. Check was for $196. A discount of $4 was taken.

  26 Borrowed $1,000 from First National Bank. Signed a note payable.

  31 Received payment on account from Jane Barr in the amount of $125. Payment was made after discount period expired.

CASH RECEIPTS JOURNAL PAGE *19*

DATE	ACCOUNT	POST. REF.	OTHER ACCOUNTS DEBIT	OTHER ACCOUNTS CREDIT	ACCOUNTS REC. CREDIT	SALES CREDIT	SALES DISCOUNT DEBIT	CASH DEBIT

Answer:

			OTHER ACCOUNTS		ACCOUNTS REC. CREDIT		SALES CREDIT		SALES DISCOUNT DEBIT		CASH DEBIT	
DATE	ACCOUNT	POST. REF.	DEBIT	CREDIT								
Aug. 1	Adam Jones				60	00			1	20	58	80
8	Cash sales for week						1,015	00			1,015	00
10	Juan Taylor, Capital			5,000 00							5,000	00
20	Cap Allen				200	00			4	00	196	00
26	Notes Payable			1,000 00							1,000	00
31	Jane Barr				125	00					125	00
31	Total			6,000 00	385	00	1,015	00	5	20	7,394	80

CASH RECEIPTS JOURNAL PAGE *19*

The subsidiary accounts receivable ledger and Other Accounts columns should be posted during the month. At the end of the month, the columns are totaled. Be sure the total of all the debit columns equals the total of all the credit columns. The column totals for Cash, Sales Discounts, Accounts Receivable, and Sales will be posted to the individual accounts in the general ledger. The account numbers will be placed below the column totals to indicate that the accounts have been posted. A check mark will be placed below the column totals for Other Accounts to indicate that the amounts were posted separately to the individual accounts. [Section 7-2]

PROBLEM 7-8: Adams Company made the following cash payments during August. Record these transactions in the cash payments journal provided below and total the columns.

Aug. 1 Paid Ewald, Inc., $490 on a $500 purchase on account, less 2% discount, Check #1841.
3 Paid Samuels, Inc., $400 on account, Check #1842.
5 Paid Sello Company $210 on account, Check #1843.
8 Bought office supplies for cash, Check #1844, for $56 from Blair Office Supplies.
15 Purchased store equipment for $5,000 from Ruff Manufacturing. $1,000 was paid by Check #1845. The balance was a note payable.
24 The owner, Juan Taylor, withdrew $2,400, Check #1846.
29 Paid utility bill to Sanford Electric for $105, Check #1847.

CASH PAYMENTS JOURNAL PAGE *44*

DATE	CHECK NO.	ACCOUNT	POST. REF.	OTHER ACCOUNTS DEBIT	CREDIT	ACCOUNTS PAYABLE DEBIT	PURCH. DISCOUNT CREDIT	CASH CREDIT

Answer:

				OTHER ACCOUNTS				ACCOUNTS PAYABLE		PURCH. DISCOUNT		CASH	
DATE	CHECK NO.	ACCOUNT	POST. REF.	DEBIT		CREDIT		DEBIT		CREDIT		CREDIT	
Aug. 1	1841	Ewald, Inc.						500	00	10	00	490	00
3	1842	Samuels, Inc.						400	00			400	00
5	1843	Sello Company						210	00			210	00
8	1844	Office Supplies		56	00							56	00
15	1845	Store Equipment		5,000	00							1,000	00
		Note Payable				4,000	00						
24	1846	Juan Taylor,											
		Drawing		2,400	00							2,400	00
29	1847	Utilities Expense		105	00							105	00
31		Total		7,561	00	4,000	00	1,110	00	10	00	4,661	00

CASH PAYMENTS JOURNAL — PAGE *44*

The amounts would be posted in the same way as for the cash receipts journal in Problem 7-7. [Section 7-2]

PROBLEM 7-9: The Dresden Company had the following transactions for October, the first month of operation. Record each transaction in the appropriate journal provided below. Total the columns in the special journals.

Oct. 1 The owner, Drew Ramirez, invested $8,000 in the business.

2 Purchased merchandise for $500 from Roth Company on account. Terms: 2/10, n/30; invoice dated 9/30.

3 Sold merchandise to Monaco Brothers, Inc., for $350, Invoice #407. Terms: 2/10, n/30; invoice dated 9/30.

4 Paid rent for the month, $750, Check #1203.

7 Purchased merchandise for $2,100 from Zanier, Inc., on account, invoice dated 10/6. Terms: 2/10, n/30.

7 Sold merchandise for $875 to Neunen Corporation on account, Invoice #408.

10 A note payable was issued in the amount of $5,000 for a loan from the bank.

13 Received payment of $343 on account from Monaco Brothers, Inc., less 2% discount.

14 Purchased office supplies for cash, $85, Check #1204.

16 Paid $200 for one-year insurance policy, Check #1205.

20 Returned damaged goods costing $200 to Zanier, Inc., and received credit.

22 Sold merchandise worth $750 to Landing Corporation on account, Invoice #410.

25 Paid Roth Company for October 2 purchase, less 2% discount, Check #1206.

26 Issued credit of $100 to Neunen Corporation for return of damaged merchandise.

28 Sold merchandise for $1,200 to Stabler Company on account, Invoice #411.

30 Cash sales for the month of $4,920.

SALES JOURNAL — PAGE *31*

DATE	ACCOUNT DEBITED	INVOICE NO.	POST. REF.	AMOUNT

PURCHASES JOURNAL PAGE 29

DATE		ACCOUNT CREDITED	INVOICE DATE	POST. REF.	AMOUNT

CASH RECEIPTS JOURNAL PAGE 44

DATE		ACCOUNT	POST. REF.	OTHER ACCOUNTS		ACCOUNTS REC. CREDIT	SALES CREDIT	SALES DISCOUNTS CREDIT	CASH DEBIT
				DEBIT	CREDIT				

CASH PAYMENTS JOURNAL PAGE 25

DATE	CHECK NO.	ACCOUNT	POST. REF.	OTHER ACCOUNTS		ACCOUNTS PAYABLE DEBIT	PURCH. DISCOUNT CREDIT	CASH CREDIT
				DEBIT	CREDIT			

GENERAL JOURNAL PAGE 51

DATE		DESCRIPTION	POST. REF.	DEBIT	CREDIT

Answer: [Section 7-2]

SALES JOURNAL   PAGE *31*

DATE		ACCOUNT DEBITED	INVOICE NO.	POST. REF.	AMOUNT	
Oct.	3	Monaco Brothers, Inc.	407		350	00
	7	Neunen Corporation	408		875	00
	22	Landing Corporation	410		750	00
	28	Stabler Company	411		1,200	00
	31	Total			3,175	00

PURCHASES JOURNAL   PAGE *29*

DATE		ACCOUNT CREDITED	INVOICE DATE	POST. REF.	AMOUNT	
Oct.	2	Roth Company	9/30		500	00
	7	Zanier, Inc.	10/6		2,100	00
	31	Total			2,600	00

CASH RECEIPTS JOURNAL   PAGE *44*

DATE		ACCOUNT	POST. REF.	OTHER ACCOUNTS DEBIT	OTHER ACCOUNTS CREDIT		ACCOUNTS REC. CREDIT		SALES CREDIT		SALES DISCOUNTS DEBIT		CASH DEBIT	
Oct.	1	Drew Ramirez, Capital			8,000	00							8,000	00
	10	Notes Payable			5,000	00							5,000	00
	13	Monaco Brothers, Inc.					350	00			7	00	343	00
	30	Cash sales for month							4,920	00			4,920	00
	31	Total			13,000	00	350	00	4,920	00	7	00	18,263	00

CASH PAYMENTS JOURNAL   PAGE *25*

DATE		CHECK NO.	ACCOUNT	POST. REF.	OTHER ACCOUNTS DEBIT		OTHER ACCOUNTS CREDIT	ACCOUNTS PAYABLE DEBIT		PURCH. DISCOUNT CREDIT		CASH CREDIT	
Oct.	4	1203	Rent Expense		750	00						750	00
	14	1204	Office Supplies		85	00						85	00
	16	1205	Prepaid Insurance		200	00						200	00
	25	1206	Roth Company					500	00	10	00	490	00
	31		Total		1,035	00		500	00	10	00	1,525	00

		GENERAL JOURNAL			PAGE *51*	
DATE		**DESCRIPTION**	**POST. REF.**	**DEBIT**		**CREDIT**
Oct.	*20*	*Accounts Payable/Zanier, Inc.*		*200*	*00*	
		Purchase Returns and Allowances				*200*	*00*
		Damaged goods returned				
	26	*Sales Returns and Allowances*		*100*	*00*	
		Accounts Receivable/Neunen Corporation				*100*	*00*
		Damaged goods returned				

PROBLEM 7-10: Post the transactions recorded in Problem 7-9 to the appropriate accounts in the accounts receivable subsidiary ledger, accounts payable subsidiary ledger, and general ledger provided. Complete the necessary posting references in the journals above as you post the amounts. When posting a general journal entry to the general ledger that affects a subsidiary ledger account as well, place a check mark in the posting reference column of the general journal to indicate that the amount was posted to the subsidiary ledger, as well as the account number in the general ledger to which the amount was individually posted.

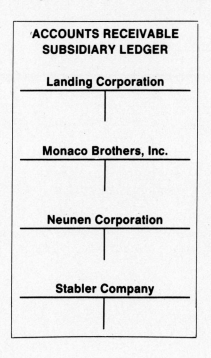

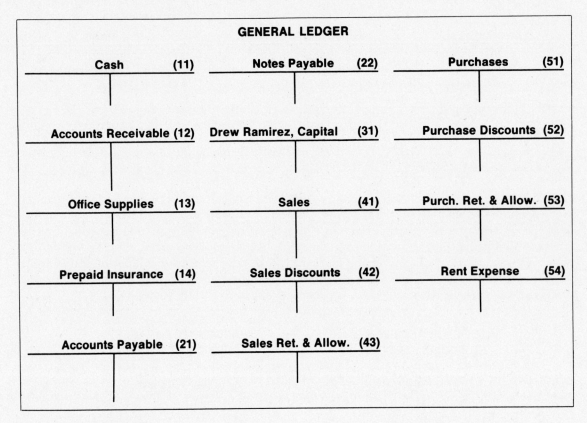

GENERAL LEDGER

Cash (11)	Notes Payable (22)	Purchases (51)
Accounts Receivable (12)	Drew Ramirez, Capital (31)	Purchase Discounts (52)
Office Supplies (13)	Sales (41)	Purch. Ret. & Allow. (53)
Prepaid Insurance (14)	Sales Discounts (42)	Rent Expense (54)
Accounts Payable (21)	Sales Ret. & Allow. (43)	

Answer: [Section 7-2]

ACCOUNTS RECEIVABLE SUBSIDIARY LEDGER

Landing Corporation

| 10/22 | 750 | |

Monaco Brothers, Inc.

| 10/3 | 350 | 10/13 | 350 |

Neunen Corporation

| 10/7 | 875 | 10/26 | 100 |

Stabler Company

| 10/28 | 1,200 | |

ACCOUNTS PAYABLE SUBSIDIARY LEDGER

Roth Company

| 10/25 | 500 | 10/2 | 500 |

Zanler, Inc.

| 10/20 | 200 | 10/7 | 2,100 |

GENERAL LEDGER

Cash (11)			
10/31	18,263	10/31	1,525

Notes Payable (22)		
	10/10	5,000

Purchases (51)		
10/31	2,600	

Accounts Receivable (12)			
10/31	3,175	10/26	100
		10/31	350

Drew Ramirez, Capital (31)		
	10/1	8,000

Purchase Discounts (52)		
	10/31	10

Office Supplies (13)	
10/14	85

Sales (41)		
	10/31	3,175
	10/31	4,920

Purch. Ret. & Allow. (53)		
	10/20	200

Prepaid Insurance (14)	
10/16	200

Sales Discounts (42)	
10/31	7

Rent Expense (54)	
10/4	750

Accounts Payable (21)			
10/20	200	10/31	2,600
10/31	500		

Sales Ret. & Allow. (43)	
10/26	100

Note that subsidiary ledger accounts should be posted and dated on a daily basis. Other Accounts columns in the special journals and general journal entries should also be posted and dated on a daily basis. Summary posting can be done for all other special journal accounts at the end of the month.

Check to see that you made the following posting reference entries in the journals in Problem 7-9.

SALES JOURNAL — PAGE *31*

DATE		ACCOUNT DEBITED	INVOICE NO.	POST. REF.	AMOUNT	
Oct.	3	Monaco Brothers, Inc.	407	√	350	00
	7	Neunen Corporation	408	√	875	00
	22	Landing Corporation	410	√	750	00
	28	Stabler Company	411	√	1,200	00
	31	Total			3,175	00
					(12)	(41)

PURCHASES JOURNAL — PAGE *29*

DATE		ACCOUNT CREDITED	INVOICE DATE	POST. REF.	AMOUNT	
Oct.	2	Roth Company	9/30	√	500	00
	7	Zanier, Inc.	10/6	√	2,100	00
	31	Total			2,600	00
					(51)	(21)

CASH RECEIPTS JOURNAL   PAGE 44

DATE	ACCOUNT	POST. REF.	OTHER ACCOUNTS DEBIT	OTHER ACCOUNTS CREDIT	ACCOUNTS REC. CREDIT	SALES CREDIT	SALES DISCOUNTS DEBIT	CASH DEBIT
Oct. 1	Drew Ramirez, Capital	31		8,000 00				8,000 00
10	Notes Payable	22		5,000 00				5,000 00
13	Monaco Brothers, Inc.	✓			350 00		7 00	343 00
30	Cash sales for month	✓				4,920 00		4,920 00
31	Total		—	13,000 00	350 00	4,920 00	7 00	18,263 00
				(✓)	(12)	(41)	(42)	(11)

CASH PAYMENTS JOURNAL   PAGE 25

DATE	CHECK NO.	ACCOUNT	POST. REF.	OTHER ACCOUNTS DEBIT	OTHER ACCOUNTS CREDIT	ACCOUNTS PAYABLE DEBIT	PURCH. DISCOUNT CREDIT	CASH CREDIT
Oct. 4	1203	Rent Expense	54	750 00				750 00
14	1204	Office Supplies	13	85 00				85 00
16	1205	Prepaid Insurance	14	200 00				200 00
25	1206	Roth Company	✓		—	500 00	10 00	490 00
31		Total		1,035 00		500 00	10 00	1,525 00
				(✓)		(21)	(52)	(11)

GENERAL JOURNAL   PAGE 51

DATE	DESCRIPTION	POST. REF.	DEBIT	CREDIT
Oct. 20	Accounts Payable/Zanier, Inc.	✓ 21	200 00	
	Purchase Returns and Allowances	53		200 00
	Damaged goods returned			
26	Sales Returns and Allowances	43	100 00	
	Accounts Receivable/Neunen Corporation	✓ 12		100 00
	Damaged goods returned			

PROBLEM 7-11: Prepare a trial balance for the Dresden Company as of October 31. You will have to determine the account balances from the general ledger in Problem 7-10.

Answer: [Chapter 4, Section 4-4]

```
                            Dresden Company
                             Trial Balance
                            October 31, 19—


Cash .......................................................  $16,738.00
Accounts Receivable .......................................     2,725.00
Office Supplies ...........................................        85.00
Prepaid Insurance .........................................       200.00
Accounts Payable ..........................................               $  1,900.00
Notes Payable..............................................                  5,000.00
Drew Ramirez, Capital......................................                  8,000.00
Sales......................................................                  8,095.00
Sales Discounts ...........................................         7.00
Sales Returns and Allowances...............................       100.00
Purchases..................................................     2,600.00
Purchase Discounts ........................................                     10.00
Purchase Returns and Allowances............................                    200.00
Rent Expense...............................................       750.00
    Totals ................................................  $23,205.00   $23,205.00
```

PROBLEM 7-12: Masse Company uses four special journals and a general journal. The special journals include a sales journal, purchases journal, cash receipts journal, and cash payments journal. Transactions for the month are summarized below.

> Sales journal: Total, $28,500
> Purchases journal: Total, $13,800
> Cash receipts journal: Cash column total, $23,150
> Accounts Receivable column total, $19,321
> Cash payments journal: Cash column total, $20,995
> Accounts Payable column total, $17,050

What account(s) in the general ledger would be posted for:

1. the sales journal total of $28,500?
2. the purchases journal total of $13,800?
3. the Cash column total of $23,150 in the cash receipts journal?
4. the Accounts Receivable column total of $19,321?
5. the Cash column total of $20,995 in the cash payments journal?
6. the Accounts Payable column total of $17,050?

Answer: [Section 7-2]

1. The Accounts Receivable control account would be debited and Sales would be credited for $28,500.
2. Purchases would be debited and Accounts Payable would be credited for $13,800.
3. Cash would be debited for $23,150.
4. The Accounts Receivable control account would be credited for $19,321.
5. Cash would be credited for $20,995.
6. Accounts Payable would be debited for $17,050.

PROBLEM 7-13: A payment in the amount of $220 is made for office supplies. The transaction is recorded in the cash payments journal incorrectly—Office Supplies is incorrectly debited for $200. The Cash column is correctly credited for $220. How will this error be found?

Answer: At the end of the month, the columns will be totaled. The total of the debit columns will not equal the total of the credit columns. The debit columns will total $20 less than the credit columns. The first step to find the error will be to re-add the columns. This will not locate the error, however. The next step will be to check each transaction by checking horizontally. This will locate the error. Debits will not equal credits for this transaction. [Section 7-2]

PROBLEM 7-14: What special journal is illustrated below? Give a brief explanation of each of the five transactions.

PAGE *40*

DATE	CHECK NO.	ACCOUNT	POST. REF.	OTHER ACCOUNTS DEBIT	CREDIT	ACCOUNTS PAYABLE DEBIT	PURCH. DISCOUNT CREDIT	CASH CREDIT
May *1*	*110*	*Taylor, Inc.*				*1,000* *00*	*20* *00*	*980* *00*
5	*111*	*Rent Expense*		*500* *00*				*500* *00*
8	*112*	*Transportation-In*		*55* *00*				*55* *00*
20	*113*	*Rose Riker, Drawing*		*2,000* *00*				*2,000* *00*
27	*114*	*Notes Payable*		*5,000* *00*				*5,000* *00*
				7,555 *00*		*1,000* *00*	*20* *00*	*8,535* *00*

Answer: The special journal is a cash payments journal. The transactions are explained as follows:

May	1	Payment of $980 was made to Taylor, Inc., with Check #110. A 2% discount was taken.
	5	Rent of $500 was paid with Check #111.
	8	Transportation expense of $55 was paid with Check #112.
	20	The owner, Rose Riker, withdrew $2,000 in cash, Check #113.
	27	Payment of $5,000 was made on a note payable, Check #114.

[Section 7-2]

PROBLEM 7-15: What are three internal control measures used to safeguard cash?

Answer: Three internal control measures used to safeguard cash are: separation of duties between two or more people; careful selection of employees; and written instructions concerning authorization of payment of cash, deposits of cash, and the recording of cash transactions. [Section 7-4]

8 ACCOUNTING FOR CASH

8-1. Internal Controls

A. In accounting, cash is defined as paper money, coins, and other items that are commonly accepted as a medium of exchange.

The caption Cash on the balance sheet includes all cash accounts or cash equivalents. For example, checking and savings accounts that are available to the company without restriction are reported as cash. If cash is restricted to a specific purpose, it should be shown on the balance sheet in an investment account.

EXAMPLE 8-1: Cash includes unrestricted money on deposit in a bank, currency, coins, checks, money orders, and traveler's checks. Cash does *not* include postage stamps, IOU's, U.S. government saving bonds, or notes. Nor does cash include cash being held for a special purpose, such as payment of long-term liabilities.

B. Internal controls over cash are necessary to prevent misuse or theft of cash.

There are various internal controls that a business can institute to safeguard cash.

1. *Separation of duties.* The various duties involving cash should be divided among two or more individuals. For example, the handling and recording of cash receipts and cash disbursements should be done by different employees. In addition, bank reconciliations of deposits and disbursements (see Section 8-4) should be prepared by someone who is not involved with cash transactions. This way, more than one person is responsible for the processing of cash, making theft more difficult.
2. *Physical control.* Safes and cash registers should be used to physically control cash. The number of employees allowed access to a safe should be limited. The use of cash registers discourages theft by providing a record of all sales that can be compared to the cash amount in the register drawer at the end of each day. The temptation to ring up a sale for less than the actual amount and pocket the difference is discouraged by the fact that most registers show the amount to the customer and the fact that the customer must be given a receipt. Thus, the customer helps to ensure that the transaction is actually recorded and is recorded in the correct amount.
3. *Daily deposits.* Deposits of all cash received should be made daily to safeguard cash. A comparison of daily cash receipts with daily cash deposits discourages employees who make deposits from "borrowing" the money for a few days.

4. *Disbursements by check.* Ideally, all disbursements should be made by check to ensure a record of the transaction and to keep the handling of cash to a minimum. When it is impractical or unacceptable to pay by check, a petty cash fund should be used (see Section 8-2).
5. *Voucher system.* A voucher system provides physical and record keeping control over cash disbursements (see Section 8-5).

8-2. Petty Cash Fund

A. A petty cash fund should be established to control disbursements when it is not practical or acceptable to write a check.

Suppose that a delivery of supplies arrives with postage due of 27 cents. Writing a check for 27 cents is impractical. It is simpler to have a small fund of money controlled by one individual for cash disbursements of this kind.

B. A relatively small amount of coins and currency should be kept on hand as petty cash.

To establish a petty cash fund, a new account called Petty Cash should be opened in the general ledger. A petty cash fund should be authorized in writing and a check written for the authorized amount. The Cash account is decreased and the Petty Cash account is increased. One person should be designated to handle the money and be responsible for its safety and disbursement.

EXAMPLE 8-2: A petty cash fund of $100 is authorized and established. The general journal entry would be

Jan.	3	Petty Cash	100	
		Cash		100
		Establish petty cash fund of $100		

C. When a disbursement is made from petty cash, a petty cash voucher is filled out with the date, amount, and reason for the disbursement.

The person receiving cash should also sign and date the voucher. At any given time, the total of all the petty cash vouchers plus coins and currency in the petty cash drawer should equal the authorized amount of the petty cash fund.

EXAMPLE 8-3: The petty cash fund established in Example 8-2 contains vouchers for postage, $37; office supplies, $12; gas for the company car, $24, and snow removal from sidewalk, $21. The vouchers total $94. The cash on hand in petty cash should be $6 ($94 + $6 = $100).

D. The petty cash fund should be replenished when the cash held by the petty cash custodian is low.

To replenish a petty cash fund, the vouchers are verified and canceled by another employee. A check is written to bring the cash to the authorized amount of the fund. The various accounts affected by the disbursements from petty cash are debited and Cash is credited. The Petty Cash account is not affected by this transaction because the Petty Cash account remains at the authorized amount until it is increased or decreased.

EXAMPLE 8-4: Based on the information in Example 8-3, the general journal entry to record the petty cash disbursements and replenish the account would be

Jan. 31	Postage Expense	37	
	Supplies Expense	12	
	Auto Expense	24	
	Maintenance Expense	21	
	Cash		94
	To replenish petty cash, verified		
	by controller's office		

A check is written for $94 and added to the $6 on hand to equal $100.

E. A Cash Short and Over account is used when errors are made in disbursing petty cash.

If the petty cash vouchers plus the cash on hand do not equal the original amount of the fund, an account called Cash Short and Over is used to record the difference.

EXAMPLE 8-4: The following journal entry to record disbursements and replenish the petty cash fund is based on the information in Example 8-2, except that the coins and currency in petty cash are only $4.

Jan. 31	Postage Expense	37	
	Supplies Expense	12	
	Auto Expense	24	
	Maintenance Expense	21	
	Cash Short and Over	2	
	Cash		96
	To replenish petty cash, verified		
	by controller's office		

In this instance, petty cash was short by $2. This shortage is a debit to Cash Short and Over. If more than $6 in cash was on hand, Cash Short and Over would be credited.

The balance of Cash Short and Over may be either a debit or credit. A debit balance in this account means there were more shortages than overages and is an expense. A credit balance means there were more overages than shortages and is a revenue. In either case, the check to replenish the fund is always written for the amount necessary to bring the cash back to the authorized amount of the fund.

8-3. Cash Sales

Cash sales should be recorded every day in the cash receipts journal and the cash should be included in the daily cash deposit to the bank. The amount recorded as cash sales should be taken from the cash register tape or from the sales invoices. This amount is compared with the cash collected from cash sales. If the amount from the cash register tape or sales invoices does not equal the cash collected on cash sales, the Cash Short and Over account is used to record the difference. This difference is usually due to minor errors in making change. Significant differences should be noted by management and corrective action taken.

EXAMPLE 8-5: The cash register tape shows cash sales of $347.20. The cash collected on cash sales is $349.60. The general journal entry to record this information would be

Feb. 4	Cash	349.60	
	Sales		347.20
	Cash Short and Over		2.40
	Cash deposits for checks and		
	register numbers		

As explained in Section 8-2, the overage is recorded as a credit to Cash Short and Over.

8-4. Bank Reconciliations

A. A bank furnishes a statement to a depositor each month.

A bank statement lists the depositor's account balance at the beginning of the month, checks and other amounts deducted from the account during the month, deposits and other amounts added to the account during the month, and the account balance at the end of the month. The bank statement balance can then be compared to the depositor's Cash account balance. However, a bank statement balance is not likely to equal a depositor's Cash account balance at a given time because of delays or errors by either party in recording transactions. It is therefore necessary to prepare a bank reconciliation.

B. A *bank reconciliation* is an analysis explaining the difference between the cash balance reported in a bank statement and the balance of the Cash account in the general ledger.

Preparing a bank reconciliation once a month is an important part of internal control over cash. Each month, recorded cash per the depositor's records is compared to the amount of cash reported by the bank, thus providing a means for finding and correcting any errors. For the greatest internal control, the bank reconciliation should be prepared by a person who is not involved in the actual handling or recording of cash each month. A bank reconciliation normally is prepared in two parts.

C. The first step in preparing a bank reconciliation is to bring the bank statement balance up-to-date with the depositor's records.

1. *Deposits.* All cash receipts recorded in the depositor's records should be deposited and shown on the bank statement. Because of time constraints, however, deposits made near the end of the month may not appear on the current month's bank statement. Although they will appear on next month's bank statement, they are nonetheless deposits of the current month. The deposits that have been recorded in the depositor's records but are not on the bank statement are called *deposits in transit.* The deposits in transit are added to the bank statement balance to bring the bank statement balance up-to-date with the amount the depositor has a right to, known as the *corrected* or *adjusted balance.*
2. *Outstanding checks.* Checks that have been written and recorded in the depositor's records but have not been presented to the bank for payment (cleared the bank) are called *checks outstanding.* Checks outstanding have been recorded in the depositor's records but do not appear on the bank statement. They are subtracted from the bank statement balance to bring the balance up-to-date with the depositor's records.
3. *Bank errors.* The only other reconciling item or items to the bank statement balance is an error or errors made by the bank. Errors are either added to or subtracted from the bank statement balance, depending on the type of error.

EXAMPLE 8-6: Cooper and Sons, Inc., maintains a company account at Last State Bank. According to a statement furnished by the bank, the balance of the account was $2,049 as of May 31. However, a comparison of the bank statement to the depositor's records reveals that a deposit of $347 recorded in the depositor's records on May 31 does not appear on the bank statement. A comparison of cancelled checks with the cash payments journal indicates that checks numbered 1937 for $50, 1952 for $25, and 1953 for $27 did not clear the bank in May. Also, the bank improperly charged the company account with a check written on another company's account for $46. Based on this information, the reconciliation of the bank statement balance would be prepared as shown on page 161.

```
                            Cooper and Sons, Inc.
                            Bank Reconciliation
                               May 31, 19––


Balance per bank statement.....................................................        $2,049
Add: Deposits in transit......................................       $347
     Improperly charged check.................................         46        393
                                                                               $2,442

Subtract: Checks outstanding
          # 1937 ............................................       $ 50
          # 1952 ............................................         25
          # 1953 ............................................         27        102
Adjusted balance..............................................                  $2,340
```

D. The second step in preparing a bank reconciliation is to bring the depositor's cash balance up-to-date with the bank statement records.

The balance per depositor's records is the amount shown in the general ledger Cash account after postings are made from the cash receipts and cash payments journals for the month.

1. *Items added to account.* Items that the bank has added to the depositor's account, but the depositor has not yet recorded in the records, are added to the balance per the depositor's records. For example, the bank may collect a customer's note for a company and deposit it directly into its account.
2. *Items subtracted from account.* Items that the bank has subtracted from a depositor's account, but the depositor has not yet recorded in the records, are subtracted from the balance per the depositor's records.

EXAMPLE 8-7: There are several instances where a bank may subtract items from a depositor's account. Banks charge for their services and notify the depositor of these charges by subtracting them on the bank statement and including a debit memo with the statement. Also, when a customer pays by check, the check is recorded in cash receipts and deposited in the depositor's bank account. If the check is returned to the depositor's bank because the customer does not have sufficient funds to cover the check (NSF check), the bank will subtract the amount of the NSF check from the depositor's account, plus any handling charges.

3. *Depositor's errors.* The only other reconciling item or items to the balance per the depositor's records are errors made in the depositor's records of cash receipts or cash payments. Errors are added to or subtracted from the depositor's balance, depending on the type of error.

EXAMPLE 8-8: Cooper and Sons, Inc., the company in Example 8-6, showed a balance in its cash account of $1,213 after posting the cash receipts and cash payments journals for May. The company received the following information with the bank statement for May.

• Customer's check for $40 was returned marked non-sufficient funds (NSF).
• Service charges were $5.
• The bank charged $8 for printing checks.
• During May, the bank collected a customer's note receivable for $1,000 (no interest included).

An examination of the cancelled checks shows that Check #1940 was written correctly for $20 to pay an account payable, but the amount recorded in the cash payments journal was $200. The reconciliation of the depositor's balance would be prepared as shown on page 162.

```
Balance per depositor's records...........................................    $1,213
Add: Note collected by bank ..............................  $1,000
     Error in recording Check #1940*......................     180     1,180
                                                                      $2,393

Subtract: Service charge..................................  $    5
          Printing charge ................................       8
          NSF check from customer ........................      40         53
Adjusted balance..........................................              $2,340
```

* The error was added because the Cash account was decreased by $200 in posting the cash payments journal when it should have been decreased by $20. It was decreased $180 too much; therefore $180 is added.

E. The adjusted balances shown for each section of the bank reconciliation must be equal.

The first section of the bank reconciliation begins with the balance per the bank statement and ends with the adjusted balance. The second section of the bank reconciliation begins with the balance per the depositor's records and ends with the adjusted balance. The two amounts shown as the adjusted balance must be equal.

EXAMPLE 8-9: The complete bank reconciliation for Cooper and Sons, Inc., is shown below. Note that the adjusted balances reached in each section of the bank reconciliation are equal.

```
                            Cooper and Sons, Inc.
                            Bank Reconciliation
                               May 31, 19--


Balance per bank statement ...............................              $2,049
Add: Deposits in transit .................................  $  347
     Improperly charged check ............................      46        393
                                                                      $2,442

Subtract:  Checks outstanding
           #1937..........................................  $   50
           #1952..........................................      25
           #1953..........................................      27        102
Adjusted balance .........................................              $2,340 ←

Balance per depositor's records ..........................              $1,213
Add: Note collected by bank...............................  $1,000
     Error in recording Check #1940 ......................     180      1,180
                                                                      $2,393

Subtract:  Service charge ................................  $    5
           Printing charge................................       8
           NSF check from customer .......................      40         53
Adjusted balance .........................................              $2,340 ←
```

F. The Cash account must be adjusted for the items affecting the balance per the depositor's records.

Bank memos for amounts not recorded by the depositor and any depositor's errors revealed by the bank reconciliation require entries to be made in the depositor's records to bring the records up-to-date.

EXAMPLE 8-10: Based on the information in Example 8-8, Cooper and Sons, Inc., must make the following general journal entries.

May 31	Cash	1,180		
	Notes Receivable		1,000	
	Accounts Payable		180	
	According to bank reconciliation for date			

This entry accounts for the amounts that were added to the depositor's balance in the bank reconciliation. The entry increases Cash by $1,180, decreases Notes Receivable by $1,000, and decreases Accounts Payable by $180.

May 31	Miscellaneous Expenses	13		
	Accounts Receivable/(name of customer)	40		
	Cash		53	
	According to bank reconciliation for date			

This entry accounts for the amounts that were subtracted from the depositor's balance in the bank reconciliation. The entry increases Miscellaneous Expenses by $13 (the $5 service charge and $8 check printing charge), increases Accounts Receivable by $40 (owed to the depositor by the customer whose check was returned NSF), and decreases Cash by $53.

The Cash account now reflects the corrected or adjusted cash balance of $2,340.

8-5. Voucher Systems

As mentioned in Chapter 7, a voucher is a document authorizing a person to pay cash. Voucher systems may vary from company to company, but in general, they require the use of a voucher form, a voucher register, and a check register. Many systems also maintain files for unpaid and paid vouchers.

A. A voucher form is used for all expenditures, except those from petty cash.

A complete voucher form usually includes

- the proper account or accounts to be debited. This is determined by the reason for the expenditure.
- the amount to credit Vouchers Payable.
- the proper amount of the check to be written when the voucher is approved.
- the approval for payment from an authorized person in the company. The person approving the voucher for payment should check the accuracy and validity of the supporting documents. Supporting documentation should be attached to the voucher (invoices, purchase orders, receiving reports).

```
                        VOUCHER

No.  434          Date  May 2, 19x1  Due    June 2, 19x1


                         PAYEE

     Allied Manufacturing Company
     1102 Fifth Avenue
     San Diego, CA  92101


            DEBIT                      |  AMOUNT

Purchases                             |  450 00
Supplies                              |
Advertising Expense                   |
Delivery Expense                      |
Insurance Expense                     |
Miscellaneous Expense                 |


Credit Vouchers Payable               |  450 00


                 VOUCHER SUMMARY

Amount                                |  450 00
Adjustment                            |
Discount                              |
Net                                   |  450 00
Approved  J.C. Nelson                 |  Controller
Recorded  B.W


                 PAYMENT SUMMARY

Date  June 2, 19x1  Amount   450.00   Check No  1942
Approved  T E Stone                   |  Treasurer
Recorded  P.E.M
```

B. After being approved by an authorized person, a voucher is recorded in a journal known as a *voucher register*.

A voucher register replaces the purchases journal discussed in Chapter 7. Vouchers are entered in numerical order and recorded as a credit to Vouchers Payable and as a debit to the account or accounts to be charged for the amount. Unpaid vouchers are often maintained in a file in the order in which they are to be paid. When a voucher is paid, the voucher is removed from the unpaid voucher file, and the date of payment and the check number are entered in the voucher register on the same line as the original voucher entry. The paid voucher is often maintained in a file for as long as company policy dictates. A voucher register is illustrated on page 165.

VOUCHER REGISTER

Date	Vou. No.	Payee	Date Paid	Check No.	Vouchers Payable Credit	Purchases Debit	Supplies Debit	Adv. Expense Debit	Delivery Expense Debit	Misc. Expense Debit	Other Accounts Debit Account	Post. Ref.	Amount
19--- May													
2	434	Allied Manufacturing	6/2	1942	450 00	450 00							
3	435	Del Mar Co.	6/3	1943	300 00			300 00					
7	436	Wong Office Supplies	6/6	1944	220 00		220 00						
10	437	Beyer Transport	6/10	1945	50 00				50 00				
13	438	Sawyer Company	6/13	1946	750 00						Equipment	15	750 00
20	439	Petty Cash	6/20	1947	34 00		8 00		10 00	16 00			
31		Totals			1,804 00	450 00	228 00	300 00	60 00	16 00			750 00
					(21)	(51)	(13)	(63)	(62)	(71)			(✓)

C. The payment of a voucher is recorded in a *check register*.

A check register replaces the cash payments journal discussed in Chapter 7. Each entry in the check register is recorded as a debit to Vouchers Payable and a credit to Cash (and Purchases Discounts when appropriate).

EXAMPLE 8-11: Under a typical voucher system, when an invoice for purchased merchandise is received, the person in charge of the voucher register prepares a voucher and attaches the purchase order, receiving report, and invoice. This information is presented to the duly authorized person, often the controller or assistant controller, for approval. In this example, the journal entry in the voucher register is a debit to Purchases and a credit to Vouchers Payable. After approval, the voucher is presented to the person in charge of the check register. This person records a debit to Vouchers Payable and a credit to Cash, writes the check, and marks the voucher paid so it cannot be used again.

D. The voucher system is a means of internal control over the payment and use of cash.

Although the voucher system presented in Section 8-5 may seem like a lot of work, it ensures that management is aware of where the company's money is being spent. It also controls the timing of payments, to ensure discounts are taken if this is company policy. Current information is also available for use in determining future cash needs, thus allowing management to make the best use of cash resources.

8-6. Marketable Securities

Cash that is not needed for immediate operations should be invested to earn a return. One way this can be accomplished is by investing idle cash in securities such as government or corporate bonds as cash or corporate stocks. These investments can be classified as current or noncurrent. Current investments will be discussed in this chapter. Noncurrent investments will be discussed in Chapter 16.

A. Two criteria must be met for an investment to qualify as a current investment.

For an investment to be current, it must be highly marketable. That is, it must be easily converted to cash. Furthermore, management must *intend* to make the security available for payment of current liabilities. That is, management must intend to make the security available for conversion to unrestricted cash as needed. Current investments are classified as a current asset on the balance sheet and usually are reported immediately following cash.

EXAMPLE 8-12: Crafty Carvers has accumulated a substantial amount of idle cash. To put this cash to work, the company purchased five Treasury Bonds for $1,000 each, and 60 percent of the stock of Strictly Steel, its major supplier of carving tools. The company's intention is to sell the bonds as cash is needed for operations and to hold the stock indefinitely to help ensure a steady supply of carving tools. The bonds would be classified as a current investment. They are readily marketable and management intends to convert them to cash as the need arises. The stock, on the other hand, is a noncurrent investment. Although it may be readily marketable, management intends to hold the stock beyond the current period.

B. Marketable securities are recorded at cost when purchased.

Normally, a brokerage fee is charged when you buy stocks or bonds. This brokerage fee is part of the cost of the marketable security.

EXAMPLE 8-13: Netherland Company has idle, excess cash and decides to buy 100 shares of ST&T common stock at $50 per share. The brokerage fee is $100. The general journal entry to record this purchase would be

July	4	Current Marketable Securities	5,100	
		Cash		5,100
		Purchased 100 shares of ST&T common stock at $50 per share plus brokerage fee of $100		

The current asset account, Current Marketable Securities, is increased $5,100 (cost of stock $50 × 100 shares = $5,000 + $100 brokerage fee), and Cash is decreased $5,100.

C. When marketable securities are sold, the net proceeds (cash received) are compared to the recorded cost and any gain or loss is recognized.

EXAMPLE 8-14: Netherland Company needs cash, so 50 shares of the ST&T stock purchased in Example 8-13 are sold for $60 per share. A brokerage fee of $70 is charged. The net proceeds are $2,930 ($60 × 50 shares = $3,000 − $70). The cost basis of the 50 shares is $51 per share ($5,100 ÷ 100 shares = $51 per share), for a total of $2,550 ($51 × 50 shares). Thus,

Proceeds	$2,930
Cost basis	− 2,550
Gain on sale	$ 380

The general journal entry to record this sale would be

Aug.	7	Cash	2,930	
		Current Marketable Securities		2,550
		Gain on Sale of Marketable Securities		380
		Sale of 50 shares of ST&T (purchased at $50 each plus $100 brokerage fee) for $60 each less $70 brokerage fee.		

Cash is increased $2,930, Current Marketable Securities is decreased $2,550, and revenue (the gain on the sale) is increased $380.

D. In addition to gains and losses on sale, current marketable securities may pay interest or dividends.

When revenue is received as interest or dividends, it should be recorded by a debit to Cash and a credit to an income account. At the end of an accounting period, if an investment has earned interest or a dividend has been declared but no cash has been received, a receivable account should be debited. Since interest or dividends are not taxable until received in cash, however, many companies do not record such earnings until received.

EXAMPLE 8-15: Netherland Company receives a $2 dividend per share on the 50 shares of ST&T stock. The general journal entry for this increase in revenue would be

Oct.	3	Cash	100	
		Dividend Income		100
		Dividend of $2 per share on 50 shares of ST&T		

Cash is increased $100 and revenue is increased $100.

E. At the end of an accounting period, current investments in marketable securities are valued at the *lower of cost or market*.

Current marketable securities are valued at the lower of cost or market on the balance sheet date to insure that these assets are not overvalued on the financial statements. At the end of each period, the current portfolio is divided into two classes: equity investments and all other (non-equity) investments. This is necessary because these two classes are treated differently. Although declines which are "other than temporary" must be recorded for both equity and non-equity investments, the treatment for equity investments restricts the computation on a stock-by-stock basis. The second difference is in the treatment of temporary declines. For equity securities, temporary declines in market value of the portfolio are recorded using an allowance account. Temporary declines in non-equity investments are not usually recorded.

1. *Equity investments*. First, for each equity security, compare the market value at the end of the accounting period with the recorded cost. If market is *below* cost and the decline is deemed to be *other than temporary*, record the decline as a loss by reducing the recorded cost of the security itself.

EXAMPLE 8-16: Assume that your company has invested in ten shares of MeToo Computers common stock at a cost of $75 per share. Because MeToo's product line has not captured an adequate share of the market, the price per share has dropped to $35 per share and is not expected to rise in the foreseeable future. The journal entry to record an adjustment to market would be

Dec. 6	Loss on Market Decline of Marketable Equity Securities	400	
	Current Marketable Securities		400
	To record an other than temporary decline in the market value of ten shares of MeToo stock below cost by $40 per share		

Next, compare the market value of the entire equity portfolio to its recorded cost as adjusted for other than temporary declines. If market value of the portfolio is *below* the portfolio's cost and the decline is deemed to be temporary, the decline is recorded in an allowance account and an unrealized loss account, as shown below.

Date	Unrealized Loss on Marketable Equity Securities	XXX	
	Allowance for Declines in Market Value of Current Marketable Equity Securities		XXX
	To record temporary decline in market value of current marketable equity securities		

The allowance account is a contra asset account that reduces the value of the current asset in the balance sheet. The unrealized loss is recognized as a loss on the income statement. Subsequent recoveries in market value of securities previously written down are recorded by debiting the allowance account and crediting a recovery account, as shown below.

Date	Allowance for Declines in Market Value of Current Marketable Equity Securities	XXX	
	Recovery in Market Value		XXX
	To record recovery in market value of current marketable equity securities		

Recoveries are only recorded up to the original cost of the securities.

EXAMPLE 8-17: On December 31, 19x1, the balance sheet date, Simco, Inc., compares the recorded cost of its current marketable equity securities to their current market value and a temporary decline of $100 in market value is determined. This decline is recorded as shown below.

19x1 Dec. 31	Unrealized Loss on Marketable Equity Securities	100	
	Allowance for Declines in Market Value of Current Marketable Equity Securities		100
	To record temporary decline in market value of current marketable equity securities		

On December 31, 19x2, another comparison shows that the market value of current marketable equity securities is now $150 below their recorded cost. The balance of the allowance account already reflects a decline of $100, so it is necessary to record a further decline of $50 ($150 − $100), so that the account shows a decline of $150 overall.

19x2 Dec. 31	Unrealized Loss on Marketable Equity Securities	50	
	Allowance for Declines in Market Value of Current Marketable Equity Securities		50
	To record further temporary decline in market value of current marketable equity securities		

On December 31, 19x3, a comparison of the recorded cost of the current marketable equity securities to their market value reveals that the securities are now valued at $50 above their recorded cost. The allowance account has a balance of $150, so it is necessary to record this recovery in market value *up to* the recorded cost of the securities, as shown below.

19x3 Dec. 31	Allowance for Declines in Market Value of Current Marketable Equity Securities	150	
	Recovery in Market Value		150
	To record recovery of temporary decline in market value of current marketable equity securities		

Note that the $150 is debited to the allowance account so that the allowance account now has a zero balance. The $50 gain above cost is not recorded. The $150 recorded in the recovery accounts offsets the $150 previously reported as unrealized losses on the income statement. The $150 recovery will be shown on the income statement to offset the previously recorded loss.

2. *Other non-equity investments.* Other than temporary declines in the market value of non-equity securities are also recorded as reductions in the cost of the investment (debit a loss account and credit the investment account). However, unlike equity securities, the other than temporary declines on other securities may be measured in three ways: by individual investment, by groups of investments, or in total. First, choose one of the measurement groupings. Then compare the market price at the end of the period with the recorded cost. If market is below cost for that group, record a loss by debiting Loss on Market Decline and crediting Current Marketable Non-Equity Securities. Temporary losses from declines in market value of non-equity securities are normally not recorded.

RAISE YOUR GRADES

Can you explain ...?

☑ the definition of cash for accounting purposes
☑ why internal control over cash is necessary
☑ why a petty cash fund is needed
☑ how petty cash is established and replenished
☑ when the Cash Short and Over account is used
☑ the difference between reconciling the balance per bank records and the balance per depositor's records
☑ which items in a bank reconciliation require journal entries
☑ how a voucher system operates as a means of internal control over cash disbursements
☑ how to adjust marketable securities to lower of cost or market
☑ the difference between accounting for temporary and other than temporary declines in market value of current marketable securities

SUMMARY

1. In accounting, cash is defined as those items that are commonly accepted as a medium of exchange.
2. Internal controls over cash are necessary to prevent misuse or theft of cash. Some means of internal control are a separation of duties, the use of safes and cash registers, daily deposits, disbursements of cash by check, the use of a petty cash fund, and a voucher system.
3. A petty cash fund should be established to control disbursements when it is not practical or acceptable to write a check.
4. To establish a petty cash fund, the Petty Cash account is debited and the Cash account is credited. To replenish a petty cash fund, the various expense accounts affected by the disbursements are debited and Cash is credited.
5. A Cash Short and Over account is used to record a shortage or overage of cash in the petty cash fund. Amounts in the Cash Short and Over account are reported as an expense on the income statement (for a debit balance), or as revenue on the income statement (for a credit balance).
6. Cash sales should be recorded every day in the cash receipts journal and included in the daily cash deposit to the bank. Any difference between the cash receipts total and the actual cash amount received is recorded in the Cash Short and Over account.
7. A bank reconciliation is an analysis explaining the difference between the cash balance reported in a bank statement and the balance of the Cash account in the depositor's general ledger.
8. The first step in preparing a bank statement is to bring the balance per bank statement up-to-date with the depositor's records. Any deposits in transit, outstanding checks, or bank errors must be added or subtracted from the bank statement balance to arrive at an adjusted balance.
9. The second step in preparing a bank statement is to bring the depositor's cash balance up-to-date with the bank statement records. Any items the bank has added to or subtracted from the depositor's account or errors in the depositor's records must be reconciled.
10. The adjusted balances shown for each section of the bank reconciliation must be equal. The depositor's Cash account must be adjusted for the items affecting the balance per the depositor's records.
11. Voucher systems may vary from company to company, but in general, they require the use of a voucher form authorizing the amount to be paid, a voucher register in which to record the

voucher and its date of payment, and a check register to record all payments by check number and amount.

12. Cash that is not needed for immediate operations should be invested to earn a return. One method of doing this is to invest in marketable securities.

13. Marketable securities may be either current or noncurrent. To be current, they must be easily converted to cash and management must intend to convert them to cash as the need arises. Current investments are classified as a current asset on the balance sheet. Noncurrent investments are reported as long-term investments on the balance sheet.

14. Marketable securities are recorded at cost when purchased, including any brokerage fees that may be charged for the purchase.

15. When marketable securities are sold, the net proceeds (cash received) are compared to the recorded cost and any gain or loss is recognized. Earnings of interest or dividends on marketable securities are recognized as income.

16. At the end of an accounting period, investments in current marketable equity securities are valued at the lower of cost or market. If there is a temporary decline in the value of current equity securities, an Allowance for Declines in Market Value account is used to record the decline and the unrealized loss is reported on the income statement. Other than temporary declines in the value of current marketable equity securities are recorded as reductions in the recorded cost of the investment. Gains above the original recorded cost of marketable securities are not recorded until the security is sold.

RAPID REVIEW   Answers

True or False

1. In accounting, the term cash includes checks, money orders, government bonds, and postage stamps. [Section 8-1]   *False*

2. Whenever possible, cash payments should be made by check. [Section 8-1]   *True*

3. The replenishment of petty cash includes a debit to the Petty Cash account. [Section 8-2]   *False*

4. If cash shortages are greater than cash overages, the Cash Short and Over account will have a debit balance. [Section 8-2]   *True*

5. Depositing cash daily is an internal control over cash. [Section 8-3]   *True*

6. Cash sales may not equal cash collected on cash sales. [Section 8-3]   *True*

7. The bank reconciliation should be prepared by a person who does not handle cash or cash transactions. [Section 8-4]   *True*

8. The main purpose of a bank reconciliation is to adjust the balance per depositor's records to the balance per bank. [Section 8-4]   *False*

9. To bring the Cash account in the general ledger up-to-date after the bank reconciliation has been prepared, a journal entry should be made for checks outstanding. [Section 8-4]   *False*

10. The voucher system provides a company with internal control over cash receipts. [Section 8-5]   *False*

11. When a voucher system is used, the person in charge of the check register will debit Vouchers Payable when a check is written. [Section 8-5]   *True*

12. Marketable securities purchased from idle cash to be held until cash is needed for operations should be classified as a long-term investment. [Section 8-6]   *False*

13. If proceeds from the sale of marketable securities exceed the cost basis, a gain should be recorded in the company's records. [Section 8-6]

True

SOLVED PROBLEMS

PROBLEM 8-1: The Drew Company controller, Suzy Drew, established a petty cash fund of $50 on September 10 to be held by B. Roach. Prepare the journal entry to record this transaction.

Answer:

Sept.	10	Petty Cash	50	00		
		Cash			50	00
		To establish petty cash fund authorized				
		by Suzy Drew, custodian B. Roach				

Petty Cash is increased by $50 and Cash is decreased by $50. Both are current assets. [Section 8-2]

PROBLEM 8-2: On September 30, the Drew Company's petty cash fund had vouchers of $8 for delivery charges, $12 for typewriter paper, $5 for flowers for a sick client, and $20 for repair of a broken office window. Cash on hand was $6. Suzy Drew verified and cancelled the vouchers. Prepare the journal entry to replenish the petty cash fund.

Answer:

Sept.	30	Delivery Expense	8	00		
		Supplies Expense	12	00		
		Miscellaneous Expense	5	00		
		Repair Expense	20	00		
		Cash Short and Over			1	00
		Cash			44	00
		To replenish petty cash, invoices verified				
		by Suzy Drew.				

The various expense accounts for which invoices were paid are debited for the appropriate amounts. You may have included delivery expense and repair expense in the Miscellaneous Expense account. When the invoices and cash are totaled, there is an overage of $1, which is credited to Cash Short and Over. Cash is credited for $44 to replenish the fund because there is $6 remaining in petty cash ($50 − $6 = $44). [Section 8-2]

PROBLEM 8-3: On December 1, Suzy Drew realized that a petty cash fund of $50 was insufficient. She authorized an increase of petty cash to $100. Prepare the journal entry to increase the fund.

Answer:

Dec.	1	Petty Cash	50	00		
		Cash			50	00
		To increase petty cash to $100 from				
		$50; authorized by Suzy Drew.				

The Petty Cash account for the Drew Company now has a $100 balance due to the decision to establish the petty cash fund at $50 and then to increase it by another $50. [Section 8-2]

PROBLEM 8-4: The owner of Mae's Dress Shop adds up the sales invoices for October 19. All sales are cash sales. The invoices total $562.50. The owner counts the cash collected for October 19. The cash collected totals $561.00. Prepare the journal entry to record the day's sales.

Answer:

Oct.	19	Cash	561	00		
		Cash Short and Over	1	50		
		Sales			562	50
		To record cash sales.				

The Cash Short and Over account is debited $1.50 because there is a shortage in the cash collected as compared to the sales invoices total. [Section 8-3]

PROBLEM 8-5: Determine the dollar amount that should be shown under the caption, Cash, on the balance sheet using the following information.

Cash on hand..	$ 52
Petty cash fund	50
IOU's from employees..	20
Cash in bank..	2,110
Traveler's check	25
Customer's NSF check being held until paid	45

_____

Answer:

Cash on hand	$ 52
Petty cash fund	50
Cash in bank	2,110
Traveler's check	25
Total cash as shown on balance sheet	$2,237

The IOU and the customer's NSF check do not qualify as cash. Both are receivables because they are owed to the company. [Section 8-1]

PROBLEM 8-6: You are assigned to prepare a bank reconciliation from the following information for Timms Company.

- The balance on the November 30 bank statement is $5,460.
- Received a memo from the Sunshine State Bank for service charges of $10.
- A deposit of $250 made November 30 did not appear on the bank statement.
- Checks written before November 30 that have not cleared the bank total $1,370.
- Check #721 was recorded in the cash payments journal for $39; the check was correctly written for $93 in payment of office supplies.
- A deposit was recorded in the cash receipts journal as a debit to Cash and a credit to Accounts Receivable of $230; the actual amount was $320 received from a customer on account.
- The company Cash account has a balance of $4,314.

Prepare the first part of the bank reconciliation reconciling the balance per bank.

Answer:

Timms Company
Bank Reconciliation
November 30, 19—

Balance per bank statement	$5,460
Add: Deposits in transit	250
	$5,710
Subtract: Checks outstanding	1,370
Adjusted balance	$4,340

Deposits in transit and checks outstanding are the only items listed because they are the only items recorded in the depositor's records that are not shown on the bank statement. No bank errors occurred. [Section 8-4]

PROBLEM 8-7: Using the information in Problem 8-6, prepare the second part of the bank reconciliation for Timms Company reconciling the bank statement balance per the depositor's records.

Answer:

Balance per depositor's records		$4,314
Add: Error in deposit ($320 − $230)		90
		$4,404
Subtract: Service charge	$10	
Error in Check #721 ($93 − $39)	54	64
Adjusted balance		$4,340

The deposit error is added because the amount entered that increased cash in the cash receipts journal was $230; it should have been $320. Thus, the Cash account is $90 less than it should be ($320 − $230), so $90 is added. The error in Check #721 is subtracted because the amount entered that decreased cash in the cash payments journal was $39; it should have been $93. Thus, the Cash account is $54 more than it should be ($93 − $29), so $54 is subtracted. The service charge of $10 is also subtracted from the depositor's cash balance. [Section 8-4]

PROBLEM 8-8: Using the information in Problem 8-7, prepare the journal entries to bring Cash to its corrected balance.

Answer:

Nov.	30	Cash	90	00		
		Accounts Receivable/Customer's Name			90	00
		Error in cash receipts journal;				
		recorded $320 receipt as $230.				
Nov.	30	Miscellaneous Expense	10	00		
		Office Supplies	54	00		
		Cash			64	00
		Bank service charge for Nov.; error in				
		recording Check #721 for $93 as $39.				

After posting, the Cash account balance in the general ledger will be $4,340. [Section 8-4]

PROBLEM 8-9: On November 6, the Ludwig Company decided to invest idle cash in 500 shares of stock in Ficus Company selling at $20 per share as a temporary investment. A brokerage fee of $500 was charged. Prepare the journal entry for this transaction.

Answer:

Nov.	6	Current Marketable Securities	10,500	00		
		Cash			10,500	00
		Purchased 500 shares of Ficus Company				
		stock at $20 per share as temporary				
		investment; $500 brokerage fee				

Note that the purchase price of the stock includes the brokerage fee. [Section 8-6]

PROBLEM 8-10: Ficus Company declared a dividend on December 20 of $.50 per share. The dividend will be paid on January 20. At Ludwig Company's year end, December 31, an adjusting entry is made to record the receivable. Prepare the journal entry that should be made at year end and on January 20 when the cash is received.

Answer:

Dec.	31	Dividend Receivable	250	00			
		Dividend Income			250	00	
		Dividend declared on investment in Ficus					
		Company stock, payable January 20					
Jan.	20	Cash	250	00			
		Dividend Receivable			250	00	
		Received dividend from Ficus Company,					
		declared December 20					

Since cash has not been received on December 31, the dividend is recorded as a receivable. [Section 8-5]

PROBLEM 8-11: On February 9 of the next year, Ludwig Company sold the stock for $9,800. A brokerage fee of $400 was charged. Prepare the journal entry for this transaction.

Answer:

Feb.	9	Cash	9,400	00			
		Loss on Sale of Marketable Securities	1,100	00			
		Current Marketable Securities			10,500	00	

The actual proceeds from the sale are $9,800 − $400 = $9,400. The loss on the sale is determined by subtracting the original cost of the stock from the amount received from the sale to get $1,100. [Section 8-6]

Cost basis	$10,500
Net proceeds	(9,400)
Loss on sale	$ 1,100

PROBLEM 8-12: Sims Company uses a voucher system. You are responsible for determining what accounts are debited and the amount of the credit to Vouchers Payable. Voucher #2351, dated June 14, is for an invoice for supplies. In examining the invoice, you determine that $150 is for paper bags for the store and $50 is for typewriter paper for the office. Prepare, in general journal form, the entry that would be made in the voucher register.

Answer: [Section 8-5]

June	14	Store Supplies	150	00			
		Office Supplies	50	00			
		Vouchers Payable				200	00
		Voucher #2351.					

PROBLEM 8-13: Voucher #2351, prepared in Problem 8-12, was approved and the person in charge of the check register paid the voucher on June 18, Check #7250. Prepare, in general journal form, the payment of the voucher.

Answer:

June	18	Vouchers Payable	200	00			
		Cash				200	00
		Voucher #2351, Check #7250.					

The entry in the check register will always include a debit to Vouchers Payable and a credit to Cash. The amounts may be different if a discount is taken. [Section 8-5]

PROBLEM 8-14: Make the journal entries necessary to record the following information.

1. On March 1, 19x2, Reed Corporation purchased 100 shares of Compuco stock at $10 per share as a current investment. A brokerage fee of $50 was charged.
2. On December 31, 19x2, the current market value of the Compuco stock was compared to the purchase price. A temporary decline of $100 in market value was determined.
3. On December 31, 19x3, a comparison of the current market value of the Compuco stock to the original purchase price revealed that there was a further temporary decline of $25 in the market value of the stock.
4. On December 31, 19x4, a comparison of the current market value of the Compuco stock to the original purchase price revealed that the market value of the stock was $50 above the purchase price.

Answer:

19x2 Mar.	1	Current Marketable Securities	1,050	00		
		Cash			1,050	00
		Purchased 100 shares of Compuco				
		stock at $10 per share plus				
		brokerage fee of $50				
Dec.	31	Unrealized Loss on Marketable Securities	100	00		
		Allowance for Declines in Market Value			100	00
		Temporary decline in market value of				
		current marketable securities				
19x3 Dec.	31	Unrealized Loss on Marketable Securities	25	00		
		Allowance for Declines in Market Value			25	00
		Temporary decline in market value of				
		current marketable securities				
19x4 Dec.	31	Allowance for Declines in Market Value	125	00		
		Recovery in Market Value			125	00
		Recovery of temporary decline in				
		market value of current marketable				
		securities				

Note that in the first entry, the brokerage fee is included in the purchase price of the stock. The market decline of $100 on December 31, 19x2 is recorded as a debit to the unrealized loss account and a credit to the allowance account. Since there is a market decline of $100 already recorded in the allowance account, then the further decline of $25 on December 31, 19x3 is recorded as a debit to the unrealized loss account and a credit to the allowance account of $25 ($125 − $100). The recovery of market value on December 31, 19x4 is recorded only *up to* the purchase price of the stock. Thus, the allowance account is debited for the $125 balance it holds and the recovery account is credited for the same amount. Gains in market value are not recorded until stock is sold. [Section 8-6]

PROBLEM 8-15: Apply the lower-of-cost-or-market principle to Big's Investment in the following marketable securities as of December 31. Big prefers to apply lower-of-cost-or-market on a group method; thus, you should try to minimize the number of computations. All the securities are available for conversion to unrestricted cash.

Company	Type	Cost	Market	Type change
Hitchhiker Guides	Common stock	$3,000	$2,000	Other than temporary
Vogon Accounting	Common stock	$6,325	$7,350	Other than temporary
Sheldon Plan	Common stock	$8,000	$7,800	Other than temporary
HAL Computers	Common stock	$1,000	$1,250	Temporary
Dune Spices	Common stock	$3,000	$2,300	Temporary
Galatic Books	Bonds	$1,500	$1,400	Other than temporary
Foundation	Bonds	$1,250	$1,300	Other than temporary
Wookie Cookies	Bonds	$1,750	$1,250	Temporary

Answer:

Dec.	31	Loss on Market Decline		1,200	00		
		Current Marketable Securities				1,200	00
		Other than temporary declines in the					
		market value of Hitchhiker Guides and					
		Sheldon Plan applied individually as					
		required (−$1,000 − $200)					
Dec.	31	Unrealized Loss on Marketable Securities		450	00		
		Allowance for Declines in Market Value				450	00
		Temporary changes in market value of					
		equity securities, HAL Computers and					
		Dune Spices, applied in aggregate as					
		required (−$700 + $250)*					
Dec.	31	Loss on Market Decline		50	00		
		Current Marketable Securities				50	00
		Other than temporary declines in the					
		market value of non-equity securities,					
		Galatic Books and Foundation, applied					
		on an aggregate basis as permitted					
		(−$100 + 50)**					

** Note that temporary losses on non-equity securities are not recorded. [Section 8-6]

	Cost	Market
* HAL Computers	$1,000	$1,250
Dune Spices	3,000	2,300
	$4,000	$3,550
Total Cost	$4,000	
Total Market	(3,550)	
Unrealized loss	$ 450	

9 SHORT-TERM RECEIVABLES, PAYABLES, AND PAYROLL

THIS CHAPTER IS ABOUT

☑ Accounts Receivable and Bad Debts
☑ Notes Receivable
☑ Accounts and Notes Payable
☑ Payroll Accounting

9-1. Accounts Receivable and Bad Debts

A. Accounts receivable are amounts owed to the company by customers who agree to pay at a later date for goods or services purchased.

The time period for payment of an account is usually 30 days after the customer is billed. A business normally evaluates a customer's financial condition before extending credit. Despite precautions, some uncollectible accounts (bad debts) arise.

B. Estimated uncollectible accounts receivable affect the balance sheet and the income statement.

The estimate of uncollectible accounts receivable is based on past experience. The estimated amount of bad debts expense should be matched against current revenues on the income statement according to the matching principle. Accounts Receivable should be reduced on the balance sheet by the amount estimated to be uncollectible. Rather than reduce Accounts Receivable directly, the estimate is recorded as a credit in a separate contra asset account called Allowance for Bad Debts (sometimes called Allowance for Uncollectible Accounts). The Allowance for Bad Debts account is a balance sheet account. It is a valuation account reducing Accounts Receivable to the expected net realizable value. A valuation account is used because the actual uncollectible accounts receivable are unknown at the time the estimate is made. When individual accounts are determined to be uncollectible, the allowance account will be debited and Accounts Receivable will be credited.

EXAMPLE 9-1: An adjusting entry is made to recognize the amount estimated to be uncollectible. The adjusting entry is shown below.

Date	Bad Debts Expense	XXX	
	Allowance for Bad Debts		XXX
	To set an allowance for the estimated		
	uncollectible accounts for the period.		

C. There are two approaches used to estimate bad debts expense.

1. *The income statement approach.* The income statement approach uses sales (an income statement account) to estimate bad debts. The estimate can be based on a percentage of total sales or on a percentage of credit sales. Total sales can be used to estimate bad debts expense if the relationship between cash sales and credit sales is fairly stable over time. Since bad debts cannot be incurred on cash sales, however, the use of only credit sales will provide a better estimate.

EXAMPLE 9-2: To illustrate the income statement approach, assume that credit sales for the year were $200,000. Assume also that based on past experience, approximately 3% of credit sales are estimated to be uncollectible. The adjusting entry for estimated bad debts expense is shown below.

Date	Bad Debts Expense	6,000	
	Allowance for Bad Debts		6,000
	Adjusting entry ($200,000 × .03)		

2. *The balance sheet approach.* The balance sheet approach uses a percentage of outstanding accounts receivable or an aging of accounts receivable schedule to estimate bad debts expense. Estimating bad debts expense using the balance sheet approach requires adjusting the Allowance for Bad Debts account to equal the estimate of current uncollectible accounts receivable.

(a) *Percentage of outstanding accounts receivable.* The estimate of bad debts expense can be based on a percentage of outstanding accounts receivable.

EXAMPLE 9-3: Assume that the allowance account has a credit balance of $500 before an adjusting entry is made for the current year. The outstanding accounts receivable balance is $120,000. It is estimated that 4% will be uncollectible, or $4,800 ($120,000 × .04). The $4,800 is the amount necessary to reduce accounts receivable on the balance sheet to its estimated net realizable value. Since the allowance account has a credit balance of $500 left over from the previous year, the amount of the adjusting entry will be $4,300 ($4,800 − $500). The adjusting entry is shown below.

Date	Bad Debt Expense	4,300	
	Allowance for Bad Debts		4,300
	To adjust accounts receivable to their net realizable value		

After the adjusting entry, the Allowance for Bad Debts account appears as follows:

Allowance for Bad Debts

500	*balance before adjusting entry*
4,300	*adjusting entry*
4,800	*balance*

(b) *Aging of accounts receivable schedule.* An aging schedule is based on the due date of the accounts. A scale of percentages is applied to the accounts. This scale is based on the experience of the company in collecting on accounts due within each payment period. The estimate is then deducted from Accounts Receivable to determine its net realizable value.

An example of an aging schedule is illustrated below.

AGING OF ACCOUNTS RECEIVABLE SCHEDULE

		Length of Time Outstanding				
Customer	Balance 12/31	1–30 Days	31–60 Days	61–90 Days	91–120 Days	120+ Days
Taylor Co.	$ 20,000	$10,000	$10,000			
O'Neal Manuf.	12,000	5,000	3,000	$4,000		
Fries Co.	35,000		35,000			
Reyer Co.	13,000	13,000				
Spotts, Inc.	40,000	35,000		1,000	$2,500	$1,500
Total	$120,000	$63,000	$48,000	$5,000	$2,500	$1,500

ESTIMATED UNCOLLECTIBLES

Age	Account Balance	× Estimated % Uncollectible =	Estimated Amount of Uncollectibles
Under 30 days	$ 63,000	2%	$1,260
31–60 days	48,000	6%	2,880
61–90 days	5,000	12%	600
91–120 days	2,500	20%	500
Over 120 days	1,500	50%	750
	$120,000		$5,990

This summary indicates a balance of $5,990 is required for the Allowance for Bad Debts account. Assuming again that the Allowance for Bad Debts account has a credit balance of $500 remaining from the previous year, the adjusting entry would be

Date	Bad Debts Expense	5,490	
	Allowance for Bad Debts		5,490
	To adjust accounts receivable to their net realizable value ($5,990–$500)		

Remember, when using the balance sheet approach, the amount of the adjusting entry must be reduced if there is is an existing credit balance in the Allowance for Bad Debts account and increased if there is a debit balance. The balance in the Allowance for Bad Debts account after the adjusting entry should be equal to the estimate of uncollectible accounts receivable. After the adjusting entry, the Allowance for Bad Debts account appears as follows:

Allowance for Bad Debts

	500	*balance before adjusting entry*
	5,490	*adjusting entry*
	5,990	*balance 12/31*

D. Some companies use the direct write-off method to determine bad debts expense.

The *direct write-off method* does not attempt to match expenses with revenue. No estimate is made of uncollectible accounts receivable at year end. Instead, the company waits until the account receivable is determined to be worthless before recording an expense. This method is not acceptable for accrual accounting unless the amount of bad debts is immaterial.

EXAMPLE 9-4: Happy Company does not estimate bad debts expense. Instead, accounts are written off directly to expense when they are determined to be worthless. The company has just learned that a credit customer, Joe Smith, is bankrupt and no payments are likely. The journal entry to write off the account receivable is shown below.

Date	Bad Debts Expense	200	
	Accounts Receivable/Joe Smith		200
	To write off account receivable due		
	to bankruptcy		

9-2. Notes Receivable

A. Notes Receivable are written promises (*promissory notes*) by the borrower (*maker*) to pay a definite sum of money on a specific date or on demand.

Notes are used to extend credit to customers or to grant additional time to pay past due accounts. Notes usually earn interest.

EXAMPLE 9-5: An illustration of a promissory note appears below. Thomas Jones promises to pay Kimberly Company $1,000 plus 12% interest on March 1 (the *maturity date*). Jones is the *maker* of the note. Kimberly Company is the *payee*.

$1,000   *September 1, 19x1*

_____*Six months*_____   after this date I promise to

pay to the order of

_____*Kimberly Company*_____

_____*One thousand and no/100*_____   dollars

for value received with interest at _____*12%*_____   payable

at _____*National Bank of Orlando*_____

#146 Due *March 1, 19x2*   *Thomas Jones*

B. *Interest* is a charge made for the use of money over a period of time.

Interest is revenue to the payee and expense to the maker. Interest rates are usually stated for a one-year period, regardless of the actual time period of the note. Thus, interest on a $1,000 note at 12% for one year is $120 ($1,000 × .12). The interest on the same note for 3 months (3/12 of the year) would be $30 ($120 × 3/12).

EXAMPLE 9-6: Interest is calculated below for the note illustrated in Example 9-5.

	Principal	Annual Rate	Time Note is
Interest =	of the Note ×	of Interest ×	Outstanding
Interest =	$1,000 ×	.12 ×	6/12
Interest =	$60		

The principal of the note ($1,000) plus the interest ($60) will be payable on March 1.

If the term of the note is expressed in days, the exact number of days is used in calculating the interest. To simplify the calculations in this chapter, 360 days in a year is assumed.

EXAMPLE 9-7: Assume that the note illustrated in Example 9-5 is due in 180 days. The interest on the note is calculated below.

$$\text{Interest} = \$1,000 \times .12 \times 180/360$$
$$\text{Interest} = \$60$$

C. Notes receivable are recorded in a Notes Receivable account in the general ledger.

The face amount of the note is recorded in the Notes Receivable account. Interest on a note receivable is revenue. An adjusting entry is made if the accounting period ends before the note matures.

EXAMPLE 9-8: Kimberly Company will record the note receivable in Example 9-5 as follows:

Sept. 1	Notes Receivable		1,000	
	Sales			1,000
	Sold merchandise, terms 6-month,			
	12% note to Thomas Jones			

EXAMPLE 9-9: To record the interest revenue on the note illustrated in Example 9-5, assume that Kimberly Company's accounting period ends on December 31. At that time, four months' interest has accrued. The journal entry to record the interest would be

Dec. 31	Interest Receivable		40	
	Interest Revenue			40
	Adjusting entry to record accrued			
	interest revenue ($1,000 ×			
	.12 × 4/12) on note			
	of Thomas Jones			

When Thomas Jones pays the note and interest on March 1, the following journal entry will be made.

Mar. 1	Cash		1,060	
	Notes Receivable			1,000
	Interest Receivable			40
	Interest Revenue			20
	To record collection of note and			
	interest from Thomas Jones			

Note that the accrued interest revenue was recorded on December 31, even though the interest had not been paid. The revenue should be recognized in the accounting period in which it is *earned* as required by the revenue realization principle. On March 1, when the full amount of interest is received, Interest Receivable is credited for the $40. The interest for January and February is recognized by crediting Interest Revenue for $20 ($1,000 × .12 × 2/12).

D. Occasionally, the maker of a note does not pay the note when it matures.

When a note passes the maturity date and it has not been paid, the note becomes *dishonored*. The dishonored note should then be transferred to Accounts Receivable along with the interest due. The dishonored note is thus recorded in the individual customer's account for future guidance in extending any further credit to the customer.

EXAMPLE 9-10: To record a dishonored note, assume Thomas Jones does not pay the note illustrated in Example 9-5 when it matures on March 1. The note would be transferred to Accounts Receivable as illustrated below.

Mar. 1	Accounts Receivable/Thomas Jones		1,060	
	Notes Receivable			1,000
	Interest Receivable			40
	Interest Revenue			20
	To record Thomas Jones'			
	dishonored note of $1,000,			
	dated September 1			

The amount transferred to Accounts Receivable includes the interest because Thomas Jones owes both the principal and the interest, and Accounts Receivable should reflect the full amount owed. If the probability of collection is low, provision should be made when computing bad debts expense at the end of the year.

E. Sometimes a company has an unexpected need for cash and decides to *discount* (sell) the note at a bank.

The payee discounts the note to a bank in exchange for cash. The bank holds the note until it matures and then collects the principal and interest from the maker. If the payee guarantees payment at maturity, the note is said to be *discounted with recourse*. During the period that the bank holds the note, the payee has a *contingent liability*. This means that if the maker pays the bank, the company (payee) has no liability. However, if the maker dishonors the note, then the company has an actual liability for the maturity value of the note.

The *discount rate* (interest rate) charged by the bank is computed on the maturity value of the note *for the period of time that the bank will hold the note*. The amount of the cash proceeds paid to the payee is the excess of the maturity value over the discount.

EXAMPLE 9-11: To illustrate discounting a note receivable, assume Kimberly Company receives a 90-day, 10% note for $5,000 from Jane Guy on June 16. On July 16, Kimberly Company discounts the note at a bank. The discount rate charged by the bank is 12%. The calculation of the cash proceeds from the bank is shown below.

Face value of note dated June 16	$5,000.00
Interest due at maturity (90 days at 10%)	
$5,000 × .10 × 90/360	125.00
Maturity value of note due Sept. 14.......................................	$5,125.00
Discount period—July 16 to Sept. 14 .... 60 days	
Discount on maturity value	
$5,125 × .12 × 60/360	102.50
Proceeds	$5,022.50

The entry on Kimberly Company's books to record this transaction is shown below. Note that the excess of the proceeds received from discounting the note over the face value of the note is recorded as Interest Revenue.

July 16	Cash	5,022.50	
	Notes Receivable		5,000.00
	Interest Revenue		22.50
	Discounted Jane Guy's note at the bank at a 12% discount rate		

If the proceeds received by Kimberly Company had been less than the face value of the note, the company would record the excess of the face value over the proceeds as Interest Expense.

9-3. Accounts and Notes Payable

A. Accounts payable represent amounts owed to suppliers for the purchase of goods or services.

The credit period for payment of an account payable is usually 30 days.

EXAMPLE 9-12: Assume that a purchase of office supplies for $120 was made on credit. To record the purchase,

Date	Office Supplies	120	
	Accounts Payable		120
	To record purchase of office supplies on account		

B. Notes payable represent amounts owed for the purchase of merchandise, equipment, past-due accounts payable, bank loans, and so on.

A note payable is a liability to the maker and an asset (note receivable) to the payee. In Example 9-5, the promissory note is a note receivable for Kimberly Company and a note payable for Thomas Jones.

EXAMPLE 9-13: To illustrate the recording of a note payable, assume that on May 1, Petta Food Company borrows $10,000 from National Bank for six months at an annual interest rate of 12%. The journal entry to record the note would be

May	1	Cash	10,000	
		Notes Payable		10,000
		Borrowed $10,000 for 6 months at 12% interest		

Assume Petta Food's fiscal year ends September 30. It is necessary to record the amount of interest expense incurred at the end of the fiscal year. Thus, on September 30, the following adjusting entry will be made.

Sept.	30	Interest Expense	500	
		Interest Payable		500
		To record accrued interest for 5 months ($10,000 $\times$ .12 $\times$ 5/12)		

The note will appear on Petta Food's September 30 balance sheet as follows:

Current liabilities:
Notes payable $10,000
Interest payable 500

The entry to record the payment of the note on November 1 will be

Nov.	1	Notes Payable	10,000	
		Interest Payable	500	
		Interest Expense	100	
		Cash		10,600
		To record payment of 12%, 6-month note and recognize interest expense for one month ($10,000 $\times$ .12 $\times$ 1/12)		

Note that when the note is paid, Interest Payable is debited for the amount of the liability recorded on September 30. The liability for Interest Payable no longer exists because Petta Food is paying the bank the $500 along with the $10,000 principal and the interest expense for October. The interest expense for October is debited to Interest Expense.

C. Interest is not always stated separately on a note.

Up until now, the promissory notes discussed have been *interest bearing notes,* so called because the face of the note specifies, or bears, the interest rate. Sometimes, however, the amount of interest to be charged is included in the face amount of the note. No reference is made to a specific interest rate. Such notes are called *non interest-bearing notes.*

EXAMPLE 9-14: Assume the same facts as stated in Example 9-13 with one exception—the interest is included in the face amount of the note. The note is shown on page 188.

```
┌─────────────────────────────────────────────────────────────────┐
│  Sanford, Florida                              May 1, 19—        │
│  Six months            after this date,   Petta Food Company     │
│                                                                   │
│  promises to pay National Bank ____ ten thousand ____            │
│                                                                   │
│  ____ and no/100 ____                                            │
│                                          George Stively          │
│                                          Diane Rodriguez         │
│  # 14                                                            │
└─────────────────────────────────────────────────────────────────┘
```

Note that interest of $600 ($10,000 × .12 × 6/12) is included in the face amount and the interest rate is not shown. The cash received by Petta Foods is $9,400 ($10,000 − $600). The interest was deducted in advance by the bank. The $600 represents future interest expense to Petta Food Company. This amount is debited to a contra liability account, Discount on Notes Payable. The face value of the note is always the amount recorded in Notes Payable. To record the note

May	1	Cash	9,400	
		Discount on Notes Payable	600	
		Notes Payable		10,000
		Borrowed $10,000 for 6 months, discounted at $600		

On September 30, the end of the fiscal year, the following adjusting entry will be made.

Sept. 30	Interest Expense	500	
	Discount on Notes Payable		500
	To record interest expense for 5 months		

As mentioned before, the Discount on Notes Payable account represents future interest. As the interest becomes due, the discount account is reduced and the expense is recognized on the income statement. The process of reducing the discount is called *amortization*.

The note will appear on Petta Food's September 30 balance sheet as shown below.

Current liabilities:
Notes payable $10,000
Less: Discount on notes payable 100 $9,900

When the note is repaid on November 1, the entry will be

Nov.	1	Notes Payable	10,000	
		Interest Expense	100	
		Discount on Notes Payable		100
		Cash		10,000
		To record payment of note and recognize interest expense for one month		

9-4. Payroll Accounting

A. The cost of labor (wages, salaries, and fringe benefits) and the related payroll taxes are a major expense for most companies.

Accounting for payroll is important because it is such a large expense and because of the government regulations that relate to payroll records. Payroll records are maintained for employees only. Employees are under the supervision and direction of the company. Others, such as independent contractors, may offer their services to a company, but they are not under the direct control of the company. Thus, no payroll records are kept for such workers.

B. The total compensation earned by an employee for a pay period is called *gross pay*.

Gross pay is the amount earned by an employee before any required or authorized deductions are made. A company may pay an overtime rate for hours worked in excess of the normal work day or week. Some companies pay a premium for work on night shifts, holidays, and Sundays.

EXAMPLE 9-15: Amy Jamison receives a regular wage of $6 per hour for a 40-hour week. She receives one and one-half times her regular wage ($9) for any hours in excess of 40. She receives twice her regular wage ($12) for holidays and Sundays. Last week she worked a total of 52 hours. Four of the hours were on Sunday. Her gross pay for the week is calculated below.

$$\begin{array}{rl}
40 \text{ hours} \times \ \ \$6 \text{ per hour} = & \$240 \\
8 \text{ hours} \times \ \ \$9 \text{ per hour} = & 72 \\
4 \text{ hours} \times \$12 \text{ per hour} = & \underline{\ \ 48} \\
\text{Gross pay} & \underline{\underline{\$360}}
\end{array}$$

C. An employee receives less than gross pay because of deductions required by law or deductions made at the request of the employee.

The amount the employee receives after all deductions are made from gross pay is called *net pay* or *take-home pay*. There are four deductions commonly made from gross pay.

1. *Federal income tax.* The federal government requires employers to withhold federal income taxes from each employee. The amount deducted depends on the employee's gross pay, marital status, and the number of exemptions claimed. Each employee is required by law to complete a Form W-4, Employee's Withholding Allowance Certificate. The number of exemptions is indicated on this form. Tables are provided by the Internal Revenue Service (IRS) to help employers calculate the amount of federal income tax to be withheld. The amount withheld is remitted by the employer to the IRS.
2. *Social security tax.* The Federal Insurance Contributions Act (FICA) provides retirement, disability, survivor, and medical benefits to those who qualify. FICA tax is paid by both the employee and the employer. The employee's is deducted from gross pay. The employer must pay a like amount on each employee. Because of financial problems with the Social Security Program, both the tax rate and the earnings subject to tax have increased in recent years. For illustration purposes, a tax rate of 7% up to a maximum income of $36,000 will be assumed.

EXAMPLE 9-16: To illustrate the calculation of FICA tax, use the data from Example 9-15 for Amy Jamison. This year-to-date, Amy has earned $12,500; therefore, the full amount of her gross pay for this pay period of $360 is subject to the 7% FICA tax. (Remember, gross pay is taxable up to $36,000 in earnings.) Thus,

$$\$360 \times .07 = \$25.20 \text{ (FICA tax)}$$

The employer will also pay $25.20 in FICA tax for Amy. The total FICA tax is therefore $50.40. The employer remits the FICA tax along with the federal income tax.

3. *State income tax.* Most states have state income taxes. The procedure for withholding state income tax is similar to the federal income tax withholding, with tables provided by the state to help employers calculate the amount of state tax to be withheld.
4. *Other deductions.* Other deductions may include group insurance, pension plans, union dues, and savings plans. The employer acts as a collection agent, remitting the deduction to the proper sources.

EXAMPLE 9-17: The calculation of Amy's net pay is shown below. Her gross pay is $360 (Example 9-15). FICA tax is $25.20 (Example 9-16). Assume the federal income tax is $35.10. There is no state tax where Amy resides. In addition, she has a deduction for hospitalization of $8.50 and a savings plan deduction of $25.00.

Gross pay		$360.00
Deductions:		
Federal income tax	$35.10	
FICA tax	25.20	
Hospitalization	8.50	
Savings plan	25.00	93.80
Net pay		$266.20

If we assume Amy is the only employee, the journal entry that the company will make to record the week's payroll is

Date	Salaries Expense	360.00	
	Federal Income Tax Payable		35.10
	FICA Tax Payable		25.20
	Hospitalization Premium Payable		8.50
	Savings Plan Withholding Payable		25.00
	Salaries Payable		266.20
	To record weekly payroll		

Amy's gross pay is recorded as a debit to Salaries Expense. The tax liability, other withholdings, and net earnings payable are recorded as credits to their proper liability accounts.

D. A payroll register (or journal) may be used to summarize the payroll data for employees.

A payroll register is used as an aid in the calculation of employees' net earnings and in determining the summary amounts to be posted to the appropriate accounts. The design of a payroll register varies according to the number of deductions, overtime, and so forth, required for a company's employees. A typical payroll register is illustrated on page 191. The information recorded in the illustrated payroll register is evident from the columnar headings. Vacant amount columns for FICA deductions in the illustration indicate that the employee's year-to-date earnings exceed the maximum earnings subject to FICA withholding.

E. In addition to the taxes paid by the employee, the employer must pay taxes on employees' gross pay.

There are three major taxes that employers must pay on employees' gross pay.

1. *Federal unemployment tax.* The Federal Unemployment Tax Act (FUTA) requires the employer to pay federal unemployment tax on all employees. This tax is normally levied against employers. This means the employer must pay this amount in addition to the gross salary of the employee. The proceeds from the tax are used to pay for programs offering temporary relief to unemployed persons. The tax is 6.2% on the first $7,000 of wages paid in a year to each employee; however, the employer is allowed a credit against the federal tax for unemployment taxes paid to the state. The maximum credit allowed is 5.4%. The federal tax is thus .8% (6.2% − 5.4%). As with the FICA tax, the rate and maximum amount taxable are subject to change by Congress.

2. *State unemployment tax.* The state unemployment compensation laws differ among the various states. Those unemployed workers eligible to receive unemployment compensation are paid out of the state fund provided by the credit allowed against the federal unemployment tax for taxes paid to the state.

3. *FICA tax.* As mentioned previously, the employer pays FICA tax equal to the amount deducted from the employee's gross pay. As with the unemployment taxes, it cannot be deducted from the employee's salary, but rather is paid in addition to the amount paid by the employee.

PAYROLL REGISTER

Week Ended November 18, 19—

Name	Total Hours	Earnings Regular Pay	Earnings Overtime Pay	Earnings Total	Deductions FICA	Federal Income Tax	Hospital Ins.	Savings Plan	Union Dues	Total Deduction	Payment Net Pay	Check No.	Account Debited Sales Salaries Expense	Office Salaries Expense
Austin, Nancy	40	450 00		450 00	31 50	58 50	10 00	22 50		122 50	327 50	781		450 00
Bates, Maria	41	650 00	22 00	672 00		100 80	10 00	33 60		144 40	527 60	782	672 00	
Carifo, Bernie	40	350 00		350 00	24 50	38 50	18 00		10 00	91 00	259 00	783		350 00
Grunwald, Ann	40	800 00		800 00		144 00	15 00	40 00		199 00	601 00	784	800 00	
Petty, Tony	40	350 00		350 00	24 50	38 50	10 00		10 00	83 00	267 00	785		350 00
Sanchez, Rob	41	500 00	18 00	518 00	36 26	72 52	12 00	25 00		145 78	372 22	786	518 00	
Simpson, Joan	43	350 00	50 00	400 00	28 00	48 00	10 00	16 00	10 00	112 00	288 00	787		400 00
Total		3,450 00	90 00	3,540 00	144 76	500 82	85 00	137 10	30 00	897 68	2,642 32		1,990 00	1,550 00

* Note that FICA tax was not withheld from Bates or Grunwald. Their earnings for the year-to-date exceeded the maximum earnings subject to FICA tax

191

EXAMPLE 9-18: To illustrate how the taxes that the employer must pay are determined, assume that Semco Products has three employees. Payroll information is shown below.

Employee	Gross Pay Current Period	Gross Pay Year-to-Date	Federal Unemployment Tax	State Unemployment Tax	FICA Tax
James Lindsay	$ 600	$9,000	$–0–	$ –0–	$ 42.00
Ruth Taylor	540	5,600	4.32	29.16	37.80
Michael Ewald	450	4,900	3.60	24.30	31.50
Total	$1,590		$7.92	$53.46	$111.30

The calculations to determine the amount of federal unemployment tax, state unemployment tax, and FICA tax withholdings for each employee are shown below.

	James	Ruth	Michael
Federal Unemployment Tax	–0–	$540 × .008 = $ 4.32	$450 × .008 = $ 3.60
State Unemployment Tax	–0–	$540 × .054 = $29.16	$450 × .054 = $24.30
FICA Tax	$600 × .07 = $42.00	$540 × .07 = $37.80	$450 × .07 = $31.50

Note that James Lindsay has earned $9,000 to date. Federal and state unemployment taxes are paid on wages up to a maximum of $7,000; therefore, no tax will be assessed during this pay period or for the balance of the year for Lindsay. Ruth Taylor and Michael Ewald have not earned the maximum of $7,000. The employer must pay the tax for these employees.

The entry to record the payroll tax expense for the week and the liability for the employer payroll taxes accrued by Semco Products is shown below.

Date	Payroll Tax Expense	172.68	
	Federal Unemployment Tax Payable		7.92
	State Unemployment Tax Payable		53.46
	FICA Tax Payable		111.30
	To record payroll taxes for current pay period		

Note that the total expense incurred by a company to employ an individual is the combination of the employee's gross salary and the employer's payroll taxes.

RAISE YOUR GRADES

Can you explain...?

☑ both the income statement approach and the balance sheet approach to calculating bad debts expense

☑ how to record notes receivable and notes payable with interest stated separately and with interest included in the face amount

☑ how to calculate interest

☑ how to calculate the proceeds for a note discounted at the bank

☑ how to calculate gross pay and net pay

☑ the difference between employee payroll taxes and employer payroll taxes

SUMMARY

1. Accounts receivable are amounts owed to a company by customers who agree to pay at a later date for goods or services purchased.
2. Some accounts receivable usually will not be collected and are referred to as uncollectible accounts receivable or bad debts.

3. Bad debts should be estimated at the end of the accounting period. The adjusting entry debits Bad Debts Expense and credits Allowance for Bad Debts (a contra asset account).

4. Two approaches used to estimate bad debts expense are the income statement approach and the balance sheet approach.

5. The income statement approach is based on a percentage of either total sales or total credit sales. A percentage of total credit sales generally provides a better estimate.

6. The balance sheet approach is based on a percentage of outstanding accounts receivable or on the aging of accounts receivable. The Allowance for Bad Debts account is adjusted to equal the estimate of current uncollectible accounts receivable.

7. A promissory note is a written promise to pay a definite sum of money on a specific date or on demand.

8. Notes receivable are used to extend credit to customers or to grant additional time to pay past due accounts.

9. Notes receivable and notes payable are recorded at their face value.

10. A note with an interest rate stated on its face is called an interest bearing note. A note that includes interest in the face amount without reference to the interest rate is called a non-interest bearing note. If stated, rates are usually for a one-year period based on 12 months. Interest can also be stated for an exact number of days.

11. Interest revenue and interest expense are recorded when received or paid and as a year-end adjustment if the accounting period ends before the note matures.

12. If the interest is included in the face amount, the interest is recorded in a discount account and amortized to Interest Expense over the life of the note.

13. A dishonored note is usually transferred to Accounts Receivable and written off as a bad debts expense, if it is not collected.

14. A note can be discounted (sold) at a bank for the maturity value of the note less the discount rate (interest) charged by the bank.

15. The cost of labor (wages, salaries, and fringe benefits) and the related payroll taxes are a major expense for most companies.

16. The total compensation earned by an employee for a pay period is called gross pay. The amount an employee receives after all deductions have been made from gross pay is called net pay.

17. Common deductions from gross pay are federal income tax, FICA tax, state income tax, and other deductions such as group insurance, pension plans, union dues, or savings plans.

18. The employer must pay taxes in addition to the employee's gross pay. Three major taxes that employers must pay are federal unemployment tax, state unemployment tax, and FICA tax.

RAPID REVIEW

Short Answer

1. What are the two approaches used to estimate bad debts expense? [Section 9-1]

2. How does the direct write-off method of determining bad debts expense differ from the allowance method? [Section 9-1]

3. What accounting principle makes the allowance method of determining bad debts expense preferable to the direct write-off method? [Section 9-1]

4. What is a note receivable? [Section 9-2]

5. What accounting principle requires an adjusting entry to record interest revenue on a note receivable if the accounting period ends before the note matures? [Section 9-2]

6. Calculate the total interest on a $5,000, 6-month note with a 14% interest rate. [Section 9-2]

7. If a company discounts (sells) a note receivable to a bank, could the company have a liability? [Section 9-2]

8. When a note (payable or receivable) is issued, how is the note recorded? [Sections 9-2 and 9-3]

9. When interest is included in the face amount (not stated separately), how is the future interest expense on a note payable recorded? [Section 9-2]

10. What is the difference between gross pay and net pay? [Section 9-4]

11. Is federal unemployment tax and state unemployment tax deducted from an employee's gross pay? [Section 9-4]

12. Is FICA tax (Social Security) deducted from gross pay or in addition to it? [Section 9-4]

Answers:

1. The balance sheet approach and the income statement approach.

2. Direct write-off does not require that an estimate be made of bad debts expense at the end of the accounting period. An individual account receivable is written off at the time it is determined to be uncollectible by debiting Bad Debts Expense and crediting Accounts Receivable.

3. The matching principle.

4. A note receivable is a promissory note, usually interest bearing, given by the borrower promising to pay a definite sum of money on a specific date or on demand.

5. The revenue realization principle.

6. $5,000 × 14% × 6/12 = $350.

7. Yes. If the note is discounted with recourse, the company has a contingent liability until the note matures. If the maker defaults, the company has an actual liability for the maturity value of the note.

8. At the face amount.

9. Future interest expense on a note payable is recorded as a debit to Discount on Notes Payable.

10. Gross pay is the amount earned by an employee before deductions for federal income tax, FICA tax, etc., are made. Net pay (take-home pay) is the amount received by the employee after deductions.

11. No. The employer must pay federal and state unemployment taxes based on the employee's gross earnings.

12. Both. The employer pays an amount equal to the amount withheld from the employee's gross pay.

SOLVED PROBLEMS

PROBLEM 9-1: The unadjusted trial balance at the end of the current year includes the following accounts.

Accounts Receivable	$90,000	
Allowance for Bad Debts		$ 300 *(credit)*
Sales	$400,000	

Calculate the bad debts expense based on the following independent assumptions.

1. Bad debts expense is estimated to be 1% of total sales.
2. Bad debts expense is estimated to be 2% of credit sales (credit sales equal 60% of total sales).
3. 3% of accounts receivable are estimated to be uncollectible.

Answer: [Section 9-1]

1. $400,000 (total sales)
   ×   .01
   $ 4,000 (estimate of bad debts expense—amount of adjusting entry)

2. $400,000 (total sales)
   ×   .60
   $240,000 (credit sales)
   ×   .02
   $ 4,800 (estimate of bad debts expense—amount of adjusting entry)

3. $ 90,000 (Accounts Receivable)
   ×   .03
   $ 2,700 (estimated uncollectible accounts receivable)

   $ 2,700 (estimate)
   −   300 (credit balance in Allowance for Bad Debts accounts)
   $ 2,400 (amount of adjusting entry)

PROBLEM 9-2: Streaker Company accepted a $1,000, 90-day, 12% note receivable. Calculate the interest Streaker Company will receive on the maturity date of the note.

Answer: [Section 9-2]

$$\text{Interest} = \frac{\text{Principal}}{\text{of the Note}} \times \frac{\text{Annual Rate}}{\text{of Interest}} \times \frac{\text{Time Note}}{\text{is Outstanding}}$$

$$= \$1,000 \times .12 \times 90/360$$
$$= \$30$$

PROBLEM 9-3: Record the following transactions in the general journal.

Nov. 1 Received a $2,000, 6-month, 12% note dated July 1 from Heathcliff Company on account.
Dec. 31 Year-end adjusting entry.
May   1 Heathcliff paid the note plus interest.

Answer: [Section 9-2]

Nov.	1	Notes Receivable	2,000	00		
		Sales			2,000	00
		Received 6-month, 12% note on				
		account from Heathcliff Company				
Dec.	31	Interest Receivable	40	00		
		Interest Revenue			40	00
		Adjusting entry to record interest				
		revenue ($2,000 × .12 × 2/12)				
May	1	Cash	2,120	00		
		Notes Receivable			2,000	00
		Interest Receivable			40	00
		Interest Revenue			80	00
		To record payment of note and interest				
		from Heathcliff Company				
		($2,000 × .12 × 4/12)				

PROBLEM 9-4: Streaker Company accepted a 180-day, 10%, $1,000 note on June 1. The note was discounted at the bank on July 31. The bank's discount rate is 14%.

1. Calculate the proceeds to the company.
2. Record the receipt of the proceeds on the books of Streaker Company.

Answer: [Section 9-2]

Face value of note... $1,000
Interest due at maturity
  $1,000 × .10 × 180/360)... 50
Maturity value of note $1,050
Discount period—July 31 to October 31................................... 120 days
Discount on maturity value
  $1,050 × .14 × 120/360 49
Proceeds $1,001

July	31	Cash	1,001	00		
		Notes Receivable			1,000	00
		Interest Revenue			1	00
		Discounted note at bank at 14%				
		discount rate				

PROBLEM 9-5: On June 1, No-Grow Nursery signed a one-year note for $5,000 with the bank. Interest (calculated at a 12% interest rate) is included in the note's face amount. Record receipt of the cash by No-Grow.

Answer: [Section 9-3]

June	1	Cash	4,400	00		
		Discount on Notes Payable	600	00		
		Notes Payable			5,000	00
		Borrowed $5,000 for one year,				
		discounted at $600				

Note that the $600 interest was deducted in advance. No-Grow Nursery received the face amount of the note less the interest ($5,000 − $600 = $4,400).

PROBLEM 9-6: Assume No-Grow has a fiscal year ending September 30. Record the adjusting entry for interest expense on September 30 for the note in Problem 9-5.

Answer: [Section 9-3]

Sept.	30	Interest Expense	200	00		
		Discount on Notes Payable			200	00
		To record interest expense at				
		year end ($600 × 4/12 = $200)				

PROBLEM 9-7: Show the liability for notes payable of No-Grow Nursery as it would appear in a partial balance sheet on September 30.

Answer: [Section 9-3]

Current liabilities:
Notes payable $5,000
Less: Discount on notes payable 400 $4,600

PROBLEM 9-8: Record the entry to be made on May 31 when No-Grow repays the note.

Answer: [Section 9-3]

May	31	Notes Payable	5,000	00		
		Interest Expense	400	00		
		Discount on Notes Payable			400	00
		Cash			5,000	00
		To record repayment of one-year note				
		and record interest expense for eight				
		months ($600 × 8/12 = $400)				

PROBLEM 9-9: Sam Palmer receives a regular wage of $10 per hour for a 40-hour week. He receives one and one-half his regular hourly rate for hours over 40 per week and twice his normal rate for Sundays and holidays. Last week Sam worked 62 hours including eight hours on a holiday. Calculate Sam's gross pay.

Answer: [Section 9-4]

$$40 \text{ hours} \times \$10 \text{ per hour} = \$400$$
$$14 \text{ hours} \times \$15 \text{ per hour}^1 = 210$$
$$8 \text{ hours} \times \$20 \text{ per hour}^2 = \underline{160}$$
$$\text{Gross pay} = \underline{\$770}$$

[1] $1\frac{1}{2}$ times regular pay: $1.5 \times \$10 = \$15$
[2] 2 times regular pay: $2 \times \$10 = \$20$

PROBLEM 9-10: Calculate the FICA tax owed by Sam Palmer based on a 7% rate and a $36,000 tax base. Sam's total gross pay for the year to date is $29,100.

Answer: Sam's total gross earnings are subject to FICA withholdings because he has not yet earned the maximum taxable amount of $36,000. Thus,

$$\$770 \times .07 = \$53.90$$

[Section 9-4]

PROBLEM 9-11: Assume the same facts as in Problem 9-10 except that Sam's total gross pay for the year to date (not including current pay) is $35,500. Calculate the FICA tax.

Answer:

$35,500	(year-to-date earnings)	$500	(wages subject to FICA tax)
+ 770	(current pay)	× .07	(FICA rate)
$36,270	(total)	$ 35	(FICA tax)

FICA taxes are paid on maximum earnings of $36,000. Once earnings reach $36,000, no more FICA tax will be paid for the balance of the year. Thus, Sam only owes FICA tax on the $500 in earnings that brought his year-to-date earnings up to the $36,000 maximum taxable amount. The maximum FICA tax paid by an employee based on a 7% rate and $36,000 tax base is $2,520 ($36,000 × .07). [Section 9-4]

PROBLEM 9-12: Calculate Sam's net pay based on the facts in Problems 9-9 and 9-10. Assume the federal income tax is $124.20, union dues are $7.00, and group insurance is $15.60.

Answer: [Section 9-4]

Gross pay		$770.00
Deductions:		
Federal income tax...	$124.20	
FICA tax..	53.90	
Union dues...	7.00	
Group insurance...	15.60	200.70
Net pay..		$569.30

PROBLEM 9-13: Tops Manufacturing Company has four employees. Payroll information for the pay period ending May 14 is shown below for each employee. Calculate the employer payroll tax expense assuming (a) an FICA tax rate of 7% on maximum earnings of $36,000, (b) federal unemployment tax rate of .8% (.008) on maximum earnings of $7,000, and (c) state unemployment tax rate of 5.4% (.054) on maximum earnings of $7,000.

Employee	Gross Pay Current Period	Gross Pay Year-to-Date
Leroy Collins	$800	$12,400
Thomas O'Neal	550	6,100
Tiffany Jones	670	10,125
Carl Ransom	220	3,200

Answer: To calculate individual amounts based on each employee's gross pay:

	Leroy	**Thomas**
FICA Tax	$800 × .07 = $56.00	$550 × .07 = $38.50
Federal Unemployment Tax	–0–	$550 × .008 = $ 4.40
State Unemployment Tax	–0–	$550 × .054 = $29.70

	Tiffany	**Carl**
FICA Tax	$670 × .07 = $46.90	$220 × .07 = $15.40
Federal Unemployment Tax	–0–	$220 × .008 = $ 1.76
State Unemployment Tax	–0–	$220 × .054 = $11.88

To determine total employer payroll tax expense:

Employee	FICA Tax	Federal Unemployment Tax	State Unemployment Tax
Leroy Collins	$ 56.00	$–0–	$–0–
Thomas O'Neal	38.50	4.40	29.70
Tiffany Jones	46.90	–0–	–0–
Carl Ransom	15.40	1.76	11.88
Total	$156.80	$6.16	$41.58

Note that Leroy and Tiffany have reached the maximum taxable earnings for federal and state unemployment tax. [Section 9-4]

PROBLEM 9-14: Prepare the journal entry to record the payroll tax expense for Tops Manufacturing Company.

Answer: [Section 9-4]

May	14	Payroll Tax Expense	204	54		
		FICA Tax Payable			156	80
		Federal Unemployment Tax Payable			6	16
		State Unemployment Tax Payable			41	58
		To record payroll taxes for the				
		current pay period				

10 INVENTORIES

THIS CHAPTER IS ABOUT

☑ **The Importance of Inventory Valuation**
☑ **Inventory Valuation: Cost Flow Assumptions**
☑ **Inventory Valuation: Lower of Cost or Market**
☑ **Estimating Inventory**

10-1. The Importance of Inventory Valuation

A. *Inventory* **consists of assets held for sale in the normal course of business and assets to be consumed, directly or indirectly, in the manufacturing process.**

Recall from Chapter 6 that a merchandising firm buys goods for resale to customers. These goods are called *merchandise inventory*. A manufacturing firm has three major types of inventory—*raw materials, work-in-process* (partially completed goods), and *finished goods*. The finished goods held for resale by a manufacturing firm are comparable to the merchandise inventory of a merchandising firm. Notice, this definition excludes long-term assets subject to depreciation, amortization, or depletion. This chapter will discuss the valuation of inventory.

B. **The valuation of inventory plays an important part in matching expired costs (expenses) to revenues for the accounting period.**

Inventory is often the largest current asset on the balance sheet. Valuing inventory is especially important because of the large dollar amount and because it appears on the balance sheet as a current asset and on the income statement in the calculation of the cost of goods sold.

       Beginning Inventory (Prior period's Ending Inventory)
+ Net Purchases
—————————————————————————
= Cost of Goods Available for Sale
— Ending Inventory
—————————————————————————
= Cost of Goods Sold
—————————————————————————

C. **Errors sometimes occur in the process of calculating ending inventory.**

Inventory items may be omitted, miscounted, or counted twice. Mathematical errors can be made in the process of calculating total inventory cost. In the current year, both the income statement and the balance sheet are affected by an error in ending inventory.

EXAMPLE 10-1:

Ending Inventory UNDERSTATED

Cost of Goods Sold	Overstated
Net Income	Understated
Current Assets	Understated
Owner's Equity	Understated

Ending Inventory OVERSTATED

Cost of Goods Sold	Understated
Net Income	Overstated
Current Assets	Overstated
Owner's Equity	Overstated

The ending inventory of the current year becomes the *beginning inventory for the next year*. Thus, the income statement will again be incorrect but the effect will be reversed.

EXAMPLE 10-2:

Beginning Inventory UNDERSTATED

Cost of Goods Sold	Understated
Net Income	Overstated
Current Assets	Correct
Owner's Equity	Correct

Beginning Inventory OVERSTATED

Cost of Goods Sold	Overstated
Net Income	Understated
Current Assets	Correct
Owner's Equity	Correct

EXAMPLE 10-3: The following income statements illustrate the effects of inventory errors on net income over two accounting periods. The first income statement shows the correct data for 19x1 and 19x2.

Kimberly Corporation
Income Statement
For Year Ended 19x1 and 19x2

(Correct)

	19x1		19x2
Sales		$11,000	$13,000
Cost of goods sold:			
Beginning inventory	$4,000		$3,000
Add: Purchases	5,000		4,000
Goods available for sale	9,000		7,000
Less: Ending inventory	3,000		1,000
Cost of goods sold		6,000	6,000
Gross profit		5,000	7,000
Operating expense		2,000	3,000
Net income		$3,000	$4,000

The following income statement shows an incorrect ending inventory in 19x1. The ending inventory is understated by $1,000. All the other accounts are correctly stated.

Kimberly Corporation
Income Statement
For Years Ended 19x1 and 19x2

<u>(Inventory Errors)</u>

	19x1		19x2	
Sales...		$11,000		$13,000
Cost of goods sold:				
Beginning inventory..............................	$4,000		→$2,000*	
Add: Purchases	5,000		4,000	
Goods available for sale	9,000		6,000	
Less: Ending inventory	2,000*		1,000	
Cost of goods sold.............................		7,000		5,000
Gross profit.......................................		4,000		8,000
Operating expenses		2,000		3,000
Net income.......................................		$ 2,000		$ 5,000

---

*Inventory should be $3,000.

By the end of 19x2, the error in the ending inventory of 19x1 has self-corrected. The effect on each year is shown below.

	With Correct Inventory	With Incorrect Inventory	Net Income Overstated (Understated)
Net income—19x1.....................................	$3,000	$2,000	($1,000)
Net income—19x2.....................................	4,000	5,000	1,000
Cumulative net income	$7,000	$7,000	$ –0–

It may seem that an error in the valuation of inventory is insignificant since it corrects itself over two accounting periods, assuming no other errors are made. However, it must be remembered that management, creditors, and owners base many decisions on the information reported on financial statements, particularly trends in net income.

EXAMPLE 10-4: Extending Example 10-3, assume the correct income from the year before the inventory error, 19x0, was $2,000 and the correct income the year after the inventory had "self-corrected" was $5,000. The trends for the correct and incorrect income would appear as follows:

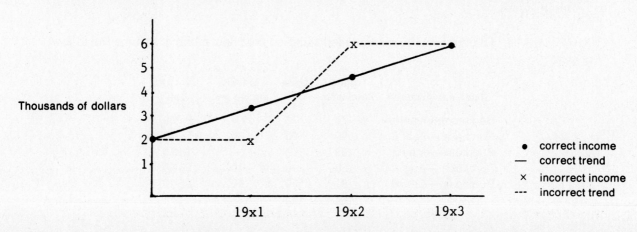

From Example 10-3, it becomes obvious that errors in the valuation of inventory cause errors in the income trend and should be avoided. For this same reason, the method chosen for valuing inventory should be carefully considered.

10-2. Inventory Valuation: Cost Flow Assumptions

A. An inventory valuation method should be selected to value ending inventory.

Before explaining four of the alternative inventory valuation methods, it should be noted that firms can, and do, use an inventory costing assumption that may not represent the actual *physical flow* of goods through a firm. In valuing inventory and the cost of goods sold, there may be more concern with the *cost flow* of goods through the firm. There is no requirement that the inventory method selected match the physical flow of goods. Under all four cost flow assumptions that we will discuss, the number of physical units available for sale, the number of units sold, and the number of units of ending inventory remain the same. The inventory valuation assumptions that will be discussed are

- Specific identification
- First-in, first-out (FIFO)
- Last-in, first-out (LIFO)
- Weighted-average

These four inventory valuation assumptions will be illustrated using the following data:

Date Units Acquired	Number of Units	× Cost per Unit =	Total Cost
Beginning inventory	70	$5.00	$ 350.00
Purchase—Feb. 6	120	5.30	636.00
May 2	100	5.75	575.00
Aug. 14	150	6.00	900.00
Dec. 6	50	6.10	305.00
Cost of goods available for sale	490		$2,766.00
Units remaining (ending inventory)	110		
Units sold	380		

B. The *specific identification* cost flow method requires a business to identify each item of merchandise with its cost.

Inventory tags with a stock number can be attached to each inventory item or the items may be identified by serial number. An accounting record is maintained showing individual stock numbers along with the item's cost. This is a useful method for companies handling *unique* items having a relatively *high cost*. Thus, specific identification is the preferred method to account for such inventory items as expensive jewelry or automobiles. The specific identification method is *not* appropriate for inventories that are *not* made up of unique items.

EXAMPLE 10-5: To illustrate the specific identification cost flow method, assume the following facts:

Date Units Acquired	Units Available	Units Sold	Units in Ending Inv.	Cost per Unit
Beginning inventory	70	70	—	$5.00
Purchase—Feb. 6	120	90	30	$5.30
Purchase—May 2	100	100	—	$5.75
Purchase—Aug. 14	150	110	40	$6.00
Purchase—Dec. 6	50	10	40	$6.10
Total	490	380	110	

The cost of ending inventory is calculated below.

Date Units Acquired	Units in Ending Inv.	× Cost per Unit =	Total Cost
Purchase—Feb. 6	30	$5.30	$159.00
Purchase—Aug. 14	40	$6.00	240.00
Purchase—Dec. 6	40	$6.10	244.00
Ending inventory	110		$643.00

The cost of the 380 units sold is calculated below.

Cost of goods available for sale	$2,766.00
Less ending inventory	643.00
Cost of goods sold	$2,123.00

EXAMPLE 10-6: The cost of goods sold can also be calculated by multiplying the number of specific units sold by their respective costs as shown below.

Date Units Acquired	Units Sold	× Cost per Unit =	Total Cost
Beginning inventory	70	$5.00	$ 350.00
Purchase—Feb. 6	90	$5.30	477.00
Purchase—May 2	100	$5.75	575.00
Purchase—Aug. 14	110	$6.00	660.00
Purchase—Dec. 6	10	$6.10	61.00
Cost of goods sold	380		$2,123.00

C. The *first-in, first-out* (FIFO) cost flow method assumes that the first items purchased (first-in) are sold first (first-out), leaving the last items purchased in ending inventory.

The FIFO method is a reasonable physical flow assumption for many companies, particularly for those that sell perishable goods or goods that have frequent style changes. However, the FIFO cost flow method may be used where the physical flow follows some other pattern if it is deemed to give a better matching of expenses with revenues.

EXAMPLE 10-7: The data at the beginning of this section is used to calculate ending inventory and cost of goods sold. The ending inventory is made up of the most recent purchases, since FIFO assumes the oldest items (those first-in) were sold. The cost of ending inventory is calculated below.

Date Units Acquired	Units on Hand	× Cost per Unit =	Total Cost
Purchase—Dec. 6 (newest)	50	$6.10	$305.00
Purchase—Aug. 14 (next newest)	60	$6.00	360.00
Ending inventory	110		$665.00

The cost of the 380 units sold is calculated as shown below.

Cost of goods available for sale	$2,766.00
Less ending inventory	665.00
Cost of goods sold	$2,101.00

The cost of goods sold can also be calculated by adding the cost of the 70 units in beginning inventory, the 120 units purchased February 6, the 100 units purchased May 2, and 90 of the 150 units purchased August 14, for a total of 380 units sold (refer to Example 10-6). Note that the *first* items in (the oldest items) go to cost of goods sold.

D. The *last-in, first-out* (LIFO) cost flow method assumes that the most recent purchases (last-in) are sold first (first-out), leaving the oldest items purchased in ending inventory.

The LIFO method assigns the *latest* costs incurred to cost of goods sold and the *earlier* costs to ending inventory. This is rarely the actual physical flow of inventory items, but the physical flow of inventory may not be as important as the cost flow, as mentioned earlier. Although the LIFO method does not follow the usual physical flow, it does a better job of matching current expenses to current revenues when prices are changing.

EXAMPLE 10-8: The data at the beginning of this section is used to calculate ending inventory and cost of goods sold. The ending inventory is made up of the earliest purchases, since LIFO assumes the newest items (those last-in) were sold. The cost of ending inventory is calculated below.

Date Units Acquired	Units on Hand	× Cost per Unit =	Total Cost
Beginning inventory (oldest)	70	$5.00	$350.00
Purchase—Feb. 6 (next oldest)	40	$5.30	212.00
Ending inventory	110		$562.00

The cost of the 380 units sold is calculated as shown below.

Cost of goods available for sale	$2,766.00
Less ending inventory	562.00
Cost of goods sold	$2,204.00

Again, the cost of goods sold can also be calculated by adding the cost of the 50 units purchased December 6, the 150 units purchased August 14, the 100 units purchased May 2, and 80 of the 120 units purchased February 6, for a total of 380 units sold (similar to Example 10-6). Note that the *last* items in (the most recent purchases) go to cost of goods sold.

E. The *weighted-average* cost flow method assumes an average cost per unit of all items available for sale during the accounting period.

The weighted-average method takes into consideration not only the cost per unit of each batch of inventory, but also the number of items in each batch. The formula to calculate cost per unit is shown below.

$$\frac{\text{Cost of goods available for sale}}{\text{Total units available for sale}} = \frac{\text{Weighted-average}}{\text{cost per unit}}$$

EXAMPLE 10-9: The weighted-average cost method is illustrated below. The data at the beginning of this section is used to calculate ending inventory and cost of goods sold.

$$\frac{\$2,766.00}{490 \text{ units}} = \$5.6449$$

The cost of ending inventory is calculated below.

$$110 \text{ units} \times \$5.6449 = \$620.94 \text{ or } \$621$$

The cost of the 380 units sold is calculated as shown below.

Cost of goods available for sale	$2,766.00
Less ending inventory	621.00
Cost of goods sold	$2,145.00

As before, the cost of goods sold can be computed directly by multiplying 380 units sold times the weighted-average cost of $5.6449 to equal $2,145.

F. A comparison of the four cost flow methods shows that each method yields a different cost of goods sold and ending inventory.

A different cost of goods sold and ending inventory results in a different net income being reported using each cost flow method. A firm should decide which cost flow method is best for its needs. The following facts should be considered.

1. *Specific identification.* Specific identification exactly matches the cost flow with the physical flow of inventory through the firm. Remember, however, that it is only practical for use by firms that deal in unique, relatively high value goods.
2. *FIFO.* The FIFO method values ending inventory at close to replacement cost since the newest purchases are assumed to be unsold. FIFO usually produces a higher net income than LIFO during a period of rising prices because it includes the oldest (lowest cost) units in cost of goods sold.
3. *LIFO.* LIFO matches the most recent costs with current revenue. Because of this, LIFO provides a better matching of revenues and expenses than FIFO or weighted-average in a period of changing prices. However, the earliest costs are used to value ending inventory; therefore, in a period of rising prices, the value of ending inventory tends to be understated. Furthermore, during a period of rising prices, LIFO will usually produce a lower net income since the most recent (higher) costs are included in cost of goods sold.
4. *Weighted-average.* The weighted-average cost method is a compromise between LIFO and FIFO. All the units sold during a period and the ending inventory are assumed to have the same unit cost. It produces a result somewhere between the LIFO and FIFO methods.

EXAMPLE 10-10: A comparison of the four cost flow methods (Example 10-4 through 10-8) and their effect on net income is shown below. Assume a selling price of $10 per unit and total operating expenses of $900.

	Specific Identification	FIFO	LIFO	Weighted-Average
Sales (380 units × $10)	$3,800	$3,800	$3,800	$3,800
Cost of goods sold:				
Beginning inventory	$ 350	$ 350	$ 350	$ 350
Add: Purchases	2,416	2,416	2,416	2,416
Goods available for sale	$2,766	$2,766	$2,766	$2,766
Less: Ending inventory	643	665	562	621
Cost of goods sold	$2,123	$2,101	$2,204	$2,145
Gross profit	$1,677	$1,699	$1,596	$1,655
Operating expenses	900	900	900	900
Net income	$ 777	$ 799	$ 696	$ 755

Note that FIFO has produced the highest net income, LIFO the lowest, and weighted-average falls somewhere between the two.

G. The periodic and perpetual inventory methods are used to record changes in inventory.

1. *Perpetual inventory method.* Recall from Chapter 6 that the perpetual inventory method keeps a continuous record of inventory on hand and the cost of goods sold. Journal entries are made to increase inventory at the time a purchase is made and to decrease inventory and record cost of goods sold at the time a sale is made. Thus, the inventory account is adjusted during the accounting period.

EXAMPLE 10-11: Assume that ten items purchased on February 6 for $5.30 each were sold on account to McCogan (Acct. #1759) on December 15 for $10 each. Using the perpetual inventory method, the following journal entry would be made.

Dec. 15	Accounts Receivable	100	
	Cost of Goods Sold	53	
	Inventory		53
	Sales		100
	To record sale		

2. *Periodic inventory method.* Recall from Chapter 6 that if the periodic method is used, the ending inventory is determined by physically counting the items on hand at the end of the accounting period. No entries are made affecting inventory and cost of goods sold at the time of a purchase or sale. Only when a periodic physical inventory is taken is the amount of inventory adjusted. The cost flow assumptions illustrated above assume the use of the periodic inventory method, although their use applies in some ways to the perpetual method. Perpetual inventory methods are covered in greater detail in advanced accounting courses.

10-3. Inventory Valuation: Lower of Cost or Market

Although inventories are generally valued at cost, circumstances sometimes arise when inventory should be valued at less than cost. Inventories can spoil, be damaged, or become obsolete. If the utility or usefulness falls below cost, the loss may be appropriately recognized in the current period. The loss in value of the inventory is calculated using the *lower of cost or market (LCM)* rule. There are four steps to the LCM rule.

1. The ending inventory cost is determined using one of the cost flow assumptions discussed in Section 10-2 (i.e., LIFO, FIFO, weighted-average, or specific identification).
2. The inventory cost is compared with market, which is normally the current replacement cost of the inventory items.
3. Any loss in inventory value may be determined on an item-by-item basis, on various categories, or on the inventory as a whole.
4. The loss (if any) is recognized in the current period and the market price becomes cost for the subsequent accounting period.

The justification for the write down of inventory below cost is that of matching the expired cost (expense) to the period in which the utility expired.

EXAMPLE 10-12: The following example illustrates the LCM rule on an item-by-item basis.

	(1)	(2) Unit	(3) Unit	(1x2) Total	(1x3) Total	
Item	Quantity	Cost	Market	Cost	Market	LCM
A	20	$24	$26	$ 480	$ 520	$ 480
B	30	15	12	450	360	360
C	15	3	4	45	60	45
D	50	10	5	500	250	250
				$1,475	$1,190	$1,135

The lower of cost or market applied on an item-by-item basis is shown in the last column. Thus, on an item-by-item basis, the inventory will be valued at $1,135. The journal entry to record the loss in inventory value is shown below.

Date	Loss on Reduction of Inventory to Market	340	
	Inventory		340
	To reduce inventory to lower of cost or market ($1,475 total cost − $1,135 market = $340 loss)		

EXAMPLE 10-13: (Based on Example 10-12). If the LCM rule is applied to the entire inventory, the inventory will be valued at market of $1,190. The loss in inventory value will be $285 ($1,475 cost − $1,190 market).

10-4. Estimating Inventory

A. There are two commonly used methods to estimate ending inventory when it is inconvenient or impossible to physically count the items on hand: the gross profit method and the retail method.

Taking a physical inventory can be time-consuming and costly. However, the cost of ending inventory is needed to prepare monthly financial statements. An *estimate* can be made to determine ending inventory. An estimate can also be made to determine the reasonableness of the physical count or to estimate the value of a destroyed inventory for insurance purposes.

B. The *gross profit method* estimates ending inventory based on the company's historical gross profit rate.

The steps in calculating ending inventory based on the gross profit method are listed below.

1. Determine the previous period's gross profit rate (gross profit as a percent of sales). The rate is based on past experience.

$$\frac{\text{Previous Period Gross Profit (\$)}}{\text{Previous Period Net Sales (\$)}} = \frac{\text{Previous Period}}{\text{Gross Profit Rate (\%)}}$$

2. Calculate estimated gross profit for the current period.

$$\frac{\text{Current}}{\text{Sales}} \times \frac{\text{Previous Period}}{\text{Gross Profit Rate}} = \frac{\text{Current Estimated}}{\text{Gross Profit}}$$

3. Calculate the estimated cost of goods sold.

$$\frac{\text{Current}}{\text{Sales}} - \frac{\text{Estimated}}{\text{Gross Profit}} = \frac{\text{Current Estimated}}{\text{Cost of Goods Sold}}$$

4. Estimate ending inventory.

$$\frac{\text{Cost of Goods Available}}{\text{(Beginning Inventory + Net Purchases)}} - \frac{\text{Estimated}}{\text{Cost of Goods Sold}} = \frac{\text{Estimated}}{\text{Ending Inventory}}$$

EXAMPLE 10-14: To illustrate how the gross profit method works, assume Petta Food Company wants to estimate ending inventory on January 31, 19x2. Sales for the month of January 19x2 were $1,500. Net purchases during the month totaled $1,200. Below is the partial income statement for the previous year, 19x1.

Petta Food Company
Partial Income Statement
For Year Ended December 31, 19x1

Sales		$10,000
Cost of goods sold:		
Beginning inventory	$2,000	
Add: Net Purchases	5,000	
Goods available for sale	$7,000	
Less: Ending inventory	1,000	
Cost of goods sold		$ 6,000
Gross profit		$ 4,000

Step 1: Determine the gross profit rate.

$$\frac{\text{Previous Period Gross Profit (\$)}}{\text{Previous Period Net Sales (\$)}} = \begin{array}{l}\text{Previous Period's}\\\text{Gross Profit Rate (\%)}\end{array}$$

$$\frac{\$\ 4{,}000}{\$10{,}000} = .40 \text{ or } 40\%$$

Step 2: Calculate gross profit.

Current Sales × Previous Period's Gross Profit Rate = Estimated Gross Profit for January 19x2

$$\$1{,}500 \times .40 = \$600$$

Step 3: Calculate estimated cost of goods sold for January 19x2.

Current Sales − Estimated Gross Profit = Estimated Cost of Goods Sold

$$\$1{,}500 - \$600 = \$900$$

Step 4: Estimate ending inventory.

$1,000	Beginning inventory (ending inventory December 31, 19x1)
+1,200	Net Purchases for January, 19x2
$2,200	Goods available for sale
− 900	Estimated cost of goods sold (Refer to Step 3)
$1,300	Estimated ending inventory January 31, 19x2

The shortcut in the gross profit method is to estimate the cost of goods sold as illustrated below. Given the gross profit rate is 40% (from Step 1 above), then the cost of goods sold rate must be 60%, as shown below.

100%	Net sales
−40%	Gross profit
60%	Cost of goods sold

Thus, the cost of goods sold can be calculated as follows:

$1,500	Net sales, Jan. 19x2
× .60	Cost of goods sold rate (100% − 40%)
$ 900	Cost of goods sold, Jan. 19x2

One weakness of the gross profit method is that it estimates this period's ending inventory, cost of goods sold, and gross profit based on the previous period's gross profit rate. This assumes conditions this period are the same as the last.

C. The *retail method* estimates ending inventory based on the relationship between this period's cost of goods available for sale and this period's retail selling price of those goods.

The retail method is used most often by merchandising firms to estimate ending inventory. Using this method, the ending inventory is first determined using retail (or selling) prices, and then is converted to cost using the ratio of cost to retail. The ending inventory using the retail method is calculated as follows:

1. Records are maintained on both costs and retail selling prices for beginning inventory and purchases.
2. Determine the goods available for sale at both cost and retail selling price.
3. Determine the cost-to-retail ratio based on the relationship between the cost of goods available for sale and the retail selling price of goods available for sale.

$$\frac{\text{Cost of Goods Available for Sale}}{\text{Retail Selling Price of Goods Available for Sale}} = \begin{array}{l}\text{Cost-to-Retail}\\\text{Ratio (\%)}\end{array}$$

4. Determine ending inventory at retail selling price by subtracting net sales for the current period from goods available for sale, both at retail selling price.

$$\begin{array}{c}\text{Retail Selling Price of}\\\text{Goods Available for Sale}\end{array} - \begin{array}{c}\text{Net Sales}\\\text{at Retail}\end{array} = \begin{array}{c}\text{Ending Inventory}\\\text{at Retail}\end{array}$$

5. Estimate ending inventory at cost by multiplying the ending inventory at retail selling price times the cost-to-retail ratio developed above.

$$\begin{array}{c}\text{Ending Inventory}\\\text{at Retail}\end{array} \times \begin{array}{c}\text{Cost-to-Retail}\\\text{Ratio (\%)}\end{array} = \begin{array}{c}\text{Estimated Ending}\\\text{Inventory at Cost}\end{array}$$

EXAMPLE 10-15: To illustrate how the retail method works, assume Dee's Sportswear wants to estimate ending inventory on March 31 before preparing quarterly financial statements. Net sales at retail selling price for the period were $67,500.

Steps 1 and 2: The records are used to determine the following information.

	Cost	Retail
Beginning inventory, Jan. 1	$12,000	$ 17,600
Net purchases, Jan. 1—March 31	55,340	86,000
Goods available for sale	$67,340	$103,600

Step 3: Determine the cost-to-retail ratio.

$$\frac{\text{Cost of Goods Available for Sale}}{\text{Retail Selling Price of Goods Available for Sale}} = \begin{array}{c}\text{Cost-to-Retail}\\\text{Ratio (\%)}\end{array}$$

$$\frac{\$\ 67,340}{\$103,600} = .65 \text{ or } 65\%$$

Step 4: Determine ending inventory at retail selling price.

$$\begin{array}{c}\text{Retail Selling Price of}\\\text{Goods Available for Sale}\end{array} - \begin{array}{c}\text{Net Sales}\\\text{at Retail}\end{array} = \begin{array}{c}\text{Ending Inventory}\\\text{at Retail}\end{array}$$

$$\$103,600 - \$67,500 = \$36,100$$

Step 5: Estimate ending inventory at cost.

$$\begin{array}{c}\text{Ending Inventory}\\\text{at Retail}\end{array} \times \begin{array}{c}\text{Cost-to-Retail}\\\text{Ratio (\%)}\end{array} = \begin{array}{c}\text{Estimated Ending}\\\text{Inventory at Cost}\end{array}$$

$$\$36,100 \times .65 = \$23,465$$

The estimated ending inventory at cost is $23,465. Markups and markdowns in the original retail selling price have been left out of the example. They are covered in advanced accounting courses. Although the retail method has the advantage of being based on current costs and revenues, it has the disadvantage of not allowing for breakage or theft.

RAISE YOUR GRADES

Can you explain ... ?

☑ the effect on the income statement and balance sheet in Year 1 and Year 2 of an error in valuing ending inventory for Year 1 (assuming ending inventory for Year 2 is correct)

☑ how to calculate ending inventory using each of the four inventory costing methods

☑ the effect on net income for each method

☑ the difference between LIFO and FIFO during a period of rising prices
☑ the lower of cost or market rule for calculating ending inventory
☑ how to estimate cost of goods sold and ending inventory using the gross profit and retail methods

SUMMARY

1. Inventory consists of assets held for sale in the normal course of business and assets to be consumed, directly or indirectly, in the manufacturing process.
2. The valuation of inventory is an important part of matching expired costs with revenue for the accounting period.
3. Inventory is often the largest current asset on the balance sheet.
4. Inventory appears on the balance sheet as a current asset and on the income statement in the cost of goods sold calculation.
5. An error in the valuation of ending inventory causes an error in cost of goods sold, gross profit, net income, current assets, and equity.
6. There are four common methods of assigning cost to the units in ending inventory: specific identification; first-in, first-out (FIFO); last-in, first-out (LIFO); and weighted-average.
7. The specific identification cost flow method requires a business to identify each item of merchandise with its cost. It may be used only for unique items that generally have a high-cost.
8. The FIFO cost flow method assumes that the first items purchased are the first items sold. The most recent costs are used to calculate ending inventory.
9. The LIFO cost flow method assumes that the most recent purchases are sold first. The newest costs incurred are assigned to cost of goods sold. The older costs are used to value ending inventory.
10. The weighted-average cost flow method assumes an average cost per unit of all the items available for sale during the accounting period. Thus, the cost per unit of ending inventory and the cost per unit of goods sold are the same.
11. The specific identification cost method exactly matches the cost flow with the physical flow of inventory through the firm.
12. FIFO values ending inventory at an amount close to replacement cost. It usually produces a higher net income during a period of rising prices than LIFO or weighted-average.
13. The LIFO method does the best job of matching revenue and expense during a period of rising prices. It usually produces a lower net income than FIFO or weighted-average if prices are rising.
14. The periodic and perpetual inventory methods are used to record changes in inventory.
15. After inventory is valued by one of the cost flow assumptions, the lower of cost or market rule (usually replacement cost) is applied, thus recognizing any loss in value in the current accounting period.
16. Sometimes it is impractical or impossible to take a physical inventory. Two widely used methods of estimating ending inventory are the gross profit method and the retail method.
17. The gross profit method estimates ending inventory based on the previous period's gross profit rate.
18. The retail method estimates ending inventory based on the relationship between the current cost of goods available for sale and the current retail selling price of those goods.

RAPID REVIEW

Multiple Choice

1. What items are included in merchandise inventory? [Section 10-1]
    (a) Raw materials
    (b) Materials in the process of production

(*c*) Goods held for resale to customers

(*d*) none of the above

2. If ending inventory is overstated in Year 1, what will be the effect on cost of goods sold in Year 1? [Section 10-1]

(*a*) No effect

(*b*) Overstated

(*c*) Understated

3. If ending inventory is overstated in Year 1, what will be the effect on equity at the end of Year 2 (assuming ending inventory for Year 2 is correct)? [Section 10-1]

(*a*) No effect

(*b*) Overstated

(*c*) Understated

4. If ending inventory is understated in Year 1, what will be the effect on net income in Year 2 (assuming ending inventory for Year 2 is correct)? [Section 10-1]

(*a*) No effect

(*b*) Overstated

(*c*) Understated

5. When would the specific identification inventory cost method be used? [Section 10-2]

(*a*) When a high net income is desired

(*b*) When a high volume of low-cost items is sold

(*c*) When a cost flow that exactly matches physical flow of goods is desired and the inventory items are unique

(*d*) All of the above

6. What items does the FIFO method assume are sold first? [Section 10-2]

(*a*) The oldest items in inventory

(*b*) The newest items in inventory

(*c*) An average of the cost of inventory

7. What costs are assigned to ending inventory when the LIFO method is used? [Section 10-2]

(*a*) The oldest items in inventory

(*b*) The newest items in inventory

(*c*) An average of the cost of inventory

8. Which cost flow method usually results in higher net income during a period of rising prices? [Section 10-2]

(*a*) Specific identification

(*b*) FIFO

(*c*) LIFO

(*d*) Weighted-average

9. Which cost flow method reports inventory on the balance sheet at closer to replacement cost? [Section 10-2]

(*a*) Specific identification

(*b*) FIFO

(*c*) LIFO

(*d*) Weighted-average

10. What does the term "market" usually mean as used in "lower of cost or market"? [Section 10-3]

(*a*) Wholesale cost

(*b*) Original market cost

(*c*) Lowest current cost

(*d*) Current replacement cost

11. Which accounting concept justifies the recognition of losses in the current accounting period using the lower of cost or market rule? [Section 10-3]

(*a*) Revenue realization

(*b*) Matching

(*c*) Cost

(*d*) Going concern

12. How is the gross profit ratio determined when using the gross profit method of estimating inventory? [Section 10-4]

(*a*) Gross profit as a percent of ending inventory

(*b*) Gross profit as a percent of cost of goods sold

(*c*) Gross profit as a percent of net sales

Answers: 1. (*c*); 2. (*c*); 3. (*a*); 4. (*b*); 5. (*c*); 6. (*a*); 7. (*a*); 8. (*b*); 9. (*b*); 10. (*d*); 11. (*b*); 12. (*c*)

SOLVED PROBLEMS

PROBLEM 10-1: The condensed income statement for Ewald Company for two years is shown below.

	Year 1	Year 2
Sales..................	$45,000	$52,000
Cost of goods sold	28,000	31,000
Gross profit	$17,000	$21,000
Operating expenses...	10,000	10,000
Net income.............	$ 7,000	$11,000

At the beginning of Year 3, it was discovered that an error had been made in Year 1. Ending inventory was incorrectly stated at $5,000, an understatement of $3,000. What effect did the error have on net income for Year 1, Year 2, and Year 3?

Answer: [Section 10-1]
Year 1: Understating ending inventory by $3,000 caused cost of goods sold to be overstated by $3,000 and net income to be understated by $3,000. Net income should have been $10,000, not $7,000.
Year 2: The ending inventory in Year 1 became the beginning inventory in Year 2. Therefore, goods available for sale was understated by $3,000. Cost of goods sold was understated by $3,000 and net income was overstated by $3,000. Net income should have been $8,000, not $11,000.
Year 3: Assuming no further errors, the error in Year 1 will self-correct by the end of Year 2, as shown below. Ending inventory was correctly stated for Year 2, thus making beginning inventory and net income correct in Year 3.

	Incorrect	Correct
Net income—Year 1.......	$ 7,000	$10,000
Net income—Year 2.......	11,000	8,000
Cumulative net income..	$18,000	$18,000

PROBLEM 10-2: The following information is available for Trumbull Corporation.

	Units ×	Cost per Unit =	Total Cost
Beginning inventory	200	$25	$5,000
Purchase—March 1	110	$29	$3,190
Purchase—June 16	160	$30	$4,800
Purchase—Oct.11	150	$34	$5,100

On December 31, 210 units were unsold. Determine the cost of ending inventory using (*a*) the FIFO cost flow assumption, (*b*) the LIFO cost flow assumption, and (*c*) the weighted-average cost flow assumption.

Answer: [Section 10-2]

(*a*) Using the FIFO method, ending inventory is made up of the last items purchased since it is assumed that the earliest items purchased were sold first.

	Units ×	Cost per Unit =	Total Cost
Purchase—Oct. 11	150	$34	$5,100
Purchase—June 16	60	$30	1,800
Ending inventory	210		$6,900

(*b*) Using the LIFO method, ending inventory is made up of the earliest items purchased since it is assumed that the last items purchased were sold first.

	Units ×	Cost per Unit =	Total Cost
Beginning inventory	200	$25	$5,000
Purchase—March 1	10	$29	290
Ending inventory	210		$5,290

(*c*) Using the weighted-average method, the total cost of goods available for sale is calculated and then divided by the number of units available for sale to determine the average cost per unit. This amount is then multiplied by the number of items on hand in ending inventory to determine the cost of ending inventory.

	Units ×	Cost per Unit =	Total Cost
Beginning inventory	200	$25	$ 5,000
Purchase—March 1	110	$29	3,190
Purchase—June 16	160	$30	4,800
Purchase—Oct. 11	150	$34	5,100
Cost of goods available for sale	620		$18,090

$$\frac{\$18,090}{620} = \$29.1774$$

$$\$29.1774 \times 210 = \$6,127.25 \text{ Ending inventory}$$

PROBLEM 10-3: The Michael Corporation sells four different products. The following information on ending inventory is availabie on December 31.

Item	Quantity	Unit Cost	Unit Market
1	100	$10	$13
2	250	$32	$30
3	60	$20	$19
4	280	$ 7	$ 9

Determine the value of ending inventory using the lower of cost or market (LCM) rule, assuming the rule is applied (*a*) on an item-by-item basis and (*b*) on inventory as a whole.

Answer: The following table shows the calculation of ending inventory both at cost and at market.

Item	(1) Quantity	(2) Unit Cost	(3) Unit Market	(1x2) Total Cost	(1x3) Total Market	LCM
1	100	$10	$13	$ 1,000	$ 1,300	$ 1,000
2	250	$32	$30	8,000	7,500	7,500
3	60	$20	$19	1,200	1,140	1,140
4	280	$ 7	$ 9	1,960	2,520	1,960
				$12,160	$12,460	$11,600

(*a*) The last column shows the LCM rule applied on an item-by-item basis. On this basis, a loss of $560 ($12,160 − $11,600) will be recognized.

(*b*) To report ending inventory using the LCM rule applied to the inventory as a whole, the two columns showing total cost and total market are compared. In this case, total cost is the lowest, so ending inventory will be reported at $12,160.

[Section 10-3]

PROBLEM 10-4: On December 31, Taylor Company has 48 units of inventory on hand. Information from the company's purchase records is shown below.

	Units	Cost per Unit
Beginning inventory	24	$6.00
Purchase—March 1	36	$7.20
Purchase—May 27	72	$7.80
Purchase—Aug. 28	60	$8.40

Determine the cost of goods sold using (*a*) the FIFO cost flow assumption, (*b*) the LIFO cost flow assumption, and (*c*) the weighted-average cost flow assumption.

	FIFO	LIFO	Weighted-Average
Cost of goods sold:			
Beginning inventory	_____	_____	_____
Add: Net Purchases	_____	_____	_____
Goods available for sale	_____	_____	_____
Less: Ending inventory	_____	_____	_____
Cost of goods sold	_____	_____	_____

Answer: Calculate the cost of beginning inventory and purchases as follows:

	Units	× Cost per Unit	= Total Cost
Beginning inventory	24	$6.00	$ 144.00
Purchase—March 1	36	$7.20	$ 259.20
Purchase—May 27	72	$7.80	561.60
Purchase—Aug. 28	60	$8.40	504.00
Total purchases	192		$1,324.80

Calculate the cost of goods sold as follows:

	FIFO	LIFO	Weighted-Average
Cost of goods sold:			
Beginning inventory	$ 144.00	$ 144.00	$ 144.00
Add: Purchases	1,324.80	1,324.80	1,324.80
Goods available for sale	$1,468.80	$1,468.80	$1,468.80
Less: Ending inventory	403.20*	316.80**	367.20***
Cost of goods sold	$1,065.60	$1,152.00**	$1,101.60

* Ending inventory using FIFO:

$$48 \times \$8.40 = \$403.20$$

** Ending inventory using LIFO:

$$24 \times \$6.00 = \$144.00$$
$$24 \times \$7.20 = \underline{\ 172.80}$$
$$\$316.80$$

*** Ending inventory using weighted-average:

$$\frac{\$1,468.80}{192} = \$7.65 \text{ Average cost per unit}$$

$$\$7.65 \times 48 = \$367.20$$

[Section 10-2]

PROBLEM 10-5: Refer to the information in Problem 10-4. Calculate net income under each cost flow assumption, assuming the selling price per unit was $12 and total operating expenses were $200.

	FIFO	LIFO	Weighted-Average
Sales			
Cost of goods sold			
Gross profit			
Operating expenses			
Net income			

Answer: [Section 10-2]

	FIFO	LIFO	Weighted-Average
Sales*	$1,728.00	$1,728.00	$1,728.00
Cost of goods sold	1,065.60	1,152.00	1,101.60
Gross profit	$ 662.40	$ 576.00	$ 626.40
Operating expenses	200.00	200.00	200.00
Net income	$ 462.40	$ 376.00	$ 426.40

* To determine sales:

192 Total units available for sale
−48 Units in ending inventory
144 Units sold

$12 × 144 = $1,728.00

PROBLEM 10-6: Using the LCM rule, prepare the journal entry (if required) under each of the following independent situations.

(a) Cost $4,560; market $4,100.
(b) Cost $6,150; market $7,000.
(c) Cost $10,500; market $9,280.

Answer: [Section 10-3]

(a)	Loss on Reduction of Inventory to Market	460	00		
	Inventory			460	00
	To reduce inventory to LCM				
	($4,560 − $4,100 = $460)				
(b)	No entry required as cost is lower than market.				
(c)	Loss on Reduction of Inventory to Market	1,220	00		
	Inventory			1,220	00
	To reduce inventory to LCM				
	($10,500 − $9,280 = $1,220)				

PROBLEM 10-7: On May 31, before the company's accountant can prepare the monthly financial statements, it will be necessary to estimate the ending inventory. The following information has been obtained from the accounting records.

Inventory balance, April 30 $ 8,400
Net purchases during May $17,100
Net sales during May $28,800

From past experience, the accountant knows the gross profit rate will be approximately 30%. Estimate the ending inventory using the gross profit method.

Answer: [Section 10-4]

1. Calculate estimated gross profit for May:

$28,800 Net sales—May
× .30 Prior period's gross profit rate
$ 8,640 Estimated gross profit—May

2. Calculate estimated cost of goods sold:

$28,800 Sales
−8,640 Estimated gross profit
$20,160 Estimated cost of goods sold—May

3. Determine estimated ending inventory:

$ 8,400 Beginning inventory
17,100 Net purchases—May
$25,500 Cost of goods available for sale
−20,160 Estimated cost of goods sold—May
$ 5,340 Estimated ending inventory

Alternative: If the prior period's gross profit rate is 30% of net sales, then the estimated cost of goods sold is 70% of net sales. Using the shortcut, you can calculate cost of goods sold without first calculating gross profit.

$28,800 Net sales—May
× .70 Estimated cost of goods sold rate
$20,160 Estimated cost of goods sold—May

PROBLEM 10-8: The inventory at Semco Tool Company was destroyed by fire on May 27. An estimate of the inventory value was needed to file an insurance claim. Determine ending inventory using the gross profit method. The following information is available.

Sales (Jan. 1—May 27) $122,000
Net purchases (Jan. 1—May 27) $ 71,750
Beginning inventory (Jan. 1) $ 31,000
Prior period's gross profit rate   45%

Answer: [Section 10-4]

1. Calculate the cost of goods sold:

$122,000 Sales
×   .55 Prior period's cost of goods sold rate
$ 67,100 Estimated cost of goods sold

2. Determine estimated ending inventory:

$ 31,000 Beginning inventory
+71,750 Net purchases
$102,750 Cost of goods available for sale
−67,100 Estimated cost of goods sold
$ 35,650 Estimated ending inventory

PROBLEM 10-9: United Retail Company takes a physical inventory at year-end. During the year, an estimate is made of ending inventory at the end of each month for monthly financial statements. The following information is available to estimate ending inventory as of April 30. Estimate ending inventory using the retail method.

	Cost	Retail
Beginning inventory, Apr. 1	$17,920	$ 25,600
Net purchases (Apr. 1–Apr. 30)	$71,659	$102,370
Net sales (Apr. 1–Apr. 30)		$105,000

Answer: [Section 10-4]

1. Determine the goods available for sale:

	Cost	Retail
Beginning inventory, Apr. 1	$17,920	$ 25,600
Net purchases	71,659	102,370
Goods available for sale	$89,579	$127,970

2. Determine the cost-to-retail ratio:

$$\frac{\$89,579}{\$127,970} = .70 \text{ or } 70\%$$

3. Determine ending inventory at retail selling price:

$127,970 Retail cost of goods available for sale
−105,000 Net sales at retail
$ 22,970 Ending inventory at retail

4. Estimate ending inventory at cost:

$22,970 Ending inventory at retail
×   .70 Cost-to-retail ratio
$16,079 Ending inventory at cost (estimate)

PROBLEM 10-10: All Sales Company has taken a physical inventory. At year-end, December 31, 80 units remain in inventory. Calculate ending inventory using the (*a*) FIFO, (*b*) LIFO, and (*c*) weighted-average methods. Use the information provided below.

	Units	Cost per Unit
Beginning	30	$6.00
Purchase—March 7	60	$6.60
Purchase—May 2	45	$7.20
Purchase—Aug. 23	75	$9.00

Answer: [Section 10-2]

(*a*) Using the FIFO method:

	Units ×	Cost per Unit =	Total Cost
Purchase—Aug. 23	75	$9.00	$675.00
Purchase—May 2	5	$7.20	36.00
Ending inventory	80		$711.00

(*b*) Using the LIFO method:

	Units ×	Cost per Unit =	Total Cost
Beginning	30	$6.00	$180.00
Purchase—March 7	50	$6.60	330.00
Ending inventory	80		$510.00

(*c*) Using the weighted-average method:

	Units ×	Cost per Unit =	Total Cost
Beginning	30	$6.00	$ 180.00
Purchase—March 7	60	$6.60	396.00
Purchase—May 2	45	$7.20	324.00
Purchase—Aug. 23	75	$9.00	675.00
Total purchases	210		$1,575.00

$$\frac{\$1,575}{210} = \$7.50 \text{ Average cost per unit}$$

$$\$7.50 \times 80 = \$600 \text{ Ending inventory}$$

PROBLEM 10-11: Refer to Problem 10-10. Assume that sales for the year are $1,900 and operating expenses are $600. Complete the income statement form below under each assumption.

All Sales Company

Income Statement

For Year Ended December 31, 19—

	FIFO	LIFO	Weighted-Average
Sales			
Cost of goods sold:			
Beginning inventory			
Add: Purchases			
Goods available for sale			
Less: Ending inventory			
Cost of goods sold			
Gross profit			
Operating expenses			
Net income			

Answer: [Section 10-2]

All Sales Company

Income Statement

For Year Ended December 31, 19—

	FIFO	LIFO	Weighted-Average
Sales	$1,900	$1,900	$1,900
Cost of goods sold:			
Beginning inventory	180	180	180
Add: Purchases	1,395	1,395	1,395
Goods available for sale	1,575	1,575	1,575
Less: Ending inventory	711	510	600
Cost of goods sold	864	1,065	975
Gross profit	1,036	835	925
Operating expenses	600	600	600
Net income	$ 436	$ 235	$ 325

11 NONCURRENT TANGIBLE AND INTANGIBLE ASSETS: ACQUISITION

THIS CHAPTER IS ABOUT

- ☑ **Plant Assets**
- ☑ **Initial Asset Cost**
- ☑ **Revenue and Capital Expenditures**
- ☑ **Sale and Exchange of Depreciable Assets**
- ☑ **Natural Resources**
- ☑ **Intangible Assets**

11-1. Plant Assets

A. Noncurrent tangible assets acquired for use in the operation of the business are usually classified on the balance sheet as *plant assets*.

The accounts that make up plant assets appear on the balance sheet after current assets and long-term investments. Other titles frequently used for plant assets are *fixed assets*, *property and equipment*, and *property, plant, and equipment*. Examples of property, plant, and equipment are land (property), buildings (plant), and office machines (equipment). Natural resources are also tangible assets. They are discussed later in Section 11-5.

To be classified as plant assets, the assets should be expected to last for more than one accounting period.

EXAMPLE 11-1: Office furniture held for sale by an office equipment store is presented in the balance sheet as *Inventory* in the current asset section. However, the same furniture, used by a real estate firm in its sales office, is presented in the balance sheet as *Office Furniture* in the plant asset section.

EXAMPLE 11-2: Land bought for future use is classified as a long-term investment. Land currently in use as a building site for a factory is classified as plant assets.

B. Plant and equipment are usually depreciable property.

These assets are shown in the balance sheet at their *net book value*. Net book value equals the recorded cost of the asset less accumulated depreciation. The cost of plant and equipment is gradually transferred to expense over the estimated life of the asset. This is because the usefulness of most plant and equipment is reduced as years go by through wear and tear or obsolescence. On the other hand, land is *not* deemed to decline in service potential over time or by use. Therefore, land is not depreciated. Depreciation is discussed in Chapter 12.

11-2. Initial Asset Cost

A. Plant assets are initially recorded at their *historical cost*.

Historical cost includes all reasonable and necessary expenditures made to get the asset in place and ready to use. Unreasonable or unnecessary costs of acquiring the asset are not considered to be a part of the cost of the asset. Unreasonable or unnecessary costs do not add utility and are expensed in the period they are incurred. For most assets: interest is considered a financing cost and is therefore not included in the acquisition cost. It is expensed in the period incurred.

EXAMPLE 11-3: Imperial Corporation purchased a piece of equipment with an invoice price of $15,000. The seller offered a cash discount of $300 for prompt payment. Other costs included sales tax of $735, freight charges of $1,000, and installation costs of $500. The firm's driver received a $50 traffic ticket for speeding while transporting the machinery from the depot. While on the factory's loading dock, the machinery was damaged and the repairs cost $240. The journal entry to record the initial cost of the equipment is

Date	Equipment	16,935	
	Cash		16,935
	To record initial cost of equipment.		

The initial cost was determined as follows:

Invoice − Cash Discount + Sales Tax + Freight + Installation = Initial Cost
$15,000 − $300 + $735 + $1,000 + $500 = $16,935

Note that the costs of the speeding ticket and of the damage on the loading dock are *not* debited to Equipment. These costs are neither reasonable nor necessary. Instead, they are debited to the appropriate expense accounts in a separate entry. Also note that the cash discount is deducted from the cost of acquiring the equipment. It is reasonable to expect prompt payment. If the payment is delayed, the lost discount is an expense of the period.

B. The cost of a lump-sum purchase should be allocated.

Several types of assets may be bought for one invoice price. The total cost should be allocated to the various assets purchased. The relative fair market value of the assets acquired is the normal basis for this allocation.

EXAMPLE 11-4: Rogue Corporation purchased land and a building for $200,000. The land was appraised at $90,000 and the building at $210,000, for a total market value of $300,000. The cost would be allocated as follows:

	Market Value	% of Market	Allocation of Cost*
Land	$ 90,000	30%	$ 60,000
Building	210,000	70%	140,000
Total	$300,000	100%	$200,000

* Calculations: Land—$90,000 ÷ $300,000 = .30 or 30%
.30 × $200,000 = $60,000
Building—$210,000 ÷ $300,000 = .70 or 70%
.70 × $200,000 = $140,000

The journal entry to allocate the costs of the land and the building would be

Date	Land	60,000	
	Building	140,000	
	Cash		200,000
	To record land and building		
	purchased at lump sum of $200,000.		
	Values allocated based on		
	appraised fair market value of		
	land, $90,000, and building,		
	$210,000.		

11-3. Revenue and Capital Expenditures

It is necessary to recognize costs related to plant assets either as expenses that benefit only the period in which they were incurred or as assets that benefit more than one accounting period. Expenditures incurred that add utility to an asset are treated as assets and are added to the recorded cost of the asset. If the utility of the expenditure expires in the current period, the expenditure is written off as an expense.

A. Costs incurred for plant assets that provide benefits only to the current accounting period are called *revenue expenditures*.

The matching principle requires that revenue expenditures be charged to expense accounts in the period in which they are incurred. They do not add to the quality of the asset or extend its life. Revenue expenditures associated with plant assets include ordinary repairs and maintenance.

B. Costs incurred for plant assets that provide benefits to more than one accounting period are called *capital expenditures*.

Expenditures made to purchase plant assets or increase the quality and/or extend the life of the asset are called capital expenditures. According to the matching principle, capital expenditures should be matched (allocated) to the periods they benefit. In addition to the original acquisition of an asset, capital expenditures include major additions, betterments, and extraordinary repairs.

1. *Major additions.* Major additions to assets include such things as adding a new wing to a factory building or a new floor to an office building. Such expenditures should be debited to the appropriate asset accounts.
2. *Betterments.* Betterments are capital expenditures that improve the quality or utility of the asset. For example, replacing narrow doors with wider, automatic doors to allow access by the handicapped is a capital expenditure because it improves the quality of service provided. The cost and accumulated depreciation of the old doors, if available, should be removed from the accounts and the cost of the new doors should be added to the asset account.
3. *Extraordinary repairs.* Extraordinary repairs are capital expenditures that extend the useful life of the asset or increase its estimated salvage value. Such expenditures are usually recorded by debiting the appropriate Accumulated Depreciation account. A debit to Accumulated Depreciation increases the book value of the asset without implying a more costly asset. Future depreciation should be determined based on the new book value (less estimated salvage value) and estimated remaining useful life of the asset.

EXAMPLE 11-5: A firm owns a machine with an original cost of $40,000 on which $17,500 of depreciation has accumulated. This equipment was overhauled at the end of five years for a cost of $4,500. It is estimated that the overhaul extended the life of the asset by four years. This extraordinary repair would be recorded as shown on page 225.

Date	Accumulated Depreciation—Equipment	4,500	
	Cash		4,500
	To record the overhaul of machine; extends estimated useful life by four years.		

Book value on the equipment would be calculated as follows:

	Before Overhaul	After Overhaul
Initial asset cost	$40,000	$40,000
Accumulated depreciation	− 17,500	− 13,000
Asset book value	$22,500	$27,000

11-4. Sale and Exchange of Depreciable Assets

A. When depreciable assets wear out or become obsolete, they may be scrapped, sold, or exchanged for similar new assets.

Some accounting entries are common to all disposals of depreciable assets. First, make sure that depreciation has been recorded up to the date of the asset disposal. Then remove both the asset account balance and the related accumulated depreciation account balance from the books.

EXAMPLE 11-6: Pixie Products, Inc., sold a piece of equipment with an original cost of $10,000 and accumulated depreciation of $6,000. It was sold for cash at its book value of $4,000. The entry would be

Date	Cash	4,000	
	Accumulated Depreciation—Equipment	6,000	
	Equipment		10,000
	To record cash sale of equipment for book value.		

B. The sale of a depreciable asset may be for book value, or for an amount above or below book value.

1. *For book value.* If a depreciable asset is sold for book value, no gain or loss is recorded (see Example 11-6).
2. *Above book value.* If a depreciable asset is sold for more than book value, a gain is recorded.

EXAMPLE 11-7: Suppose that Pixie Products (Example 11-6) sold its equipment to Dixie on account for $7,000. A $3,000 gain would result. This gain is the difference between the account receivable of $7,000 and the $4,000 book value ($10,000 less $6,000). The entry would be

Date	Accounts Receivable	7,000	
	Accumulated Depreciation—Equipment	6,000	
	Equipment		10,000
	Gain on Sale of Plant Assets		3,000
	To record sale of equipment to Dixie on account at a gain. Sale price ($7,000) − Book value ($10,000 − $6,000) = $3,000 gain.		

3. *Below book value.* If a depreciable asset is sold for less than book value, a loss is recorded.

EXAMPLE 11-8: Suppose that Pixie Products (Examples 11-6 and 11-7) sold its equipment to Trixie for $3,000 cash. A $1,000 loss would result. This loss is the difference between the $3,000 cash received and the $4,000 book value. The entry would be

Date	Cash	3,000	
	Accumulated Depreciation—Equipment	6,000	
	Loss on Sale of Plant Assets	1,000	
	Equipment		10,000
	To record cash sale of equipment		
	at a loss. Sale price ($3,000) —		
	Book value ($10,000 − $6,000) =		
	$1,000 loss.		

C. One depreciable asset may be exchanged for another.

Old equipment may be traded for new equipment. The list price of the new asset less the trade-in allowed for the old asset equals the amount to be paid. Although losses may always be recognized, the recognition of gains requires the earning process to be complete.

EXAMPLE 11-9: An old asset is exchanged for a similar new asset with a list price of $26,000. A trade-in allowance of $14,000 is given on the old asset. Thus,

$26,000 List price
−14,000 Trade-in allowance on old asset
$12,000 Amount paid

1. *Exchanges of similar assets—gains.* Gains on the exchange of similar assets are *not* recognized. If the assets are similar, the earning process is not complete and it is improper to realize revenue. Instead, the new asset is recorded at the book value of the old asset plus the amount paid.

EXAMPLE 11-10: An old delivery truck with a $12,000 book value ($30,000 cost less accumulated depreciation of $18,000) and a fair market value of $14,000 is traded in for a new delivery truck with a list price of $40,000. A $14,000 trade-in allowance is given. The amount paid is $26,000 ($40,000 cost less $14,000 trade-in). The gain of $2,000 ($14,000 fair market value less $12,000 book value) is *not* recorded. Instead, the new asset is recorded at $38,000 ($12,000 book value of old asset plus $26,000 cash paid). The entry would be

Date	Delivery Truck (New)	38,000	
	Accumulated Depreciation—Equipment	18,000	
	Delivery Truck (Old)		30,000
	Cash		26,000
	To record exchange of old delivery		
	truck with a book value of $12,000		
	and a trade-in of $14,000 for a new		
	delivery truck with a list price of		
	$40,000.		

2. *Exchange of similar assets—losses.* Losses incurred in the exchange of similar assets are recognized. The new asset is recorded at the fair market value of the assets exchanged.

EXAMPLE 11-11: Suppose that in Example 11-10 the fair market value of the old delivery truck was only $9,000, and the trade-in-allowance was only $9,000. Cash paid equals $31,000 ($40,000 cost of the new asset less $9,000 trade-in). The loss is $3,000 ($9,000 fair market value less $12,000 book value). *Note:* It is not unusual for dealers to allow inflated trade-ins in certain industries.

The entry would be

Date	Delivery Truck (New)	40,000	
	Accumulated Depreciation—Equipment	18,000	
	Loss on Exchange of Plant Assets	3,000	
	Cash		31,000
	Delivery Truck (Old)		30,000
	To record exchange and the loss incurred in the exchange.		

3. *Exchanges of dissimilar assets—gains.* Gains on the exchange of dissimilar assets are recognized. If the assets are dissimilar, accountants believe the earning process is complete when the transaction has taken place. If the transaction cannot be measured objectively by the amount of cash given or received, the accountant must rely on other evidence.

   (a) First, the accountant checks to see if one of the items given or received has a fair market value more objective or verifiable. For example, the published daily prices of stocks sold on the stock exchanges provide a more objective, verifiable fair market value than the appraisal value of real estate.

   (b) Second, if both the item given and the item received have equally objective, verifiable fair market values, the accountant normally uses the fair market value of the item given up.

   (c) Third, if the item given up lacks an objective, verifiable fair market value, the accountant uses the fair market value of the item received.

   (d) Fourth, if neither the item given up nor the item received has an objective, verifiable fair market value, the accountant uses appraisals, book values, list prices, or estimates.

EXAMPLE 11-12: Stock with a book value of $12,000 is given in exchange for land east of Yeehaw Junction. The land has an asking price of $15,000. Because the earning process is complete (an exchange of dissimilar items), the accountant could record a gain, if any. If the stock had a quoted price of $14,000, the accountant would record a gain of $2,000 ($14,000 − $12,000), ignoring the asking price on the land. Lacking a quoted price on the stock, the accountant might rely on appraisals. If appraisals of equal quality were available for both the stock and the land, the accountant would use the appraisal for the stock (the item given up). The accountant would use the appraisal for the land (the item received) only if it gave better evidence of the fair market value of the transaction or if it was the only evidence available. The $12,000 book value of the stock or the $15,000 asking price of the land would only be used as a last resort.

11-5. Natural Resources

A. Natural resources represent assets that are created by nature.

Natural resources have utility by use or sale only after being removed from the tract or deposit from which they evolved. Natural resources are recorded at their historical (acquisition) cost. Development costs, if any, are added to the cost of the natural resources.

EXAMPLE 11-13: Examples of natural resources are oil and gas fields, mineral deposits, and tracts of standing timber. Development costs for these natural resources include drilling (oil), mine shafts (minerals), and seedlings (timber).

B. Natural resources are listed on the balance sheet at cost less accumulated *depletion.*

Depletion is the term used to describe the allocation of the cost of the natural resource to the units removed. Depletion is discussed in more detail in Chapter 12.

11-6. Intangible Assets

A. *Intangibles* **are noncurrent assets that lack physical substance but confer benefits or rights that are useful to the business.**

Common types of intangible assets are patents, copyrights, goodwill, trademarks, leaseholds, and leasehold improvements.

1. *Patents.* Patents represent the exclusive right to manufacture, use, or sell a product. They are granted for a period of 17 years. Although the legal life of a patent is 17 years, the economic (useful) life may be shorter. The amortization period for the cost of patents should be its economic life if shorter than the legal life.

2. *Copyrights.* Copyrights represent the exclusive right to publish and/or sell artistic, musical, or literary works. They are granted for the lifetime of the author of the work, plus 50 years. Like patents, the economic life of a copyright may be shorter than its legal life. The accounting profession has stated that intangible assets should be amortized over a period not to exceed forty years. Copyrights should therefore be amortized over their economic life, their legal life, or a period of forty years, whichever is shorter.

3. *Goodwill.* Goodwill is that part of the purchase price of an operating entity that cannot be identified with particular assets. Goodwill may result from good management, good location, customer habits, or other similar traits. Only purchased goodwill is recorded and presented in the financial statements because it is the only type of goodwill that can be objectively determined. Goodwill equals the amount by which the purchase price exceeds the appraised value of the identifiable net assets. Goodwill should be allocated over its useful life, not to exceed forty years.

4. *Trademarks.* Trademarks are names, symbols, or devices used to identify a product or a firm. Like goodwill, a trademark normally appears as an asset only if it is acquired through purchase. In most instances, the costs of developing a trademark are minimal and should be expensed when incurred.

5. *Leaseholds.* Leaseholds are contracts granting the right to use specific property for a specific period of time. Leaseholds are allocated over the life of the lease.

6. *Leasehold improvements.* Leasehold improvements are additions and/or improvements to property leased under long-term leases. Leasehold improvements are allocated over the anticipated life of the lease or the life of the improvements, whichever is less. Such improvements stay with the property when it reverts to the owner at the end of the lease unless the lease specifies otherwise.

7. *Research and development.* Although substantial costs may be incurred through research and development of new products, the cost of product-related research and development must be expensed in the period incurred. Although future benefits may be realized, the matching of these costs to future revenue would be difficult, if not impossible, to objectively verify.

B. Intangible assets are recorded at historic cost.

Intangible assets appear on the balance sheet immediately after plant assets. They are reported at their unamortized cost; that is, the portion of the cost not previously amortized to expense.

1. *Purchase cost.* Generally, only the cost of *purchasing* an intangible asset is recorded in the asset account. If an intangible asset, such as a copyright, is internally developed, its costs must be expensed when incurred.

2. *Defense costs.* The cost of successfully defending the right granted by patents, copyrights, and trademarks is added to the intangible asset account. If such a defense is unsuccessful, the legal cost should be expensed in the current year. In addition, the balance in the asset account may have to be reduced or eliminated if the asset's value is affected as a result of the unsuccessful defense.

RAISE YOUR GRADES

Can you explain...?

☑ the difference between noncurrent tangible and intangible assets
☑ how to present tangible assets on a balance sheet
☑ what is included in the cost of a tangible asset
☑ how to record lump-sum purchases of tangible assets
☑ the difference between capital and revenue expenditures
☑ how to calculate and record the gain or loss on the sale of a tangible asset
☑ how to record the exchange of one tangible asset for another of similar use
☑ how to record natural resources
☑ how intangible assets are presented on the balance sheet

SUMMARY

1. Noncurrent tangible assets acquired for use in the operation of the business rather than for resale are usually classified on the balance sheet as plant assets.

2. Noncurrent tangible assets appear on a balance sheet after current assets and investments. They may also be described as fixed assets, property, plant and equipment, or plant and equipment.

3. Most noncurrent tangible assets are depreciated. Land is an exception.

4. Noncurrent tangible assets are reported at their original cost less accumulated depreciation (net book value). Original cost includes all reasonable and necessary expenditures made to get the asset in place and ready to use.

5. The cost of a lump-sum purchase of tangible assets should be allocated to each type of asset based on relative fair market value.

6. Costs incurred for plant assets that provide benefits only to the current accounting period are called revenue expenditures. Revenue expenditures include ordinary repairs and maintenance and are expensed immediately.

7. Costs incurred for plant assets that provide benefits to more than one accounting period are called capital expenditures. Capital expenditures include the original acquisition, major additions, betterments, and extraordinary repairs.

8. When assets are disposed of, depreciation is recorded up to the date of sale and both the asset cost and the accumulated depreciation are removed from the firm's books.

9. Gains or losses on the sale of depreciable assets are recorded.

10. Gains on the exchange of similar assets are not recognized. The new asset is recorded at the book value of the old asset plus the amount paid.

11. Losses on the exchange of similar assets are recognized. The new asset is recorded at the fair market value of the assets exchanged.

12. Gains and losses on the exchange of dissimilar items are recognized. Accountants believe that the earning process is complete when the exchange of dissimilar items has taken place.

13. Natural resources represent physical assets that are created by nature. They have utility by use or sale only after being removed from the tract or deposit where they evolved.

14. Natural resources are recorded at historical cost and appear on the balance sheet in the noncurrent assets section at cost less accumulated depletion.

15. Intangible assets are noncurrent assets which lack physical substance but confer benefits and rights that are of value to the business. Common types of intangible assets are patents, copyrights, goodwill, trademarks, leaseholds, and leasehold improvements.

16. Intangible assets are accounted for at cost and appear on the balance sheet at cost or at that portion of cost not previously amortized.

RAPID REVIEW   Answers

True or False

1. Noncurrent tangible assets are expected to be used for more than one accounting period. [Section 11-1]   *True*

2. Amortization of intangible assets is similar to depreciation of plant assets. [Section 11-6]   *True*

3. The same type of physical asset may be classified as inventory to one firm and as a plant asset to is another firm. [Section 11-1]   *True*

4. Land is depreciable property. [Section 11-1]   *False*

5. The cost of noncurrent tangible assets is usually charged to expense over more than one accounting period. [Section 11-1]   *True*

6. Noncurrent tangible assets appear on the balance sheet at their market value. [Section 11-1]   *False*

7. Plant and equipment are recorded at their historical cost that includes all reasonable and necessary costs to get the asset in place and ready to use. [Section 11-2]   *True*

8. The cost of a lump-sum purchase of noncurrent tangible assets should be allocated, usually based on fair market value. [Section 11-2]   *True*

9. Net book value is equal to the historical cost of an asset plus accumulated depreciation. [Section 11-1]   *False*

10. Revenue expenditures benefit more than one accounting period. [Section 11-3]   *False*

11. The complete overhaul of a piece of machinery which extends the life of the asset would be an extraordinary repair and increase the net book value of the asset. [Section 11-3]   *True*

12. Intangible assets lack physical substance. [Section 11-6]   *True*

13. The accumulated depreciation account is debited at the time the related asset is sold. [Section 11-4]   *True*

14. Sales of plant and equipment may be for book value or for an amount greater than or smaller than book value. [Section 11-4]   *True*

15. Book value is the difference between the recorded cost of an asset and the accumulated depreciation. [Section 11-1]   *True*

16. When one noncurrent tangible asset is exchanged for another similar asset, a gain is recorded if the trade-in allowance is greater than book value. [Section 11-4]   *False*

17. Depletion is the term used to describe the allocation of the cost of a natural resource to the units removed. [Section 11-5]   *True*

SOLVED PROBLEMS

PROBLEM 11-1: Dog-Gone Company, a company selling dog food and dog supplies, recently opened for business. During the first month of operation, it acquired the following articles: 5,000 pounds of dog food, 100 dog collars of various sizes and styles, two typewriters for use in the office, a cash register, three months' supply of paper bags in which to place customers' merchandise, an adding machine for use in the office, two months' supply of stationery, and 50 dog leads. Which of these items should be considered depreciable assets by the firm?

Answer: Only the typewriters, cash register, and the adding machine should be considered depreciable assets. Although the paper bags and stationery will be used in the operation of the business, the company expects to use these supplies in less than one accounting period. The dog food, dog collars, and dog leads represent merchandise for resale, and thus will be carried as inventory. [Section 11-1]

PROBLEM 11-2: Practical Company purchased a large piece of equipment with a list price of $100,000. The firm took advantage of a 2% discount offered for prompt payment. In order to move the equipment to its place of business, Practical Company had to pay $900 for a special permit to use the county roads; rent a special crane to position the equipment on the firm's truck, for a cost of $500; and pay $300 for a county escort through the business district. While unloading the equipment at the firm's place of business, damage occurred which cost $800 to repair. Special electrical wiring, costing $1,100, and additional concrete reinforcement, costing $700, had to be provided so the equipment could be installed. The company financed the acquisition with a note payable and paid $635 interest. What is the acquisition cost of the equipment?

Answer: $101,500

List price	$100,000	
Less discount	2,000	$ 98,000
Permit		900
Crane rental		500
County escort		300
Special wiring		1,100
Concrete reinforcement		700
Total cost		$101,500

The damage is not considered to be a normal and reasonable cost. Interest costs are financing costs, not a cost of the acquired asset. [Section 11-2]

PROBLEM 11-3: Do-Good Company purchased some office equipment, trucks, and store equipment at an auction. The firm paid a total of $100,000 for all of the assets. Valuation of these assets for property tax purposes was as follows: office equipment, $30,000; trucks, $4,000; and store equipment, $6,000. How should the firm record the acquisition cost of these assets?

Answer: [Section 11-2]

Office equipment	$75,000
Trucks	$10,000
Store equipment	$15,000

The property tax valuation could serve as the basis for allocating the acquisition cost, as follows:

	Tax Value	% of Value*	Cost Allocation*
Office equipment	$30,000	75%	$ 75,000
Trucks	4,000	10%	10,000
Store equipment	6,000	15%	15,000
Total	$40,000	100%	$100,000

*Calculations: Office equipment—$30,000 ÷ $40,000 = .75 or 75%
.75 × $100,000 = $75,000
Trucks—$4,000 ÷ $40,000 = .10 or 10%
.10 × $100,000 = $10,000
Store equipment—$6,000 ÷ $40,000 = .15 or 15%
.15 × $100,000 = $15,000

PROBLEM 11-4: New Company decided to replace its window unit air conditioners with a central air-conditioning unit. This was done primarily to make customers more comfortable; the building life would not be extended as a result. The net cost of the central air unit amounted to $5,400. How should this capital expenditure be recorded?

Answer:

Date	Building	5,400	00		
	Cash			5,400	00
	To record the cost of purchasing and				
	installing an air-conditioning unit.				

The installation of the central air-conditioning unit would be considered a betterment because it improves the quality of service that New Company can provide to its customers. The cost should be added to the Building asset account. If the estimated useful life of the air conditioner is less than the useful life of the building, the cost should be debited to a separate account. [Section 11-3]

PROBLEM 11-5: New Company (Problem 11-4) also overhauled some of its equipment, replacing an engine with a newer engine. The net cost of the new engine amounted to $1,800, and extended the life of the equipment by two years. How should this capital expenditure be recorded?

Answer:

Date	Accumulated Depreciation — Equipment	1,800	00		
	Cash			1,800	00
	To record the replacement of engine				
	in equipment.				

The new engine would be considered an extraordinary repair because it extended the useful life of the equipment. Thus, the expenditure should be recorded by debiting the Accumulated Depreciation account and crediting Cash. [Section 11-3]

PROBLEM 11-6: Re-New Company sold a machine with a cost of $12,000 and accumulated depreciation of $3,000 for $9,000 cash. How should this sale be recorded?

Answer:

Date	Cash	9,000	00		
	Accumulated Depreciation — Equipment	3,000	00		
	Machine			12,000	00
	To record sale of machine at book value.				

The company received an amount equal to the machine's book value. No gain or loss occurred. [Section 11-4]

PROBLEM 11-7: Suppose that Re-New Company (Problem 11-6) sold its machine for $11,000. How should this sale be recorded?

Answer:

Date	Cash	11,000	00		
	Accumulated Depreciation — Equipment	3,000	00		
	Machine			12,000	00
	Gain on Sale of Plant Assets			2,000	00
	To record gain on sale of machine.				
	Sale price ($11,000) − Book value				
	($12,000 − $3,000) = $2,000 gain.				

The firm received $2,000 more than the book value for the machine. Thus, a gain is recorded. [Section 11-4]

PROBLEM 11-8: Assume now that Re-New's machine (Problem 11-6) was sold for $7,500. How should this sale be recorded?

Answer:

Date	Cash	7,500	00		
	Accumulated Depreciation — Equipment	3,000	00		
	Loss on Sale of Plant Assets	1,500	00		
	Machine			12,000	00
	To record loss on sale of machine.				
	Sale price ($7,500) − Book value				
	($12,000 − $3,000) = $1,500 loss.				

The firm received $1,500 less than the machine's book value. Thus, a loss is recorded. [Section 11-4]

PROBLEM 11-9: Basic Company exchanged a truck used in its operations for a new truck. The old truck originally cost $10,000; $4,000 of accumulated depreciation had been recorded on the asset. The new truck sold for a list price of $14,000. The firm received a $7,500 trade-in allowance. How should the exchange be recorded for book purposes?

Answer:

Date					
	Truck (New)	12,500	00		
	Accumulated Depreciation—Truck	4,000	00		
	Truck (Old)			10,000	00
	Cash			6,500	00
	To record exchange of old truck with a				
	book value of $6,000 and a				
	trade-in of $7,500 for a new truck				
	with a list price of $14,000.				

The book value of the old truck was $6,000 ($10,000 − $4,000). The gain on the exchange of similar items is deferred because the earning process is not complete. The new asset is recorded at the amount given up—cash of $6,500 plus the book value of the old asset, $6,000. [Section 11-4]

PROBLEM 11-10: Boulder Company exchanged a truck (original cost, $10,000; accumulated depreciation, $6,000) for a new truck which had a fair market value of $12,000. A $3,000 trade-in allowance was given by the seller. How should this exchange be recorded?

Answer:

Date					
	Truck (New)	12,000	00		
	Accumulated Depreciation—Equipment	6,000	00		
	Loss on Exchange of Plant Assets	1,000	00		
	Truck (Old)			10,000	00
	Cash			9,000	00
	To record loss on exchange of truck.				

The company must pay $9,000 cash for the new truck ($12,000 cost of new truck less $3,000 trade-in allowance). The trade-in allowance can be assumed to be the fair market value of the old truck. Therefore, the loss on the truck is $1,000 ($3,000 fair market value of old truck less $4,000 book value). A loss is recorded. [Section 11-4]

PROBLEM 11-11: New Product Company was involved in litigation, defending its patents. The cost of the firm's successful defense amounted to $2,500. How should the firm record these costs?

Answer:

Date	Patent	2,500	00		
	Cash			2,500	00
	To record cost of successful defense				
	of patent rights.				

The cost of a successful patent defense is added to the asset account. [Section 11-6]

12 NONCURRENT TANGIBLE AND INTANGIBLE ASSETS: AMORTIZATION

THIS CHAPTER IS ABOUT

☑ **Plant and Equipment Cost Allocation**
☑ **Journal Entry for Depreciation**
☑ **Depreciation Methods**
☑ **Revising Depreciation Rates**
☑ **Natural Resource Cost Allocation**
☑ **Intangible Asset Cost Amortization**

12-1. Plant and Equipment Cost Allocation

A. The cost of tangible plant assets, except for land, is gradually allocated to expense as the assets are used in accordance with the matching principle.

Amortization is the general term used to describe the process of systematically allocating cost to expense. This process allows a firm to transfer the cost of an asset to expense over the expected life of the asset in a rational and systematic way.

B. The allocation process for plant assets is called depreciation.

Depreciation is the process of transferring the cost of plant and equipment to expense. It is not a valuation process. It is a systematic method of allocating an asset's cost over its estimated useful life.

EXAMPLE 12-1: Assume that Matz Company purchases a truck for use in its operations. When the truck is used in the operation of the business, it helps produce revenues. A portion of the cost of the truck should be transferred from the balance sheet (asset) to the income statement (expense) over the years the truck provides service.

C. Depreciation is based on asset cost, estimated useful life, and estimated salvage value.

As discussed in Chapter 11, depreciable assets are recorded at historical cost. The estimated useful life is the length of time the firm expects to be able to use the asset in normal operations. The salvage value (sometimes referred to as residual value) is the amount the firm estimates the asset will bring if sold at the end of its useful life.

EXAMPLE 12-2: Estimated useful life is usually expressed in years and fractions of years. However, the lives of some assets can better be described in terms of how many units of output they can produce, such as how many miles a vehicle can be driven during its useful life.

12-2. Journal Entry for Depreciation

A. Regardless of the method of calculating depreciation, the adjusting entry to record depreciation is the same.

The asset's cost remains intact in the asset account. This allows the users of financial statements to determine the original asset cost. The depreciation for the period is credited to the contra asset account, Accumulated Depreciation. Accumulated depreciation continues to increase until it equals the asset cost less estimated salvage value. Accumulated depreciation is subtracted from the asset account on the balance sheet to show the net book value of the asset. If the asset is sold, traded, or scrapped, the asset and the accumulated depreciation are both removed, as discussed in Chapter 11.

EXAMPLE 12-3: Assume that store equipment has an original cost of $15,000. The Accumulated Depreciation account balance totals $6,000. Book value of $9,000 will be presented on the balance sheet as follows:

```
Plant assets:
  Store Equipment................................................  $15,000
  Less:  Accumulated Depreciation ...............................    6,000   $9,000
```

B. The adjusting entry to record depreciation results in a debit to Depreciation Expense and a credit to Accumulated Depreciation.

EXAMPLE 12-4: Assume depreciation for the period amounts to $1,000. The adjusting entry would be

Date	Depreciation Expense	1,000	
	Accumulated Depreciation		1,000
	Adjusting entry to record		
	depreciation expense for current		
	accounting period		

C. Initial depreciation on assets is usually calculated to the nearest full month.

Management often adopts a simplifying policy for recording depreciation. For example, depreciation is commonly disregarded in the month of purchase if the asset is acquired after the 15th of the month. Under this policy, a full month's depreciation is recorded in the month of acquisition if the asset is purchased in the first half of the month.

12-3. Depreciation Methods

Four depreciation methods are commonly used by firms.

A. The *straight-line method* spreads the depreciable amount (cost minus salvage) evenly over the years the asset is used.

The straight-line method is the easiest method for calculating depreciation. It assumes the asset is equally used over time. Using this approach, an equal amount of cost is allocated to expense each period of the asset's useful life. Straight-line depreciation is calculated as follows.

$$\frac{\text{Cost} - \text{Salvage}}{\text{Useful Life in Years}} = \frac{\text{Depreciation}}{\text{per Year}}$$

Depreciation for one month would, of course, be calculated by dividing annual depreciation by twelve.

EXAMPLE 12-5: A machine with a cost of $16,000 is expected to have a useful life of five years. Its estimated salvage value is $1,000. Straight-line depreciation for a year would be calculated as follows:

$$\frac{\$16,000 - \$1,000}{5} = \$3,000$$

Monthly depreciation would be

$$\frac{\$3,000}{12} = \$250$$

B. The *units-of-production* method bases periodic depreciation on output.

The units-of-production method is based on the assumption that an asset depreciates only as it is used. The asset life is expressed in expected units of output, such as hours, miles, or number of units. There are two steps to this method.

1. *Calculate the depreciation per unit.* The first step is to calculate the per unit cost as follows:

$$\frac{\text{Cost} - \text{Salvage}}{\text{Estimated Units of Useful Life}} = \frac{\text{Depreciation per}}{\text{Unit of Output}}$$

2. *Calculate the depreciation for total units produced.* The second step is to calculate the amount of depreciation expense recorded in any one period by multiplying depreciation per unit by the number of units of output for that period.

EXAMPLE 12-6: A machine with a cost of $16,000 and an estimated salvage value of $1,000 is expected to be useful in producing 50,000 units of output. Depreciation per unit would be:

$$\frac{\$16,000 - \$1,000}{50,000} = 30¢ \text{ per unit}$$

Depreciation during a period in which 12,000 units were produced would amount to

$$12,000 \text{ units} \times 30¢ \text{ per unit} = \$3,600$$

C. The *declining balance* method and *sum-of-the-years'-digits* method allocate a larger amount of depreciation to the early years of useful life.

These methods assume that more utility is used up early in the asset's life. Both are accelerated methods because a larger portion of the asset's cost is allocated to expense in the early years of use and lesser amounts in the later years.

1. *The declining balance method.* Although salvage value does not enter into the depreciation calculations using the declining balance method, the asset should not be depreciated to a book value below its estimated salvage value. The most common form of this depreciation method is the *double-declining balance approach.* Using this approach, the annual straight-line rate is doubled. The straight-line rate is determined by dividing 100% by the estimated useful life (in years). This straight-line rate is then multiplied by 2 to determine the annual double-declining balance rate. Once determined, this annual rate does not change. The annual double-declining balance rate is then multiplied by the asset's book value (cost − accumulated depreciation) to determine the annual depreciation expense. Since book value decreases each year, the depreciation expense each year will decrease.

EXAMPLE 12-7: An asset with a cost of $16,000 and a salvage value of $1,000 is expected to be useful for five years. The straight-line depreciation rate would be 20% (1 ÷ 5 years = .20 or 20%). The double-declining balance rate would be 40% (.20 × 2 = .40 or 40%). Annual depreciation would be calculated as follows:

Year	Annual Calculation*	Annual Depreciation Expense	Accumulated Depreciation	Remaining Book Value
1	.40 × $16,000 = $6,400	$ 6,400	$16,000 − $ 6,400 = $9,600
2	.40 × $ 9,600 = $3,840	$10,240	$16,000 − $10,240 = $5,760
3	.40 × $ 5,760 = $2,304	$12,544	$16,000 − $12,544 = $3,456
4	.40 × $ 3,456 = $1,382	$13,926	$16,000 − $13,926 = $2,074
5		$1,074**	$15,000	$16,000 − $15,000 = $1,000

* Double declining rate times the book value.

** The depreciation expense in the fifth year would be limited to no more than $1,074. The company is entitled to $1,074 depreciation expense in Year 5. Book value would then equal $1,000, the estimated salvage value. The asset's book value should not be depreciated below the salvage value.

2. *The sum-of-the-years'-digits method.* The sum-of-the years'-digits method, like the declining balance method, is an accelerated depreciation method. The rate for the sum-of-the-years'-digits method is determined as follows:

$$\text{Fraction} = \frac{\text{Number of Years of Estimated Life at Beginning of Period}}{\text{Sum of the Years of the Asset's Estimated Life}}$$

The numerator of the fraction decreases each year. This fraction is multiplied by the asset cost minus salvage value to determine annual depreciation expense.

EXAMPLE 12-8: The asset with a cost of $16,000 and a salvage value of $1,000 is expected to be useful for five years. The denominator of the fraction would be $5 + 4 + 3 + 2 + 1$, or 15 (sum of the years of estimated useful life). There is also a formula that can be used: $[(N)(N + 1)] \div 2$ with N equaling the total number of years of useful life. The calculation for this example is $[(5)(5 + 1)] \div 2 = 15$ (denominator of fraction). Annual depreciation expense would be calculated as follows:

Year	Annual Depreciation Calculation	Annual Depreciation Expense
1	5/15 × ($16,000 − $1,000) =	$5,000
2	4/15 × ($16,000 − $1,000) =	$4,000
3	3/15 × ($16,000 − $1,000) =	$3,000
4	2/15 × ($16,000 − $1,000) =	$2,000
5	1/15 × ($16,000 − $1,000) =	$1,000

When using the sum-of-the-years'-digits method of depreciation, it is necessary to record depreciation expense for one full calendar year at one year's rate before using the next year's rate. This becomes important when an asset is acquired at some time other than the beginning of the fiscal year. In that case, fractions of the year must be allocated to the fiscal year.

EXAMPLE 12-9: Assume that the asset described in Example 12-8 is acquired April 1, 19x1, three months after the start of the fiscal year. Using the sum-of-the-years'-digits method, the annual depreciation expense for each fiscal year would be as follows:

Fiscal Year	Depreciation Calculation	Annual Depreciation Expense
19x1	(5/15 × $15,000) × 3/4* = $3,750	$3,750
19x2	(5/15 × $15,000) × 1/4 = $1,250	
	(4/15 × $15,000) × 3/4 = $3,000	$4,250
19x3	(4/15 × $15,000) × 1/4 = $1,000	
	(3/15 × $15,000) × 3/4 = $2,250	$3,250
19x4	(3/15 × $15,000) × 1/4 = $ 750	
	(2/15 × $15,000) × 3/4 = $1,500	$2,250
19x5	(2/15 × $15,000) × 1/4 = $ 500	
	(1/15 × $15,000) × 3/4 = $ 750	$1,250
19x6	(1/15 × $15,000) × 1/4 = $ 250	$ 250

* The asset has been in use for 9/12 of the year (or 3/4). The remaining 3/12 or 1/4 is recognized in the following period. Note that the numerator does not change until a full year's depreciation expense has been recorded.

12-4. Revising Depreciation Rates

Occasionally, circumstances occur which require revising the amount of annual depreciation expense. Errors may be made in estimating the asset's useful life or in estimating the salvage value. The book value of the asset may change as the result of a betterment or an extraordinary repair (see Chapter 11). When this occurs, the remaining book value is allocated over the asset's remaining useful life.

EXAMPLE 12-10: An asset with a cost of $11,500 and an estimated salvage value of $1,500 has been depreciated over three of the five years of its estimated life using the straight-line method. At the end of the third year of its life, the asset's book value is $5,500 as shown below.

$11,500 Original cost
− 6,000 3 years' depreciation ($2,000 per year)
$ 5,500 Book value

At the beginning of the fourth year, an extraordinary repair costing $2,000 extended the life of the asset by two more years. The estimated salvage value was reduced to $1,000. Depreciation for each of the remaining four years of the asset's life would be calculated as follows:

$5,500 Book value before extraordinary repairs
+2,000 Extraordinary repairs
$7,500 New book value

$$\frac{\$7,500 \text{ New book value} - \$1,000 \text{ Current estimated salvage}}{4 \text{ years remaining life}} = \$1,625 \text{ Adjusted depreciation expense per year}$$

12-5. Natural Resource Cost Allocation

A. The cost of natural resources is allocated on a units-of-production basis.

The estimated life of the asset is expressed in terms of the number of units of output the firm expects to extract.

B. The process of allocating the cost of a natural resource is called *depletion.*

Natural resources are listed on the balance sheet at cost less accumulated depletion. If all the units extracted (removed) from the natural resource are sold during the year they are extracted, the entire depletion cost appears as an expense on the income statement. If a portion of the units extracted remains unsold at year end, the depletion cost of the unsold units is shown on the balance sheet as inventory.

EXAMPLE 12-11: A mineral deposit with an estimated 750,000 tons of ore is acquired for $1,500,000. There is no estimated salvage value. The depletion cost per unit is $2 per ton ($1,500,000 ÷ 750,000 tons). If 60,000 tons are extracted during the first year, the depletion charge will be $120,000 (60,000 tons × $2 cost per ton). The asset would appear on the balance sheet as follows:

Mineral deposit	$1,500,000
Less: Accumulated depletion	120,000
	$1,380,000

If all 60,000 tons were sold during the same year, a depletion expense of $120,000 would appear on the income statement. If only 40,000 tons were sold, an $80,000 depletion expense (40,000 tons × $2) would appear on the income statement and $40,000 (20,000 tons × $2) would appear on the balance sheet as inventory.

12-6. Intangible Asset Cost Amortization

A. The process of allocating the cost of an intangible asset over its useful life is called *amortization.*

Intangible assets should be amortized over their estimated useful lives. If the legal life of an intangible asset exceeds its estimated useful life, the asset should be amortized over the shorter estimated useful life. An intangible asset should not be amortized over more than 40 years or its legal life, whichever is shorter. If an intangible asset is determined at any time to be worthless, it should be written off in the current period.

B. Amortization of intangible assets is calculated using the straight-line method.

Amortization Expense is debited to record the cost allocation. The intangible asset account is normally credited directly, although a contra asset account can be used.

EXAMPLE 12-12: A patent is purchased from another firm for $3,400. Although this new patent has all 17 years of its legal life remaining, it has an estimated useful life of 10 years. The asset cost of $3,400 would be amortized over 10 years using the straight-line method. The adjusting entry to record annual amortization is shown below.

Date	Amortization Expense	340	
	Patents		340
	To record the patent amortization over its estimated useful life of 10 years		

RAISE YOUR GRADES

Can you explain . . . ?

☑ depreciation
☑ what three components are the basis for the depreciation of tangible assets

☑ how to record the adjusting entry for depreciation
☑ how to calculate depreciation using each of the four methods illustrated
☑ how to revise annual depreciation expense if one of the three basic components changes
☑ how the cost of natural resources is transferred to expense as the asset is depleted
☑ how intangible assets are amortized

SUMMARY

1. Amortization is the general term for the allocation of an asset's cost to expense.
2. Amortization of plant and equipment is called depreciation.
3. Depreciation is based on the asset cost, its expected useful life, and its estimated salvage value.
4. When depreciation is recorded, the asset account balance remains intact. Depreciation Expense is debited and Accumulated Depreciation is credited. On the balance sheet, the Accumulated Depreciation account (a contra asset account) is subtracted from the asset to show the book value of the asset.
5. Depreciation is usually calculated to the nearest full month.
6. Four common methods are used to calculate depreciation. They are straight-line, units-of-production, declining balance, and sum-of-the-years'-digits.
7. The straight-line method spreads the depreciable amount evenly over the years the asset is used.
8. The units-of-production method bases periodic depreciation on the period's output.
9. The declining balance method and sum-of-the-years'-digits method allocate a larger amount of depreciation to the early years of useful life.
10. If changes are made in the asset's book value, estimated useful life, or its estimated salvage value, the new book value is allocated over the new remaining life of the asset.
11. As a natural resource is used up, the cost is allocated to expense on a units-of-production basis and is called depletion.
12. The cost of intangible assets is amortized over their estimated useful lives on the straight-line basis. Amortization is normally credited directly to the asset account.

RAPID REVIEW   Answers

True or False

1. Amortization is the general term used to describe the allocation of asset cost to expense. [Section 12-1]   *True*

2. Depreciation is an allocation process, not a valuation process. [Section 12-1]   *True*

3. Land is depreciated over one hundred years. [Section 12-1]   *False*

4. Each method of calculating depreciation requires a different type of adjusting entry. [Section 12-2]   *False*

5. Depreciation is credited directly to the asset account. [Section 12-2]   *False*

6. Net book value or book value represents the undepreciated portion of the asset cost. [Section 12-2]   *True*

7. The adjusting entry to record depreciation consists of a debit to the Depreciation Expense account and a credit to the Accumulated Depreciation account. [Section 12-2]   *True*

8. Accelerated depreciation methods allocate larger portions of depreciation to the earlier years of life. [Section 12-3]   *True*

9. A revision in the asset's useful life or in the estimate of salvage value has no effect on the depreciation expense in future years. [Section 12-4] *False*

10. The units-of-production method of depreciation is used to amortize the cost of natural resources. [Section 12-5] *True*

11. Intangible assets require no amortization. [Section 12-6] *False*

SOLVED PROBLEMS

PROBLEM 12-1: Shadow Company owns factory equipment with an original cost of $64,000. It is expected to have a useful life of four years. At the end of its estimated useful life, the equipment is expected to have a salvage value of $4,000. Using straight-line depreciation, calculate the annual depreciation expense.

Answer: $15,000

$$\frac{\text{Cost} - \text{Salvage}}{\text{Years of Life}} = \frac{\$64,000 - \$4,000}{4}$$

$$\frac{\$60,000}{4} = \$15,000$$

The same amount of depreciation expense would be recorded each year using the straight-line method. [Section 12-3]

PROBLEM 12-2: If Shadow Company (Problem 12-1) depreciated the factory equipment using the units-of-production method, assuming an expected total output of 100,000 units, how much depreciation expense should be recorded during a period in which 30,000 units were produced and sold?

Answer: $18,000

$$\frac{\text{Cost} - \text{Salvage}}{\text{Total Units of Output}} = \frac{\text{Depreciation}}{\text{Per Unit}}$$

$$\frac{\text{Depreciation}}{\text{Per Unit}} \times \frac{\text{Units}}{\text{Produced}} = \frac{\text{Depreciation}}{\text{Expense}}$$

$$\frac{\$64,000 - \$4,000}{100,000 \text{ units}} = 60¢$$

$$60¢ \times 30,000 \text{ units} = \$18,000$$

[Section 12-3]

PROBLEM 12-3: Would Shadow Company (Problem 12-1) record the same amount of depreciation expense each year using the units-of-production method?

Answer: No. While the cost per unit would be the same each period, the total amount of depreciation expense recorded would change according to the number of units produced during each period. [Section 12-3]

PROBLEM 12-4: Assume that Shadow Company (Problem 12-1) uses the double-declining balance method to calculate depreciation. How much depreciation expense would be recorded in each of the four years of the asset's life?

Answer: $32,000; $16,000; $8,000; $4,000

$$\frac{1}{\text{Years of Life}} = \frac{\text{Straight-Line}}{\text{Rate}} \times 2 = \frac{\text{Double-Declining}}{\text{Balance Rate}}$$

$$1/4 = .25 \times 2 = .50 \text{ or } 50\%$$

$$\frac{\text{Book Value at}}{\text{Start of Year}} \times \frac{\text{Double Declining}}{\text{Balance Rate}} = \frac{\text{Annual Depreciation}}{\text{Expense}}$$

Book Value × Rate	=	Annual Depreciation Expense	Book Value
$64,000 × .50	=	$32,000	$32,000
$32,000 × .50	=	16,000	16,000
$16,000 × .50	=	8,000	8,000
$ 8,000 × .50	=	4,000	4,000

[Section 12-3]

PROBLEM 12-5: Assume that Shadow Company (Problem 12-1) uses the sum-of-the-years'-digits method for calculating depreciation. How much depreciation expense would be recorded in each of the four years of the asset's life?

Answer: $24,000; $18,000; $12,000; $6,000

$$\frac{\text{Number of Years Life at Beginning of Year}}{\text{Sum of the Years of the Asset Life}} \times (\text{Cost} - \text{Salvage}) = \frac{\text{Annual Depreciation}}{\text{Expense}}$$

$4/10^* \times \$60,000 = \$24,000$

$3/10 \times \$60,000 = \$18,000$

$2/10 \times \$60,000 = \$12,000$

$1/10 \times \$60,000 = \$ 6,000$

$$^*4 + 3 + 2 + 1 = 10 \text{ or } \frac{4(4 + 1)}{2} = 10 \qquad \text{[Section 12-3]}$$

PROBLEM 12-6: Assume that Shadow Company (Problem 12-1) acquired its factory equipment on April 30, 19x1, four months after the start of the fiscal year. If it uses sum-of-the-years'-digits depreciation, how much depreciation would be recorded during each calendar year of the asset's life?

Answer: $16,000; $20,000; $14,000; $8,000; $2,000

Fiscal Year	Depreciation Calculation		Annual Depreciation Expense
19x1	4/10 × $60,000 × 2/3*	= $16,000	$16,000
19x2	4/10 × $60,000 × 1/3	= $ 8,000	
	3/10 × $60,000 × 2/3	= $12,000	$20,000
19x3	3/10 × $60,000 × 1/3	= $ 6,000	
	2/10 × $60,000 × 2/3	= $ 8,000	$14,000
19x4	2/10 × $60,000 × 1/3	= $ 4,000	
	1/10 × $60,000 × 2/3	= $ 4,000	$ 8,000
19x5	1/10 × $60,000 × 1/3	= $ 2,000	$ 2,000

* The asset has been in use for 8/12 of the year (or 2/3).

[Section 12-3]

PROBLEM 12-7: An asset with a cost of $12,000 and a salvage value of $2,000 has been depreciated over three of its four years of expected life using the straight-line method. At the beginning of the fourth year, an extraordinary repair of $1,500 extended the asset life by one year. What is the annual depreciation expense for each of the remaining years of the asset's life?

Answer: $2,000

Prior annual depreciation expense was $2,500 [($12,000 − 2,000 = $10,000)/4 years]. Thus, book value before the extraordinary repairs amounted to $4,500 ($12,000 − 7,500). After the extraordinary repairs, book value would amount to $6,000 ($4,500 + $1,500), and the estimated remaining life would be two years. New book value minus salvage value spread evenly over the adjusted estimated life would equal the new annual depreciation expense.

$$\frac{\$6,000 - 2,000}{2} = \frac{\$4,000}{2} = \$2,000$$

[Section 12-4]

PROBLEM 12-8: A firm acquired a coal mine with an estimated deposit of 1,000,000 tons of coal at a total cost of $3,500,000 with no estimated salvage value. If 40,000 tons are extracted and sold during the first year, what would the depletion expense be?

Answer: $140,000

$$\frac{\$3,500,000 \text{ cost}}{1,000,000 \text{ tons}} = \$3.50 \text{ per ton}$$

$3.50 per ton × 40,000 tons = $140,000

[Section 12-5]

PROBLEM 12-9: If the firm in Problem 12-8 sold only 30,000 of the extracted tons during the first year, how much depletion expense would appear on the income statement?

Answer: $105,000

$3.50 per ton × 30,000 tons = $105,000. The remaining depletion amount of $35,000 would appear on the balance sheet as inventory. [Section 12-5]

PROBLEM 12-10: A copyright with a remaining legal life of ten years is acquired for a cost of $10,000. It is estimated that the useful life of the copyright will be five years. How much annual amortization expense should be recorded?

Answer: $2,000

The copyright would be amortized over the shorter of the legal or estimated useful life. Thus, $10,000 ÷ 5 = $2,000. [Section 12-6]

PROBLEM 12-11: Prepare the journal entries for the following adjusting entries:

Dec. 31 Office equipment that costs $3,000 and has a salvage value of $1,000 was depreciated for the first year of its estimated five-year life using the straight-line method.

Dec. 31 A bauxite deposit (original cost of $2,000,000; estimated deposit, 1,000,000 tons) yielded 80,000 tons and 60,000 tons of bauxite were sold during the first year of operation.

Dec. 31 A patent (original cost of $5,000; estimated useful life of five years) was amortized. The patent was acquired on January 1.

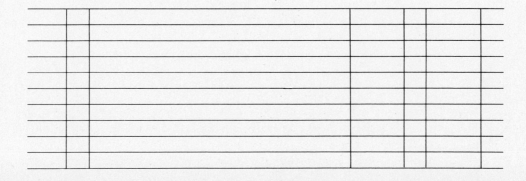

Answer: [Sections 12-2, 12-3, 12-4, and 12-5]

Dec.	31	Depreciation Expense	400	00		
		Accumulated Depreciation—Equipment			400	00
		(3,000 − 1,000)/5 years				
	31	Depletion Expense	120,000	00		
		Inventory—Bauxite	40,000	00		
		Accumulated Depletion—Mineral Deposit			160,000	00
		($2,000,000 ÷ 1,000,000 tons) ×				
		80,000 tons				
	31	Amortization Expense	1,000	00		
		Patents			1,000	00
		($5,000 ÷ 5 years)				

PROBLEM 12-12: Show how the assets in Problem 12-11 would appear on the firm's balance sheet as of December 31, after adjusting entries have been prepared.

Answer: [Sections 12-2, 12-4, and 12-5]

Current assets:
Inventory .... $ 40,000

Plant assets:
Office equipment .... $ 3,000
Less: Accumulated depreciation   400   2,600
Mineral deposit $2,000,000
Less: Accumulated depletion   160,000   1,840,000

Intangible assets:
Patent   4,000

EXAMINATION II (CHAPTERS 6 THROUGH 12)

True or False

1. Sales returns and allowances are added to gross sales to arrive at net sales. (Chapter 6)
2. Ending inventory appears on the balance sheet as a current asset. (Chapter 6)
3. Separation of duties is an internal control. (Chapter 8)
4. A debit balance in the Cash Short and Over account at the end of the period is shown as revenue on the income statement. (Chapter 8)
5. The entry to replenish Petty Cash requires a debit to Petty Cash and a credit to Cash. (Chapter 8)
6. Federal unemployment tax and state unemployment tax are deducted from the employee's gross pay. (Chapter 9)
7. During a period of rising prices, the LIFO method will result in a lower net income than the FIFO method. (Chapter 10)
8. If a depreciable asset is sold for more than book value, a gain is recorded. (Chapter 11)
9. Intangible assets are amortized over their legal life or forty years, whichever is longer. (Chapter 12)

Fill in the blanks

Fill in the missing word or words.

1. A company will have a net _____ if gross profit is greater than operating expenses. (Chapter 6)
2. A company with a large number of accounts receivable will probably maintain an accounts receivable _____ . (Chapter 7)
3. The sales journal is posted at the end of the month by debiting _____ and crediting _____ . (Chapter 7)
4. When a voucher system is used, the voucher register replaces the _____ . (Chapter 8)
5. The adjusting entry to record the estimated uncollectible accounts receivable requires a debit to _____ and a credit to _____ . (Chapter 9)
6. If ending inventory is overstated in the current year, cost of goods sold will be _____ , net income will be _____ , and equity will be _____ . (Chapter 10)
7. Costs incurred for plant assets that provide benefits to more than one accounting period are called _____ expenditures. _____ expenditures only provide benefits to the current accounting period. (Chapter 11)
8. Noncurrent assets which lack physical substance but confer benefits and rights that are of value to the business are referred to as _____ assets. (Chapter 11)

Problems

PROBLEM 1: Use the following information to calculate the cost of goods sold:

Beginning Inventory	$ 9,000
Ending Inventory	10,100
Purchases	62,300
Purchase Discounts	1,200
Purchase Returns and Allowances	800
Transportation in	2,500

PROBLEM 2: Sun Company uses the following journals: general, cash receipts, cash payments, sales and purchases. Name the journal in which each of the following transactions would be recorded:

(a) Purchase of merchandise for cash
(b) Adjusting entry for expired insurance
(c) Purchase of office equipment for cash
(d) Sale of merchandise for cash
(e) Payment of rent
(f) Payment of salaries
(g) Return of merchandise purchased on credit
(h) Sales of merchandise on credit
(i) Purchase of merchandise for credit
(j) Closing entries

PROBLEM 3: Prepare a bank reconciliation for Charles Tuna Company for May, 19x5, using the following information:

(a) The balance per the May 31, 19x5 bank statement is $10,150.
(b) The service charge for May is $15.
(c) A deposit of $526 made on May 31 did not appear on the bank statement.
(d) Checks written before May 31 that have not cleared the bank total $2,162.
(e) The balance per the company's records on May 31 is $7,029.
(f) The bank collected a customer's note receivable for $1,500.

PROBLEM 4: The adjusted trial balance at the end of the current year includes the following accounts:

	Debit	Credit
Accounts Receivable	76,000	
Allowance for Bad Debts		$ 250
Sales		350,000

Calculate the bad debts expense based on the following independent assumptions and prepare the general journal entry:

(a) Bad Debts expense is estimated to be 1% of total sales.
(b) Bad Debts expense is estimated to be 3% of credit sales (credit sales equal 60% of total sales).
(c) 4% of accounts receivable are estimated to be uncollectible.

PROBLEM 5: Orange Computer Company accepted a $2,500, six-month, 14% note receivable. Calculate the interest Orange Computer will receive on the maturity date.

PROBLEM 6: The following information is available for Tabby Company:

Beginning Inventory	100 units @ $10 =	$1,000
Purchase (Feb. 15)	350 units @ $12 =	4,200
Purchase (May 6)	510 units @ $13 =	6,630
Purchase (Oct. 31)	250 units @ $15 =	3,750

On December 31, 160 units were unsold. The company uses a periodic inventory method. Compute the ending inventory under each of the following cost flow assumptions.

(a) First-in, first-out (FIFO)
(b) Last-in, first-out (LIFO)
(c) Weighted-average cost

PROBLEM 7: On July 31, an estimate of ending inventory is necessary before monthly financial statements can be prepared. The gross profit rate in the past has been approximately 35%. Estimate ending inventory using the gross profit method.

Inventory, July 1	$ 63,000
Net purchases during July	210,000
Net sales during July	380,000

PROBLEM 8: Seminole Company sold a truck with a cost of $10,000. Accumulated depreciation up to the date of sale was $6,000. The truck was sold for $3,500. Record the sale in the journal below.

	DATE	DESCRIPTION	POST. REF.	DEBIT	CREDIT	
1						1
2						2
3						3
4						4
5						5

JOURNAL **PAGE**

PROBLEM 9: Billings Company exchanged a machine (original cost − $35,000; accumulated depreciation − $27,000) for a new machine with a list price of $50,000. A trade-in allowance of $6,000 was given. How should the exchange be recorded?

JOURNAL **PAGE**

	DATE	DESCRIPTION	POST. REF.	DEBIT	CREDIT	
1						1
2						2
3						3
4						4
5						5

PROBLEM 10: Emerald Industries acquired a new machine at a cost of $35,000. The useful life is estimated to be five years. Estimated salvage value is $5,000. Compute the depreciation for the five years using the following methods:

(a) straight-line
(b) double-declining balance
(c) sum-of-years'-digits

ANSWERS

True or False

1. False   2. True   3. True   4. False   5. False   6. False   7. True   8. True   9. False

Fill in the Blanks

1. income
2. subsidiary ledger
3. accounts receivable; sales
4. purchases journal
5. bad debts expense; allowance for bad debts
6. understated; overstated; overstated
7. capital; revenue
8. intangible

Problems

Problem 1: (Chapter 6)

Beginning Inventory			$ 9,000
Purchases		$62,300	
Less: Purchase Discounts	$1,200		
Purchase Returns and Allowances	800	2,000	
Net Purchases		$60,300	
Add: Transportation in		2,500	62,800
Cost of goods available for sale			$71,800
Less: Ending Inventory			10,100
Cost of Goods Sold			$61,700

Problem 2: (Chapter 7)

(a) Cash Payments		(f) Cash Payments
(b) General		(g) General
(c) Cash Payments		(h) Sales
(d) Cash Receipts		(i) Purchases
(e) Cash Payments		(j) General

Problem 3: (Chapter 8)

Charles Tuna Company
Bank Reconciliation
May 31, 19x5

Balance per bank statement...	$10,150
Add: Deposit in transit	526
	$10,676
Subtract: Checks outstanding	2,162
Adjusted balance...	$ 8,514
Balance per depositor's records...	$ 7,029
Add: Note collected by bank	1,500
	$ 8,529
Subtract: Service charge..	15
Adjusted balance...	$ 8,514

Problem 4: (Chapter 9)

(a) $350,000 Total Sales
    ×   .01
    $ 3,500 Estimate of Bad Debts Expense

Date	Bad Debts Expense	3,500	
	Allowance for Bad Debts		3,500

(b) $350,000   Total Sales
   ×   .60
$210,000   Credit Sales
   ×   .03
$ 6,300   Estimate of Bad Debts Expense

Date	Bad Debts Expense	6,300	
	Allowance for Bad Debts		6,300

(c) $76,000   Accounts Receivable
   ×   .04
$ 3,040   Estimated Uncollectible Accounts Receivable
− 250   Credit balance in Allowance for Bad Debts
$ 2,790   Amount of Adjusting Entry

Date	Bad Debts Expense	2,790	
	Allowance for Bad Debts		2,790

Problem 5: (Chapter 9)

$$\text{Interest} = \begin{array}{c}\textbf{Principal}\\\textbf{of the note}\end{array} \times \begin{array}{c}\textbf{Annual rate}\\\textbf{of interest}\end{array} \times \begin{array}{c}\textbf{Time note is}\\\textbf{outstanding}\end{array}$$

$$\$175 = \$2{,}500 \times .14 \times 6/12$$

Problem 6: (Chapter 10)

(a) FIFO

     Purchased Oct. 31   160 units @ 15   = $2,400 Ending Inventory

(b) LIFO

Beginning Inventory	100 units @ $10	=	$1,000
Purchased Feb. 15	60 units @ $12	=	720
	Ending Inventory		$1,720

(c) Weighted Average

Beginning Inventory	100 units @ $10	=	$ 1,000
Purchase (Feb. 15)	350 units @ $12	=	4,200
Purchase (May 6)	510 units @ $13	=	6,630
Purchase (Oct. 31)	250 units @ $15	=	3,750
Total Available Units	Total Cost of Goods Available		$15,580

$$\frac{\$15{,}580}{1{,}210 \text{ units}} = \$12.876 \text{ (rounded)}$$

$12.876 × 160 units = $2060.16 Ending Inventory

Problem 7: (Chapter 10)

1. Calculate estimated gross profit for July:

     $380,000   Net sales —July
     ×   .35   Prior period's gross profit rate
     $133,000   Estimated gross profit—July

2. Calculate cost of goods sold:

$380,000   Net sales
− 133,000   Estimated gross profit
$247,000   Estimated cost of goods sold   July

3. Determine ending inventory:

$ 63,000   Beginning inventory
+ 210,000   Purchases
$273,000   Cost of goods available for sale
− 247,000   Estimated cost of goods sold
$ 26,000   Estimated ending inventory

Problem 8: (Chapter 11)

	DATE	DESCRIPTION	POST. REF.	DEBIT	CREDIT	
JOURNAL					**PAGE**	
1	Date	Cash		3 5 0 0 00		1
2		Accumulated Depreciation		6 0 0 0 00		2
3		Loss on Sale of Truck		5 0 0 00		3
4		Truck			1 0 0 0 0 00	4
5						5

Problem 9: (Chapter 11)

	DATE	DESCRIPTION	POST. REF.	DEBIT	CREDIT	
JOURNAL					**PAGE**	
1	Date	Machine (new)		5 0 0 0 0 00		1
2		Accumulated Depreciation		2 7 0 0 0 00		2
3		Loss on Exchange of machine*		2 0 0 0 00		3
4		Cash			4 4 0 0 0 00	4
5		Machine (old)			3 5 0 0 0 00	5

* $35,000   original cost
   − 27,000   accumulated depreciation
   $ 8,000   book value
   − 6,000   trade-in allowance
   $ 2,000   loss on exchange of machine

Problem 10: (Chapter 10)

(a) Straight-line

$$\frac{\$35,000 - \$5,000}{5 \text{ years}} = \$6,000 \text{ depreciation expense per year}$$

(*b*) double-declining balance

Year	Annual Calculation		Annual Depreciation Expense	Accumulated Depreciation	Remaining Book Value
1	$35,000 × .40	=	$14,000	$14,000	$35,000
2	$21,000 × .40	=	$ 8,400	$22,400	$12,600
3	$12,600 × .40	=	$ 5,040	$27,440	$ 7,560
4			$ 2,560*	$30,000	$ 5,000
5			0		

* *The machine cannot be depreciated below the estimated salvage value of $5,000. Therefore, the depreciation expense for Year 4 will be $2,560 for a total depreciation expense in Years 1–4 of $30,000.*

(*c*) sum-of-years'-digits

Year	Annual Depreciation Calculation		Annual Depreciation Expense
1	5/15 × $30,000*	=	$10,000
2	4/15 × $30,000	=	$ 8,000
3	3/15 × $30,000	=	$ 6,000
4	2/15 × $30,000	=	$ 4,000
5	1/15 × $30,000	=	$ 2,000

* ($35,000 − $5,000)

13 PARTNERSHIP ACCOUNTING

THIS CHAPTER IS ABOUT

☑ **Characteristics of Partnerships**
☑ **Partnership Accounting**
☑ **Starting a Partnership**
☑ **Dividing Profit or Loss**
☑ **Adding a Partner**
☑ **Liquidating a Partnership**

13-1. Characteristics of Partnerships

There are three common types of business organizations in the United States—sole proprietorships, partnerships, and corporations. Partnerships will be discussed in this chapter.

A. The Uniform Partnership Act defines a partnership as "an association of two or more persons to carry on as co-owners a business for profit."

The Uniform Partnership Act has been adopted by most states and governs the formation, operation, and dissolution of partnerships. An *association* is a voluntary arrangement formed by agreement. The agreement may be verbal or written. The term *persons* includes individuals, other partnerships, corporations, and other types of associations. The purpose of forming the partnership must be to earn a *profit*. A non-profit organization cannot be a partnership.

B. There are five main characteristics of partnerships.

1. *Ease of formation.* A partnership is easy to form. As mentioned before, a partnership can be formed by either a verbal or written agreement. It should be written to prevent future misunderstanding. The agreement should include the name, address, and purpose of the business; the names and duties of each partner; the amount to be invested by each; the method for distributing profits and losses; provisions for the admission and withdrawal of partners; and the method for dissolving the partnership.
2. *Limited life.* A partnership has a limited life. The partnership is formed by agreement between the partners. The agreement ends and the partnership dissolves when a change of partners occurs. This happens when a partner withdraws, goes bankrupt, becomes incapacitated, or dies; a new partner is admitted; an existing partner retires; or the purpose of forming the partnership is completed.
3. *Unlimited liability.* The partners have unlimited liability. Each partner is personally responsible for all the debts of the partnership. Creditors must first make claims against the assets of the business. If the partnership assets are not enough to satisfy creditors, then the creditors may make claims against the personal assets of the partners.
4. *Mutual agency.* Each partner acts as an agent for the partnership. Any partner can enter into contracts to buy and sell goods and services. As long as the partner acts within the scope of normal business operations, the partnership is bound to the contract. This is called mutual agency.
5. *Co-ownership of partnership property.* When a partner invests property in a partnership,

he or she gives up all personal rights to the property. The property becomes jointly owned by all partners.

C. There are advantages and disadvantages that should be considered before forming a partnership.

One of the most important advantages of a partnership is the ease of formation. This allows two or more persons to bring together needed capital and special skills without the cost or formality of forming a corporation. There may also be tax advantages. The disadvantages include limited life, unlimited liability, and mutual agency.

13-2. Partnership Accounting

Accounting for a partnership is similar to accounting for a proprietorship. The major difference is in owners' equity because a separate capital account and drawing account are maintained for each partner. Accounting for assets and liabilities is the same as for a sole proprietorship.

EXAMPLE 13-1: Dee O'Neal and Michael Lindsay agree to form a partnership and call it D&M Video. The only difference in the accounting equation between a sole proprietorship and a partnership is in owners' equity, as shown below.

$$\text{Assets} = \text{Liabilities} + \underline{\text{Owners' Equity}}$$
$$\text{D. O'Neal, Capital}$$
$$\text{M. Lindsay, Capital}$$

Dee and Michael will each have a capital and a drawing account as illustrated below.

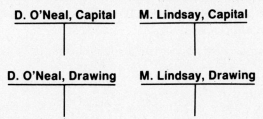

13-3. Starting a Partnership

A. To start a partnership, the new partners may contribute cash or assets other than cash.

The noncash assets should be valued at their fair market value on the day the partner transfers ownership of the assets to the partnership. The appropriate asset accounts are debited and the capital accounts are credited for any contributions.

EXAMPLE 13-2: On May 1, Dee contributes $40,000 in cash to the new partnership, D&M Video. Michael contributes $10,000 in cash, plus land and a building with fair market values of $20,000 and $30,000 respectively. To record the contributions, the following entries are made.

May	1	Cash	40,000	
		D. O'Neal, Capital		40,000
		To record cash contribution		
		for the new partnership		
	1	Cash	10,000	
		Land	20,000	
		Building	30,000	
		M. Lindsay, Capital		60,000
		To record cash and noncash		
		contributions at fair market		
		value for the new partnership		

B. Additional investments can be made by the partners.

The asset account is debited and the capital account is credited for any additional investments.

EXAMPLE 13-3: D&M Video needs additional capital. Dee and Michael each agree to invest an additional $5,000 in the business. The journal entry is shown below.

June 30	Cash	10,000	
	D. O'Neal, Capital		5,000
	M. Lindsay, Capital		5,000
	To record additional investments by partners		

Note that the capital accounts of the partners do not have to be equal. Any limitations on amounts that can be invested and withdrawn by each partner should be included in the partnership agreement.

13-4. Dividing Profit or Loss

A. The net income of a partnership can be distributed equally or in any other manner upon which the partners agree.

The net income or loss may be distributed to the partners in any manner they agree upon. If the partnership agreement does not state how profits and losses are to be distributed, the law assumes they are to be shared equally. There are several methods of distribution that partners may agree upon.

1. *Fixed ratio.* The partners may agree to share the income or loss equally or unequally, such as 60% and 40%.

EXAMPLE 13-4: Assume D&M Video earns $20,000 net income in the first year. The partnership agreement states that the income or loss will be divided on a fixed ratio of 70% to Dee and 30% to Michael. Dee's capital account will increase by $14,000 ($20,000 × .70) and Michael's will increase by $6,000 ($20,000 × .30).

2. *Recognition of services and the balance in a fixed ratio.* One partner may devote more time to the business or have special skills. This may be recognized by distributing a portion of the net income as a salary allowance. The remainder can then be divided in a fixed ratio.

EXAMPLE 13-5: Assume that the partnership agreement allows for a salary of $3,000 to Dee and $5,000 to Michael. The balance is to be shared equally. The distribution of net income of $20,000 is shown below.

Distribution of Net Income	Dee	Michael	Total
Salary:			
Dee..	$3,000		$ 3,000
Michael..		5,000	5,000
Remainder divided equally:			
(20,000 − $8,000) ÷ 2 = $6,000 each	6,000	6,000	12,000
Total	$9,000	$11,000	$20,000

After the distribution has been determined, the journal entry to transfer the net income to the individual partners' capital accounts is shown on page 257.

Dec. 31	Income Summary	20,000	
	D. O'Neal, Capital		9,000
	M. Lindsay, Capital		11,000
	To record the distribution of net income according to the partnership agreement		

3. *Interest on investment.* Differences in the balance of each partner's capital account may be recognized in the income distribution, usually in the form of interest.

EXAMPLE 13-6: Assume that the partnership agreement has the following features:

* Salary of $3,000 to Dee and $5,000 to Michael.
* Interest of 10% on the beginning capital balances (refer to Example 13-2).
* Any remaining balance to be divided equally.

The distribution of the net income of $20,000 is shown below.

Distribution of Net Income	Dee	Michael	Total
Salary:			
Dee..	$3,000		$ 3,000
Michael..		$ 5,000	5,000
Interest:			
Dee ($40,000 × .10)..	4,000		4,000
Michael ($60,000 × .10)...................................		6,000	6,000
Remainder divided equally:			
($20,000 − $18,000) ÷ 2 = $1,000 each..................	1,000	1,000	2,000
Total	$8,000	$12,000	$20,000

Dee's capital account will be credited for $8,000 and Michael's will be credited for $12,000.

B. The partnership may incur a loss or the net income may be insufficient to cover the salary and interest allowed in the partnership agreement.

The partnership agreement is still followed. If the partnership agreement allows for salary and/or interest payments, these allocations are made. The total deficiency after these allocations is allocated according to the fixed ratio.

EXAMPLE 13-7: Assume the same facts given in Example 13-6 except that the net income is $15,000.

Distribution of Net Income	Dee	Michael	Total
Salary:			
Dee..	$3,000		$ 3,000
Michael..		$5,000	5,000
Interest:			
Dee..	4,000		4,000
Michael..		6,000	6,000
Deficiency divided equally:			
($15,000 − $18,000) ÷ 2 = −$1,500 each..............	(1,500)	(1,500)	(3,000)
Total	$5,500	$9,500	$15,000

If a net loss had been incurred, the same procedure would have been followed. Salary and interest would have been allocated and the remaining deficiency allocated on a fixed ratio.

13-5. Adding a Partner

A person can be admitted to a partnership in one of two ways.

A. An incoming partner can purchase an interest from one or more of the existing partners.

The only accounting entry on the partnership books will be to transfer the capital account from the selling partner to the incoming partner. The assets and liabilities of the partnership do not change and total owners' equity does not change. This is because the transaction is a personal one between the selling and incoming partners.

EXAMPLE 13-8: Dee and Michael agree to admit a third partner, Lory Smith. Michael will sell Lory 50% of his interest for $50,000. Dee is not selling any of her interest. Before admitting Lory, Dee's capital balance is $55,000 and Michael's is $80,000. The journal entry is shown below.

Date	M. Lindsay, Capital	40,000	
	L. Smith, Capital		40,000
	To record the transfer of 50% of		
	M. Lindsay's interest to L. Smith		
	($80,000 × .50 = $40,000)		

The capital balances after Lory is admitted are listed below.

	Dee	**Michael**	**Lory**
Capital Balance	$55,000	$40,000	$40,000

Note: A new partnership agreement should be made for the three partners as the old partnership ended when the new partner was admitted.

B. An incoming partner can make an investment in the partnership.

If an incoming partner makes an investment in the partnership, the assets and capital accounts increase because the payment is being made directly to the partnership.

EXAMPLE 13-9: Assume that Michael does not sell 50% of his interest to Lory as illustrated in Example 13-8. Instead, Dee and Michael agree to admit Lory with a one-fourth interest for an investment of $45,000. Before Lory is admitted, Dee has a capital balance of $55,000 and Michael has $80,000. After Lory makes an investment of $45,000, the total owner's equity will be $180,000.

	Capital
Dee	$ 55,000
Michael	80,000
Lory...	45,000
Balance...	$180,000

Lory has a one-fourth interest ($180,000 ÷ 4 = $45,000). Lory did not pay anything extra to join the partnership. The journal entry is shown below.

Date	Cash	45,000	
	L. Smith, Capital		45,000
	To record investment by L. Smith to		
	gain a one-fourth interest in		
	partnership		

1. *Bonus paid to existing partners.* Sometimes the new partner is required to pay a bonus to the existing partners in order to join the partnership. The asset account is debited for the full amount paid by the new partner and the partners' capital accounts are credited for the respective amounts they are allowed, based on the partnership agreement.

EXAMPLE 13-10: D&M Video has been very profitable. Assume now that Dee and Michael agree to let Lory join the partnership, but only if she agrees to pay $65,000 for a one-fourth interest. Lory will be paying a $15,000 bonus to the existing partners. Dee and Michael share profits and losses equally and, therefore, they each receive a $7,500 bonus from Lory when she is admitted ($15,000 ÷ 2 = $7,500).

	Capital
Dee	$ 55,000
Michael	80,000
	$135,000
Investment by Lory	65,000
Total	$200,000

The amount to be recorded in Lory's capital account is $50,000 ($200,000 ÷ 4). The bonus is the difference between the amount invested ($65,000) and the amount credited to Lory's capital account ($50,000). The journal entry is shown below.

Date	Cash	65,000	
	D. O'Neal, Capital		7,500
	M. Lindsay, Capital		7,500
	L. Smith, Capital		50,000
	To record bonus paid to existing partners and admission of L. Smith into partnership		

After the investment the capital balances are: Dee, $62,500; Michael, $87,500; and Lory, $50,000.

2. *Bonus paid to new partner.* At times, existing partners may decide to pay a bonus to a new partner who will bring needed capital or special skills to the partnership. The new partner is given a larger interest than his or her capital contribution. The bonus is deducted from the existing partners' capital accounts according to the partnership agreement and credited to the new partner's capital account along with the amount of his or her investment.

EXAMPLE 13-11: Assume the same facts given in Example 13-10 except Lory will invest only $25,000 for a one-fourth interest. Dee and Michael will each contribute $7,500 to Lory's capital account. The journal entry is shown below.

Date	Cash	25,000	
	D. O'Neal, Capital	7,500	
	M. Lindsay, Capital	7,500	
	L. Smith, Capital		40,000
	To record bonus paid to L. Smith and admission of L. Smith into partnership		

Total capital after Lory's investment is $160,000 ($55,000 + $80,000 + $25,000). One-fourth interest is $40,000 ($160,000 ÷ 4 = $40,000). The $40,000 is the amount recorded as Lory's initial investment in the partnership.

13-6. Liquidating a Partnership

A. **When the business operations of a partnership are to be discontinued, the process is called *liquidation*.**

Liquidation only happens when the partnership will no longer be operating as a business.

B. **There are three steps in the liquidation process.**

The first step in the liquidation process is to sell the noncash assets. The profit (or loss) from the sale of noncash assets is distributed to the partners according to their profit and loss sharing ratio. The creditors are then paid and the remaining cash (if any) is distributed to the partners according to the balance in their respective capital accounts. It is *not* distributed according to their income-sharing ratio.

EXAMPLE 13-12: At the end of the sixth year of operation, all three partners of D&M Video decided to liquidate the business. The balance sheet on December 31, 19x6 is shown below.

Assets		Liabilities and Owner's Equity	
Cash	$ 22,000	Accounts payable	$ 34,000
Other assets	252,000	D. O'Neal, Capital	78,000
		M. Lindsay, Capital	100,000
		L. Smith, Capital	62,000
Total	$274,000	Total	$274,000

STEP 1: Sell noncash assets. Assume that the noncash assets are sold for $240,000, which results in a $12,000 loss ($252,000 − $240,000). Any profit or loss on liquidation is shared by the partners according to their profit and loss sharing ratio. Dee, Michael, and Lory share profits and losses equally; therefore, each will absorb a $4,000 loss ($12,000 ÷ 3). The journal entry for the sale of Other Assets is shown below.

Date	Cash	240,000	
	D. O'Neal, Capital	4,000	
	M. Lindsay, Capital	4,000	
	L. Smith, Capital	4,000	
	Other Assets		252,000
	To record the sale of other assets at a loss of $12,000		

The loss could have been recorded in a separate loss account and then distributed to the partners. Since the business is being liquidated, however, recording it in a loss account, first is unnecessary. There is now $262,000 in the Cash account after the sale of noncash assets ($22,000 + $240,000).

STEP 2: Pay liabilities. The journal entry to settle Accounts Payable is shown below.

Date	Accounts Payable	34,000	
	Cash		34,000
	To record payment of liabilities		

There is now $228,000 in the Cash account after payment of liabilities ($262,000–$34,000).

STEP 3: Distribute cash to partners. Distribution of cash is based on the balance in each partner's capital account. The journal entry to record distribution of cash is shown below.

Date	D. O'Neal, Capital	74,000	
	M. Lindsay, Capital	96,000	
	L. Smith, Capital	58,000	
	Cash		228,000
	To record cash distribution to partners upon liquidation		

Note that a loss of $4,000 was distributed to each partner in Step 1. This reduced their capital accounts to the amounts shown in Step 3. A liquidation schedule illustrating the transactions just described is shown on page 261.

D&M Video

Liquidation Schedule

December 31, 19x6

	Cash	+	Other Assets	=	Liabilities	+	D. O'Neal, Capital	+	M. Lindsay, Capital	+	L. Smith, Capital
Balance Before Liquidation	$ 22,000		$252,000		$34,000		$78,000		$100,000		$62,000
Sale of Other Assets	240,000		(252,000)				(4,000)		(4,000)		(4,000)
	$262,000		–0–		$34,000		$74,000		$ 96,000		$58,000
Payment of Liabilities	(34,000)				(34,000)						
	$228,000		–0–		–0–		$74,000		$ 96,000		$58,000
Distribution of Cash to Partners	(228,000)						(74,000)		(96,000)		(58,000)
	–0–		–0–		–0–		–0–		–0–		–0–

C. Any losses incurred during liquidation must be absorbed by the partners.

If one of the partners has a debit balance after absorbing a loss during liquidation, that partner must contribute enough cash to eliminate the debit balance. If the partner is bankrupt and unable to eliminate the deficit, the remaining partners absorb the deficiency according to their profit and loss sharing ratio.

RAISE YOUR GRADES

Can you explain ...?

☑ the characteristics of a partnership
☑ how a partnership differs from a sole proprietorship
☑ three ways in which net income may be divided among partners and calculate the distribution under each method
☑ how to record the addition of a partner who has purchased an interest from an existing partner
☑ how to record the addition of a partner who has invested in the partnership
☑ the liquidation process

SUMMARY

1. The Uniform Partnership Act governs the formation, organization, and dissolution of partnerships.
2. A partnership is defined as "an association of two or more persons to carry on as co-owners a business for profit."
3. The characteristics of a partnership include ease of formation, limited life, unlimited liability, mutual agency, and co-ownership of partnership property.
4. A partnership agreement can be verbal or written, but should be written to prevent future misunderstanding.
5. The advantages of a partnership are ease of formation and possible tax advantages.
6. There are also disadvantages: limited life, unlimited liability, and mutual agency.

7. Each partner has a separate capital and drawing account.
8. Partners may contribute cash and noncash assets. Noncash assets should be recorded on the partnership's books at fair market value at the time they are transferred to the partnership.
9. The partnership agreement should state how profits and losses are to be distributed. If the agreement does not specify, then the profits and losses are shared equally.
10. Some of the common ways of dividing net income or loss are fixed ratio; salary allowance and the balance in a fixed ratio; or interest based on the balances in capital accounts, a salary allowance, and the balance in a fixed ratio.
11. A person can be admitted to the partnership in one of two ways: purchase an interest in the partnership from one or more existing partners, or make an investment in the partnership.
12. When an incoming partner purchases an interest from an existing partner, the only accounting entry made is to transfer the capital account from the selling partner to the incoming partner.
13. When the incoming partner invests in the partnership rather than purchasing an interest from an existing partner, assets and equity increase.
14. A bonus can be paid to the existing partners to gain admittance into the partnership, or the existing partners may pay a bonus to bring a person with needed capital or special skills into the business.
15. When a partnership is liquidated, the noncash assets are sold and the liabilities are paid. The remaining cash is distributed to the partners according to their respective capital accounts.
16. Any partner with a debit balance must contribute cash to eliminate the debit. If unable to do so, the remaining partners are responsible for the loss according to their profit and loss sharing ratio.

RAPID REVIEW   Answers

True or False

1. The Uniform Partnership Act governs the formation, organization, and dissolution of partnerships in the United States. [Section 13-1] — *True*

2. A partnership agreement must be written to be legal. [Section 13-1] — *False*

3. A partnership has a continuous life. [Section 13-1] — *False*

4. Mutual agency refers to the fact that each partner acts as an agent for the partnership. [Section 13-1] — *True*

5. An advantage of a partnership is that it is easy to form. [Section 13-1] — *True*

6. Disadvantages of a partnership include unlimited liability and mutual agency. [Section 13-1] — *True*

7. The only major difference between accounting for a sole proprietorship and a partnership is in the asset section. [Section 13-2] — *False*

8. When a partnership is formed, any noncash assets should be valued at their fair market value when transferred to the partnership. [Section 13-3] — *True*

9. The partners' capital accounts must always be equal. [Section 13-3] — *False*

10. If the partnership agreement does not state how profits and losses should be distributed, they should be distributed equally. [Section 13-4] — *True*

11. If a partnership incurs a net loss, the entire loss is distributed in a fixed ratio. [Section 13-4] — *False*

12. If an incoming partner purchases an interest directly from an existing partner, assets and equity of the partnership increase. [Section 13-5]   *False*

13. When a partnership is liquidated, the cash remaining after all liabilities have been paid is distributed according to the balances in the respective capital accounts. [Section 13-6]   *True*

SOLVED PROBLEMS

PROBLEM 13-1: On January 2, Chris Wagner and Erika Weisman are starting a partnership to be called W & W Company. Chris is contributing land, building, and office equipment that have a fair market value of $10,000, $20,000, and $5,000, respectively. Erika is contributing cash of $20,000. Prepare the general journal entry to record the transfer of assets to the partnership.

Answer: [Section 13-3]

Jan.	2	Land	10,000	00		
		Building	20,000	00		
		Office Equipment	5,000	00		
		C. Wagner, Capital			35,000	00
		To record the transfer of assets to the				
		partnership				
	2	Cash	20,000	00		
		E. Weisman, Capital			20,000	00
		To record the investment of cash				
		in the partnership				

PROBLEM 13-2: Chris and Erika each invest an additional $10,000 in W & W Company on September 1. Prepare the general journal entry.

Answer: [Section 13-3]

Sept.	1	Cash	20,000	00		
		C. Wagner, Capital			10,000	00
		E. Weisman, Capital			10,000	00
		To record additional investment in the				
		partnership				

PROBLEM 13-3: On December 31, W & W Company has a net income of $30,000. Assume the partnership agreement states that profits and losses will be divided with 60% to Chris and 40% to Erika. Prepare the journal entry to record the distribution of net income.

Answer: [Section 13-4]

Dec.	31	Income Summary	30,000	00		
		C. Wagner, Capital			18,000	00
		E. Weisman, Capital			12,000	00
		To record distribution of net income				
		according to partnership agreement				

Calculations: Chris—$30,000 × .60 = $18,000
Erika—$30,000 × .40 = $12,000

PROBLEM 13-4: Assume that the partnership agreement between Chris and Erika allows a salary of $6,000 to Chris and $4,000 to Erika. The balance is to be distributed equally. Calculate the distribution of net income of $30,000 to Chris and Erika.

Answer: [Section 13-4]

Distribution of Net Income	Chris	Erika	Total
Salary:			
Chris...	$ 6,000		$ 6,000
Erika...		$ 4,000	4,000
Remainder divided equally:			
($30,000 − $10,000) ÷ 2 = $10,000 each..............	10,000	10,000	20,000
Total...	$16,000	$14,000	$30,000

PROBLEM 13-5: Assume the same facts given in Problem 13-4 except interest of 10% is paid on the beginning capital balances of $35,000 for Chris and $20,000 for Erika. Calculate the distribution of net income to Chris and Erika.

Answer: [Section 13-4]

Distribution of Net Income	Chris	Erika	Total
Salary:			
Chris...	$ 6,000		$ 6,000
Erika...		$ 4,000	4,000
Interest:			
Chris ($35,000 × .10)...............................	3,500		3,500
Erika ($20,000 × .10)...............................		2,000	2,000
Remainder divided equally:			
($30,000 − $15,500) ÷ 2 = $7,250 each..............	7,250	7,250	14,500
Total...	$16,750	$13,250	$30,000

PROBLEM 13-6: Assume the same facts given in 13-5 except the net income for the year was only $8,000. Calculate the distribution of net income to Chris and Erika.

Answer: [Section 13-4]

Distribution of Net Income	Chris	Erika	Total
Salary:			
Chris	$ 6,000		$ 6,000
Erika...		$ 4,000	4,000
Interest:			
Chris ($35,000 × .10).....................................	3,500		3,500
Erika ($20,000 × .10)..................................		2,000	2,000
Deficiency divided equally:			
($8,000 − $15,500) ÷ 2 = −$3,750 each.............	(3,750)	(3,750)	(7,500)
Total	$ 5,750	$ 2,250	$ 8,000

Remember that you still follow all the steps agreed upon in the partnership agreement, even though net income is not sufficient to cover the distribution of salary and interest allowances. The total deficiency is distributed in the last step—the fixed ratio. When you have finished the distribution, you can check to make sure that the amount you have allocated to the partners equals the net income (or loss) you started out to distribute.

Check: Chris	$5,750
Erika	2,250
Net income........................	$8,000

PROBLEM 13-7: A year later, Chris and Erika have agreed to admit Dottie Dougherty to the partnership. The new partnership will be called W, W, & D Company. Chris now has a capital balance of $40,000 and Erika has a capital balance of $60,000 before Dottie is admitted. Dottie will invest $50,000 in the partnership for a one-third interest. Prepare the general journal entry for this transaction.

Answer: [Section 13-5]

Date	*Cash*	50,000	00		
	D. Dougherty, Capital			50,000	00
	To record D. Dougherty's investment in				
	the partnership				

Calculations: C. Wagner, Capital	$ 40,000
E. Weisman, Capital	60,000
D. Dougherty, Capital	50,000
Total capital	$150,000

$150,000 × 1/3 = $50,000. No bonus is paid.

PROBLEM 13-8: Assume the same facts given in Problem 13-7 except that Dottie will pay a bonus to Chris and Erika. Assume now that Chris and Erika share profits at 60% and 40%, respectively. Dottie will invest $40,000 for a one-fourth interest. Prepare the general journal entry to record this transaction using the form on page 265.

Answer: [Section 13-5]

Date	Cash	40,000	00			
	C. Wagner, Capital				3,000	00
	E. Weisman, Capital				2,000	00
	D. Dougherty, Capital				35,000	00
	To record bonus paid to existing partners					
	and admission of D. Dougherty into					
	partnership					

Calculations:

C. Wagner, Capital	$ 40,000
E. Weisman, Capital	60,000
D. Dougherty, Capital	40,000
Total capital	$140,000

$140,000 × 1/4 = $35,000

A bonus of $5,000 ($40,000 − $35,000) will be paid to Chris and Erika and will be distributed according to their profit and loss sharing ratio, as follows:

Chris $5,000 × .60 = $3,000
Erika $5,000 × .40 = $2,000

PROBLEM 13-9: Chris, Erika, and Dottie decide to liquidate the partnership on December 31 of the following year. The balance sheet before the liquidation is shown below.

Assets		Liabilities and Owner's Equity	
Cash	$ 10,000	Accounts payable	$ 13,000
Other assets	128,000	C. Wagner, Capital	50,000
		E. Weisman, Capital	43,000
		D. Dougherty, Capital	32,000
Total	$138,000	Total	$138,000

Prepare a liquidation schedule assuming the noncash assets are sold for $98,000 and that the partners share profits and losses equally, using the form provided.

W, W, & D Company

Liquidation Schedule

December 31, 19—

	Cash	+	Other Assets	=	Liabilities	+	C. Wagner, Capital	+	E. Weisman, Capital	+	D. Dougherty, Capital
Balances Before Liquidation											
Sale of Other Assets											
Balance											
Payment of Liabilities											
Balance											
Distribution of Cash to Partners											
Balance											

Answer: [Section 13-6]

W, W, & D Company

Liquidation Schedule

December 31, 19—

	Cash	+	Other Assets	=	Liabilities	+	C. Wagner, Capital	+	E. Weisman, Capital	+	D. Dougherty, Capital
Balances Before Liquidation	$ 10,000		$128,000		$13,000		$50,000		$43,000		$32,000
Sale of Other Assets*	98,000		(128,000)				(10,000)		(10,000)		(10,000)
Balance	$108,000		–0–		$13,000		$40,000		$33,000		$22,000
Payment of Liabilities	(13,000)				(13,000)						
Balance	$ 95,000		–0–		–0–		$40,000		$33,000		$22,000
Distribution of Cash to Partners**	(95,000)						(40,000)		(33,000)		(22,000)
Balance	–0–		–0–		–0–		–0–		–0–		–0–

  * The loss on the sale of Other Assets is distributed equally to the three partners according to their partnership agreement.
 ** The cash is distributed to the partners based on the balance in their capital accounts. This represents their total investment at the time of liquidation.

PROBLEM 13-10: Alice Jones and Kimberly Taylor have been partners in Great Interiors for five years. Alice decides to sell her interest to her sister, Lisa Jones. Kimberly agrees to admit Lisa to the partnership. Alice's capital account has a balance of $15,000. She sells her interest to Lisa for $20,000. Prepare the general journal entry to record this transaction.

Answer:

Date	A. Jones, Capital	15,000	00		
	L. Jones, Capital			15,000	00
	To record the transfer of ownership of				
	partnership from A. Jones to L. Jones				

Note that the assets did not change. [Section 13-5]

PROBLEM 13-11: Cindy Spotts and Jeff Goen have capital balances in their partnership of $30,000 and $40,000 respectively. They share profits as follows: Cindy, 60%, and Jeff, 40%. The business is very profitable. On May 1, Cindy and Jeff agree to admit Don Emery to the partnership. Don will have a one-third interest for an investment of $50,000. Calculate the bonus and prepare the journal entry.

Answer: [Section 13-4]

$ 30,000 Cindy
40,000 Jeff
50,000 Don
$120,000 Total capital after Don's investment

$120,000 × 1/3 = $40,000 (amount to be credited to Don's capital account)

$50,000 − $40,000 = $10,000 (bonus to Cindy and Jeff)

The bonus is distributed according to the profit and loss sharing ratio, as shown below.

$10,000 × .60 = $6,000 (bonus to Cindy)
$10,000 × .40 = $4,000 (bonus to Jeff)

May	1	Cash	50,000	00		
		C. Spotts, Capital			6,000	00
		J. Goen, Capital			4,000	00
		D. Emery, Capital			40,000	00
		To record investment by D. Emery to				
		gain one-third interest in partnership				

14

CORPORATIONS: CHARACTERISTICS AND CAPITAL STOCK

THIS CHAPTER IS ABOUT

☑ **Characteristics of Corporations**
☑ **Corporate Accounting**
☑ **Capital Stock**
☑ **Treasury Stock**
☑ **Stockholders' Equity Section**

14-1. Characteristics of Corporations

A. A corporation is a legal entity having many of the same rights and responsibilities as a natural person.

A corporation may own property, sue and be sued, borrow money, and enter into contracts. It also pays income taxes on its income.

B. A corporation offers some advantages that are not available in a sole proprietorship or partnership.

1. *Transfer of ownership.* Ownership of a corporation is divided into shares of stock. The shares of stock can be transferred from one investor to another without disrupting the business operations. Owners of a corporation are called *stockholders.*
2. *Continuous life.* A corporation has continuous life because ownership is usually easily transferred. As noted above, ownership can change without disrupting business operations.
3. *Limited liability.* The stockholders have limited liability. Because it is a separate legal entity, the maximum amount a stockholder can lose is the amount of his or her investment. Creditors can only make claims against the assets of the corporation.
4. *Raising capital.* It is fairly easy for a corporation to raise capital. Limited liability and the ease of transferring shares of stock make investment in a corporation more attractive to investors.

C. A corporation has some disadvantages that are not present in a sole proprietorship or partnership.

1. *Income taxes.* Corporations are required to pay income taxes on earnings. Federal and state income taxes often take about 50% of taxable income. Any income distributed to stockholders as dividends is income to the individual stockholder and is subject to the individual stockholder's personal income tax. This is sometimes called double taxation.
2. *Regulation of operations.* Corporations are subject to heavier regulation than sole proprietorships and partnerships.

D. A corporation is created by obtaining a charter from one of the states.

An application called the *articles of incorporation* is submitted to the proper state official. After the *charter* is obtained, the stockholders meet to elect the *board of directors* and to pass the *bylaws* that will govern the operation of the business. The formation of a corporation is more costly and involved than forming a sole proprietorship or partnership. There are legal fees for preparing the articles of incorporation, filing fees to the state, and numerous other costs. These costs are debited to an asset account called Organization Costs. This is an intangible asset and must be amortized over a maximum of 40 years. Most corporations amortize these costs over five years—the minimum length of time allowed under current income tax laws.

14-2. Corporate Accounting

The major difference in accounting for a corporation and accounting for a sole proprietorship or partnership is in the owners' equity. The owners' equity is called *stockholders' equity*, but the name change is not the only difference. There are two sources of capital for a corporation that are reported in two subsections in the stockholders' equity section on the balance sheet— contributed (or paid-in) capital and earned capital (retained earnings).

Contributed capital includes the investment made by the owners. Earned capital or retained earnings represents the earnings of the company from its beginning, less any losses and less any distribution of earnings in the form of dividends. Retained earnings are explained in more detail in Chapter 15.

EXAMPLE 14-1:

Assets = Liabilities + Owners' Equity

becomes

Assets = Liabilities + Stockholders' Equity
1. Contributed Capital
(investments by owners)
2. Earned Capital
(earnings retained in
the corporation)

14-3. Capital Stock

A. Ownership in a corporation is represented by shares of stock.

The corporate charter specifies the types of stock and the number of shares the corporation is authorized to issue. Normally, the number of shares authorized is greater than the number of shares to be issued at the time of organization. Two types of stock can be issued— common stock and preferred stock. The term *capital stock* includes both common and preferred stock.

B. If only one type of stock is issued by a corporation, it is called *common stock*.

The owners of common stock usually have the following rights:

1. To elect the board of directors and to vote on particular issues.
2. To share in the distribution of earnings in the form of dividends.
3. To share in the distribution of assets if the corporation is liquidated. Creditors have first claim on the assets. Stockholders share in the distribution of assets only after creditors have been paid.
4. To subscribe to additional shares of stock if the corporation decides to issue more shares. This is called the *preemptive right*. This enables stockholders to maintain their percentage of ownership. A stockholder currently owning 10% of the shares would be offered the right to purchase 10% of the new issue. Preemptive rights are not granted by corporations organized in some states. In addition, stockholders sometimes waive their preemptive rights.

C. A second type of stock called *preferred stock* may be issued by a corporation.

Preferred stock has preferential rights over common stock in some ways. However, some rights are given up in return. Preferred stockholders usually have no voting rights. Some of the characteristics of preferred stock are listed below.

1. Preferred stockholders are entitled to receive a specified amount of dividend each year before any dividends are paid to common stockholders.
2. Most preferred stocks are *cumulative*. This means that if all or part of a preferred dividend is not paid in the current year, it is in arrears. The dividend accumulates. Before dividends can be paid on common stock, all dividends in arrears plus the current year's dividend on preferred stock must be paid.

EXAMPLE 14-2: To illustrate the cumulative feature of preferred stock, assume that Tabby Company has two types of stock—common and preferred. Each share of cumulative preferred stock is entitled to a $9 dividend each year. No dividends are paid in Year 1. At the end of Year 1, a $9 dividend per share on preferred stock is in arrears.

Year 2 is more profitable. Tabby Company plans to pay a dividend to common stockholders. Before the common stock dividend can be paid, however, a dividend of $18 per share must be paid on preferred stock ($9 for Year 1, plus $9 for the current year).

Preferred stock can be *noncumulative*. Any omitted dividends are lost forever. In the example above, if the preferred stock had been noncumulative, the preferred stockholder in Example 14-2 would only receive $9 per share in Year 2.

3. Preferred stock also has preference at the time of liquidation. Preferred stockholders share in the distribution of assets after creditors have been paid, but before common stockholders.
4. Some preferred stock is *convertible* into shares of common stock at the option of the stockholder. The exchange ratio is stated on the preferred stock certificate.
5. Preferred stock may also be *callable* at the option of the company. When preferred stock is callable, the issuing corporation has the right to reacquire (call) the stock at a specified price (call price). The call price is usually set slightly above the original issue price. This allows the corporation to retire the stock when the capital is no longer needed or when financing can be obtained at a lower cost.
6. Preferred stock can also be *participating*, which means it can share in dividends beyond the stipulated amount. This is rarely encountered.

D. A share of stock can be either a par-value stock or a no-par stock.

1. *Par-value stock*. Par-value stock has an amount per share printed on the stock certificate and the par value is specified in the corporate charter. It can be any amount decided upon by the corporation. The significance of par value is that it represents the *legal capital*. Legal capital is a minimum amount required by each state to be retained by a corporation for protection of its creditors. Dividends cannot be declared if it causes total stockholders' equity to be reduced below the amount of legal capital.

   The par value for common stock is usually set low. It is not an indication of market value.

EXAMPLE 14-3: To illustrate par-value stock, a portion of Vetter Company's stockholders' equity section on the balance sheet is shown below.

Common stock, $5 par value (10,000 shares
authorized, 5,000 shares issued)... $25,000

The par value of $5 is multiplied times the number of shares issued—5,000 shares. This equals the legal capital for common stock. Stock can be issued for an amount greater than par. The excess is recorded in a separate account. This is discussed later in the chapter.

2. *No-par stock*. No-par stock can be issued in most states. Some states require that the board of directors place a *stated value* on no-par stock. Accounting for par-value stock and

no-par stock with a stated value is the same. The stated value for no-par stock becomes the legal capital. If a corporation issues no-par stock without a stated value, the total amount paid for the stock is usually reported as legal capital.

E. Accounting for the issuance of common stock and preferred stock is the same.

1. *Issuance of stock for cash in excess of par.* At the time the stock is issued, the Cash account is debited and the par value or stated value is credited to the legal capital account. Any amount in *excess* of the par value or stated value is credited to an account called Paid-in Capital in Excess of Par. A separate legal capital account and paid-in capital in excess of par account are maintained for each type of stock—common and preferred. The names, addresses, and numbers of shares owned by each stockholder are maintained by the corporation in a separate *stockholders ledger* in order to issue dividends, proxy forms, and financial reports. (An independent stock registrar and transfer agent may provide this service.)

EXAMPLE 14-4: One hundred shares of common stock with a par value of $5 per share are issued at $15 per share by Vetter Company. The journal entry to record this transaction is shown below.

Date	Cash	1,500	
	Common Stock		500
	Paid-in Capital in Excess of Par:		
	Common		1,000
	Issued 100 shares of $5 par value		
	common stock at $15 per share		

The Common Stock account (legal capital) is credited for the $5 par value for each share issued ($5 × 100 shares = $500). The balance, or $10 per share, is credited to the Paid-in Capital in Excess of Par account ($10 × 100 shares = $1,000).

2. *Issuance of stock for cash below par.* Most states do not allow stock to be issued below par or allow it only under certain conditions. If the corporation is liquidated and there are not enough assets to pay creditors, the original purchaser of stock issued below par may be held contingently liable to the creditors for the amount up to the par value of their stock.

3. *Issuance of stock for assets other than cash.* Stock is usually issued in exchange for cash, but a corporation may issue stock in exchange for land, buildings, or other assets. Stock may also be issued in exchange for services of attorneys and promoters in organizing the corporation. The transaction should be recorded at the current market value of the asset or service received or the current market value of the stock, whichever is more clearly discernible. (Stock must be actively traded to have a reliable market value.)

EXAMPLE 14-5: To record the issuance of stock in exchange for land, suppose that Vetter Company issues 500 shares of $5 par value common stock in exchange for land. The stock is currently selling on the market for $20 per share. The market price of actively traded stock is more objective than the appraisal value of land, so the land will be recorded at $10,000 ($20 market price per share × 500 shares) as shown below.

Date	Land	10,000	
	Common Stock		2,500
	Paid-in Capital in Excess of Par:		
	Common		7,500
	Issued 500 shares of $5 par value		
	common stock in exchange for land;		
	market value of stock was $20		

14-4. Treasury Stock

Sometimes corporations find it advantageous to reacquire shares of their own stock. These shares are called *treasury stock*. Treasury stock is the corporation's own capital stock that has been issued, reacquired by the corporation, but not cancelled or reissued. A corporation may purchase treasury stock for a variety of reasons, such as to have stock available to issue as bonuses, for employee stock purchase plans, or to boost earnings per share. (Earnings per share is discussed in Chapter 15.) Treasury stock is still considered issued but not outstanding and, therefore, is not included in computing earnings per share and does not receive dividends. The term *outstanding* refers to shares of stock that have been issued and are in the hands of owners (stockholders) of the corporation. Treasury shares are issued, but are not outstanding because they are no longer in the hands of stockholders. The purchase of treasury stock is usually recorded at cost in a Treasury Stock account. Treasury Stock is a contra stockholders' equity account. The cost of the treasury stock held by a corporation is deducted from the total of capital stock, additional paid-in capital and retained earnings on the balance sheet.

EXAMPLE 14-6: To illustrate the purchase of treasury stock by the Vetter Company, assume 500 shares are purchased at $16 per share. The journal entry to record the transaction is shown below.

Date	Treasury Stock	8,000	
	Cash		8,000
	Purchased 500 shares of company's $5 par value common stock at $16 per share		

Assets and stockholders' equity have been reduced by the transaction.

If the treasury stock is reissued at a price greater than cost, the excess is credited to Paid-In Capital from Treasury Stock.

EXAMPLE 14-7: Assume that 250 of the shares of treasury stock purchased in Example 14-6 are sold for $20 per share. The journal entry to record the sale is shown below.

Date	Cash	5,000	
	Treasury Stock		4,000
	Paid-In Capital from Treasury Stock		1,000
	Reissued 250 shares of treasury stock at $20 per share		

The Treasury Stock account is credited for the cost (250 shares × $16 per share = $4,000). The Paid-in Capital from Treasury Stock account is credited for the excess received above cost ($5,000 − $4,000 = $1,000).

If the treasury stock is reissued at a price less than cost, the difference is debited to the Paid-In Capital from Treasury Stock account. If there is no paid-in capital from treasury stock, or if it is insufficient, any remaining amount may be debited to Retained Earnings.

14-5. Stockholders' Equity Section

As mentioned at the beginning of this chapter, the stockholders' equity section on the balance sheet has two subsections—paid-in capital and retained earnings. Recall that retained earnings represent the earnings of the company from its beginning, less any losses and less any distributions of earnings in the form of dividends.

EXAMPLE 14-8: The stockholders' equity section as it would be presented on the balance sheet of Vetter Company is illustrated on page 274.

Stockholders' Equity

Paid-in capital:
Preferred 8% stock, cumulative, $50 par (5,000 shares
  authorized, 1,000 shares issued and outstanding) $50,000
Common stock, $5 par value (10,000 shares authorized,
  5,000 shares issued) $25,000
Paid-in capital in excess of par: common   40,000   65,000

Paid-in capital from sale of treasury stock   1,000

Total paid-in capital $116,000
Retained earnings   210,000
Total paid-in capital and retained earnings $326,000
Less treasury stock (250 shares at cost)   4,000

Total stockholders' equity $322,000

Note that the cost of the treasury stock that has not been reissued ($250 shares × $16 per share) is deducted from total paid-in capital and retained earnings.

RAISE YOUR GRADES

Can you explain . . . ?

☑ the characteristics of a corporation and how it is formed
☑ the advantages and disadvantages of a corporation
☑ the two sections in stockholders' equity as reported on the balance sheet of a corporation
☑ the characteristics of common stock
☑ the characteristics of preferred stock
☑ how to account for the sale of capital stock
☑ how to account for the purchase and sale of treasury stock
☑ how to prepare the stockholders' equity section of the balance sheet

SUMMARY

1. A corporation is a legal entity having many of the same rights and responsibilities as a natural person.
2. A corporation offers some advantages that are not available in a sole proprietorship or partnership, such as transfer of ownership without disruption of operations, limited liability of stockholders, and ease of raising capital.
3. A corporation has some disadvantages that are not present in a sole proprietorship or partnership, such as higher taxation and heavier regulation of operations.
4. A corporation is created by obtaining a charter from one of the states after submitting articles of incorporation to the proper state official. Stockholders then elect a board of directors and pass bylaws to govern the operations of the business. The cost of forming a corporation is debited to Organization Costs, an intangible asset account, and amortized usually over a five-year period.
5. The stockholders' equity section on the balance sheet of a corporation is divided into two subsections—contributed (or paid-in) capital and earned capital (retained earnings).

6. Contributed capital includes the investment made by the owners (stockholders).

7. Retained earnings represent the earnings of the company from its beginning, less any losses and less any distribution of earnings in the form of dividends.

8. Ownership of a corporation is represented by shares of stock.

9. There are two types of stock that can be issued by a corporation—common stock and preferred stock.

10. Common stock usually confers the right to elect the board of directors, to vote on particular issues, to share in the distribution of earnings in the form of dividends, and to share in the distribution of assets upon liquidation.

11. Preferred stock has preferential rights over common stock as to dividends and distribution of assets upon liquidation. Most preferred stock is cumulative. It may also be callable at the option of the company and/or convertible into common stock.

12. A share of stock can be either a par-value stock or a no-par stock. Par value (or stated value in the case of no-par stock) is an arbitrary amount that represents the legal capital required by the state to be retained by a corporation for protection of its creditors. If no-par stock does not have a stated value, the total amount paid for the stock is usually reported as legal capital.

13. At the time stock is issued, the par value is credited to the Common Stock or Preferred Stock legal capital account. Any excess received over par is credited to Paid-in Capital in Excess of Par.

14. Separate legal capital and paid-in capital in excess of par value accounts are maintained for common and preferred stock and are reported separately in the paid-in capital section of stockholders' equity.

15. Stock can also be issued for assets other than cash. The transaction is recorded at the current market value of the asset or service received or the current market value of the stock, whichever is more clearly discernible.

16. Treasury stock is the corporation's own capital stock that has been issued, reacquired by the corporation, but not cancelled or reissued. The purchase of treasury stock is usually recorded at cost and is deducted from the total of capital stock, paid-in capital in excess of par value and retained earnings on the balance sheet. When treasury stock is sold, any excess received over cost is credited to Paid-In Capital from Treasury Stock.

RAPID REVIEW   Answers

True or False

1. A corporation is a separate legal entity. [Section 14-1]   *True*

2. Stockholders have unlimited liability. [Section 14-1]   *False*

3. One of the advantages of a corporation is the ease of formation. [Section 14-1]   *False*

4. Stockholders' equity is divided into two subsections on the balance sheet—paid-in capital and retained earnings. [Section 14-2]   *True*

5. Ownership in a corporation is represented by shares of stock. [Section 14-3]   *True*

6. A corporation can only issue one class of stock. [Section 14-3]   *False*

7. Common stockholders have the right to elect the board of directors. [Section 14-3]   *True*

8. Common stockholders must receive their dividends before preferred stockholders can receive their distribution. [Section 14-3]   *False*

9. Par value on common stock represents market value at the time the stock is issued. [Section 14-3]   *False*

10. Legal capital for common stock is equal to par value times the number of shares issued. [Section 14-3]   *True*

11. Stock can only be issued in exchange for cash. [Section 14-3]   *False*

12. Treasury stock is considered to be outstanding and receives dividends. [Section 14-4]   *False*

13. Treasury stock is a contra stockholders' equity account. [Section 14-4]   *True*

SOLVED PROBLEMS

PROBLEM 14-1: A summary of the stockholders' equity sections for Year 1 and Year 2 on the balance sheet of Ramco Corporation is shown below.

	Year 2	Year 1
Preferred 10% stock, $100 par value	$100,000	$ 60,000
Common stock, $5 par value	150,000	80,000
Paid-in capital in excess of par: common	620,000	190,000
Retained earnings	115,000	35,000
Total paid-in capital and retained earnings	$985,000	$365,000

(a) How many shares of preferred stock were issued in Year 2?

(b) How many shares of common stock were issued in Year 2?

(c) What was the total paid-in (contributed) capital at the end of Year 2?

Answer: [Section 14-3]

(a) $100,000 Year 2 balance
  −60,000 Year 1 balance
  $ 40,000 Increase in preferred stock

  $40,000 ÷ $100 par = 400 shares of preferred stock sold in Year 2.

(b) $150,000 Year 2 balance
  −80,000 Year 1 balance
  $ 70,000 Increase in common stock

  $70,000 ÷ $5 par = 14,000 shares of common stock sold in Year 2.

(c) $100,000 Preferred stock at par
  150,000 Common stock at par
  620,000 Paid-in capital in excess of par: common
  $870,000 Total paid-in capital

PROBLEM 14-2: Garfield Company paid $170,000 in dividends in Year 2. The company has 5,000 shares of 10%, $100 par value, cumulative preferred stock and 10,000 shares of $5 par-value common stock. The dividend on preferred stock is one year in arrears. What is the total amount paid to preferred stockholders in the current year? to common stockholders?

Answer: [Section 14-3]

Preferred:

  5,000 shares × .10 × $100 par value × 2 years = $100,000 paid to preferred stockholders

The one year in arrears and the current year's dividend must be paid on preferred stock before a dividend can be paid on common stock.

Common:

$170,000 Dividends paid during Year 2
— 100,000 Preferred dividends
$ 70,000 Paid to common stockholders

PROBLEM 14-3: Discuss the advantages of a corporation over other types of business formations.

Answer: There are several advantages that a corporation has that are not available in a sole proprietorship or partnership. For example, shares of stock (representing ownership in the corporation) can be transferred without disrupting business operations. Thus, a corporation is said to have continuous life. Furthermore, stockholders have limited liability for the debts of the corporation. The maximum amount a stockholder can lose is the amount of his or her investment. Also, it is fairly easy for a corporation to raise capital. The limited liability feature and the ease of transferring ownership make investment in a corporation attractive. [Section 14-1]

PROBLEM 14-4: Discuss the disadvantages of a corporation that are not present in other types of business formations.

Answer: There are several disadvantages that a corporation has that are not present in a sole proprietorship or partnership. Corporations must pay income taxes on earnings that often take about 50% of taxable net income. Furthermore, any income distributed to stockholders as dividends is considered income to the individual stockholder and is subject to the individual stockholder's personal income tax, resulting in double taxation of a portion of the corporation's income. Also, corporations are subject to heavier regulation than other types of businesses. [Section 14-1]

PROBLEM 14-5: Ace Corporation was incorporated in April. The corporation was authorized to issue 10,000 shares of $10 par-value common stock. Journalize the following transactions.

April 1   Sold 4,000 shares to the organizers of the corporation for $14 per share.
April 4   Issued 100 shares to Phil Thorpe, attorney, for legal services during the organization of the corporation. The charge for legal services was $1,500.
April 24   Sold an additional 1,000 shares to investors at $18 per share.

Answer: [Sections 14-1 and 14-3]

Apr.	1	Cash	56,000	00		
		Common Stock			40,000	00
		Paid-In Capital in Excess of Par: Common			16,000	00
		Issued 4,000 shares to organizers at $14				
		per share				
	4	Organization Costs	1,500	00		
		Common Stock			1,000	00
		Paid-In Capital in Excess of Par: Common			500	00
		Issued 100 shares as payment of legal				
		services				
	24	Cash	18,000	00		
		Common Stock			10,000	00
		Paid-In Capital in Excess of Par: Common			8,000	00
		Issued 1,000 shares to investors at $18				
		per share				

PROBLEM 14-6: On June 16, Jones Corporation issued 1,000 shares of $1 par-value common stock for land appraised at $20,000. The stock is not actively traded. Record the transaction.

Answer: [Section 14-3]

June	16	Land	20,000	00		
		Common Stock			1,000	00
		Paid-In Capital in Excess of Par: Common			19,000	00
		Purchased land in exchange for 1,000				
		shares of $1 par-value common stock				

PROBLEM 14-7: 1,000 shares of $10 par-value common stock of Campbell Company were reacquired on April 14. The market price of the stock on that date was $50. Record the purchase.

Answer: [Section 14-4]

Apr.	14	Treasury Stock	50,000	00		
		Cash			50,000	00
		Reacquired 1,000 shares of $10				
		par-value common stock at $50 per				
		share				

PROBLEM 14-8: On June 30, the company sold 500 shares of the treasury stock purchased in Problem 14-7. The price of the stock on June 30 was $60. Record the sale.

Answer: [Section 14-4]

June	30	Cash	30,000	00			
		Treasury Stock			25,000	00
		Paid-In Capital from Treasury Stock			5,000	00
		Sold 500 shares of Treasury stock at				
		$60 per share—cost $50 per share				

PROBLEM 14-9: For each of the transactions below, indicate the effect on total stockholders' equity in the space provided.

	Increase	Decrease	No Effect
Issued 100 shares of common stock	_____	_____	_____
Purchased 50 shares of treasury stock	_____	_____	_____
Sold 30 shares of treasury stock	_____	_____	_____

Answer: [Sections 14-3 and 14-4]

	Increase	Decrease	No Effect
Issued 100 shares of common stock	X		
Purchased 50 shares of treasury stock		X	
Sold 30 shares of treasury stock	X		

PROBLEM 14-10: Orth Corporation was organized on February 6. The corporation was authorized to issue 1,000 shares of 10%, $50 par-value, cumulative preferred stock and 5,000 shares of $10 par-value common stock. Record the following journal transactions.

Feb. 6 Sold 500 shares of preferred stock at par.

Feb. 8 Issued 100 shares of common stock to an attorney for legal fees in organizing corporation. The bill for these services was $2,000. The stock is not actively traded.

Feb. 20 Sold 1,000 shares of common stock to investors at $21 per share.

Feb. 28 Sold 100 shares of preferred stock at $53 per share.

Answer: [Section 14-3]

Feb.	6	Cash	25,000	00				
		Preferred Stock				25,000	00
		Sold 500 shares preferred at $50 par					
	8	Organization Costs	2,000	00			
		Common Stock				1,000	00
		Paid-In Capital in Excess of Par: Common				1,000	00
		Issued 100 shares of $10 par-value common					
		stock in exchange for legal services					
	20	Cash	21,000	00			
		Common Stock				10,000	00
		Paid-In Capital in Excess of Par: Common				11,000	00
		Sold 1,000 shares $10 par-value					
		common stock at $21 per share					
	28	Cash	5,300	00			
		Preferred Stock				5,000	00
		Paid-In Capital in Excess of Par: Preferred				300	00
		Sold 100 shares $50 par-value preferred					
		stock at $53 per share					

PROBLEM 14-11: What are the rights of common stockholders?

Answer: Common stockholders usually have the right to elect the board of directors of the corporation and to vote on particular issues. They also have the right to share in the distribution of earnings in the form of dividends and to share in the distribution of assets (after creditors and preferred stockholders) if the corporation is liquidated. They may also have the preemptive right to subscribe to additional shares of stock if the corporation decides to issue more shares, thus maintaining their percentage of ownership. [Section 14-3]

PROBLEM 14-12: What are some of the characteristics of preferred stock?

Answer: Preferred stockholders are entitled to receive dividends before dividends are paid to common stockholders, and to receive their distribution of assets upon liquidation of the corporation after creditors but before common stockholders. Most preferred stocks are cumulative, which means that if all or part of a preferred dividend is not paid in the current year, it is in arrears and the accumulated amount of dividends plus the current year's dividend must be paid to preferred stockholders before common stockholders' dividends are paid. Some preferred stock is convertible into shares of common stock at the option of the stockholder, with the exchange ratio stated on the preferred stock certificate. Preferred stock may also be callable at the option of the company, meaning that the corporation has the right to reacquire the stock at a specified price. Some preferred stock may also be participating, which means it can share in dividends beyond the stipulated amount, but this is rarely encountered. [Section 14-3]

15 CORPORATIONS: DISCLOSURE OF EARNINGS AND DIVIDENDS

THIS CHAPTER IS ABOUT

☑ **Net Income**
☑ **Unusual and Nonrecurring Items**
☑ **Earnings Per Share**
☑ **Retained Earnings**
☑ **Retained Earnings Appropriated (Reserved)**
☑ **Dividends**

15-1. Net Income

A. The amount of net income earned by corporations is important information to investors and other users of financial statements.

For example, net income is the basis for determining dividend distributions. Users also look at net income for trends in earnings. Various financial statistics are based on earnings. Because of these and other reasons, the income statement should show the components of net income in a format that is informative and useful.

B. All events effecting net income for a period should be disclosed on the income statement.

From time to time, unusual and nonrecurring events may occur that effect the net income of a company. In order to present a clear picture of current earnings, accounting practice requires that such events be shown separate from normal "everyday" operations. These unusual and nonrecurring transactions include discontinued operations, extraordinary items, and accounting changes. Earnings per share should also be shown for these items.

EXAMPLE 15-1: On page 282 is an illustration of a corporate income statement. Income from unusual and nonrecurring items are shown separately from income from continuing (normal) operations. For the purposes of this statement, a 40% income tax rate has been assumed.

15-2. Unusual and Nonrecurring Items

Items affecting net income that are unusual and nonrecurring should be reported on the income statement after income from continuing operations. Since these items appear on the income statement after taxes have been deducted from income from continuing operations, they must also be reported on an after tax basis.

Lessing Corporation

Income Statement

For Year Ended December 31, 19x3

Revenues		$100,000
Less costs and expenses		40,000
Income from continuing operations before taxes		$ 60,000
Income taxes		24,000
Income from continuing operations		$ 36,000
Discontinued operations:		
Income from discontinued operations (net of taxes of $2,000)	$3,000	
Gain on sale of discontinued operations (net of taxes of $4,000)	6,000	9,000
Income before extraordinary items and cumulative effect of change		
in accounting principle		$ 45,000
Extraordinary gain (net of taxes of $1,800)		2,700
Subtotal		$ 47,700
Cumulative effect of a change in accounting principle (net of		
taxes of $480)		(720)
Net income		$ 46,980
*Earnings per share of common stock		
Income from continuing operations	$1.80	
Discontinued operations	.45	
Income before extraordinary items and cumulative effect of change in		
accounting principle	$2.25	
Extraordinary gain	.14	
Cumulative effect of change in		
accounting principle	(.04)	
Net income	$2.35	

---

* Earnings per share is calculated based on 20,000 shares outstanding for the year.

A. **The operating results and any gains or losses from *discontinued operations* should be disclosed separately on the income statement.**

A corporation may be divided into segments. A segment may be a division, department, product line, or separate class of customer. Normally, the assets and operating results are clearly identifiable for a segment. When a corporation decides to sell, abandon, or otherwise dispose of a segment, it is accounted for as a discontinued operation. The operating results and any gain or loss on disposal of the segment are shown separately on the income statement, net of the income tax effect.

EXAMPLE 15-2: In Example 15-1, income from discontinued operations was $5,000. The income taxes were $2,000 ($5,000 × .40), resulting in a net of tax income of $3,000. The gain on the disposal of the segment was $10,000 and the income taxes were $4,000 ($10,000 × .40), resulting in a net of tax gain of $6,000. Remember that *net of taxes* simply means that the amount shown on the income statement is reported as an *after-tax* amount.

B. *Extraordinary gains or losses* **should be disclosed separately on the income statement.**

To be extraordinary, the event causing the gain or loss must be material, unusual in nature, and not expected to recur in the foreseeable future. To determine if a gain or loss is extraordinary, the environment in which the business operates must be considered. Examples of extraordinary gains and losses include losses from major casualties such as earthquakes and floods, expropriation of assets by foreign governments, gains and losses from the enactment of a new law, and gains and losses from early retirement of debt. These gains and losses should be shown net of taxes and below the operating results and any gain or loss from discontinued operations. In Example 15-1, the extraordinary gain was $4,500. The income taxes were $1,800.

C. The *cumulative effect of a change in accounting principle* **should be disclosed separately on the income statement.**

The consistency quality states that companies should apply the same accounting method from year to year. However, a change is allowed if the new method provides more useful information and the cumulative effect of the change on the net income and the reason for the change are fully disclosed in the financial statements. Examples are changing from double declining balance to straight-line depreciation or from FIFO to LIFO inventory method. Example 15-1 illustrates a change in depreciation methods. The tax savings was $480. The change had the cumulative effect of reducing net income by $720.

15-3. Earnings Per Share (EPS)

A. Earnings per share is one of the most widely quoted financial statistics.

Earnings per share can be used in evaluating the performance of the company and to compare its performance to other companies. It is based on the current year's income and should be disclosed on the face of the income statement (see Example 15-1). An earnings per share amount should be shown for income from continuing operations, income before extraordinary items and cumulative effect of a change in accounting principle, and net income. Earnings per share amounts may be presented for the operating results and any gains or losses from discontinued operations and extraordinary items as well. The formula for calculating earnings per share is

$$\frac{\text{Annual Net Income Available to Common Stockholders}}{\text{Weighted-Average Number of Common Shares Outstanding}} = \text{EPS}$$

B. The simplest EPS calculation is found when a company has only common stock and the same number of shares are outstanding for a full year.

EXAMPLE 15-3: Assume that Day Corporation has only one type of capital stock—common. The current net income was $100,000 and there were 10,000 shares of common stock outstanding all year. The EPS is calculated below.

$$\frac{\$100,000}{10,000} = \$10 \text{ EPS}$$

C. If the number of shares outstanding changes during the year, it is necessary to compute a weighted-average number of shares outstanding.

EXAMPLE 15-4: Assume that some of the 10,000 shares of Day Corporation were issued during the year. Suppose that 6,000 were outstanding all year, 2,000 additional shares were issued on April 1, and 2,000 were issued on October 1. The company reports on a calendar-year basis. It is necessary to determine the weighted-average number of common shares outstanding, as shown below.

$$
\begin{array}{lll}
 & 6{,}000 \text{ shares} \times 1 \text{ year} & = 6{,}000 \\
\text{(Issued 4/1)} & 2{,}000 \text{ shares} \times 9/12 \text{ year} & = 1{,}500 \\
\text{(Issued 10/1)} & 2{,}000 \text{ shares} \times 3/12 \text{ year} & = \underline{\ \ 500} \\
 & \text{Weighted-average number of} & = \underline{8{,}000} \\
 & \text{common shares outstanding} &
\end{array}
$$

The EPS calculation is

$$\frac{\$100{,}000}{8{,}000} = \$12.50 \text{ EPS}$$

D. If a company has preferred stock outstanding, the preferred dividend requirement for the current year is subtracted from net income before computing EPS for common stock.

EXAMPLE 15-5: Now assume that Day Corporation has two types of capital stock—common and preferred. The net income must be adjusted for the current year's preferred dividend requirement. Preferred stockholders are entitled to $10,000 in preferred dividends. The calculation is shown below.

$$\frac{\$100{,}000 - \$10{,}000}{8{,}000^*} = \$11.25 \text{ EPS}$$

*Weighted average calculated in previous example.

E. If a company has convertible bonds or preferred stock outstanding, the potential effect of conversion to common stock may need to be disclosed.

A corporation may have bonds and preferred stock outstanding that can be converted into shares of common stock in the future. If these securities are converted into common stock, the earnings per share may be diluted because of the additional number of common shares outstanding.

EXAMPLE 15-6: Assume that each share of Day Corporation's preferred stock can be converted into four shares of common stock. Day Corporation has 1,000 shares of 10%, $100 par, cumulative preferred stock outstanding. If all the preferred shares were converted into common stock, there would be an additional 4,000 shares of common stock outstanding (1,000 shares of preferred × 4).

When a corporation has convertible securities, earnings per share could be reduced if the securities were converted to common stock. Corporations are sometimes required to present two separate earnings per share figures. The first figure is called *primary* earnings per share. The calculations in Example 15-5 were primary earnings per share. A second figure, called *fully diluted* earnings per share, may be required for any corporation with convertible securities (bonds or preferred stock) outstanding. This is only a "what if" calculation; i.e., what if the bonds or preferred shares were converted?

EXAMPLE 15-7: Examples 15-5 and 15-6 are continued below by calculating fully diluted earnings per share.

$$\frac{\$100,000}{12,000} = \$8.33 \text{ Fully diluted EPS}$$

Note: If the preferred shares were converted, there would be no preferred dividend paid; therefore, the total net income of $100,000 is used in the calculation. To calculate fully diluted earnings per share, it is assumed the shares were converted at the beginning of the year. The weighted-average number of common shares of 8,000 calculated in Example 15-4 was used in the example (4,000 converted preferred + 8,000 weighted average common shares outstanding = 12,000). The primary EPS is $11.25. The fully diluted EPS is $8.33.

15-4. Retained Earnings

A. Retained earnings represent the earnings of a corporation that have not been distributed to stockholders.

Retained earnings are a part of stockholders' equity. A corporation may distribute some of its net income to stockholders in the form of dividends. Any distribution of net income reduces retained earnings. Retained earnings are equal to the total net income, less any losses and less any dividends distributed since the corporation began operations.

EXAMPLE 15-8: J. G. Corporation began operating three years ago. The corporation had a net income of $5,000 in the first year and a net loss of $2,000 in the second year. In the third year, it earned a net income of $6,000 and distributed a dividend of $1,500. The retained earnings balance at the end of Year 3 was $7,500, as shown below.

$5,000	Net income, Year 1
−2,000	Net loss, Year 2
$3,000	Retained earnings, beginning Year 3
+6,000	Net income, Year 3
−1,500	Dividend distribution, Year 3
$7,500	Retained earnings, end of Year 3

B. A statement of retained earnings is prepared at the end of the accounting period.

A statement of retained earnings is a summary of the changes in retained earnings during the year.

EXAMPLE 15-9: A statement of retained earnings for J. G. Corporation as it would be prepared at the end of Year 3 is shown below.

J. G. Corporation
Statement of Retained Earnings
For Year Ended December 31, 19x3

Retained earnings, January 1, 19x3	$3,000
Add December 31, 19x3 net income	6,000
Subtotal	$9,000
Deduct dividends	1,500
Retained earnings, December 31, 19x3	$7,500

15-5. Retained Earnings Appropriated (Reserved)

A. A corporation may need to restrict the amount of dividends paid to stockholders.

The board of directors may decide to expand, build a new plant, or purchase new equipment. For this reason, they may want to retain a portion or all of the retained earnings of the corporation. A restriction on retained earnings may be due to contractual or legal requirements as well. For example, state law may require an appropriation of the retained earnings balance equal to the cost of any purchases of treasury stock.

B. Any restriction on retained earnings must be disclosed on the balance sheet.

Stockholders can be informed of restrictions on retained earnings by a footnote or by dividing retained earnings into two parts.

EXAMPLE 15-10: Pear Computer Corporation needs to expand. The board of directors has approved plans for a new plant. Construction is to begin next year. Pear Computer Corporation can notify its stockholders of the restriction on retained earnings by adding a footnote to the balance sheet similar to the one below.

> *Note 4:* The corporation is limiting the payment of dividends because the board of directors has approved plans for a new plant. Construction will begin next year. The amount of retained earnings restricted for this construction project is $500,000.

The corporation may also inform stockholders of the restriction by dividing retained earnings into two sections on the balance sheet as shown below.

Retained earnings:
Appropriated for new plant construction	$500,000
Unappropriated	110,000
Total retained earnings	$610,000

C. A journal entry is needed to divide retained earnings into appropriated and unappropriated.

The appropriated amount is transferred from the Retained Earnings account to a special account designating its purpose. Total retained earnings does not change with the entry, it is just divided into two sections. When the need for the appropriation no longer exists, the appropriated amount should be transferred back to the Retained Earnings account.

EXAMPLE 15-11: The journal entry to record a restriction of retained earnings for the plant construction by Pear Computer Company is shown below.

Date	Retained Earnings	500,000	
	Retained Earnings Appropriated for New Plant		500,000
	Appropriation for new plant by action of the board of directors		

15-6. Dividends

A. Dividends are a distribution of a corporation's earnings to the stockholders.

The distribution may be in the form of cash, other assets, or stock. Dividends may be paid quarterly, semiannually, annually, or at any time the board of directors decides to declare a dividend. There are three important dates related to a dividend declaration.

1. *Date of declaration.* All dividends must be declared by the board of directors. This is the date the board takes formal action.

2. *Date of record.* All stockholders whose names appear on the records of the corporation on this date will receive a dividend. This date is usually two to three weeks after the date of declaration.

3. *Date of payment.* This is the date the dividend is distributed to stockholders. Payment usually occurs a few weeks after the date of record.

B. The most common type of dividend is a cash dividend.

A journal entry is required to record the declaration of a cash dividend. Retained Earnings is debited and Dividends Payable is credited. Note that when dividends are declared, they become a current liability of the corporation. When the dividend is paid, Dividends Payable is debited and Cash is credited.

EXAMPLE 15-12: Assume that Southern Corporation declares a $1 per share dividend on $10 par value common stock on December 15. There are 5,000 shares outstanding on the date of declaration. The entry to record the declaration is shown below.

Dec. 15	Retained Earnings	5,000	
	Dividends Payable		5,000
	To record declaration of cash dividend of $1 per share on 5,000 shares of $10 par, common stock outstanding ($1 × 5,000 shares)		

The entry to record the payment of January 15, the date of payment, is shown below.

Jan. 15	Dividends Payable	5,000	
	Cash		5,000
	To record distribution of $1 per share dividend on common stock		

Some corporations debit an account called Cash Dividends or Dividends Declared when the dividend is declared. This account is then closed to Retained Earnings at the end of the accounting period.

C. The preferred stockholder is entitled to receive cash dividends before any dividend is paid to common stockholders.

The dividend on preferred stock is based on a stated amount per share or on a percentage of par value. If the preferred stock is cumulative, all dividends in arrears plus the current dividend on preferred stock must be paid before a dividend can be paid on common stock.

EXAMPLE 15-13: A portion of the stockholders' equity of Wood Corporation is shown below.

Preferred stock, 10% cumulative, $100 par value, 2,000 shares
authorized and outstanding. $200,000
Common stock, $5 par value, 10,000 shares authorized and
8,000 shares outstanding 40,000

If the corporation declares a $1 per share dividend on common stock in Year 1, a dividend of $10 per share must also be paid on the preferred shares outstanding. The calculation is shown below.

Preferred stock:
$100 par value × .10 × $2,000 shares outstanding = $20,000

Common stock:
$1 per share × 8,000 shares outstanding   =   8,000
Total dividend declared in Year 1   = $28,000

If no dividends are declared in Year 1, the preferred dividends will be in arrears for Year 1. The preferred stock is cumulative in this example; therefore, dividends for both Year 1 and Year 2 will have to be paid on preferred stock before a dividend can be paid on common stock in Year 2.

Dividends in arrears are not a liability of the corporation because no liability exists until the board of directors declares a dividend. However, dividends in arrears as of a balance sheet date should be disclosed by a footnote.

D. Corporations may also distribute dividends in the form of additional shares of the corporation's own stock.

There are several reasons why a corporation may issue stock dividends, such as to conserve cash, to allow a nontaxable distribution to stockholders (the stock dividend is not taxed until the shares are sold), or to decrease the market price of the stock, thus making the stock more attractive to a larger number of stockholders. Additional shares are issued to stockholders in proportion to the number of shares they currently own.

EXAMPLE 15-14: Equity Corporation declared a 10% stock dividend on common stock. The corporation had 10,000 shares of common stock outstanding on the date of declaration; thus, 1,000 shares of stock will be issued (10,000 × .10). Sandra Hoover owns 5% of the stock outstanding, or 500 shares (.05 × 10,000). Therefore, Sandra will receive 50 shares of the stock dividend (.05 × 1,000). After the stock dividend is issued, the corporation will have 11,000 shares outstanding (10,000 + 1,000). Sandra will have 550 of those shares (500 + 50).

E. There are some important differences between stock dividends and cash dividends.

No assets are distributed with a stock dividend; therefore, the corporation does not incur a liability to pay a dividend when the stock dividend is declared. Furthermore, there is no change in total stockholders' equity when a stock dividend is declared. The effect of a stock dividend on stockholders' equity is to transfer retained earnings to paid-in capital and to increase the number of shares outstanding. Thus, some of the accounts within stockholders' equity change, but total stockholders' equity remains unchanged.

F. Accounting for a stock dividend depends on the size of the distribution.

When a small stock dividend is declared (less than 20–25%), the *market price* on the date of declaration is debited to Retained Earnings. The *par value* is debited to Retained Earnings for large stock dividends (greater than 20–25%). Market price per share is used on small stock dividends because it is assumed that the price of the shares will not decrease very much as a result of the issuance of additional shares. A large stock dividend, however, will probably cause the market price to decline substantially because of the large increase in the number of shares outstanding after the dividend is distributed.

1. *Accounting for a small stock dividend.* When accounting for a small stock dividend, the market value of the stock on the date of declaration is debited to Retained Earnings. The par value of the stock is credited to Common Stock Dividend to be Distributed. Any excess of market value over par is credited to Paid-In Capital from Stock Dividends. At the time of distribution, the Common Stock Dividend to be Distributed account is debited and the Common Stock account is credited.

EXAMPLE 15-15: Assume that Catco, Inc., declares a 10% stock dividend on all outstanding shares of common stock on June 30. There are 5,000 shares outstanding; thus, 500 new shares will be issued (.10 × 5,000 shares). The market price on the date of declaration is $20 and par value is $5. The journal entry on the date of declaration is shown on page 289.

June 30	Retained Earnings	10,000	
	Common Stock Dividend to be Distributed		2,500
	Paid-In Capital from Stock Dividends		7,500
	To record declaration of 10% stock dividend		
	Market price is $20; par value is $5		

Retained Earnings is debited for the market value of the stock dividend (500 shares × $20). The par value is credited to the Common Stock Dividend to be Distributed account (500 × $5) and the excess of market value over par is credited to the Paid-in Capital from Stock Dividends account (500 shares × $15). Note that market value has been used to reduce Retained Earnings. The journal entry at the time of distribution on July 30 is shown below.

July 30	Common Stock Dividend to be Distributed	2,500	
	Common Stock		2,500
	To record issuance of 500 shares of $5 par value common stock		

2. *Accounting for a large stock dividend.* When accounting for a large stock dividend, the par value of the stock is debited to Retained Earnings and credited to Common Stock Dividend to be Distributed. Upon distribution, the account is debited and Common Stock is credited.

EXAMPLE 15-16: Assume that Catco, Inc., declares a large stock dividend of 50% on its 5,000 outstanding shares on December 31; thus, 2,500 shares will be issued (5,000 shares × .50). Par value is $5 per share and the market price is $20 on the date of declaration. Par value, *not* market price, is used to reduce Retained Earnings when a large stock dividend is declared. The journal entry is shown below.

Dec. 31	Retained Earnings	12,500	
	Common Stock Dividend to be Distributed		12,500
	To record declaration of 50% stock dividend on $5 par value common stock (2,500 × $5)		

G. A *stock split* increases the number of shares outstanding and reduces the par value of the stock.

A stock split is done primarily to reduce the market price per share of stock, making it affordable to more investors. A stock split is not the same as a stock dividend. No ledger accounts are affected by a stock split. However, a memorandum entry is appropriate.

EXAMPLE 15-17: Spotts, Inc., has 10,000 shares of $10 par value common stock outstanding when the corporation declares a 2-for-1 stock split. This means that an additional share will be issued for every share outstanding and the par value of each share will drop to $5.

Before the split:
Common stock, $10 par value, 10,000 shares outstanding $100,000

After the split:
Common stock, $5 par value, 20,000 shares outstanding $100,000

RAISE YOUR GRADES

Can you explain...?

☑ how to report unusual and nonrecurring items on the income statement
☑ how to calculate earnings per share
☑ how appropriated retained earnings can be reported on the balance sheet
☑ how to calculate and record a cash dividend declaration and distribution
☑ the difference between a stock dividend and a cash dividend
☑ how to record the declaration and distribution of a small and a large stock dividend
☑ the difference between a stock dividend and a stock split.

SUMMARY

1. Because net income provides important information to investors and other users, the accounting profession requires that unusual and nonrecurring items be reported separately from the income resulting from normal "everyday" operations on the income statement.
2. The categories that should be shown separately on the income statement are discontinued operations, extraordinary items, and the cumulative effect of changes in accounting principle.
3. Earnings per share is one of the most widely quoted financial statistics. The formula for calculating earnings per share is

$$\frac{\text{Annual Net Income Available to Common Stockholders}}{\text{Weighted-Average Number of Common Shares Outstanding}} = \text{Earnings per Share}$$

4. Retained earnings represent the earnings of a corporation that have not been distributed to stockholders. Retained earnings are equal to the total net income, less any losses and less any dividends distributed since the corporation began operations.
5. A corporation may need to restrict the amount of dividends paid to stockholders. The corporation can inform stockholders of this restriction by a footnote or by dividing retained earnings into two parts on the balance sheet—appropriated and unappropriated.
6. Dividends are a distribution of a corporation's earnings to the stockholders. The distribution may be in the form of cash, other assets, or stock.
7. A cash dividend creates a liability on the date of declaration.
8. Preferred dividends must be paid before dividends are paid on common stock. If the preferred stock is cumulative, dividends in arrears must also be paid before the dividends are paid on common stock.
9. Corporations may distribute dividends in the form of additional shares of the corporation's own stock. The effect of a stock dividend is to transfer retained earnings to paid-in capital and to increase the number of shares outstanding. Total stockholders' equity remains unchanged.
10. For a small stock dividend (less than 20–25%), Retained Earnings is debited for the market price of the stock on the day the stock dividend is declared.
11. For a large stock dividend (greater than 20–25%), Retained Earnings is debited for the par value of the stock.
12. A stock split increases the number of shares outstanding and reduces the par value of the stock.

RAPID REVIEW

Short Answer

1. What are the three categories of unusual and nonrecurring items that must be reported separately below "income from continuing operations" on the income statement? [Section 15-2]

2. Under what circumstances is an event causing a gain or loss considered extraordinary? [Section 15-2]

3. What is the formula for calculating earnings per share? [Section 15-3]

4. To calculate primary earnings per share, what adjustment is made to net income if there are preferred and common stockholders? [Section 15-3]

5. If 2,000 shares of common stock are outstanding for the full year and 1,000 shares are issued on July 1, what is the weighted-average number of common shares outstanding on December 31? [Section 15-3]

6. What are the two types of earnings per share figures that are required? [Section 15-3]

7. What are the types of dividends a corporation can distribute? [Section 15-6]

8. When does a cash dividend become a liability? [Section 15-6]

9. What effect does the declaration of a cash dividend have on stockholders' equity? [Section 15-6]

10. Are dividends in arrears on cumulative preferred stock a liability? [Section 15-6]

11. When a 10% stock dividend is declared, is Retained Earnings debited for the market price or par value? [Section 15-6]

12. What is the effect on total stockholders' equity when a stock dividend is declared? [Section 15-6]

13. When does a cash dividend affect stockholders' equity? [Section 15-6]

Answers:

1. Discontinued operations, extraordinary items, and the cumulative effect of a change in accounting principle.

2. The event must be material, unusual in nature, and not expected to recur in the foreseeable future.

3. $$\frac{\text{Annual Net Income Available to Common Stockholders}}{\text{Weighted-Average Number of Common Shares Outstanding}} = \text{Earnings per Share}$$

4. The current year's dividend requirement on preferred stock is deducted from net income before calculating earnings per share.

5. 2,500 [2,000 + (1,000 × 6/12)]

6. Primary and fully diluted earnings per share.

7. Cash, other assets, or stock dividends.

8. On the date of declaration.

9. Stockholders' equity is decreased.

10. No.

11. Market price.

12. No effect.

13. On the date of declaration.

SOLVED PROBLEMS

PROBLEM 15-1: Thorsen Corporation has one class of stock (common) and earned a net income of $20,000 in Year 2. There were 5,000 shares of common stock outstanding all year. Calculate earnings per share for Year 2.

Answer: [Section 15-3]

$$\frac{\$20,000}{5,000} = \$4.00 \text{ Earnings per share}$$

PROBLEM 15-2: Assume that Thorsen Corporation still has only one class of stock and earned $20,000 during Year 2. For this problem, 5,000 shares were outstanding on January 1, 5,000 additional shares were issued July 1, and 2,000 additional shares were issued on October 1. Calculate earnings per share.

Answer: It is necessary to calculate the weighted-average number of shares outstanding during Year 2.

	5,000 shares × 1 year	= 5,000
(Issued 7/1)	5,000 shares × 6/12 year	= 2,500
(Issued 10/1)	2,000 shares × 3/12 year	= 500
	Weighted-average number of common shares outstanding	8,000

Now calculate earnings per share.

$$\frac{\$20,000}{8,000} = \$2.50 \text{ Earnings per share}$$

[Section 15-3]

PROBLEM 15-3: Assume the same facts as in Problem 15-2 except that Thorsen Corporation also has preferred stock outstanding. The dividend requirement on the preferred stock is $2,000. Calculate earnings per share on common stock.

Answer: Subtract the dividend requirement for the current year on preferred stock from net income and then calculate EPS on common stock.

$$\frac{\$20,000 - \$2,000}{8,000} = \$2.25 \text{ earnings per share}$$

[Section 15-3]

PROBLEM 15-4: Garfield Corporation had the following stock outstanding for the full year.

10% preferred stock, $50 par value, 4,000 shares issued and outstanding ... $200,000
Common stock, $10 par value, 40,000 shares issued and outstanding........ 400,000

Net income for the year was $80,000. Each share of preferred stock can be converted into six shares of common stock. Calculate primary earnings per share and fully diluted earnings per share. (Assume common stock has been outstanding for a full year.)

Answer: [Section 15-3]

Primary EPS:

$$\frac{\$80,000 - \$20,000}{40,000} = \$1.50 \text{ Primary earnings per share}$$

The preferred dividend requirement is $20,000 (.10 × $50 par value × 4,000 shares), which must be subtracted from net income in calculating primary earnings per share.

Fully diluted EPS:

$$\frac{\$80,000}{64,000} = \$1.25 \text{ Fully diluted earnings per share}$$

40,000	Common shares
+ 24,000	Preferred (4,000 shares × 6 = 24,000)
64,000	Potential common shares outstanding

The preferred dividend requirement of $20,000 is not deducted because it is assumed that all the preferred stock is converted into common stock.

PROBLEM 15-5: Prepare a statement of retained earnings for Fenco Corporation for the year ended December 31, 19x4. Retained earnings on December 31, 19x3 were $56,500. Net income for 19x4 was $12,300. Dividends declared and paid amounted to $5,000 in 19x4.

Answer: [Section 15-4]

Fenco Corporation

Statement of Retained Earnings

For Year Ended December 31, 19x4

Retained earnings, January 1, 19x4	$56,500
Add December 31, 19x4 net income	12,300
Subtotal	$68,800
Deduct dividends	5,000
Retained earnings, December 31, 19x4	$63,800

PROBLEM 15-6: On December 15, 19x2, Day Corporation declared a 50¢ per share dividend on its $5, par-value, common stock. There were 30,000 shares outstanding. The date of payment is January 15, 19x3. Record the declaration and the payment of the dividend.

Answer: [Section 15-6]

Dec.	15	Retained Earnings	15,000	00		
		Dividends Payable			15,000	00
		To record declaration of 50¢ dividend on				
		common stock (30,000 shares				
		outstanding × .50)				
Jan.	15	Dividends Payable	15,000	00		
		Cash			15,000	00
		To record payment of dividends				
		declared 12/15/x2				

PROBLEM 15-7: Palmer Corporation has two classes of stock: 8% preferred stock, cumulative, $50 par value, 20,000 shares outstanding; and common stock, $10 par value, 50,000 shares outstanding. There are no dividends in arrears. If $130,000 in dividends is declared in Year 2, how much will common stockholders receive?

Answer: Preferred stockholders must be paid a dividend first. The balance will be paid to common stockholders.

$50 par value × .08 × 20,000 shares = $80,000 Preferred dividend

$130,000 Total amount declared
−80,000 Preferred dividend
$ 50,000 Common dividend

[Section 15-6]

PROBLEM 15-8: Refer to Problem 15-7. What is the amount of dividend that will be paid per share of preferred and common stock?

Answer: [Section 15-6]

Preferred: $80,000 ÷ 20,000 shares = $4
Common: $50,000 ÷ 50,000 shares = $1

PROBLEM 15-9: Refer to Problem 15-7. If dividends were not paid in Year 1, would the answer to Problem 15-7 change?

Answer: Yes. If dividends were not paid in Year 1, the preferred dividends would be in arrears. Dividends for Year 1 and the current year on preferred stock must be paid before a dividend can be paid on common stock. Preferred stockholders would be entitled to $160,000 ($80,000 × 2 years). Since only $130,000 was available for dividends, the full amount of $130,000 would be paid to preferred stockholders. [Section 15-6]

PROBLEM 15-10: Accounting, Inc., has one class of stock—common stock, $6 par value, 20,000 shares outstanding. The board of directors has approved a 3 to 1 stock split. What will the effect be on the legal capital (Common Stock) account?

Answer: Three shares will be issued for every share outstanding. Thus, the par value will decrease to $2 per share ($6 ÷ 3) and 60,000 shares will be outstanding (20,000 × 3). There is only a decrease in par value and an increase in the number of shares outstanding. [Section 15-6]

PROBLEM 15-11: Indicate the effect of each of the following transactions on assets, liabilities, and total stockholders' equity. Use the following to indicate the effect: Increase (I), Decrease (D), or No Effect (NE).

	Assets	Liabilities	Stockholders' Equity
Cash dividend declared			
Cash dividend paid			
Stock dividend declared			
Stock dividend distributed			
Stock split declared			
Stock split distributed			

Answer: [Section 15-6]

	Assets	Liabilities	Stockholders' Equity
Cash dividend declared	NE	I	D
Cash dividend paid	D	D	NE
Stock dividend declared	NE	NE	NE
Stock dividend distributed	NE	NE	NE
Stock split declared	NE	NE	NE
Stock split distributed	NE	NE	NE

16 LONG-TERM PAYABLES AND INVESTMENTS

16-1. Long-Term Investments

A. A corporation may invest in securities issued by other corporations or in U.S. Government bonds.

The purpose of the investments may differ. The corporation (*investor*) may be investing idle cash in marketable securities. This type of investment was discussed in Chapter 8. A corporation may decide to invest in the common stock of another corporation (*investee*) in order to expand the investor's operation or for other reasons. This type of investment is considered *long-term* because the investment either is not readily marketable or is made for reasons other than just putting idle cash to work.

B. Accounting for investments in equity securities differs depending on the percentage of ownership involved and the degree of control over the investee company.

Percent Ownership in Common Stock	Accounting Method
Less than 20%	Recorded at cost and adjusted to lower-of-cost-or-market (LCM) on balance sheet date (Cost Method)
20% – 50%	Recorded at cost, but adjusted each year for changes in stockholders' equity of investee company (Equity Method)
More than 50%	Consolidated Financial Statements (Equity Method)

1. *Less than 20%.* The Accounting Principles Board in Opinion 18 stated that a corporation usually lacked significant influence when the investor owned less than 20% of the common stock of another corporation. *Significant influence* was defined as the ability to affect operating policies. Referring to the chart shown above, you can see that an investment of less than 20% would be recorded at cost and adjusted to LCM on the balance sheet date.

   The cost method was discussed in Chapter 8 for securities classified as current. This section will discuss investments in *noncurrent* equity securities, pointing out any differences. Both current and noncurrent investments are recorded at cost. Dividends are reported as investment income to the investor under the cost method. On the balance sheet date the securities are valued at the lower of cost or market. The *portfolios of current and noncurrent securities are valued separately.* Declines considered to be other than temporary are recorded as a loss by reducing the recorded cost of the security itself. (Refer to page 168.)

Next, the market value of each portfolio (current and noncurrent) is compared to cost. Any decline considered to be temporary is recorded in an unrealized loss account and an allowance account. Up to this point, current and noncurrent portfolios are treated alike. However, the unrealized loss account is treated differently for noncurrent securities under the cost method. The unrealized loss is reported on the income statement for the *current* portfolio. Unrealized losses are included in the stockholders' equity section of the balance sheet for the *noncurrent* portfolio. The journal entry would be:

Unrealized Loss on Noncurrent Securities	XX	
Allowance for Declines in Market Value of		
Noncurrent Marketable Equity Securities		XX

The unrealized loss account reduces stockholders' equity, but has no effect on net income.

A recovery in the market value of the noncurrent securities is recorded up to the cost of the securities. The entry for the recovery would be:

Allowance for Declines in Market Value of		
Noncurrent Marketable Equity Securities	XX	
Unrealized Loss on Noncurrent Securities		XX

When the equity securities are sold, the treatment is the same as for the current equity securities. You may want to review Section 8-6, keeping in mind the one difference—the treatment of the unrealized loss account.

2. *20%–50%.* Unless there is evidence to the contrary, it is assumed that there is significant influence with ownership of 20% or more of the common stock in another corporation.

An ownership interest of 20%–50% is initially recorded at cost (including brokerage commission). Under the equity method, the investor company records its share of the investee net income as an increase to the investment account. Dividends received are a distribution of income already recorded. Therefore, the investment account is decreased for any dividends received.

EXAMPLE 16-1: On January 3, 19x3, Big Corporation purchased 40% of the common stock of Little Corporation for $50,000. Little Corporation's net income for 19x3 was $10,000. A cash dividend of $1,600 was received by Big Corporation on December 31. The journal entries to record the above transactions are illustrated below.

Jan. 3	Investment in Little Corporation	50,000	
	Cash		50,000
	To record the purchase of		
	a 40% interest in Little		
	Corporation		
Dec. 31	Investment in Little Corporation	4,000	
	Investment Income		4,000
	To record a 40% share of net		
	income recorded by Little		
	Corporation ($10,000 × .40)		
Dec. 31	Cash	1,600	
	Investment in Little Corporation		1,600
	To record receipt of cash		
	dividend		

298 Principles of Accounting I

The balance in the Investment account at the end of the first year is $52,400 ($50,000 + $4,000 − $1,600). Investments recorded using the equity method (the method illustrated above) are not adjusted to the lower-of-cost-or-market.

3. *More than 50%.* When more than 50% of the common stock in a corporation is owned by the investor, the investor is said to have a *controlling interest.* When a controlling interest exists, the investor is called the *parent company* and the investee is called the *subsidiary company.* Consolidated financial statements are prepared by the parent company. Accounting for a controlling interest is the subject of an advanced accounting course.

C. A corporation may also invest in debt securities issued by another corporation.

Investments in debt securities can be classified as current or noncurrent. Accounting for current investments was discussed in Chapter 8. Noncurrent investments in debt securities are recorded at cost (including brokerage commissions).

EXAMPLE 16-2: On June 1, Sun Corporation purchased 5-year bonds issued at a discount by Moon Corporation. (Bonds issued at a discount are discussed in Section 16-5.) Sun intended to hold the bonds until maturity. Sun bought ten $1,000 bonds at 96. There was a brokerage commission of $300. The entry to record the purchase is shown below.

June	Investment in Bonds	9,900	
	Cash		9,900
	To record the purchase of Moon Corporation bonds at 96 plus brokerage commission of $300 ($10,000 × .96 = $9,600 + $300 brokerage commission)		

A separate discount account is usually not maintained. The difference between cost and maturity value is amortized by debiting Investment in Bonds and crediting Interest Revenue. The entry would be reversed if the bond had been purchased at a premium. At maturity the Investment in Bonds account should equal the maturity value of the bonds. The straight-line method of amortization can be used if the difference between the straight-line and the effective-interest methods is immaterial. (The effective-interest method is discussed in Section 16-5.)

16-2. Long-Term Payables: Bonds

A. A corporation may issue capital stock or bonds payable when it needs to raise a large amount of long-term capital.

Accounting for the issuance of capital stock was discussed in Chapter 14. By issuing bonds, a large number of creditors (bondholders) furnish needed capital.

EXAMPLE 16-3: Osher Corporation plans to build a $10 million office complex. A bond issue is planned to raise the needed capital.

B. There are several characteristics of bonds.

1. *Long-term.* Bonds usually have a maturity date of ten to fifty years.
2. *Interest-bearing.* Most bonds are issued with a stated rate of interest.
3. *Secured or unsecured.* Bonds may be *mortgage bonds* secured by a pledge of specific assets as collateral. *Debenture bonds* are unsecured. Their value rests on the general credit of the corporation.
4. *Term or serial bonds.* A bond issue may have a fixed maturity date—all bonds mature on the same date. These are called *term bonds.* *Serial bonds* have more than one maturity date.

EXAMPLE 16-4: Assume Osher Corporation plans to retire all of the bonds in ten years. They are issued on January 1, Year 1, and will mature on December 31, Year 10. The bonds are called term bonds. Assume instead that Osher Corporation wants to retire $2 million at the end of Year 10, $2 million at the end of Year 11, and so on, until the full $10 million bond issue has been retired. These bonds are called serial bonds.

5. *Registered or coupon bonds.* Most bonds being issued now are *registered bonds.* The name and address of the present owner is recorded with the corporation. Interest checks are mailed to the current bondholder. *Coupon bonds* have coupons attached. On each interest payment date, a coupon is detached and turned into a bank for collection. The corporation usually has no record of the name and address of the current owner of coupon bonds.

C. The contract between the bondholder and the corporation is called a *bond indenture.*

The indenture describes the rights, privileges, and limitations of bondholders. It usually gives the maturity date, interest rate, interest payment dates, and other characteristics, along with the obligations of the corporation.

D. Bonds Payable should appear as a long-term liability on the balance sheet.

Bonds are usually issued with a face value of $1,000. Over the life of the bonds, the corporation makes periodic payments of interest to the bondholders. Interest is usually paid semiannually. The interest rate is stated on the bond. The price of bonds is quoted as a percent of the face (or par) value. Bonds may sell at 100% of face value or they may sell at a price less than or greater than the face value. When a bond sells for less than face value, it is said to be selling at a *discount.* When it sells for more than the face value, it is selling at a *premium.* Discounts and premiums are discussed in more detail later in the chapter.

EXAMPLE 16-5: Assume that on January 1, 19x1, J.G. Corporation issues $100,000 of five-year bonds with a face value of $1,000 each, and a stated interest rate of 10%.

1. If the bonds sell at 100 (100% of their face value), they will be selling at par.

$$\$1,000 \times 1.00 = \$1,000$$

An investor will pay $1,000 for the bond.
2. Now assume that the bonds sell at 93(93% of the face value). They will be selling at a discount (less than par).

$$\$1,000 \times .93 = \$930$$

The investor will pay $930 for a bond with a maturity value of $1,000.
3. If the bonds sell at 108(108% of face value), they will be selling at a premium.

$$\$1,000 \times 1.08 = \$1,080$$

In this instance, the investor will pay an amount greater than the maturity value.

16-3. Bonds Issued at Par

A. A bond issued at par sells at 100% of the face value.

When issued, Cash is debited and Bonds Payable is credited for the face amount of the bonds issued. Interest payments over the life of the bonds are debited to Bond Interest Expense and credited to Cash. Upon maturity, Bonds Payable is debited for the maturity value of the bonds and Cash is credited.

EXAMPLE 16-6: In Example 16-5, J.G. Corporation issued $100,000, 10%, five-year bonds, with a face value of $1,000 each. Interest is payable semi-annually on January 1 and July 1. Assume the bonds are sold at par on January 1, 19x1. The journal entry to record the issue is shown on page 300.

	19x1			
Jan.	1	Cash	100,000	
		Bonds Payable		100,000
		To record the issuance of 10%,		
		5-year bonds at par		

On July 1, the first semiannual interest payment is made. The journal entry follows.

	19x1			
July	1	Bond Interest Expense	5,000	
		Cash		5,000
		To record the semiannual		
		interest payment at 10% on		
		$100,000 face value bonds		
		($100,000 × .10 × 1/2 year		
		= $5,000)		

When the bonds mature in five years, the entry will be

	19x5			
Dec.	31	Bonds Payable	100,000	
		Cash		100,000
		To record payment to		
		bondholders on maturity date		

As mentioned before, Bonds Payable usually appears on the balance sheet as a long-term liability. When the bonds are due to mature, however, they should be shown as a current liability if current assets will be used to retire the bonds.

B. Bonds may be issued between interest payment dates.

Example 16-6 assumed that the bonds were issued on one of the interest payment dates. When bonds are issued between the interest payment dates, the investor pays the interest accrued to the date of the issuance. This practice allows the corporation to pay a full six month's interest on the stated interest date. The amount of accrued interest is credited to Bond Interest Payable at the time of issuance.

EXAMPLE 16-7: If J.G. Corporation does not issue the bonds until April 1, three months after the interest date shown on the bonds, the investors will pay $1,000 for each bond plus $25 accrued interest ($1,000 × .10 × 3/12). The journal entry is shown below.

April	1	Cash	102,500	
		Bonds Payable		100,000
		Bond Interest Payable		2,500
		To record issuance of $100,000,		
		10%, 5-year bond issue sold at		
		par plus accrued interest for		
		three months		

On July 1, the corporation will send bondholders a check for six months' interest that represents the return of interest received by the corporation when the bond was issued, plus three months of interest earned (April 1 to July 1). The entry is shown below.

July	1	Bond Interest Expense	2,500	
		Bond Interest Payable	2,500	
		Cash		5,000
		To record payment of		
		semiannual interest on $100,000,		
		10%, 5-year bonds		

Note that only three months of interest expense is recorded. The other $2,500 (Bond Interest

Payable) is a return of accrued interest the bondholders paid at the time they purchased the bonds. This example assumes the bonds are sold at par.

16-4. The Effect of Market Rate of Interest on Bond Prices

So far, bonds selling for 100% of their face value have been discussed. Investors are willing to pay this amount if the stated rate of interest on the bond is the same as the current market or *effective rate of interest* on a bond with similar features and risks.

The corporation must decide on the interest rate for the bond in advance of the issue date. If interest rates change between the time the interest rate for the bond is set and the bond issue date, the bond will not sell at par (face value).

EXAMPLE 16-8: Recall that J.G. Corporation is selling their $100,000 bond issue with a stated rate of interest of 10%. Suppose that the bonds are being marketed when interest rates on bonds with similar features and risks are selling with an effective (market) rate of interest of 12%. Investors will be unwilling to pay $1,000 for J.G.'s bonds for a $100 interest payment each year ($1,000 × .10) when they can receive a return of $120 per year ($1,000 × .12) for a similar bond. Investors may be willing to buy J.G.'s bonds for less than their face value, however, at an amount that will give the investor a rate of return equal to the effective (or market) rate of 12%. The bonds will thus be selling at a discount.

EXAMPLE 16-9: Now, assume that the effective rate of interest is only 8% when the bonds are sold. J.G. Corporation will be able to sell the bonds at an amount greater than par because bonds with similar features and risks are only paying a rate of return of 8%. The bonds will thus be selling at a premium.

16-5. Bonds Issued at a Discount

A. Bonds are issued at a price below par when the stated interest rate is lower than the effective interest rate for similar bonds.

The bonds are thus issued at a discount. The amount of discount is debited to a Discount on Bonds Payable account.

EXAMPLE 16-10: Assume instead that on January 1, J.G. Corporation issues $100,000, 10%, 5-year bonds at 93. The journal entry to record the sale is shown below

Jan.	1	Cash	93,000	
		Discount on Bonds Payable	7,000	
		Bonds Payable		100,000
		To record the issuance of bonds—10%, 5-year, at 93 ($100,000 × .93 = $93,000)		

B. The discount amount is amortized over the life of the bonds.

Straight-line amortization is the simplest method. An equal amount of discount is allocated to each interest period. The discount is usually amortized twice a year—on the semiannual interest payment dates. The discount amount to be amortized is debited to Bond Interest Expense along with the amount of the interest payment. Discount in Bonds Payable is credited for the amortization amount. The amortization per period is calculated as follows:

$$\frac{\text{Bond discount}}{\text{Total number of interest periods}} = \text{Discount amortized per period}$$

EXAMPLE 16-11: Recall from Example 16-10 that the discount on the bonds issued by J.G. Corporation is $7,000. The bonds will mature in 5 years.

$$\frac{5 \text{ Years} \times 2 \text{ Interest payments per year}}{} = 10 \text{ Interest periods}$$

$$\frac{\$7,000}{10} = \$700 \text{ Discount amortized per period}$$

To record the first semiannual interest payment and discount amortization on July 1, J.G. Corporation will make the following journal entry:

July	1	Bond Interest Expense	5,700	
		Discount on Bonds Payable		700
		Cash		5,000
		To record semiannual interest payment to bondholders and straight-line amortization of discount		

Two separate entries can be made instead of the compound entry shown above. The two separate entries are shown below.

July	1	Bond Interest Expense	5,000	
		Cash		5,000
		To record semiannual cash payment to bondholders ($100,000 × .10 × 1/2 year)		
	1	Bond Interest Expense	700	
		Discount on Bonds Payable		700
		To record semiannual amortization of the discount ($7,000 ÷ 10 interest periods)		

The total interest expense for the period is $5,700.

C. The unamortized discount amount is subtracted from the face value to arrive at the net liability.

As the discount is amortized, the discount decreases and the net liability (or carrying value) increases.

EXAMPLE 16-12: If J.G. Corporation had issued financial statements immediately after issuing the bonds, the liability for bonds payable would have appeared in the long-term liability section of the balance sheet as shown below.

Long-term liabilities:
Bonds payable $100,000
Less: Discount on bonds payable............................ 7,000 $93,000

After the July 1 interest payment, the liability would appear as follows:

Long-term liabilities:
Bonds payable $100,000
Less: Discount on bonds payable* 6,300 $93,700

*(Discount = $7,000 − $700 = $6,300)

On the maturity date, the balance in Discount on Bonds Payable is zero. The net liability equals the face value of the bonds.

D. The amount of discount can be amortized each period using the *effective-interest method*.

The straight-line method is the simplest method to amortize a discount, but there is a conceptual weakness in the method. An equal amount of interest expense is recognized each period. However, as the discount is amortized, the net liability increases (see Example 16-12 above). If the liability is increasing, the interest expense should also be increasing. The *effective-interest method* overcomes the problem. Using the effective-interest method, the amount of discount amortized each period is based on the net liability (or carrying value) of the bonds and the effective rate of interest at the time the bonds were issued. The difference between the total interest expense calculated using this method and the amount of the periodic cash interest payment is the amount of discount to be amortized for the period.

EXAMPLE 16-13: To illustrate the effective interest method, let's continue our example of J.G. Corporation. Assume the $100,000 of 5-year bonds with a 10% stated interest rate were issued when the effective (market) rate was *approximately* 12%. The bonds sold for $93,000. The table below shows the amortization of the discount semiannually over the 5-year life of the bonds using the effective-interest method.

Semi-Annual Interest Period	A Carrying Value at Beginning of Period	B Effective Semiannual Interest Expense* (6% × A)	C Semiannual Interest Paid to Bondholders (5% of Face Value)	D Discount Amortization (B − C)	E Bond Discount Balance at End of Period	F Carrying Value at End of Period (A + D)
Issue Date					$7,000	
1	$93,000	$5,580	$5,000	$580	6,420	$ 93,580
2	93,580	5,615	5,000	615	5,805	94,195
3	94,195	5,652	5,000	652	5,153	94,847
4	94,847	5,691	5,000	691	4,462	95,538
5	95,538	5,732	5,000	732	3,730	96,270
6	96,270	5,776	5,000	776	2,954	97,046
7	97,046	5,823	5,000	823	2,131	97,869
8	97,869	5,872	5,000	872	1,259	98,741
9	98,741	5,924	5,000	924	335	99,665
10	99,665	5,335**	5,000	335	—	100,000

* Rounded to nearest dollar.
** Interest expense equals interest paid to bondholders for the period plus the remaining balance of the unamortized discount. This adjusts for rounding.

To help you understand the table, each column is explained as follows:

1. *Column A.* The carrying value at the beginning of the period is used to calculate the discount to be amortized. The carrying value for a discounted bond increases each period as the Discount on Bonds Payable decreases.
2. *Column B.* The effective semiannual interest rate is one-half of the annual effective rate of 12%, or 6%. The *total* interest expense for the period is based on the effective rate. Column A × effective semiannual rate = total interest expense for the period. (Period 1: $93,000 × .06 = $5,580)
3. *Column C.* The semiannual interest *paid to bondholders* equals one-half of the stated annual rate of 10%, or 5%. The semiannual rate is multiplied times the face value of the bonds ($100,000 × .05 = $5,000 interest paid to bondholders).
4. *Column D.* The amount of discount to be amortized is determined by subtracting Column C from Column B. Total interest was calculated in Column B. Total interest expense for a period equals the cash payment to bondholders plus the amount of the discount to be amortized. (Period 1: $5,580 − $5,000 = $580 amount of discount to be amortized at the end of Period 1.)

5. *Column E.* The Bond Discount at the end of the period has been reduced by the amount of discount amortized in the current period. (Period 1: $7,000 − $580 = $6,420)
6. *Column F.* The carrying value at the beginning of the period is increased by the amount of the discount amortized in the current period. (Period 1: $93,000 + $580 = $93,580)

As you can see, the effective-interest method calculates the interest expense for the current period based on the net liability for the current period. The interest expense as a percent of the net liability is constant over the life of the bonds. If you use the straight-line method, interest expense as a percent of the net liability decreases over time when the bond is issued at a discount. (Total interest expense remains constant as the net liability increases).

EXAMPLE 16-14: Based on the table in Example 16-13, the following entry will be made to record the first interest payment and the amortization of the related amount of discount.

July	1	Bond Interest Expense	5,580	
		Discount on Bonds Payable		580
		Cash		5,000
		To record semiannual interest expense on 10%, 5-year bonds sold at a discount.		

Note that the amortization of the discount is calculated by multiplying the carrying value of the bonds payable at the beginning of the period by the effective interest rate. This gives you the *total* interest expense for the period. Subtract the cash payment to bondholders from the total interest expense to arrive at the amount of discount being amortized in the current period.

16-6. Bonds Issued at a Premium

A. Bonds are issued at a price above par when the stated interest rate is higher than the effective interest rate for similar bonds.

The bonds are thus issued at a premium. The amount of premium is credited to a Premium on Bonds Payable account.

EXAMPLE 16-15: Assume the $100,000, 10%, 5-year bonds issued by J.G. Corporation sell at 108. The journal entry to record the sale of the bonds is shown below.

Jan.	1	Cash	108,000	
		Premium on Bonds Payable		8,000
		Bonds Payable		100,000
		To record the issuance of 10%, 5-year bonds at 108 ($100,000 × 1.08 = $108,000)		

B. The premium is amortized over the life of the bonds.

Premium on Bonds Payable is debited for the premium amount. Again, straight-line amortization is the easiest method.

EXAMPLE 16-16: The premium on the bonds issued in the previous example is $8,000. Using the straight-line method, $800 will be amortized each six-month period ($8,000 ÷ 10 = $800). The journal entry for the first interest period is shown below.

July	1	Bond Interest Expense	4,200	
		Premium on Bonds Payable	800	
		Cash		5,000
		To record semiannual interest payment to bondholders and straight-line amortization of premium		

C. The unamortized premium is added to the face value of the bonds to arrive at the net liability.

As the premium is amortized, the net liability decreases. On the date the bonds mature, Premium on Bonds Payable will have a zero balance and the net liability will equal the face value of the bonds.

EXAMPLE 16-17: To continue Example 16-16, assume that the balance sheet is prepared on the day the bonds are issued. The net liability would appear as shown below.

Long-term liabilities:
Bonds payable $100,000
Add: Premium on bonds payable 8,000 $108,000

After the July 1 interest payment and amortization of the premium, the liability will appear as follows:

Long-term liabilities:
Bonds payable $100,000
Add: Premium on bonds payable*........................... 7,200 $107,200
 * $8,000 − $800 = $7,200

D. The premium can be amortized each period using the effective interest method.

The above examples assumed the use of the straight-line method. If the effective-interest method is used, the amount of the premium amortized each interest period is based on the net liability at the beginning of each period. The procedure is similar to amortizing a discount except the Premium on Bonds Payable is *added* to the face value of the bonds to determine the net liability. As the premium is amortized, the net liability *decreases* and, therefore, the total interest expense *decreases* each period. An amortization schedule for bonds issued at a premium is shown in Example 16-18.

EXAMPLE 16-18: The table below shows the amortization of the premium semiannually over the 5-year life of the $100,000, 10% bonds issued by J.G. Corporation at 108.

Semi-Annual Interest Period	(A) Carrying Value At Beginning of Period	(B) Effective Semiannual Interest Expense** (4%* × A)	(C) Semiannual Interest Paid to Bondholders (5% of Face Value)	(D) Premium Amortization (C—B)	(E) Bond Premium Balance at End of Period	(F) Carrying Value at End of Period (A—D)
Issue date					$8,000	
1	$108,000	$4,320	$5,000	$680	7,320	$107,320
2	107,320	4,293	5,000	707	6,613	106,613
3	106,613	4,265	5,000	735	5,878	105,878
4	105,878	4,235	5,000	765	5,113	105,113
5	105,113	4,205	5,000	795	4,318	104,318
6	104,318	4,173	5,000	827	3,491	103,491
7	103,491	4,140	5,000	860	2,631	102,631
8	102,631	4,105	5,000	895	1,736	101,736
9	101,736	4,069	5,000	931	805	100,805
10	100,805	4,195***	5,000	805	—	100,000

 * Approximately

 ** Rounded to nearest dollar.

 *** Interest expense equals interest paid to bondholders for the period plus the remaining balance of unamortized premium. This adjusts for rounding.

Note that the total interest expense for each period (Column B) is *less* than the interest payment being made to bondholders (Column C). Remember that the amortization of a premium *reduces* total interest expense from the stated rate (5% semiannually) to the effective rate (4% semiannually). The bondholders always receive a cash payment for the stated rate (5% semiannually in this example).

EXAMPLE 16-19: The journal entry to record the payment of interest and amortization of the premium on the first interest payment date (refer to the first line of the table) is shown below.

July 1	Bond Interest Expense	4,320	
	Premium on Bonds Payable	680	
	Cash		5,000
	To record semiannual interest expense on 10%, 5-year bonds issued at 108		

The total interest expense will decrease each period as the net liability decreases.

16-7. Retirement of Bonds

Bonds are sometimes retired before the maturity date. If interest rates decline, the corporation may be better off retiring the bonds and issuing new bonds at a lower interest rate. To allow a corporation this flexibility, most bonds have a *call feature*. This feature allows the corporation to retire the bonds by paying the bondholders an amount that is usually above the face value. This amount is referred to as the *call price*. A loss is incurred if a corporation retires bonds at a call price above their carrying value. A gain is realized if the bonds are retired at a call price below their carrying value.

EXAMPLE 16-20: Assume that J.G. Corporation decides to retire the 5-year bonds issued at 108 at the end of the third year. The bonds are retired at a call price of 105 ($100,000 × 1.05 = $105,000). The carrying value of the bonds at the end of the third year (6th interest period) is $103,491 (refer to the table in Example 16-18). The journal entry to retire the bonds is shown below.

19x3			
Dec. 31	Bonds Payable	100,000	
	Premium on Bonds Payable	3,491	
	Loss on Retirement of Bonds	1,509	
	Cash		105,000
	To record retirement of $100,000, 10%, 5-year bonds at the end of Year 3 for 105		

There is a loss in this example because the net liability was less than the call price of 105.

16-8. Other Long-Term Liabilities

There are other ways by which a corporation can obtain long-term financing. The corporation may obtain long-term financing in the form of a note payable. In this case, the financing is obtained from a single creditor. A type of note payable is a mortgage note payable. The borrower pledges title to specific assets as collateral for the loan. A long-term lease (*capital lease*) also provides long-term financing. This has become a popular way to finance equipment used by the business. Many companies pay retirement benefits to employees. Accounting for pension plans is complex. The Retirement Security Act of 1974 (ERISA) requires extensive reporting on pension plans. Capital leases and pensions are covered in more advanced accounting courses.

RAISE YOUR GRADES

Can you explain...?

☑ the different methods of accounting for investments in securities
☑ the characteristics of bonds
☑ why bonds are sometimes issued at a discount or a premium
☑ how to record a bond issued at par, at a discount, or at a premium
☑ how to amortize the discount or premium using the straight-line method
☑ how to amortize the discount or premium using the effective-interest method
☑ how to record interest expense including the amortization of a discount or premium
☑ where and how bonds appear on the balance sheet
☑ how to record the retirement of a bond before the maturity date

SUMMARY

1. A corporation may invest in securities issued by other corporations or in U.S. Government bonds. The purpose may be to put idle cash to work, or to expand the corporation's operations.

2. Accounting differs for investments in equity securities depending on the percentage of ownership involved and the degree of control over the investee company: less than 20% = cost method; 20% or more = equity method.

3. Noncurrent investments in debt securities are recorded at cost. The difference between cost and maturity value is amortized over the life of the bonds.

4. When a corporation needs to raise a large amount of long-term capital, it may issue capital stock or bonds payable. By issuing bonds, a large number of creditors (bondholders) furnish the needed capital.

5. Bonds are long-term, usually interest-bearing, and normally have a face value of $1,000.

6. Bonds may sell at par (face value), at a discount (less than face value), or at a premium (greater than face value).

7. When the stated or contract rate equals the effective or market rate of interest, the bonds will sell at par.

8. When the stated rate is greater than the effective rate of interest, the bonds will sell at a premium.

9. When the stated rate is less than the effective rate of interest, the bonds will sell at a discount.

10. The discount or premium should be amortized over the life of the bond using the straight-line method or the effective-interest method. The straight-line method amortizes an equal amount of premium or discount over the life of the bond. The effective-interest method bases the amount amortized each period on the net liability of the bonds.

11. The amortization of the discount increases total interest expense above the amount of the cash payment. The amortization of the premium reduces total interest expense below the amour. of the cash payment.

12. Interest payments to bondholders are usually made semiannually and are based on the stated interest rate.

13. Bonds are sometimes retired before the maturity date. The corporation pays the bondholder the call price to redeem the bond.

14. Other long-term liabilities include mortgage notes payable, long-term (capital) leases, and pensions.

RAPID REVIEW	Answers

True or False

1. A long-term investment in equity securities is always recorded at cost and adjusted to lower-of-cost-or-market on the balance sheet date. [Section 16-1]   *False*

2. The difference between cost and maturity value should be amortized when a corporation regards its investment in debt securities as long-term. [Section 16-1]   *True*

3. Bonds are usually issued with a $1,000 face value. [Section 16-2]   *True*

4. Bonds are sold at par when the stated rate of interest equals the effective rate of interest for bonds with similar features and risks. [Section 16-4]   *True*

5. Bonds Payable usually appears in the current liability section of the balance sheet. [Section 16-3]   *False*

6. A bond sells at a discount if the stated rate of interest is greater than the effective (market) rate for bonds with similar features and risks. [Section 16-5]   *False*

7. When the premium on bonds payable is amortized, total interest expense is less than the semiannual cash interest payment to bondholders. [Section 16-6]   *True*

8. The straight-line method of amortizing a discount or premium is preferred because the amount of amortization is based on the net liability of the bonds at the beginning of the period. [Section 16-5]   *False*

9. When a discount is amortized using the effective-interest method, the amount of the discount amortized each period increases as the net liability increases. [Section 16-5]   *True*

10. The journal entry to record the amortization of a premium on bonds payable includes a debit to Interest Expense and a debit to Premium on Bonds Payable. [Section 16-6]   *True*

11. The unamortized premium is deducted from bonds payable to arrive at the net liability. [Section 16-6]   *False*

12. If a bond has a call feature, the corporation has the option of retiring the bonds before the maturity date by paying the call price to bondholders. [Section 16-7]   *True*

13. Bondholders are owners of the corporation. [Section 16-2]   *False*

14. A secured bond is secured by a pledge of specific assets as collateral. [Section 16-2]   *True*

15. Term bonds all mature on the same date. [Section 16-2]   *True*

16. A bond that sells for more than the face value is said to be selling at a discount. [Section 16-2]   *False*

17. Bond prices are quoted as a percent of the face (or par) value. [Section 16-2]   *True*

SOLVED PROBLEMS

PROBLEM 16-1: On January 5, 19x5, Irwin, Inc., purchased 30% of the common stock of Baker Tool Company for $10,000. At the end of Year 5, Baker Tool Company reported a net income of $5,000 and paid a cash dividend of $2,000 to stockholders. The payment date was December 15. Record all of the above transactions in the general journal of Irwin, Inc.

Answer:

Jan.	5	Investment in Baker Tool Company	10,000	00		
		Cash			10,000	00
		To record purchase of 30% of common				
		stock of Baker Tool				
Dec.	15	Cash	600	00		
		Investment in Baker Tool Company			600	00
		To record receipt of cash dividend from				
		Baker Tool ($2,000 × .30)				
Dec.	31	Investment in Baker Tool Company	1,500	00		
		Investment Income			1,500	00
		To record 30% share of net income of				
		Baker Tool				

Irwin, Inc., owns 30% of the common stock of Baker Tool Company and therefore uses the equity method to record the investment. 30% of the net income of Baker Tool is recorded as an increase in the investment account. However, the payment of dividends is a distribution of net income. The receipt of the dividend decreases the investment. [Section 16-1]

PROBLEM 16-2: Refer to the information in Problem 16-1. Calculate the balance in the investment account at the end of Year 5.

Answer: [Section 16-1]

   $10,000 Original Cost
   −   600 Cash Dividend
  +1,500 30% Share of Net Income
   $10,900 Balance on 12/31/x5

PROBLEM 16-3: Morris Company plans to issue $100,000, 10-year, 12% bonds. Calculate the amount of cash received by Morris under each of the following assumptions: (*a*) bonds sell at par; (*b*) bonds sell at 103; (*c*) bonds sell at 96.

Answer: [Section 16-2]
(*a*) $100,000 × 1.00 = $100,000
(*b*) $100,000 × 1.03 = $103,000
(*c*) $100,000 × .96 = $ 96,000

PROBLEM 16-4: On January 1, 19x1, Tusca Corporation issued $500,000 of 10-year, 12% bonds. Interest is payable semiannually on January 1 and July 1. Assume the bonds sell at par.

Record the issue on January 1 and the first interest payment on July 1.

Answer: [Section 16-3]

Jan.	1	Cash	500,000	00		
		Bonds Payable			500,000	00
		To record the issue of 12%,				
		10-year bonds at par				
July	1	Bond Interest Expense	30,000	00		
		Cash			30,000	00
		To record semiannual interest payment				
		($500,000 × .12 × 1/2 year)				

PROBLEM 16-5: Assume the same facts as given in Problem 16-4 except that the bonds sell at a discount at 98. Record the bond issue, the first semiannual interest payment, and the semiannual amortization of the discount using the straight-line method.

Answer:

Jan.	1	Cash	490,000	00		
		Discount on Bonds Payable	10,000	00		
		Bonds Payable			500,000	00
		To record the issue of 12% 10-year bonds				
		at 98 ($500,000 × .98 = $490,000)				
July	1	Bond Interest Expense	30,000	00		
		Cash			30,000	00
		To record the semiannual interest				
		payment ($500,000 × 12% ×				
		1/2 year)				
	1	Bond Interest Expense	500	00		
		Discount on Bonds Payable			500	00
		To record the semiannual amortization				
		of discount ($10,000 ÷ 20				
		payment periods = $500)				

You may have combined the interest payment and amortization of discount into one entry with a debit to Interest Expense for the total expense of $30,500 and a credit to Cash for $30,000 and Discount on Bonds Payable for $500. The discount should be amortized semiannually over the 10-year life of the bonds, which equals twenty amortization periods. [Section 16-4]

PROBLEM 16-6: Refer to Problem 16-5. If Tusca Corporation issued financial statements immediately after issuing the bonds, show how the liability for bonds payable would appear on the balance sheet.

Answer: [Section 16-4]

Long-term liabilities:
Bond payable $500,000
Less: Discount on bonds payable 10,000 $490,000

PROBLEM 16-7: Again assume the same facts as given in Problem 16-4 except that the bonds sell at a premium of 104. Record the bond issue, the first semiannual interest payment, and the semiannual amortization of the premium using the straight-line method.

Answer: [Section 16-5]

Jan.	1	Cash	520,000	00		
		Premium on Bonds Payable			20,000	00
		Bonds Payable			500,000	00
		To record issuance of 12%, 10-year				
		bonds at 104 ($500,000 × 1.04 =				
		$520,000)				
July	1	Bond Interest Expense	30,000	00		
		Cash			30,000	00
		To record semiannual interest payment				
July	1	Premium on Bonds Payable	1,000	00		
		Bond Interest Expense			1,000	00
		To record semiannual amortization of				
		premium ($20,000 ÷ 20 payment				
		periods = $1,000)				

Note that the amortization of the premium reduces total interest expense below the cash payment.

$30,000 Cash payment
−1,000 Premium amortization
$29,000 Total interest expense

The discount amortization in Problem 16-5 increases total interest expense above the cash payment.

$30,000 Cash payment
    500 Discount amortization
$30,500 Total interest expense

PROBLEM 16-8: Refer to Problem 16-7. Show how the liability for bonds payable would appear on the balance sheet after the first interest payment on July 1.

Answer:

Long term liabilities:
  Bonds Payable $500,000
  Add: Premium on bonds payable 19,000 $519,000

The Premium on Bonds Payable account was reduced $1,000 when the amortization was recorded on July 1. The new balance is $19,000. As the premium is amortized, the liability is reduced until the liability equals the maturity value. [Section 16-6]

PROBLEM 16-9: On January 1, Lee, Inc., issued $100,000 of 5-year bonds with a stated interest rate of 12%. The market rate for bonds with similar features and risks was approximately 16%. The bonds sold at 87. Complete an amortization table for the first two years using the effective-interest method. Interest is payable semiannually.

Semi-Annual Interest Period	Carrying Value at Beginning of Period	Effective Semiannual Interest Expense (8%)	Semiannual Interest Paid to Bondholders (6%)	Discount Amortization	Bond Discount Balance at End of Period	Carrying Value at End of Period
Issue date						
1						
2						
3						
4						

Answer: [Section 16-6]

Semi-Annual Interest Period	Carrying Value at Beginning of Period	Effective Semiannual Interest Expense (8%)	Semiannual Interest Paid to Bondholders (6%)	Discount Amortization	Bond Discount Balance at End of Period	Carrying Value at End of Period
Issue date					$13,000	
1	$87,000	$6,960	$6,000	$ 960	$12,040	$87,960
2	87,960	7,037	6,000	1,037	11,003	88,997
3	88,997	7,120	6,000	1,120	9,883	90,117
4	90,117	7,209	6,000	1,209	8,674	91,326

PROBLEM 16-10: Prepare two journal entries to record the first semiannual interest payment and the amortization of the discount given in Problem 16-9. You may omit explanations with the journal entries.

Answer: [Section 16-6]

July	1	Bond Interest Expense	6,000	00			
		Cash				6,000	00
		Bond Interest Expense	960	00			
		Discount on Bonds Payable				960	00

PROBLEM 16-11: Refer to Problem 16-9. Show how the bond liability would appear on the balance sheet of Lee, Inc., at the end of Year 2.

Answer: [Section 16-6]

Long-term liabilities:
Bonds payable $100,000
Less: Discount on bonds payable.............................. 8,674 $91,326

PROBLEM 16-12: Baxter Company has decided to retire $50,000 in bonds before maturity. The bonds originally sold at a discount. The balance in the Discount on Bonds Payable account at the time of retirement is $2,000. The call price on the bonds is 103. The bonds are retired on July 1, the interest payment date. Assume the interest and the amortization of the discount have been recorded. Prepare the journal entry to retire the bonds.

Answer: [Section 16-7]

July	1	Bonds Payable	50,000	00			
		Loss on Retirement**	3,500	00			
		Discount on Bonds Payable				2,000	00
		Cash*				51,500	00
		To record early retirement of bonds					
		payable at call price of 103.					

* $50,000 × 1.03 = $51,500 Call price
** $51,500 Cash paid − $48,000 Net liability = $3,500 Loss on retirement

Assuming that interest rates had dropped substantially since the bonds were issued, the company is better off retiring the bonds at a loss and reissuing at a lower interest rate.

17 FINANCIAL STATEMENT ANALYSIS

THIS CHAPTER IS ABOUT

- ☑ How to Read a Financial Statement
- ☑ Ratio Analysis
- ☑ Financial Condition
- ☑ Capital Utilization
- ☑ Measures of Performance
- ☑ Limitations of Financial Statement Analysis

17-1. How to Read a Financial Statement

A. The place to start in any financial statement is at the back with the report of the independent Certified Public Accountant.

The report of the independent Certified Public Accountant tells you if the report has been *audited*, *reviewed* (but not audited), or *merely compiled* (neither audited nor reviewed). Audited financial statements offer the highest degree of assurance that the operations and financial position of the company have been appropriately reported.

B. Virtually all large and medium sized companies, as well as many small companies, obtain audited financial statements.

The auditor examines the financial statements and the supporting data using *Generally Accepted Auditing Standards (GAAS)* to determine if the financial statements *"present fairly"* in accordance with *Generally Accepted Accounting Principles (GAAP)*. Upon completion of the audit, the auditors issue a letter stating their opinion of the financial statements. There are key phrases to watch for in the auditor's report.

1. *Presents fairly except for.* The phrase *"presents fairly except for"* indicates that the auditor does not feel the item is presented fairly or, at a minimum, the auditor feels the item warrants further attention.
2. *Does not present fairly.* Another phrase to watch for is *"does not present fairly."* In this case, the independent auditor believes the financial statements prepared by management do not fairly present the results of operations and financial position of the company.

C. After the auditor's report, the next section to be reviewed is the footnotes.

The footnotes give nonquantitative information necessary to interpret the quantitative items appearing in the body of the financial statements.

EXAMPLE 17-1: The fact that taxes may be lower this year because of a favorable court settlement on a previous year's taxes would be revealed in the footnotes.

D. Next review the chairman's letter.

The chairman's letter contains information on the future prospects of the company and his stance on its economic and political environment. Look for new products or lines, and lines or products that have been discontinued. Also look for phrases such as "Except for..." Now you are ready to examine the numbers.

17-2. Ratio Analysis

Financial ratios are used to evaluate the financial condition of the company, to evaluate how well the company used the resources entrusted to it, and to evaluate the company's operating performance. The majority of this traditional analysis is made up of comparisons of *ratios*. Without comparisons, you can learn very little.

EXAMPLE 17-2: Would you accept a job with a salary of $100 a day? Finding $100 a day attractive, you might be tempted to say yes, but what if there were an identical job that paid $150? By comparison, the first job is relatively less attractive.

Most comparisons require the use of ratios rather than absolute numbers. For example, it is difficult, if not impossible, to evaluate a $1,000 increase in income without a ratio. You are better able to evaluate the $1,000 increase if you know that it is a 20% increase over last year's income of $5,000. The information given on the balance sheet and the income statement presented below will be used to illustrate ratio analysis throughout this chapter.

Argus Company
Income Statement
For Year Ended December 31, 19--

Gross sales		$43,620.00	
Less: Sales discounts	$ 2,130.00		
Sales returns	1,590.00	3,720.00	
Net sales			$39,900.00
Cost of goods sold:			
Inventory, January 1		$ 9,630.00	
Purchases	$21,795.00		
Less: Purchase discounts $408.00			
Purchase returns 660.00	1,068.00		
Net purchases		20,727.00	
Add: Transportation-in		567.00	
Cost of goods available for sale		$30,924.00	
Less: Inventory, December 31		10,950.00	
Cost of goods sold			19,974.00
Gross profit			$19,926.00
Operating expenses:			
Rent expense		$ 1,560.00	
Salary expense		8,107.50	
Utilities expense		978.00	
Interest expense		360.00	
Depreciation expense		2,040.00	13,045.50
Net income			$ 6,880.50

Argus Company
Balance Sheet
December 31, 19--

Assets

Current assets:

Cash	$ 3,180.00	
Accounts receivable	3,435.00	
Inventory	10,950.00	
Prepaid insurance	720.00	
Total current assets		$18,285.00

Plant assets:

Equipment	$20,400.00	
Less: Accumulated depreciation	8,160.00	12,240.00
Total assets		$30,525.00

Liabilities

Current liabilities:

Accounts payable	$8,451.00	
Salaries payable	457.50	
Total current liabilities		$ 8,908.50

Long-term liabilities:

Bonds payable	10,000.00	
Total liabilities		$18,908.50

Stockholders' Equity

Common stock, 1,000 shares at $1 par	$1,000.00	
Paid-in capital in excess of par	2,000.00	
Total paid-in capital	$ 3,000.00	
Retained earnings	8,616.50	
Total stockholders' equity		11,616.50
Total liabilities and stockholders' equity		$30,525.00

17-3. Financial Condition

The balance sheet provides the information necessary to evaluate the financial condition of the company. The financial condition is evaluated in terms of its liquidity and its solvency.

A. Liquidity is a company's ability to meet current obligations.

There are three methods of evaluating the liquidity of the company.

1. *Net working capital.* Net working capital is the difference between the current assets and the current liabilities. Net working capital, or simply working capital, shows the current assets that would remain if the current liabilities were paid immediately. The larger the

net working capital, the greater the safety margin the company has in paying its current obligations.

EXAMPLE 17-3: Net working capital for Argus Company is calculated below.

Current assets...	$18,285.00
Current liabilities...	−8,908.50
Net working capital......................................	$ 9,376.50

2. *Current ratio.* The current ratio indicates the relative short-term liquidity of a firm. Generally, it is a more useful indicator than the amount of working capital because it allows for a comparison of the liquidity of different sizes of firms or of the same firm as it changes size. The current ratio is determined by dividing the current assets by the current liabilities.

EXAMPLE 17-4: The current ratio calculation for Argus Company is shown below.

Current assets............................ $\dfrac{\$18,285.00}{\$ 8,908.50}$ = 2.0525 or 2.05 Current ratio
Current liabilities.........................

There is no correct ratio. The needs of a particular firm dictate what is appropriate. A current ratio for a firm with stable cash flows, such as a utility, would generally be lower than that for a firm with irregular cash flows, such as a construction company.

3. *Acid-test ratio.* The acid-test ratio, or *quick ratio*, is used where a measure of "immediate" liquidity is desired. Quick assets are cash and those assets that can be converted into cash quickly. The ratio is determined by dividing quick assets by current liabilities. Quick assets include cash, short-term marketable securities, net current accounts receivable, and net current notes receivable.

EXAMPLE 17-5: The acid test ratio calculation for Argus Company is shown below.

Cash	$3,180.00
Accounts receivable...	3,435.00
Quick assets	$6,615.00

Quick assets................................ $\dfrac{\$6,615.00}{\$8,908.50}$ = .7425 or .74 Acid-test ratio
Current liabilities...........................

B. Solvency is a company's ability to meet long-term obligations.

There are two common methods of evaluating the solvency of the company.

1. *Debt-to-equity ratio.* The ratio of debt-to-equity indicates the relative safety of the resources provided by creditors. The ratio is determined by dividing total liabilities by total stockholders' equity. As the percentage of debt declines, the creditors have a higher degree of assurance that the company will be able to meet its obligations to them.

EXAMPLE 17-6: The debt-to-equity ratio for Argus Company is determined below.

Total liabilities............................... $\dfrac{\$18,908.50}{11,616.50}$ = 1.63 Debt-to-equity ratio
Total stockholders' equity....................

2. *Times-interest-earned.* The times-interest-earned ratio indicates the risk of bankruptcy associated with the debt. The ratio shows the number of times that interest charges are

earned during the year by dividing income (before interest and taxes) by interest expense. The higher the ratio, the lower the risk of not being able to meet interest payments in a period of decreased earnings.

EXAMPLE 17-7: The calculation for times-interest-earned for Argus Company is shown below.

$$\frac{\text{Income before interest and taxes}\dots\dots\dots}{\text{Interest expense}\cdots\cdots\cdots} \quad \frac{\$6,880.50 + \$360.00}{\$360.00} = 20.11 \text{ Times-interest-earned}$$

17-4. Capital Utilization

Measures of capital utilization indicate how well the company uses its resources and how hard these resources are being worked. There are three common methods of measuring capital utilization.

A. *Days' receivables* is a measure of the average age of the receivables.

By comparing the average age of the receivables to the credit terms extended to customers, an idea of the credit worthiness of the receivables can be obtained. A measurement of the credit policies for a period is determined by dividing the average net receivables for the period by net credit sales and multiplying by 365 to get the average length of time that receivables are outstanding.

EXAMPLE 17-8: Assuming that Argus Company has net credit sales of $25,000, the days' receivables is

$$\frac{\text{Net receivables}\dots\dots\dots\dots\dots}{\text{Net credit sales}\dots\dots\dots\dots\dots} \quad \frac{\$3,435}{\$25,000} \times 365 = 50.1 \text{ or } 50 \text{ Days}$$

A measure as of the end of the period uses the ending balance of net receivables.

B. *Inventory turnover* indicates the relative liquidity of the inventory and gives an overall indication of how active the inventory is.

The higher the turnover, the faster the inventory sells on average. Inventory turnover is determined by dividing the cost of merchandise sold by average inventory. It is necessary to use the average of the beginning and ending inventory balances if monthly data are not available.

EXAMPLE 17-9: The average inventory for Argus Company is $10,290 ($9,630 + $10,950/2). The inventory turnover is shown below.

$$\frac{\text{Cost of goods sold}\dots\dots\dots\dots\dots}{\text{Average inventory}\dots\dots\dots\dots\dots} \quad \frac{\$19,974}{\$10,290} = 1.94 \text{ Inventory turnover}$$

C. *Asset turnover* gives an overall indication of how assets are being used to generate sales.

As with the inventory turnover, the higher the turnover, the more active the assets are. Asset turnover is determined by dividing net sales by total assets. Long-term investments should be excluded from total assets, as they are not related to sales of goods or services. Total assets used in the ratio can be the balances at the end of the period, the average of the beginning and ending balances, or the average monthly totals.

EXAMPLE 17-10: The asset turnover for Argus Company is shown below. Total assets are taken from the balance sheet at the end of the period.

Net sales .... $\dfrac{\$39,900}{\$30,525}$ = 1.31 Asset turnover
Average total assets* ....

* Only ending assets were given in this example; therefore average assets were not used.

17-5. Measures of Performance

Measures of performance indicate the overall effectiveness of the company's operations. There are four common measures of performance.

A. *Profit margin percentage* **indicates the number of cents of each dollar of sales that were earned as profit.**

The profit margin percentage is determined by dividing net income by net sales.

EXAMPLE 17-11: The profit margin percentage for Argus Company is calculated below.

Net income .... $\dfrac{\$6,880.50}{\$39,900.00}$ = .17 Profit margin percentage
Net sales ....

B. *Return on owners' investment* **provides the best overall measure of the company's performance from the stockholders' point of view.**

The higher the return, the more profitable the investment. Note, however, that high returns are generally associated with high risk. The return on owners' investment is determined by dividing net income by average common stockholders' equity. Preferred dividend requirements for the period should be excluded from net income. Furthermore, the par value and any additional paid-in capital on preferred stock should be excluded from stockholders' equity to get common stockholders' equity.

EXAMPLE 17-12: The return on owners' investment for Argus Company is calculated below.

Net income .... $\dfrac{\$6,880.50}{\$11,616.50}$ = .59 Return on owners' investment
Average common stockholders' equity* ....

* Only ending stockholders' equity was given in this example, therefore, average stockholders' equity was not used.

C. *Earnings per common share* **(EPS) indicates the amount of earnings that remain for each share of a common stock after preferred dividend requirements have been met.**

Note that this number is dependent on the number of shares outstanding. A two-for-one stock split would decrease EPS by one half. EPS is determined by dividing net income (less preferred dividends, if any) by the number of shares of common stock outstanding.

EXAMPLE 17-13: The EPS for Argus Company is calculated below.

Net income .... $\dfrac{\$6,880.50}{1,000}$ = $6.88 EPS
1000 shares of common stock...............................

D. *Price earnings ratio* **indicates the relative attractiveness of the stock to investors.**

The price earnings ratio is determined by dividing the market price per share of common stock by earnings per share.

EXAMPLE 17-14: Assuming a market price of $103.20 per share for Argus Company's stock, the price earnings ratio would be

Market price per share $103.20
Earnings per share .... ───────── = 15 Price earnings ratio
$6.88

17-6. Limitations of Financial Statement Analysis

The financial statements of companies are necessarily limited to the reporting of financial items. These items are further limited to those that can be reported in monetary terms. Any valuations (such as inventory costs) are based on past transactions and estimates of what will happen. Furthermore, assets and liabilities are reported based on historical cost. Thus, the financial numbers do not reflect either price changes in the general economy or the specific price changes related to the reported items. There is currently a trend toward reporting values other than historical cost as supplemental information in financial statements. This information can be useful in analyzing trends.

EXAMPLE 17-15: If cash of $100 is held during a period of inflation, the purchasing power of the cash declines during the period. The $100 will not buy as much as it would a year ago. Thus, economic purchasing power is lost. This loss is not reported except perhaps as supplemental information.

The thing to remember about financial statement analysis is that all of the analytical methods discussed in this chapter are *helpful* in judging the present performance of a company and in determining future trends. They are not definitive guides, however. Conditions in the general economic and business environment and conditions peculiar to the company itself or to the industry of which it is a part should also be considered. When comparing the data of a company to competing firms, any differences in accounting methods should be determined, as this may influence the comparison.

RAISE YOUR GRADES

Can you explain...?

☑ the difference between an audit, a compilation, and a review
☑ the importance of an independent CPA's audit report and give several key phrases to look for
☑ how footnotes are useful in financial analysis
☑ what is found in the chairman's letter
☑ why comparisons are necessary when analyzing financial reports
☑ the difference between liquidity and solvency
☑ what capital utilization ratios measure
☑ the limitations of financial statement analysis

SUMMARY

1. By starting at the back of the financial statements, a user can determine the level of assurance associated with a particular set of financial statements. Statements that have been audited by an independent Certified Public Accountant offer the highest level of assurance that they "present fairly in accordance with generally accepted accounting principles".

2. The phrases "except for" or "does not present fairly" indicate that the auditor feels that the item is not presented fairly or, at a minimum, that the item warrants further attention.
3. The chairman's letter provides information about the future prospects of the company.
4. Traditional financial analysis makes use of comparisons of ratios.
5. Liquidity is a company's ability to meet it's current obligations. Measures of liquidity include net working capital, current ratio, and acid-test ratio.
6. Solvency is a company's ability to pay it's long-term debt obligations as they mature. Measures of solvency include debt-to-equity and times-interest-earned.
7. Capital utilization indicates how well the company uses its resources and how hard the assets are being worked. Measures of capital utilization include days' receivables, inventory turnover, and asset turnover.
8. Measures of performance indicate the overall effectiveness of the company's operations. Measures of performance include profit margin percentage, return on owners' investment, earnings per share, and price earnings ratio.
9. Ratio analysis is limited by its restriction to quantitative financial accounting data.

RAPID REVIEW   Answers

True or False

		Answers
1.	A review gives the highest level of assurance that management's financial statements "present fairly in accordance with generally accepted accounting principles". [Section 17-1]	*False*
2.	Special insight into the company can be found in the chairman's letter. [Section 17-1]	*True*
3.	Ratios allow the comparison of companies of different sizes. [Section 17-2]	*True*
4.	Net working capital is computed by adding current assets and current liabilities. [Section 17-3]	*False*
5.	Quick assets include cash, short-term marketable securities, net current accounts receivable, and net current notes receivable. [Section 17-3]	*True*
6.	The debt-to-equity ratio is computed by dividing total liabilities by total stockholders' equity. [Section 17-3]	*True*
7.	The higher the debt ratio, the lower the risk of bankruptcy associated with the debt [Section 17-3]	*False*
8.	Days' receivables is determined by dividing net receivables by net credit sales and multiplying by 365. [Section 17-4]	*True*
9.	Inventory turnover is determined by dividing cost of goods sold by average inventory. [Section 17-4]	*True*
10.	Return on owners' investment is one of the least important ratios. [Section 17-5]	*False*
11.	The earnings per share ratio is not affected by a stock split. [Section 17-5]	*False*
12.	The price earnings ratio indicates the relative attractiveness of the stock to investors. [Section 17-5]	*True*
13.	Ratio analysis is limited by the conventions of financial accounting. [Section 17-6]	*True*
14.	There is a trend toward including values other than historical cost as supplemental information. [Section 17-6]	*True*

SOLVED PROBLEMS

Use the following financial statements to work the problems that follow for 19x2:

Peter's Pickle Packers
Comparative Balance Sheet
As of December 31, 19x2 and 19x1

	19x2	19x1
Assets		
Current assets:		
Cash...	$ 618	$ 332
Accounts receivable (net)............................	1,050	1,710
Inventory...	3,990	3,412
Prepaid insurance...................................	60	56
Total current assets...............................	$5,718	$5,510
Plant assets:		
Equipment.. $4,351		$3,677
Less: Accumulated depreciation.................... 1,435		1,711
Net equipment......................................	2,916	1,966
Total assets...	$8,634	$7,476
Liabilities		
Current liabilities:		
Accounts payable....................................	$ 394	$1,108
Salaries payable.....................................	446	430
Total current liabilities............................	$ 840	$1,538
Long-term liabilities:		
Bonds payable......................................	3,196	2,996
Total liabilities......................................	$4,036	$4,534
Stockholders' equity		
Common stock, 1,090 shares at $2 par................	2,180	2,180
Paid in capital in excess of par......................	420	420
Total contributed capital...........................	$2,600	$2,600
Retained earnings...................................	1,998	342
Total stockholders' equity............................	$4,598	$2,942
Total liabilities and stockholders' equity...............	$8,634	$7,476

```
                        Peter's Pickle Packers
                          Income Statement
                   For Year Ended December 31, 19x2


Cash sales.....................................................    $10,863
Credit sales...................................................     15,387
   Net sales ..................................................               $26,250

Cost of goods sold:
   Inventory, January 1.......................................    $ 3,412
   Net purchases .............................................     20,186
   Cost of goods available for sale ..........................    $23,598
   Less: Inventory, December 31..............................      3,990
       Cost of goods sold ....................................                 19,608
Gross profit..................................................                $ 6,642

Operating expenses:
   Rent expense...............................................    $ 1,055
   Salary expense.............................................      2,378
   Utilities expense..........................................        703
   Interest expense...........................................        252
   Depreciation expense......................................        276
       Total operating expenses..............................                  4,664
Net income ..................................................                 $ 1,978
```

PROBLEM 17-1: Compute net working capital.

Answer: [Section 17-3]

Current assets...	$5,718
Current liabilities	− 840
Net working capital......................................	$4,878

PROBLEM 17-2: Compute the current ratio.

Answer: [Section 17-3]

Current assets...
Current liabilities .... $\frac{\$5,718}{\$840} = 6.8071$ or 6.81

PROBLEM 17-3: Compute the acid-test ratio (quick ratio).

Answer: [Section 17-3]

Cash	$ 618
Accounts receivable	1,050
Quick assets..	$1,668

Quick assets...
Current liabilities .... $\frac{\$1,668}{\$840} = 1.9857$ or 1.99

PROBLEM 17-4: Compute the debt-to-equity ratio.

Answer: [Section 17-3]

Total liabilities...
Total stockholders' equity .... $\frac{\$4,036}{\$4,598} = 0.878$ or $.88$

PROBLEM 17-5: Compute the times-interest-earned ratio.

Answer: [Section 17-3]

Income before interest .... $\dfrac{\$1,978 + \$252}{\$252} = 8.85$
Interest expense...

PROBLEM 17-6: Compute the days' receivables.

Answer: [Section 17-4]

Average net receivables:

$$\frac{\text{Beginning receivables} + \text{Ending receivables}}{2} = \frac{\$1,710 + \$1,050}{2} = \$1,380$$

Average net receivables.......................... $\dfrac{\$\,1,380}{\$15,387} \times 365 = 32.7 \text{ or } 33 \text{ days}$
Net credit sales...................................

PROBLEM 17-7: Compute the inventory turnover ratio.

Answer: [Section 17-4]

Average inventory:

$$\frac{\text{Beginning inventory} + \text{Ending inventory}}{2} = \frac{\$3,412 + \$3,990}{2} = \$3,701$$

Cost of goods sold .... $\dfrac{\$19,608}{\$\,3,701} = 5.30$
Average inventory...

PROBLEM 17-8: Compute the asset turnover ratio.

Answer: [Section 17-4]

Average total assets:

$$\frac{\text{Beginning total assets} + \text{Ending total assets}}{2} = \frac{\$7,476 + \$8,634}{2} = \$8,055$$

Net sales .... $\dfrac{\$26,250}{\$\,8,055} = 3.26$
Average total assets..

PROBLEM 17-9: Compute the profit margin percentage.

Answer: [Section 17-5]

Net income .... $\dfrac{\$\,1,978}{\$26,250} = .075$
Net sales ....

PROBLEM 17-10: Compute the return on owners' investment.

Answer: [Section 17-5]

Average common stockholders' equity:

$$\frac{\text{Beginning common equity} + \text{Ending common equity}}{2} = \frac{\$2,942 + \$4,598}{2} = \$3,770$$

Net income .... $\dfrac{\$1,978}{\$3,770} = .52$
Average common stockholders' equity ....

PROBLEM 17-11: Compute earnings per common share.

Answer: [Section 17-5]

Net income (less preferred dividends if any) . . . . $\dfrac{\$1{,}978}{1{,}090} = \$1.81$

1090 shares of \$2 par common stock . . . .

PROBLEM 17-12: Compute the price earnings ratio given a market price per share of \$16.29.

Answer: [Section 17-5]

Market price per share . . . . $\dfrac{\$16.29}{\$\ 1.81} = 9$

Earnings per share . . . .

EXAMINATION III (CHAPTERS 13 THROUGH 17)

True or False

1. If an incoming partner purchases an interest from an existing partner, the assets of the partnership do not change. (Chapter 13)

2. If the partnership agreement does not specify how profits are to be divided, profits are divided equally. (Chapter 13)

3. Organization costs for a corporation are expensed in the period incurred. (Chapter 14)

4. Dividends in arrears for preferred stock will appear in the current liability section of the balance sheet. (Chapter 14)

5. A stock dividend decreases total assets and stockholders' equity. (Chapter 15)

6. When a small stock dividend is declared, the retained earnings account is debited for the market price of the stock on that date. (Chapter 15)

7. If an investor owns less than 20% of the common stock in the investee corporation, the investment is usually adjusted to the lower of cost or market on the balance sheet date. (Chapter 16)

8. Using the effective interest method, an equal amount of interest expense is recognized each period. (Chapter 16)

9. Net working capital is computed by dividing current assets by current liabilities. (Chapter 17)

10. Ratios allow the comparison of companies of different sizes. (Chapter 17)

Fill in the blank

Fill in the missing word or words.

1. The disadvantages of a partnership include _____, _____, and _____.

2. The corporation's own capital stock that has been issued, reacquired by the corporation, but not retired is called _____ _____.

3. Unusual and nonrecurring items shown separately on the income statement include _____, _____, and _____. (Chapter 15)

4. If a bond is issued at a discount, the net liability _____ as the discount is amortized. (Chapter 16)

5. A bond issue with more than one maturity date is referred to as _____ bonds. (Chapter 16)

6. Cost of goods sold divided by average inventory is an indication of the _____ of the inventory and an indication of how active the inventories. (Chapter 17)

Solved Problems

PROBLEM 1: On May 31, 19x1, the end of the fiscal year, the XYZ partnership had a net income of $40,000. Profits and losses are divided in a fixed ratio as follows: 50% to X, 30% to Y, and 20% to Z. Compute the distribution of net income.

PROBLEM 2: X, Y, and Z decide to liquidate the partnership on May 31, 19x6. The balance sheet before the liquidation is shown below:

Assets		Liabilities and Owners' Equity	
Cash	$ 25,000	Accounts Payable	$ 32,000
Other Assets	198,000	X, Capital	75,000
		Y, Capital	56,000
		Z, Capital	60,000
Total	$223,000	Total	$223,000

Prepare a liquidation schedule assuming the noncash assets are sold for $155,000. The partners share profits and losses as follows: 50% to X, 30% to Y and 20% t Z.

PROBLEM 3: The stockholders' equity sections of CoCo Corporation for year 1 and 2 appear below:

	Year 2	Year 1
Preferred stock, $100 par value 10%	$ 50,000	$ 20,000
Common stock, $10 par value	70,000	50,000
Paid-in capital in excess of par:		
common	300,000	180,000
Retained Earnings	31,000	18,000
	$451,000	$268,000

(a) How many shares of preferred stock were issued in year 2?
(b) How many shares of common stock were issued in year 2?
(c) If there were no dividends paid in year 2, what was the net income or loss?
(d) What is the total paid-in (contributed) capital at the end of year 2?

PROBLEM 4: Clearwater Corporation has one class of stock (common) and earned a net income of $6,000 in year 2. There were 3,000 shares of common stock outstanding all year. Calculate earnings per share for year 2.

PROBLEM 5: Assume Clearwater Corporation still has only one class of stock and earned $26,000 during year 3. 3,000 shares were outstanding on January, 19x3, 2,000 additional shares were issued July 1, 19x3, and 1,500 additional shares were issued on October 1, 19x3. Calculate earnings per share.

PROBLEM 6: Princess Corporation plans to issue $500,000, 5-year, 10% bonds. Calculate the amount of cash received by Princess under each of the following assumptions:

(a) bonds sell at par
(b) bonds sell at 106
(c) bonds sell at 93

PROBLEM 7: Goen Corporation issued $100,000, 10-year, 12% bonds on July 1, 19x1. The semi-annual interest dates are July 1 and January 1. The bonds sold at 96. Prepare the journal entries to record the bond issue on July 1, and the interest payment and amortization of the discount on January 1, 19x2. (Ignore year-end accruals and use the straight-line method.) Use the journal on page 328.

	JOURNAL			PAGE /
DATE	DESCRIPTION	POST. REF.	DEBIT	CREDIT

(Blank journal form with rows numbered 1 through 12)

PROBLEM 8: The following information relates to MGT Corporation:

Assets	19x3	19x2
Current Assets	$12,000	$10,000
Noncurrent Assets	17,000	15,000
Total Assets	$29,000	$25,000
Liabilities & Equity		
Current Liabilities	$ 6,500	$ 8,000
Noncurrent Liabilities	14,500	10,000
Stockholders' Equity	8,000	7,000
Total Liabilities and Equity	$29,000	$25,000

Sales	$24,000
Cost of Goods Sold	16,000
Gross Profit	$ 8,000
Operating Expenses	5,000
Net Income, 19x3	$ 3,000

Compute the following for 19x3:

(a) working capital
(b) current ratio
(c) debt ratio
(d) asset turnover
(e) profit margin percentage
(f) return on investments

ANSWERS

True or False

1. True   2. True   3. False   4. False—not a liability until declared   5. False   6. True
7. True   8. False   9. False   10. True

Fill in the Blank

1. limited life, unlimited liability, and mutual agency
2. treasury stock
3. discontinued operations, extraordinary items, and cumulative effect of accounting changes
4. increases
5. serial
6. relative liquidity

Solved Problems

PROBLEM 1: X:$40,000 × .50 = $20,000
Y:$40,000 × .30 = $12,000
Z:$40,000 × .20 = $ 8,000   (Chapter 13)

PROBLEM 2: (Chapter 13)

XYZ Partnership
Liquidation Schedule
May 31, 19x6

	Cash	+	Other Assets	= Liabilities	+	X, Capital	+	Y, Capital	+	Z, Capital
Balances Before										
Liquidation	$ 25,000		$198,000	$32,000		$75,000		$56,000		$60,000
Sale of Other Assets	155,000		(198,000)			(21,500)		(12,900)		(8,600)
	$180,000		–0–	$32,000		$53,500		$43,100		$51,400
Pay Liabilities	32,000			(32,000)						
	$148,000		–0–	–0–		$53,500		$43,100		$51,400
Distribute Cash to Partners	(148,000)					(53,500)		(43,100)		(51,400)
	–0–		–0–	–0–		–0–		–0–		–0–

PROBLEM 3: (Chapters 14 and 15)

(*a*) $50,000   Year 2 balance
(20,000)   Year 1 balance
$30,000   Increase in Preferred Stock

$30,000 ÷ $100 par = 300 shares of preferred stock issued in year 2

(*b*) $70,000   Year 2 balance
(50,000)   Year 1 balance
$20,000   Increase in Common Stock

$20,000 ÷ $10 par = 2,000 shares of common stock issued in year 2

(*c*) $31,000   Retained Earnings – Year 2 balance
(18,000)   Retained Earnings – Year 1 balance
$13,000   Increase in Retained Earnings

Since no dividends were paid, the increase in retained earnings was due to net income of $13,000.

(*d*) $ 50,000   Preferred Stock at par
70,000   Common stock at par
300,000   Paid-in Capital in excess of par: common
420,000   Total Paid-in Capital

PROBLEM 4: (Chapter 15)

$$\frac{\$6,000}{3,000 \text{ shares}} = \$2.00 \text{ Earnings per share}$$

PROBLEM 5: (Chapter 16)
Calculating the weighted average number of shares outstanding:

	3,000 shares × 1 year	= 3,000
(Issued 7/1)	2,000 shares × 6/12 year	= 1,000
(Issued 10/1)	1,500 shares × 3/12 year	= 375
	Weighted Average Shares	4,375
	Outstanding	

Calculating earnings per share

$$\frac{\$26,000}{4,375} = \$5.94 \text{ (rounded)}$$

PROBLEM 6: (Chapter 16)

(a) $500,000 × 1.00 = $500,000
(b) $500,000 × 1.06 = $530,000
(c) $500,000 × .93 = $465,000

PROBLEM 7: (Chapter 16)

	DATE		DESCRIPTION	POST. REF.	DEBIT	CREDIT	
		JOURNAL				**PAGE** *1*	
1	19x1 July	1	*Cash*		9 6 0 0 0 00		1
2			*Discount on Bonds Payable*		4 0 0 0 00		2
3			*Bond Payable*			100 0 0 0 00	3
4			*($100,000 × .96 =*				4
5			*$96,000)*				5
6	19x2 Jan	1	*Bond Interest Expense*		6 0 0 0 00		6
7			*Cash*			6 0 0 0 00	7
8			*($100,000 × .12 × ½ =*				8
9			*$6,000)*				9
10		1	*Bond Interest Expense*		2 0 0 00		10
11			*Discount on Bonds Payable*			2 0 0 00	11
12			*($4,000 ÷ 20 periods =*				12
13			*$200)*				13

PROBLEM 8: (Chapter 17)

(a) $12,000 − $6,500 = $5,500 Working capital
(b) $12,000 ÷ $6,500 = 1.85 current ratio
(c) $21,000 ÷ $8,000 = 2.625 debt ratio
(d) (29,000 + $25,000) ÷ 2 = $27,000 average total assets
    $24,000 ÷ $27,000 = .89 asset turnover
(e) $3,000 ÷ $24,000 = .125 profit margin percentage
(f) ($8,000 + $7,000) ÷ 2 = $7,500 average equity
    $3,000 ÷ $7,500 = .40 return on investment

INDEX

E

Earnings per share, 283-285, 319
Effective-interest method
  in amortizing bond discounts, 303, 304
  in amortizing bond premiums, 304-306
Electronic data processing, 137-138
Employee's Withholding
  Allowance Certificate (W-4), 189
Entity assumption, 18
Equations
  basic accounting, 2-4
  income statement, 16
Equity, *def.*, 3, 14
  statement of, 17, 28, 69, 111
Equity method, 296-298
Expenses, *def.*, 5

F

Federal income tax, 189-192
Federal Insurance Contributions
  Act (FICA), 189-192 *passim*
Federal Unemployment Tax Act
  (FUTA), 190-192
Financial accounting, *def.*, 2
Financial statements
  analysis of, 314-320
  guideline for preparing, 17-19
  for merchandising firms, 111-112
First-in, first-out (FIFO) cost flow
  method, 205, 207
Fixed assets, *def.*, 222
Footing, 30
Full disclosure principle, 18
Fully diluted earnings per share, 284-285

G

Gains, *def.*, 5
General journal, 136
General ledger, 42, 45-46
Generally Accepted Accounting
  Principles, 17-19, 314
Generally Accepted Auditing
  Standards, 314
Goodwill, 228
Governmental accounting, *def.*, 2
Gross pay, 189
Gross profit method, 209-210

H

Historical cost
  of intangible assets, 228
  of plant assets, 223
Historical-cost principle, 18

I

Income statement, *def.* and *illus.*, 14-16
  corporate, *illus.*, 281-283

equation, 16
  worksheet for, 27, 69, 110
Income statement approach, 182
Income Summary account, 70
Income tax, employee's, 189-192
Industry practices constraint, 19
Intangible assets, *def.*, 13, 228
  amortization of, 241
Interest
  accounting for, 167
  on bonds, 299-306
  on marketable securities, 167
  on notes payable, 187-188
  on notes receivable, 184-186
Internal control, 138, 157-158
Inventory, *def.*, 102, 201
  cost flow assumptions in valuing, 204-208
  estimation of, 209-211
  internal control of, 138
  turnover of, 318
  valuation of, 106-107, 201-209
Investments, *def.*, 4
  long-term, 13, 296-298

J

Journal, general, 42-45, 136
  special, *def.* and *illus.*, 129-136

L

Last-in, first-out (LIFO) cost flow
  method, 206, 207
Leaseholds and leasehold
  improvements, 228
Liabilities, *def.*, 3, 13-14
Liquidity, 316-317
Loss, *def.*, 5
Lower of cost or market
  in valuing inventories, 208-209
  in valuing marketable securities, 168-169, 296-297

M

Managerial accounting, *def.*, 2
Marketable securities, 166-169
  dividends on, 167
  valuation of, 168-169
Matching principle, 18, 59
Materiality constraint, 19
Merchandising firms, 102-111
Monetary-unit assumption, 18
Mortgage bond, 298
Mortgage note payable, 306

N

Natural resources, 13, 227
  cost allocation of, 240-241
Net book value, *def.*, 222
Net income, *def.*, 5
  in income statement equation, 16
Net working capital, 316-317
Noncurrent assets, *def.*, 13
No-par stock, 271-272
Notes payable, 187-188

Non interest-bearing, 187-188
Notes receivable, 184-186
  discounted, 186
  dishonored, 185-186
Not-for-profit accounting, *def.*, 2

O

Operating cycle, 12
Operational assets, 3
Other assets, 3
Owner elements, 4

P

Parent company, 298
Partnership accounting
  adding a partner, 258-259
  dividing profit/loss, 256-257
  liquidation of, 259-261
  start-up of, 255-256
Partnerships, 254-255
Par-value
  bonds, 299-300
  stock, 271-272
Patents, 228
Payroll accounting, 188-192
Pension plans, 306
Performance elements, 4-5
Performance measures, 319-320
Periodic inventory, 107, 208
Periodicity assumption, 18
Perpetual inventory, 106-107, 207-208
Petty cash fund, 158-159
Plant assets *def.*, 13, 222
  historical cost of, 233
  sale and exchange of, 225-227
Posting, 46-49, 129
Preemptive right, 270
Preferred stock, 271-274 *passim*, 287-288
Premiums on bonds, 299, 300-303
Price earnings ratio, 319-320
Primary earnings per share, 284
Principles
  full disclosure, 18
  generally accepted accounting, 314
  historical cost, 18
  matching, 18, 59
  revenue realization, 18, 59
Profit margin percentage, 319
Promissory notes, *illus.*, 184-186, 188
Purchases journal, 131-132

Q

Quick ratio, 317

R

Ratio analysis, 315-316
Ratios,
  cost to retail, 210-211
  current, 317
  debt to equity, 317